D1713386

Botany, sexuality and women's writing 1760–1830

Manchester University Press

This book is dedicated to the memory of Anita George

Botany, sexuality and women's writing 1760–1830

From modest shoot to forward plant

Sam George

Manchester University Press
Manchester and New York
distributed exclusively in the USA by Palgrave

Published by Manchester University Press
Oxford Road, Manchester M13 9NR, UK
and Room 400, 175 Fifth Avenue, New York, NY 10010, USA
www.manchesteruniversitypress.co.uk

Distributed exclusively in the USA by
Palgrave, 175 Fifth Avenue, New York,
NY 10010, USA

Distributed exclusively in Canada by
UBC Press, University of British Columbia, 2029 West Mall,
Vancouver, BC, Canada V6T 1Z2

British Library Cataloguing-in-Publication Data
A catalogue record for this book is available from the British Library

Library of Congress Cataloging-in-Publication Data applied for

ISBN 978 0 7190 7697 8 *hardback*

First published 2007

16 15 14 13 12 11 10 09 08 07 10 9 8 7 6 5 4 3 2 1

Typeset
by Frances Hackeson Freelance Publishing Services, Brinscall, Lancs
Printed in Great Britain
by MPG Books Ltd, Bodmin, Cornwall

Contents

Illustrations

Acknowledgements

I would like to thank the staff of the Library and Herbarium at the Royal Botanic Gardens, Kew; the Linnaean Society of London Library; the John Rylands Library, Manchester; the Bodleian Library, Oxford; and the British Library, London and Boston Spa for their help and expertise. I am grateful to Revd Peter Bowles for giving me access to rare books in the Library of the Church of St Edmund, Castleton and to York Public Library for allowing me access to the minute books of the Ancient Society of York Florists. I would also like to acknowledge the interlibrary loans division at the University of York library and the staff at the King's Manor Library in York. Thanks also to Steve Corbett and to Gordon Smith of the University of York Library Photographic Department for help in preparing scanned images. I would like to express my gratitude to Peter Miller and Tony Fothergill at Ken Spelman's Antiquarian Booksellers in York for training me in handling early printed books and for offering me gainful employment when my funding ran out in York. Thanks are especially due to Peter Miller for his encouragement and advice.

I wish to thank Professor Harriet Guest for her rigorous reading of the early drafts of this book in thesis form and Dr Angela Keane at the University of Sheffield for inspiring me to undertake a Ph.D. in eighteenth-century studies in the first place. I am indebted to the interdisciplinary culture at the Centre for Eighteenth-Century Studies, University of York, for stimulating my research.

My greatest debt in writing the book is to Bill Hughes for his continued support and unwavering enthusiasm for my project. He read and commented on all the chapters in different stages of completion. I am also indebted to Ulrika Maude, who I met on day one of my Ph.D. on a cold October day in York and who has remained a firm friend ever since. Thank you for supporting me through the highs and lows: I cannot imagine completing this without having met you. I would like to thank Martin Green whose small act of kindness allowed me to complete this project. Thanks are also due to my late grandmother, my father, David George, and my sisters, Rowena, Demelza and Caroline. Special thanks go to Jonathan who inspired me and made me believe in myself enough to see the book through to the end. Thank you for keeping the wolves from my door. My cats, Hatty and Arrietty made my study a more inviting place and provided comfort in the final stages of my research. Finally I would like to dedicate this book to my late mother, Anita George, who cultivated a love of gardening and literature in me, the cross-fertilization of which was the inspiration for this work.

An earlier version of Chapter 1 appeared as 'The cultivation of the female mind', *History of European Ideas*, 31 (2005). Material from Chapter 2 has been published as 'Linnaeus in Letters', *British Journal for Eighteenth-Century Studies*, 28:1 (2004). A shortened version of sexuality debates in relation to botany from Chapter 4 has been published as 'Not Strictly Proper for a Female Pen', *Comparative Critical Studies*, 2:2 (2005).

Introduction

Botany has become fashionable; in time it may become useful, if it be not so already.[1]

THE STEREOTYPE of the forward, sexually precocious female botanist made its first appearance in literature in the turbulent revolutionary climate of the 1790s, though women had, in fact, been avidly botanising earlier in the century. The emergence of this figure illustrates both the contemporary appeal, particularly to women, of the Linnaean Sexual System of botanical classification, and the anxieties surrounding female modesty that it provoked. Thus, in the reactionary poem, *The Unsex'd Females* (1798), the Reverend Richard Polwhele (1760–1838) warned that botanising girls, in scrutinising the sexual parts of the flower, were indulging in acts of wanton titillation. In the same year James Plumptre (1770–1832) conceived a comic opera entitled *The Lakers* in which the heroine is a female botanist, 'Miss Beccabunga Veronica of Diandria Hall'.[2] Veronica's precocious search for botanical specimens parallels her immodest search for a husband. With only Erasmus Darwin's provocative account of *The Loves of the Plants* (1789) to guide her, 'she has been studying the system of plants, till she now wishes to know the system of man' (I.1.2). Botany, we are reminded in the preface, 'is by no means a proper amusement for the more polished sex' (xii). The botanising activities of Veronica's maid, Anna, suggest that the fashion for women's botany has, deplorably, even reached the servant classes. Anna has been learning something of Linnaean classification and she later confides to the aptly named Billy Sample that 'all ladies who know anything study botamy [sic] now' (III.1.43). The punning malapropism alerts the reader to the supposed sauciness of the activity. And this is not all: Anna goes on to enumerate the many varieties of sexual union in the plant kingdom and how they are analogous to human sexuality. The father of modern botany, Carl von Linné, or Linnaeus (1707–78), founded a classification system based on the male and female parts of the flower; it focused attention on the organs of generation and was termed the 'Sexual System' or *systema sexuale*. Linnaeus famously made use of human–plant analogies; his nomenclature was inspired by traditional wedding imagery and marriage metaphors permeate his botanical taxonomy in *Systema Naturae* (1735) in which he explained the concept of *nuptiae plantarum* (or 'The Marriage of Plants'). However, Linnaeus disclosed that in general such propriety was inapplicable to plants, whose sexual union was uncontrolled. Plumptre's Anna is clearly drawing on Linnaean ideas in her dialogue with Billy:

> *Anna*: Oh such an enlightened study! such hard names! [...] Such curious truths too contained in it—why, plants are all men and women.
> *Sample*: Aye, there are sweet-williams; I'm a sweet-william. And coxcombs, and painted ladies, and lords and ladies, and naked ladies, and—
> *Anna*: No, no, I mean that they drink and sleep, and are like man and wife.
> *Sample*: What, sleep in the same bed?
> *Anna:* Yes, and in different beds, and live sometimes in different houses.
> *Sample*: Have a separate *maintenance*! They must be your fashionable plants then. What and some have their misses, I reckon, as well as their wives?
> *Anna*: O yes! A great many: and some ladies have their gallants too.
> *Sample*: Upon my word, Miss, a very pretty study this seems to be that you've learnt: I can't say I should much like my wife to know anything about it.
> *Anna*: That you'll find a difficult matter to get one who's ignorant of it; for all ladies that know any thing study botamy [sic] now. (III.1. 43–4)

The Lakers and *The Unsex'd Females* show how fashionable women's botany had become. They demonstrate the spread of Linnaean ideas in England and the anxieties surrounding the figure of the female botanist in the last decade of the eighteenth century. Plumptre differs from Polwhele in that his discouragement of Linnaean botany for women is humorous, yet still his preface locates such botanising within 'the false taste of a licentious age, which is gaining ground, and corrupting the soft and elegant manners of the otherwise loveliest part of creation' (xii). This debate around taste and propriety is central to my exploration of women's literary interaction with botany.

As we have seen, Plumptre informs us that his heroine's botanical knowledge is gleaned from her reading of Darwin's *The Loves of the Plants*, a poem inspired by the Linnaean system. Darwin (1731–1802) was certainly instrumental in popularising Linnaean botany for women. His 'Key of the Sexual System' (Appendix 1) was appended to the Lichfield Botanical Society's *The Families of Plants* in 1787 and it makes explicit the language used to describe the marriage of plants in Linnaean texts in English in the eighteenth century.[3] Here, the male and female parts of the flower, the stamens and pistils, are 'husbands' and 'wives'. Plants whose flowers contain different numbers of male stamens and female pistils are described in terms of 'houses' or 'marriages'. The Linnaean nomenclature rests on contemporary marriage practices, with marriages divided into two groups, either 'public' (those whose flowers are visible) or 'clandestine' (flowers scarce visible to the naked eye). Darwin informs us that in clandestine marriages flowers may be 'concealed within the fruit' and that 'Nuptials are celebrated privately' (lxxix). It is this imagery of nuptials, spouses and marriages which captured the public imagination in the mid to late eighteenth century and caused botany to be caught up in debates around sexuality and propriety.

Flowers are traditionally emblematic of the female sex in literary texts; however, a particular, complex refinement of this is taking place here. I will thus explore how botany becomes a discourse of female sexuality in eighteenth-century literature. I will investigate the moral backlash against female botanists and the problems of representation facing literary women who practised the modern, sexual system of botany. This will involve interrogating a small group of interrelated texts and teasing out connections, influences, revisions and resistances. I examine a number of authors who have been overlooked, setting my readings within the context of broader debates on botany and gender. Botany would never again be quite so topical or fashionable and these texts serve to remind us of this, while allowing us to consider the reasons why women's botany in particular became so prominent and so controversial.

There was an enormous growth in the number of botanical and horticultural books – literary, scientific and artistic – published in Britain in the eighteenth century. They covered an increasingly wide field of interest: herbals; books on medical botany, plant physiology and anatomy; floras, including local and foreign floras; gardening books, covering botanic, private and nursery gardens, and including garden design; works on planting; letters on botany; botanical dialogues; long poems on botanical and horticultural themes, and botanical drawing books.

There had been an extraordinary influx of new plants into Britain at this time. Sir Joseph Banks (1743–1820), the botanist, and Linnaeus's pupil, Daniel Solander, discovered and collected new species of plant on various voyages of discovery. On Banks's return from the South Seas on board Cook's *Endeavour* voyage, he was employed by George III at the Royal Botanic Gardens at Kew. Kew boasted some 5500 species of plant as listed by William Aiton in *Hortus Kewensis* in 1789. The number of species had doubled by the second edition of this work in 1814. Banks gained fame (and some notoriety) when John Hawkesworth's *Account of the Voyages* was published in 1773 and his celebrity in aristocratic circles added to the fashion for plant collecting and botanising.

The public's interest in flower painting was boosted by the appointment in 1790 of one of the most famous botanical artists of the day, Francis Bauer (1758–1840), at Kew. Bauer instructed Queen Charlotte and Princess Elizabeth in botanical drawing, making the drawing and collecting of plants socially desirable. At this time, women embarked on a new kind of floriculture; daughters were instructed in botanical drawing in the manner of the royal princesses, and floral pursuits such as flower gardening, pressing, moulding or embroidering flowers were promoted in manuals and in periodicals such as *The Lady's Monthly Museum* and *The Lady's Magazine.*

The new interest in botany and floriculture was even reflected in women's fashion. David Allen remarks that:

> a marked rise in interest in botany and horticulture can be shown to have coincided with an outbreak of highly naturalistic floral designs on silks, a trend which began in the late 1720s and which originally came from Lyons. Kitty, Duchess of Queensbury is said to have become famous around this time for a dress so perfectly representative of nature's beauties that it gave her the appearance of a walking botanic garden.[4]

Floral fashions continued well into the century and there were elaborate hairstyles and headdresses featuring flowers, leaves, feathers, fruits and even artificial birds. Such extravagance of taste was the subject of a number of satirical prints by Darly featuring preposterous coiffures. *The Flower Garden* of 1777 (see cover illustration) is one such caricature: a lady of fashion sporting a towering wig adorned with floral boughs, silk flowers, giant shells and fashioned into a miniature flower garden at the top complete with husbandman, formal beds, hedgerows, trees and a summerhouse. Such satires show the associations that had developed concerning women and flowers in fashionable society in the 1770s.

Mary Delany (1700–88), a close friend of Queen Charlotte, pioneered the art of crafting paper flowers after nature and classifying them according to the system of Linnaeus.[5] Delany's paper mosaics began as a genteel female pursuit, developing from the new interest in floriculture, but what was new about Delany's paper cut-outs is how botanically accurate they were. They brought her public recognition and allowed her access to exclusive botanical circles. After the death of her second husband she spent an increasing amount of time with Margaret Cavendish Bentinck, the Duchess of Portland (1715–85), at her estate, Bulstrode in Buckinghamshire. The Duchess herself was a great collector and her natural history collection was the largest in Britain. As Delany gained prominence she received gifts of plants from Kew, from the Chelsea Physic garden, and from the most famous British botanist of the day, Joseph Banks. Her unique skill in floral imitation led to her being celebrated by Darwin in *The Loves of the Plants* (itself a favourite with enlightened British women). Delany kept careful records of her elegant representations of flowers listing the Latin name and classification of each. Thus, what had begun as an aesthetic exercise or feminine accomplishment had developed into a scientific project. The decorative paper cut-outs served to mask this genteel woman's interest in Enlightenment science and in the Linnaean sexual system of classification. The scientific and aesthetic are inextricably linked here through a minute exploration of flowers. Such progressions from floriculture to Linnaean botany, from the particular to the universal, changed the way many women thought about flowers and helped generate new genres of women's writing such as the botanical dialogue or conversation and the botanical poem with scientific notes. Many of these works are as generically unstable as Delany's *hortus siccus* or paper garden, and blur the distinctions between aesthetic representation and scientific classification. I will focus on the cross-fertilisation of these ideas in eighteenth-century women's writing with the escalation of women's involvement in scientific botany being a central concern of my study.

This book shares some parallels with work by Barbara T. Gates, Ann Shteir and Londa Schiebinger. Barbara Gates has surveyed Victorian and Edwardian women and their relationship to nature and anthologised women's nature illustration and writing.[6] Schiebinger first posed the question, 'Was botany feminine?' in 1989 in her exploration of women in the origins of modern science. In 1996, Shteir produced a history of women and botany in England from the mid-eighteenth century through to the late Victorian period.[7] While I acknowledge these pioneering studies, I depart from their approach in that, as a literary critic, I am primarily concerned not with academies, salons, botanical societies and plant collectors, but with texts – texts which illustrate the literary representation of botanical science in the eighteenth century. Shteir and Gates's studies of women and natural history are broad and sweeping; as a scholar of the eighteenth century I focus on the Linnaean years in England during the Enlightenment which, I argue, is when the most progressive texts by and for women were produced. I suggest, for example, that Jean-Jacques Rousseau's botanical letters addressed to a young woman (translated into English in 1785) are vital to our understanding of women as both the producers and consumers of botanical texts. This crucial work has been given little consideration in studies such as Shteir's.[8] I depart from Shteir in that I argue that the feminisation of botany first occurred in texts written by men. These botanical texts were often reinterpreted in significant ways by women, but there had already been a distinctive female orientation of the texts by the male writers themselves. Hence I am concerned with a wider understanding of the discourse and practice of 'female botany' than Shteir.

This study will explore the cultivation of the female mind and its implications for the theories of the feminised discourse of botanical literature. I offer detailed readings of epistolary, dialogic and poetical introductions to botany by eighteenth-century British women. I situate these unique texts within the literature of the eighteenth century where they can be seen to be in dialogue with the writings of the key figures, Jean-Jacques Rousseau, Erasmus Darwin and Mary Wollstonecraft, people who straddle the complicated boundary between Enlightenment and Romanticism, and all of whom were closely involved in discussions of the cultivation of women and the culture of botany.

As I have said, Rousseau (1712–78) is one such male figure who takes on a particularly important role. I have selected him rather than other *philosophes* for a number of reasons. Rousseau was a keen botanist and he was instrumental in shaping the feminisation of botany in the eighteenth century. He turned to botany with renewed enthusiasm during his persecution and exile, seeking solace in the flowers and plants that inhabited his immediate surroundings. He began notes towards a botanical dictionary in 1764 and he botanised so avidly on the island of St Pierre during his confinement there in 1765 that he fantasised about compiling a complete flora of the island that would occupy his entire life.[9] He is rumoured to have botanised in Derbyshire with the Duchess of Portland[10] and it is here that he was introduced to the British botanist Sir Brooke Boothby (1744–1824), the cousin of the botanist and author Maria Jacson. Boothby was a member of the Botanical Society at Lichfield, whose founding member was Erasmus Darwin. The scholars who made up the Botanical Society at Lichfield, who I give much attention to, were all fervid Rousseauvians.

Most crucially, one of the most popular eighteenth-century texts on botany in England was a translation of Rousseau's *Lettres elementaires sur la botanique* (1771–74). Rousseau wrote the botanical letters for Madame Madelaine Catherine Delessert (born Madelaine Catherine de la Tour in Neuchâtal in 1747) who was the owner of a famous herbarium and botanical library. Madelaine married Etienne Delessert of Lyon, a member of the Huguenot family, in 1776. She had written to Rousseau in his exile and in 1771 she asked for his help in introducing her daughter, Marguerite-Madelaine (known as Madelon), to botany.

The letters offer guidance to Madelaine, a young mother, over the instruction in botany of her daughter, Madelon. The received image of Rousseau as a botanist is usually that of the solitary herboriser; however, the *Letters* show a new kind of sociability in relation to Rousseau and botany through a dialogue or exchange of knowledge between a tutor, mother and daughter. The *Letters* were published in the *Collection complëte des Œuvres de J.J. Rousseau* in 1782 and translated (using this edition) into English by Thomas Martyn, Professor of Botany at Cambridge, in 1785. Martyn's book, entitled *Letters on the Elements of Botany Addressed To A Lady,* became a surprise bestseller in England and went through many editions. It was addressed to, and widely read by, British women. As an example of this profound influence, Priscilla Wakefield – another key figure in my narrative – recognisably modelled her own botanical letters of 1796 on Rousseau's.[11]

British women were familiar with Rousseau the botanist. Charlotte Smith (1749–1801), whose work I look at closely, strongly identified with the solitary botanising figure of the *Rêveries du promeneur solitaire* (composed 1776–78, published posthumously in 1782). The lone walker and herboriser of *Rêveries* is reincarnated as a botanising mother and aunt engaged in a familial dialogue in her *Rural Walks in Dialogues* (1795) and *Rambles Farther* (1796), echoing Rousseau's own more sociable botanising in the *Letters.*

Finally, Rousseau's sentimental novel, *Julie ou la Nouvelle Héloïse* (1761)[12], was also enormously popular amongst British women and offered positive images for women that belied his often misogynist – but ambivalent – attitudes towards women.[13] A central trope in this novel is the image of Julie tending her garden; this is an obvious botanical image in itself, but the peculiarly uncultivated nature of Julie's garden found a receptive audience among certain women – notably, Eleanor Butler and Sarah Ponsonby, 'The Ladies of Llangollen'.[14] These women were famous for their garden at Plas Newydd in Llangollen where they entertained a number of distinguished guests. Among the visitors to Llangollen was the poet Anna Seward (1742–1809). Botany was the main topic of conversation at Plas Newydd and Rousseau too was much debated at the soirées the women held in their library.[15] Seward was to publish a volume of verse dedicated to these women in 1796 (*Llangollen Vale with Other Poems*).

More contentiously, there was the engagement by many British women with Rousseau's educational text, *Emile* (1762), and its rather passive heroine, Sophy. Mary Wollstonecraft, for instance, was both inspired by his general theories and exasperated by the separate treatment accorded to Sophy, reacting against this in her *Vindication of the Rights of Woman* (1792).

Wollstonecraft (1759–97) is another figure who is crucial to debates around women and botany. Wollstonecraft took lessons in flower drawing from James Sowerby (1757–1822), the illustrator of the influential *English Botany* (1790–1814). She defended botany against prudery in *A Vindication*, attacking those who would limit women's access to Linnaean knowledge. She approved of botany as a female pursuit but she deplored sentimental analogies between women and flowers. She uses hackneyed-sounding floral epithets ironically in *A Vindication*, launching an attack on flowery diction in works for female education. I trace her involvement in debates around sexuality and botany in the 1790s and explore how she came to inspire a number of botanical satires, appearing as an adulterous female plant in a dialogue between Polwhele and Thomas Mathias, author of *The Pursuits of Literature* (1794–97).

Wollstonecraft's *A Vindication* raises questions about women's access to Linnean botany. Previous Linnaean studies by scholars such as Wilfrid Blunt, William Stearn, Frans Stefaleu, Tore Frängsmyr and Lisbet Koerner have neglected to mention female Linnaeans in England in the eighteenth century.[16] Elsewhere, debates have focused on the public role of Linnaean botany in the voyages of discovery.[17] I have redressed the balance by examining 'indigenous botany' – the botany of native plants – by women in the private domestic sphere of the home, garden and hedgerow. I show how this public/private divide is broken down in a complex and interesting way by women whose texts register these conflicts and tensions. Many women, for example, paraded their botanical knowledge in published texts while simultaneously apologising for obtruding their work upon the public in the prefatory material of their works.

Studies of women and science in the eighteenth century, with the exception of Shteir's, have tended to overlook botany and have focused instead on astronomy and chemistry, telescopy and microscopy.[18] Patricia Phillips's study of *The Scientific Lady* mistakenly states that in the mid- to late eighteenth century,

> natural history and Buffon in particular, had a wide popularity among women ... Botany, on the other hand, was a field not yet appropriated by the ladies, although the Queen, her mother-in-law, the Dowager Princess of Wales and George III were keen botanists.[19]

Botany has been neglected in these accounts of the 'scientific lady' and, while texts such as Elizabeth Carter's translation of Algarotti, *Sir Isaac Newton's Philosophy Explain'd for the Use of the Ladies* (1739), Aphra Behn's translation from Fontenelle, *A Discovery of New Worlds* (1688), and Jane Marcet's *Conversations on Chemistry* (1806) have rightly been explored, the pioneering botanical works of Priscilla Wakefield (1751–1832), Maria Elizabetha Jacson (1755–1829), and Frances Arabella Rowden (1770–1840[?]) have all but been forgotten.

The microscope offered women access to other worlds as much as did narratives of voyaging and exploring the globe. Marjorie Hope Nicholson has discussed the influence of Newton's *Optics* on the poetry of the eighteenth century, but the influence of Linnaeus on women's poetry and the use of microscopy in the woman's botanical poem have never been addressed in any detail.[20] I have covered new ground here and rescued from obscurity texts by authors such as Arabella Rowden and Sarah Hoare (1767–1855) who have rarely been considered in the field of literature. Since I began this study, however, there has been a resurgence of interest in Charlotte Smith, and Loraine Fletcher has written on the importance of botany to our understanding of Smith in her recent biography.[21] Judith Pascoe was the first to examine Smith as a botanist and one or two articles have since appeared on the natural history in Smith's *Beachy Head* (1807).[22] I have been able to place Smith within a tradition of eighteenth-century literary women who cultivated an interest in botany and examine her botanical poetry alongside that of Sarah Hoare and Arabella Rowden, together with poetry from Robert Thornton's *Temple of Flora* (1807) which includes work by relatively unknown poets such as Cordelia Skeeles, all of who are important to this study.

Janet Browne, Alan Bewell, Londa Schiebinger and Tim Fulford have all explored botany's role in the sexual politics of the 1790s.[23] However, these works have centred upon Erasmus Darwin, Carl Linnaeus, and Joseph Banks. I explore important new territory in investigating how female Linnaeans dealt with the delicate issue of plant sexuality. I address the problems of representation facing literary women who practised the sexual system of botany and demonstrate how women struggled to give voice to a subject which was judged 'not strictly proper for a female pen'.[24] Vivien Jones has brought botany into her discussion of Mary Wollstonecraft and sex education.[25] I have been able to illuminate the late eighteenth-century debate between Wollstonecraft, Darwin, Polwhele and Barbauld with some new material from Anna Seward and lesser known authors such as Elizabeth Moody and Arabella Rowden. Important work emerges out of my attention here to genre and the networks of sociability from which these authors emerge.

There has been much textual criticism covering the related area of women and gardens. Sue Bennett and Stephen Bending's books are recent examples of scholarship in this area.[26] I focus on a group of published texts by women in the culture of botany rather than on actual gardens and plant collections. I am primarily concerned with middle-class women: those who wrote for profit, and women educators who entered professional writing through botany. Lady Charlotte Murray (1754–1808) is perhaps an exception, due to her elevated position, but she did publish in the field of botany. Her *British Garden* (1799) was a flora rather than the book on gardening that the title suggests. It was written for the use of ladies on trips to botanical gardens and was published commercially in an expensive two-volume edition in 1799. Botany and gardening do converge in one or two of the published texts by women that I study. Maria Jacson's *Florist's Manual* (1816), for example, combines systematic botany with instructions on flower gardening for women. This text in particular raises an interesting debate around the tensions between the aesthetic and the scientific and the privileging of botany over floristry. Female botanists often dissociated themselves from the practices of florists and horticulturalists, following Rousseau and Linnaeus, and this opposition of botany to floristry is the subject of my final chapter. I uncover this opposition in the writings of Charlotte Smith, a Rousseauvian, and Maria Jacson, a Linnaean. However, Rousseau's Julie (from *La Nouvelle Héloïse*) and her wild flower garden form an integral part of my discussion on cultivation in Chapter 1 and I draw on the published work of the gardener Jane Loudon in my concluding section to illustrate anti-Linnaean texts by women in the Victorian era. Contemporary debates on horticulture and gardening form the subject matter for many of the long poems of the eighteenth century: I cover new ground here examining the Linnaean poem by women.

The Linnaean system of botany was promoted as a form of rational amusement for women in the latter part of the eighteenth century. The vogue for botanical texts for women had been anticipated by William Withering's *Botanical Arrangement of All Vegetables Naturally Growing in Great Britain* in 1776, but was developed largely by later writers. Women's texts emerged in the late 1790s, adding to the feminisation of botany that male authors had cultivated. The Reverend Charles Abbot closely observed the development of women's botany; his *Flora bedfordiensis* (1798) celebrated Britain's botanical 'daughters' who:

> have evinced a zeal and ardour in Botanical researches which have not only done the highest honor [*sic*] to themselves, but have eminently contributed to rescue these pursuits from unmerited reproach, to elevate them into reputation, and to impart to them, if not a superior value, at least a superior currency and fashion. – That such excellence should have been attained in this branch of science by so many of the female sex, notwithstanding the disadvantages they labour under from the want of scholastic and technical instruction, is a convincing proof of the liberality with which Nature has endowed the female mind: and how little reason there is to suppose that their intellectual [sic] are from any other cause than want of cultivation, in any degree inferior to their personal accomplishments.[27]

Thus Abbot records the rise of the woman botanist in England in the eighteenth century.

There were, of course, women plant collectors too; Anna Blackburne (1726–93)[28] and Lady Margaret Cavendish Bentinck, the Duchess of Portland. Anna Blackburne learned about botany from the library of the family seat, Orford Hall in Lancashire. She taught herself Latin so that she could study the Linnaean system of classification and developed a well known natural history collection. Orford Hall boasted a well stocked and much admired garden, established by Anna's father, John Blackburne. The Blackburnes benefited from their close proximity to the Warrington Academy, receiving naturalist visitors such as Johann Reinhold Forster (1754–94) who taught at the school in the 1760s. The Duchess of Portland kept a botanical garden in the grounds of her house at Bulstrode. She employed naturalists such as James Bolton (1735–99) and the Reverend John Lightfoot (1725–83), author of *Flora scotica* (1777), who was engaged in arranging and documenting her collection. The Duchess and Mrs Delany frequented London and Bath society and regularly held soirées in which literary and botanical conversations took place. Guests at such gatherings included the botanist, Daniel Solander (1733–82), who had also assisted with the collections at Bulstrode, and the Linnaean, Benjamin Stillingfleet (1702–71), a favourite with these women. His habit of wearing blue stockings at these meetings, where literary and scientific dialogue took the place of card-playing, led to the term 'Bluestocking' being coined, referring to the circle of learned women. Women who were instructed in botany by Linnaeans such as Stillingfleet or Solander speak of a flirtatious initiation into botanical knowledge. Mary Berry (1763–1852), the author and friend of Horace Walpole, who claimed to have learnt botany from Solander, was already familiar with botanical sexual innuendo, though she only employed this herself in private correspondence:

> I must at last own with blushes ... I was early initiated into all the amours and loose manners of the plants by that very guilty character, Dr Solander, and passed too much time in the society and observance of some of the most abandoned vegetable coquettes.[29]

The botanical dialogue or conversation, in its printed form, which came to exemplify the role of women in the culture of eighteenth-century botany, originated in such meetings.

The genre of the familial dialogue was important among published texts on botany. Fontenelle's *Entretiens sur la pluralité des mondes* (1686) spurred the growth of a market for scientific dialogues addressed to women, and botany, too, proved popular in a dialogic format. Priscilla Wakefield, one of the pioneers of the botanical dialogue in England, saw dialogue as fulfilling an educational ideal:

> The form of dialogue has been adopted as best suited to convey instruction blended with amusement; being desirous that it should be read rather from choice than from compulsion, and be sought by my young readers as an entertainment not shunned as a mere dry preceptive lesson.[30]

In Wakefield's *Mental Improvement* (1794) botany is taught through a series of instructive conversations. The transformative influence of good conversation is demonstrated by the figure of Augusta, the twelve-year-old motherless child who, prior to her stay with the Harcourt family, has only received formal lessons from a governess. After her access to informal conversation in the Harcourt household, Augusta is cured of her wayward habits. She is ultimately transformed by an informal introduction to natural history and announces that she wishes to become a botanist like her interlocutor, Sophia:

> *Augusta*. I have walked a great deal, and in some of my rambles have availed myself of your directions, to become acquainted with the nature of plants and flowers. I have learned the names of the different parts that compose them; and, if Sophia will give me her kind assistance, I hope, in time, to become a botanist.
> *Sophia*. You cannot propose any thing more agreeable to me, than that we should pursue this delightful study together. Our walks will become more interesting, by having a particular object in view; every step we advance will supply new entertainment; from the humble moss, that creeps upon the thatch, to the stately oak, that adorns the forest.[31]

Charlotte Smith's *Rural Walks* (1795) and *Rambles Farther* (1796) are largely comprised of botanical dialogues and *Conversations Introducing Poetry Chiefly on the Subject of Natural History* (1804) elaborated on this theme. Maria Jacson's *Botanical Dialogues Between Hortensia and Her Four Children* appeared in 1797. Other examples of this genre are Elizabeth and Sarah Mary Fitton's *Conversations on Botany* (1818), Harriet Beaufort's *Dialogues on Botany* (1829) and Jane Marcet's *Conversations on Vegetable Physiology* (1829).

The familiar letter played an important role in the feminisation of botany. Jean-Jacques Rousseau's botanical letters were, as already stated, translated and published as *Letters on the Elements of Botany Addressed to a Lady* in 1785. The epistolary format was adopted by Priscilla Wakefield in *An Introduction to Botany in a Series of Familiar Letters* (1796). Examples of the botanical letter as a genre of women's writing can also be found in the nineteenth century in texts such as Sarah Waring's *A Sketch of the Life of Linnaeus in a Series of Letters Designed for Young Persons* (1827).

Poetical studies came into vogue after the publication of Erasmus Darwin's *The Loves of the Plants* (1789) which was to form the second part of the epic poem, *The Botanic Garden*, in 1791. This text was to have a profound effect on women, and a new genre of women's writing, the botanical poem with scientific notes, emerged after Darwin. Charlotte Smith's 'Flora' from *Conversations Introducing Poetry* (1804) and Sarah Hoare's 'The Pleasures of Botanical Pursuits, A Poem', appended to the eighth edition of Wakefield's *An Introduction to Botany* in 1818 and later appearing as *A Poem on the Pleasures and Advantages of Botanical Pursuits* (1826), are examples of this new genre as is Frances Arabella Rowden's *A Poetical Introduction to the Study of Botany* (1801).

The figure of the Swedish naturalist Carl Linnaeus haunts this study. Linnaeus is known to have corresponded with British women botanists, most notably Anna Blackburne of Orford Hall. However, his involvement with British women in the culture of botany went far deeper than this polite exchange of letters. Linnaeus influenced British women's engagement with botany in dramatic and contradictory ways. Conventional morality dictated that women should not become too familiar with the terminology of the Sexual System and by the early nineteenth century there was a movement to ensure that no botanical textbook would bring 'the blush of injured modesty to the innocent fair'; simultaneously, the Linnaean sexual system was becoming unacceptable in England.[32] I introduced sexuality debates in relation to botany earlier in my discussion of literary texts written in the last decade of the eighteenth century. Eighteenth-century botany remained associated with sexuality due to Darwin's libidinous account of *The Loves of the Plants* (1789, 1791) and the Linnaean Joseph Banks's reputation as a libertine.[33] Darwin caused controversy by addressing his colourful descriptions of Linnaeus's floral harems to women, and Banks's reputation for sexual promiscuity arose from Hawkesworth's unreliable account of the visit to Tahiti on Cook's *Endeavour* voyage.[34]

To understand the impact of the Sexual System on the botanical culture of the 1790s it is necessary to look at the development of such a system and to explore Linnaeus's contribution to British botany in the eighteenth century. Linnaeus was the founder of the Sexual System but he was not the first to teach the theory of plant sexuality; his contribution was to popularise this and give it a solid empirical foundation. The ancients were not ignorant of the existence of sex in plants, nor were seventeenth-century naturalists such as Sir Thomas Millington (1628–1703) and John Ray (1627–1705). The English gardener Philip Miller had written about plant fertilisation by bees in 1721 and addressed the sexuality of plants in his *Catalogus Plantarum* of 1730. However, it was the Frenchman, Sébastien Vaillant (1669–1722), who had first brought plant sexuality to Linnaeus's attention. Vaillant had studied under botanist and explorer Joseph Fitton de Tournefort (1656–1708) and held an appointment as botanist at the Jardin du Roi in Paris.[35] At the opening of the garden in 1717, he gave an address entitled *Discours sur la structure des fleurs*, an exposition of the sexual function of flowers, which was rendered shocking by his use of vernacular terminology. Vaillant had spoken of flowers as the sexual organs of plants, comparing the stamens to the penis, yet he had never demonstrated his theory by experiment.[36] Vaillant's ideas were communicated to Linnaeus in an academic oration by the Dutch botanist and physician Hermann Boerhaave (1668–1738) in 1717.[37] From this time onwards, Linnaeus laboured to develop his understanding of plant sexuality. He confirmed that plants reproduce sexually in a prize-winning essay to the St Petersburg Academy in 1759. This dissertation on the sexes of plants was published in 1760 and James Edward Smith (1755–1828) translated the pioneering work from Latin into English in 1786.[38]

Linnaeus demonstrated that the generation of plants was sexual in an experiment on hemp. When male plants from one lot of seedlings are removed, and a pot is kept which contains only female plants, the female plants are only fertilised by pollen carried by the wind. Linnaeus thus identified pollen as the 'impregnating powder'. He employed his humanised imagery in the description of the experiment itself where female plants are 'widows' or 'virgins'.[39] The idea of pollen being carried 'promiscuously' aloft by the wind shocked William Smellie (1740–95), compiler of the first edition of the *Encyclopaedia Britannica* (1771) and author of *Philosophy of Natural History* (1790), who refused to believe that the Creator would leave something as important as reproduction to mere chance.[40] Smellie asserted that, contrary to the theory of pollination expressed by Linnaeus, 'all the laws of nature are fixed, steady and uniform, in their operations'.[41] The idea that the laws of nature governing reproduction in plants could be abandoned to apparent uncertainties proved controversial at a time when social order and natural order were considered interdependent.

I have already mentioned that Linnaeus made use of human–plant analogies; his nomenclature was inspired by traditional wedding imagery and marriage metaphors permeate his botanical taxonomy. However, despite this emphasis on marriage, Linnaeus disclosed that there is only one monogamous class of plants. This scarcity of monogamy outraged Johann Siegesbeck of St Petersburg who could not comprehend how anyone could teach so 'licentious' a method. Siegesbeck had much in common with the best-known British critic of Linnaeus, Charles Alston (1685–1760).[42] Alston had studied under Boerhaave at the University of Leyden and favoured Tournefort's system of classification (Tournefort did not admit the existence of sex in plants and divided plants into twenty-two classes according to the general form of the flower). Both men found the Sexual System inadequate but also morally repulsive. Siegesbeck, for example, argued in 1737 that the Creator of the vegetable kingdom would never have permitted such 'loathsome harlotry' as several males fertilising one female.[43]

Religious debates in relation to botany resurface in the late eighteenth century: the country clergy, many of whom were amateur naturalists following in the footsteps of John Ray, did not like the direction botany had taken since Linnaeus. An example was the Reverend Richard Polwhele, author of *The Unsex'd Females* (1798), which as I declared earlier, contained an attack on women botanists. Polwhele exemplified the country clergy's claims on botany as a virtuous pastime associated with the local knowledge of the amateur naturalist. He produced topographical works including *The History of Devonshire* (1793–97) and the *History of Cornwall* (1803–08). In poems such as 'The Influence of Local Attachment with Respect to Home', Polwhele demonstrates how 'the mind is acted upon by localities' and, he argued, this particularised knowledge could be extended to an observation of plants in a particular geographical area. Polwhele's emphasis on geographical location and the centrality of local habitat to botanical study is at odds with Linnaeus, who sought principles that would hold universally. An uncritical advocate of 'local knowledge', Polwhele expressed that hostility to universalism which is often connected to reactionary and nationalistic ideologies.[44]

Satirical and parodic attacks on Linnaeus appeared in the mid-eighteenth century, differing in content from those that would be inspired by the later upsurge in popularity of botany for women, but prefiguring them by providing their general form. Unconcerned with morality, they mocked instead the ancient idea of a plant as an inverted animal which Linnaeus had adopted: 'the stomach of plants is the earth, the lacteal vessels the root, the bones the trunk, the lungs are the leaves, and the heart is heat'.[45] These comparisons inspired La Mettrie's *L'Homme plante* (1748).[46] The 'human plant' of this satire is described according to the rules of Linnaean botany and belongs to the class *Dioecia* (derived from the Greek for 'two homes or houses') and order *Monandria* ('one husband'), with only one stamen or pistil. The pistil and stilus (penis and vagina) are classified, and given measurements and definitions in the manner of flora.[47]

The Man Plant: Or, Scheme for Increasing and Improving the British Breed (1752) is a British satire of botanical treatises clearly inspired by La Mettrie (1709–51). The author, Vincent Miller, adopting the persona of a professor of philosophy, describes a scheme of 'maturing the Man-foetus by artificial heat'.[48] His instructions for the propagation of a human ovum in a hothouse specifically satirise Linnaean analogies between the animal and vegetable kingdoms. 'In the following Formulary', states Miller, 'the Female of the human species is described, as a Flower Plant, in the Method of *Linnaeus*'.[49] The gardener's daughter, Sally, a woman of easy virtue selected for the purposes of the experiment, is described in suitably clichéd floral epithets:

> She was in that critical Season, when the integrity of a Girl hangs upon a single Hair, and her Virgin flower sits so loose, that it drops with the least shake, or warm Breath, as one sees a Peach-blossom blown away with the lightest puff of a Western Breeze.[50]

Sally is seduced, prescribed 'a proper regimen, of light, digestible, and analeptic food'[51] and produces an egg after thirty-nine days. The human egg, planted in a basket of earth and hatched after a period of eight months, is described as belonging to the class *Dioecia*, order *Monandria* and is of the genus *Homo*.

The sexual imagery in Linnaeus invited such parodies; similarly, for the translators of Linnaeus, the persuasiveness of the Sexual System was often due more to its rhetoric rather than its empirical validity. In Chapter 1 I demonstrate how Linnaeus offered what appeared to be a boudoir version of botany where 'male' stamens and 'female' pistils were likened to brides and bridegrooms on their nuptial bed. Hugh Rose's translation of Linnaeus's *Philosophia botanica* (1775) elaborates on Linnaeus's theme of consummation within marriage:

> The *calyx* then is the marriage bed, the *corolla* the curtains, the filaments the spermatic vessels, the *antherae* the testicles, the dust the male sperm, the *stigma* the extremity of the female organ, the *style* the *vagina*, the *germen* the ovary.[52]

Such analogies between the anatomy of flowers and the human reproductive organs offended Charles Alston, the King's botanist, who complained that 'no imagined analogy between plants and animals can warrant or excuse the fulsome and obscene names, imposed by the sexualists on the different parts of the fructification of vegetables'.[53]

The Sexual System both inspired and provided the formal methodology for a diverse range of texts in English from Withering's *Botanical Arrangement* to Darwin's *Botanic Garden* and Robert Thornton's *Temple of Flora* (1807) These texts were female centred and it was this approach that popularised Linnaean botany as a female pursuit in the eighteenth century. The Linnaean society did not open its doors to women until as late as 1919, but British women were practising the modern system of botany in the late eighteenth century, despite fears that the sexual system of classification threatened feminine modesty.[54] The idea that sexuality was the key to classification proved controversial at a time when the laws of nature were conventionally appealed to as the justification for social mores.

British women writers' engagement with Linnaean methodology and Linnaean ideas is the main subject of this book. Before I introduce the Linnaean texts that are the focus of this study, I undertake a wider investigation into the culture of botany and the cultivation of female minds in the Enlightenment in order to establish the background. Chapter 1 thus explores women's problematic relationship to Enlightenment culture through an investigation of contemporary literary analogies between women and flowers. Rousseau features prominently but other writers appear. Floral metaphors contrasting cultivation and decadence with naturalness and simplicity flourish. Conversely, botanical imagery that binds culture, social progress and education proliferates, opposing these themes to nature and underdevelopment; all this rhetoric is invariably gendered. Centrally, I emphasise Mary Wollstonecraft's strategy of appropriating the language of botany to expose the contradictions underlying Enlightenment universalism with regard to women.

Chapter 2 investigates the initiation of a process of feminisation of botany in Rousseau's and Priscilla Wakefield's letters on botany; these were literary and educational texts addressed specifically to women. This feminisation is examined in relation to the gendered dichotomy of the public and private spheres. During the course of this study, contradictory tendencies emerge: women's botany could have a repressive, domesticating, ideological function but was simultaneously liberating, allowing women to participate to some extent in the public community of Enlightenment scientific discovery.

Linnaean classification exemplified order, making botany an ideal discipline for young British women in the eighteenth century. Chapter 3 pursues these themes of order and nationality. The ordered nature of botanical taxonomic systems conveniently lent itself to ideological constructions of social hierarchy. Rivalries with France drove this botany in 'an English dress', introducing nationalistic strands which contrasted with the disinterested global nature of Linnaeus's system. For instance, the work of William Withering – whose botany was localised and desexualised – proliferated with military imagery. Lady Charlotte Murray and others followed Withering in this undermining of Linnaean principles by similarly concentrating on the local and down-playing problematic sexual reproduction. Maria Jacson would restore the original universalising impulse to botanical study, though ambiguously. Erasmus Darwin, in *The Botanic Garden*, controversially emphasised the sexual dimension in a way that had obvious and disturbing implications for human society; various women's texts of the period responded in a complex way to this subversive text.

Chapter 4 expands upon these responses: Darwin's explicit discussion of sexuality related to the aura of illicit sexuality that had surrounded Sir Joseph Banks. Botany, from being a reputable and chaste enterprise for women, had suddenly become dangerous. Popular botanical texts rigorously suppressed the sexual aspect, so crucial to the scientific advance made by Linnaeus. Reactionary opponents of Darwin and other radicals – often religiously inspired – denounced women botanists and the Linnaean system. The outcome was an unfortunate regression to a sanitised, unscientific and politically conservative feminine botany that, in the early nineteenth century, came to replace the enlightened women's botany that – despite some ambivalence – had had a genuinely emancipatory character. I argue that the most progressive botanical texts by and for women were produced during the Linnaean years in England.

Chapter 5 focuses on early nineteenth-century debates and demonstrates how scientific botany came into conflict with the craft of floristry. The preference for indigenous botany and favouring of British flora over cultivated exotics and hybrids took on nationalistic overtones and there was a class dimension too. Caught up in this opposition was the parallel dichotomy of the universal and the particular that appeared in the aesthetics of Reynolds, Johnson and others. Inevitably, this debate had a gendered aspect: botanical texts by Maria Jacson and Robert Thornton and the poetry of Charlotte Smith, Arabella Rowden and others (which employed botanical discourse) reveal these themes in a context of anxiety about women and social order.

I conclude by returning to botany's role in the rational education of young women. Native flowers were invested with virtue and used for moral teaching in periodical literature for women and in pedagogical texts featuring young female protagonists. Charlotte Smith's *Rural Walks* (1797) and Wollstonecraft's *Original Stories* (1788) are examples of this. Despite some didacticism, these are enlightened and progressive works and, while they anticipate the language of flowers in nineteenth-century texts 'for ladies', they remain generically and scientifically distinct from the Victorian flower books that succeed them.

Notes

1 Maria Edgeworth, *Letters for Literary Ladies to which is added an Essay on the Noble Science of Self-Justification*, ed. Claire Connnolly (2nd edn 1798; London: J. M. Dent, 1993), p. 21.

2 James Plumptre, *The Lakers: A Comic Opera in Three Acts*, intr. Jonathan Wordsworth (London: printed for W. Clarke, 1798; facs. repr. Woodstock Books: Oxford and New York, 1990), I.1.2)). All further references are to this edition and are given in parentheses in the text as act and scene numbers followed by page. 'Lakers' was the name locals gave to the first tourists who visited Cumberland, as it was then known, in search of the picturesque. In Plumptre's text these visitors include the poet, the painter, and the botanist. Veronica, the heroine, is described as 'a great botanist and picturesque traveller'; she frequently cites Gilpin and is well versed in Erasmus Darwin's *The Loves of the Plants*. Plumptre is satirising these fashionable pursuits, and recommends that readers familiarise themselves with *West's Guide to the Lakes* (1795) and Darwin's *The Botanic Garden* (1791) (*The Loves of the Plants* formed the second part of this and was first published in 1789).

3 Erasmus Darwin, 'Key of the Sexual System', in *The Families of Plants, with Their Natural Characters* ..., 2 vols (London: printed by John Jackson; sold by J. Johnson, 1787), I, lxxvii–lxxx. Further references are given in parentheses in the text.

4 David Elliston Allen, *The Naturalist in Britain: A Social History* (London: Allen Lane, 1976), pp. 30–1.

5 See Ruth Hayden, *Mrs Delany and Her Floral Collages* (London: British Museum Press, 1980).

6 See Barbara T. Gates, *Kindred Nature: Victorian and Edwardian Women Embrace the Living World* (Chicago and London: University of Chicago Press, 1998) and Barbara T. Gates (ed.), *In Nature's Name: An Anthology of Women's Writing and Illustration 1780–1930* (Chicago and London: University of Chicago Press, 2002).

7 Ann B. Shteir, *Cultivating Women, Cultivating Science: Flora's Daughters and Botany in England 1760–1860* (Baltimore, MD and London: Johns Hopkins University Press, 1996); Londa Schiebinger, *The Mind Has No Sex? Women In the Origins of Modern Science* (Cambridge, MA and London: Harvard University Press, 1989).

8 Shteir's study only contains two brief references to Rousseau's botanical letters (Shteir, *Cultivating Women*, pp. 19, 82).

9 Rousseau, *The Confessions* in *The Collected Writings of Rousseau*, V, ed. Christopher Kelly, Roger D. Masters and Peter G. Stillman, trans. Christopher Kelly (Hanover, NH and London: University Press of New England, 1995), p. 537.

10 See Dave Edmunds and John Eidinow, *Rousseau's Dog: Two Great Thinkers at War in the Age of Enlightenment* (London: Faber and Faber, 2006), p. 287.

11 There are obvious similarities between these two texts. Both explain the Linnaean system in a series of letters, one for each class, and centre on an intimate exchange of knowledge between two women. Rousseau's text is written for a young woman and her daughter and Wakefield's is comprised of a correspondence between two sisters. They also each feature a botanising teacher or governess who superintends the letters.

12 The first edition was published under the title *Julie ou la Nouvelle Héloïse: Lettres de deaux amants, habitants d'une petite ville au pied des Alps*, 6 vols (Amsterdam: Marc Michel Rey, 1761). The first English edition was published as *Eloisa: Or, a Series of Original Letters Collected and Published by J. J. Rousseau. Translated from the French. In four volumes*, 4 vols (London: R. Griffiths, T. Becket, P. A. De Hondt, 1761).

13 See Jane Rendall's remarks about this in *The Origins of Modern Feminism: Women in Britain, France and the United States, 1780–1860* (London: Macmillan, 1985), pp. 15–18.

14 These Irish women ran away from their aristocratic homes and took a cottage together in Wales. Their favourite book was *La Nouvelle Héloïse* and they are believed to have modelled their unusually aristocratic cottage garden at Plas Newydd on Julie's Elysium. For a discussion of this garden, see Anne Scott-James, *The Cottage Garden* (London: Allen Lane, 1981), pp. 29–33. For an account of their friendship see Elizabeth Mavor, *The Ladies of Llangollen: A Study in Romantic Friendship* (London: Michael Joseph, 1971).

15 Seward's visit to Llangollen is recounted by John Brewer in *The Pleasures of the Imagination: English Culture in the Eighteenth Century* (London: Harper Collins, 1997), p. 606. The volume of verse she dedicated to them was published in 1796 (*Llangollen Vale with other Poems* (London: G. Sael, 1796)).

16 Wilfrid Blunt, *The Compleat Naturalist: A Life of Linnaeus* (London: Collins, 1971); Wilfrid Blunt and William T. Stearn, *The Art of Botanical Illustration* (first pub. London: Collins, 1950; rev. edn Woodbridge, Suffolk: Antique Collector's Club, 1994); William T. Stearn, 'Linnaeus's "Species Plantarum" and the Language of Botany', *Proceedings of the Linnaean Society of London*, 165, part 2 (1955), 158–64; William T. Stearn, 'Carl Linnaeus: Classifier and Namer of Living Things', *New Scientist*, 4 (1958), 401–3; William T. Stearn, 'The Origin of the Male and Female Symbols of Biology', *Taxon*, 11:4 (1962), 109–13; Frans Stafleau, *Linnaeus and the Linnaeans: The Spreading of their Ideas in Systematic Botany 1735–1789* (Utrecht: Oosthoek's Uitgeversmaatschappis N.V. for the International Society of Plant Taxonomy, 1971); Lisbet Koerner, *Linnaeus: Nature and Nation* (Cambridge, MA and London: Harvard University Press, 1999); Tore Frängsmyr (ed.), *Linnaeus: The Man and the Work* (Berkeley, CA and London: University of California Press, 1983).

17 See Mary Louise Pratt, *Imperial Eyes: Travel Writing and Transculturation* (London: Routledge, 1992); Barbara Stafford, *Voyage Into Substance: Art, Science, Nature and the Illustrated Travel Account, 1760–1840* (Cambridge, MA: MIT Press, 1984); Beth Fowkes Tobin, 'Imperial Designs, Botanical Illustration and the British Empire', *Studies in Eighteenth-Century Culture*, 25 (1996), 265–92; David Phillip Miller and Peter Hanns Reill (eds), *Visions of Empire: Voyages, Botany and Representations of Nature* (Cambridge: Cambridge University Press, 1996).

18 See Gerald Dennis Meyer, *The Scientific Lady in England 1650–1760: An Account of Her Rise With Emphasis on the Major Roles of the Telescope and Microscope*

(Berkeley, CA and Los Angeles: University of California Press, 1955); Patricia Phillips, *The Scientific Lady: A Social History of Women's Scientific Interests 1520–1918* (London: Weidenfeld and Nicholson, 1990); Myra Reynolds, *The Learned Lady in England 1650–1760* (Gloucester, MA: Peter Smith, 1964).

19 Patricia Phillips, *The Scientific Lady*, p. 97.

20 Marjorie Hope Nicolson, *Newton Demands the Muse: Newton's Opticks and the Eighteenth-Century Poets* (Princeton, NJ: Princeton University Press, 1966).

21 Loraine Fletcher, *Charlotte Smith: A Critical Biography* (London: Macmillan, 1998).

22 See Judith Pascoe, 'Female Botanists and the Poetry of Charlotte Smith', in Carol Shiner Wilson and Joel Haefner (eds), *Re-Visioning Romanticism: British Women Writers, 1776–1837* (Philadelphia: University of Pennsylvania Press, 1994), pp. 193–209; Donelle R. Ruwe, 'Charlotte Smith's Sublime: Feminine Poetics, Botany and Beachy Head', *Prism(s): Essays in Romanticism*, 7 (1999), 117–32; Anne D. Wallace, 'Picturesque Fossils, Sublime Geology? The Crisis of Authority in Charlotte Smith's Beachy Head', *European Romantic Review*, 13 (2002), 77–93; Donna Landry, 'Green Languages? Women Poets As Naturalists in 1653 and 1807', *Huntington Library Quarterly*, 63:4 (2000), 467–89.

23 Janet Browne, 'Botany for Gentleman: Erasmus Darwin and the Loves of the Plants', *ISIS: Journal of the History of Science Society*, 80:304 (December 1989), 593–621; 'Botany in the Boudoir and Garden: The Banksian Context', in Miller and Reill (eds), *Visions of Empire*, 153–72; Alan Bewell, 'Jacobin Plants: Botany As Social Theory in the 1790s', '"On the Banks of the South Sea": Botany and Sexual Controversy in the Late Eighteenth Century', in Miller and Reill (eds), *Visions of Empire*, pp. 173–91; Londa Schiebinger, 'The Private Life of Plants: Sexual Politics in Carl Linnaeus and Erasmus Darwin', in Marina Benjamin (ed.), *Science and Sensibility: Gender and Scientific Enquiry 1780–1945* (Oxford: Oxford University Press, 1991), pp. 121–43; *Nature's Body: Sexual Politics and the Making of Modern Science* (London: Pandora, 1993); Tim Fulford, 'Coleridge, Darwin, Linnaeus: The Sexual Politics of Botany', *Wordsworth Circle*, 28:3 (1997), 124–30.

24 Anna Seward, *Memoirs of the Life of Dr Darwin* (London: J. Johnson, 1804), p. 131.

25 Vivien Jones, 'Advice and Enlightenment: Mary Wollstonecraft and Sex Education', in Sarah Knott and Barbara Taylor (eds), *Women, Gender and Enlightenment* (Basingstoke: Palgrave Macmillan, 2005), pp. 140–55.

26 Sue Bennett's book *Women and Gardens* (London: National Portrait Gallery, 2000) was accompanied by a special exhibition. Stephen Bending is currently completing a research project on women and gardens in the long eighteenth century (*Retirement and Disgrace: Women and Gardens in the Eighteenth Century*).

27 Charles Abbot, 'Preface', *Flora bedfordiensis* ... (Bedford: Printed and sold by W. Smith, and G. G. & J. Robinson, 1798), p. vi.

28 See V. P. Wystrach, 'Anna Blackburne (1792–93): a neglected patroness of natural history', *Journal of the Society for the Bibliography of Natural History*, 8 (1976–78), 148–68.

29 Mary Berry to Horace Walpole, 29th April, 1789, in *The Yale Edition of Horace Walpole's Correspondence*, ed. W. S. Lewis and A. Dayle Wallace, 31 vols (London: Oxford University Press; New Haven: Yale University Press, 1937–61), XI, p. 12.

30 Priscilla Wakefield, 'Preface', *Mental Improvement*, 2 vols (London: Darton and Harvey, 1794), I, p. ii.

31 *Ibid.*, pp. 39–40.

32 See W. T. Stearn, 'Preface', Carl Linnaeus, *Species Plantarum* (Uppsala: [n. pub], 1753; repr. Ray Society: London, 1957), p. 25.

33 A number of critics, notably Philip Ritterbush, François Delaporte, Londa Schiebinger, Janet Browne, Tim Fulford and Alan Bewell, have explored botany and sexual politics in the late eighteenth century. For a general discussion, see Philip Ritterbush, *Overtures to Biology: The Speculations of Eighteenth-Century Naturalists* (New Haven, CT: Yale University Press, 1964) and François Delaporte, *Nature's Second Kingdom: Explorations of Vegetality in the Eighteenth Century*, trans. Arthur Goldhammer (Cambridge, MA: MIT Press, 1982). For Erasmus Darwin and Linnaeus, see Schiebinger, 'The Private Life of Plants'; Browne, 'Botany For Gentleman'; Fredrika J. Teute, 'The Loves of the Plants; or, the Cross Fertilization of Science and Desire at the End of the Eighteenth-Century', *Huntington Library Quarterly*, 63:3 (2000), 319–45; Fulford, 'Coleridge, Darwin, Linnaeus'. Luisa Calé has covered some of the texts that I will be exploring here such as those by Darwin, William Smellie, and Richard Polwhele; however, she does not include any of the women's texts and she has adopted a poststructuralist approach which I have avoided ('"A Female Band Despising Nature's Law": Botany, Gender and Revolution in the 1790s', *Romanticism on the Net*, 17 (February 2000). For Banks, botany and sexuality, see Alan Bewell, '"On the Banks of the South Seas"', and Browne, 'Botany in the Boudoir and Garden'.

34 John Hawkesworth, *An Account of the Voyages Undertaken by the Order of His Present Majesty For Making Discoveries in the Southern Hemisphere*, 3 vols (London: W. Strahan & T. Cadell, 1773). Commenting on Hawkesworth's account, Jonathan Lamb writes: 'in short, it was whatever approximated to the novelistic without seeming too improbable' (Jonathan Lamb, *Preserving the Self in the South Seas 1680–1840* (Chicago and London: University of Chicago Press, 2001), p. 100).

35 Joseph Pitton de Tournefort was Professor of Botany at the Jardin des Plantes from 1688, and was in charge of a scientific expedition to Asia and parts of Europe. In *Institutiones Rei Herbariae*, 3 vols (Paris: [n. pub.], 1700) he defined 698 genera principally on the basis of characters of the corolla and fructification. Many of his genera continued to be recognised though re-defined and re-named by Linnaeus. In *Elémens de botanique, ou methode pour connoître les plantes*, 3 vols (Paris: [n. pub.], 1694) he criticised Ray for using more characters than were essential in defining genera and species. Ray's *De variis plantarum methodis dissertatio brevis* (London: [n. pub.], 1696) was a defence of the principles of natural classification against such artificial 'essentialist' classifications as Tournefort and others. See A. G. Morton, *History of Botanical Science* (London: Academic Press, 1981), p. 228. See also my account of Linnaeus's rejection of Tournefort in Chapter 1 above, p. 20.

36 For Sebastien Vaillant, see Morton, *History of Botanical Science*, pp. 241–2.

37 The 1717 oration by Boerhaave was entitled *Sermo de Structura Florum.*

38 [Carl Linnaeus,] *A Dissertation on the Sexes of Plants Translated From the Latin of Linnaeus By James Edward Smith, F. R. S.* (London: George Nicol, 1786). James Edward Smith's 1786 translation of Linnaeus's 'Dissertation on the Sexes of Plants' (1760) celebrated the triumph of the Sexual System over the work of Linnaeus's opponents such as Adanson (Smith, 'Preface', in Linnaeus, *A Dissertation*, pp. xiii–xiv). Smith became the most prominent English Linnaean after Joseph Banks, purchasing Linnaeus's herbarium collections and manuscripts and founding the Linnaean Society of London in 1788. For a comprehensive list of Smith's botanical works and collaborations, see Blanche Henrey, *British Botanical and Horticultural Literature*

before 1800, 3 vols (Oxford: Oxford University Press, 1975), III, pp. 115–17. For the Linnaean Society, see Andrew Thomas Gage, *A History of the Linnaean Society of London* (London: Taylor & Francis for the Linnaean Society, 1938). For biographical details, see *Memoir and Correspondence of Sir James Edward Smith*, ed. Lady Pleasance Smith, 2 vols (London, Longman, Rees, Orme, Brown, Green, 1832).

39 Linnaeus, *Dissertation*, pp. 33–4.

40 William Smellie, *The Philosophy of Natural History* (Edinburgh: Printed for the Heirs of Charles Elliot and T. Kay; London: T. Cadell and G. G. & J. Robinson, 1790), p. 251.

41 Smellie, *Philosophy*, p. 251.

42 Charles Alston was appointed King's Botanist in 1716; he succeeded George Preston as Professor of Botany at the University of Edinburgh in 1738. When Linnaeus introduced his Sexual System of classification, Alston argued against it in a paper entitled 'A Dissertation on the Sexes of Plants' which was read before the Edinburgh Medical Society and published in 1754.

43 Siegesbeck on Linnaeus as cited in W. T. Stearn, 'Preface', in Linnaeus, *Species Plantarum*.

44 After the anthropologist, Clifford Geertz. See David Simpson, 'Being There?: Literary Criticism, localism and local knowledge', *Critical Quarterly*, 35:3 (Autumn 1993), 3–17 (p. 3).

45 Hugh Rose, *The Elements of Botany*... (London: T. Cadell & M. Hingeston, 1775), p. 151.

46 La Mettrie, *L'Homme plante* (Potsdam: [n. pub.] 1748). There is a modern edition by F. L. Rougier (New York: The Institute of French Studies, 1936). For a discussion of La Mettrie in connection to Linnaeus, see Gunnar Broberg, 'Linnaeus's Classification of Man', in Frangsmyr (ed.), *Linnaeus: The Man and His Work*, p. 174. La Mettrie's better-known *L'Homme machine*, an extremely mechanistic explanation of human behaviour, was published in the same year. La Mettrie listed Linnaeus in his *Ouvrage de Pénélope ou Machiavel en Médecine* (Geneva: Heirs of Cramer & P. Philibert, 1748), a scathing compendium of eminent men of science.

The Natural History of the Arbor Vitae, or Tree of Life and *The Natural History of the Frutex Vulvaria, or Flowering Shrub* were both published in 1732, the latter by an evocatively named Philogynes Clitorides. Both pamphlets are botanical skits and are often attributed to Thomas Stretser. The tree of life and the flowering shrub represent male and female genitalia (the *vulvaria* is defined as the female *Arbor Vitae*). There are a range of puns, double entendre, sexual allusions and innuendos at work in these texts.

47 Botanical allegory has been largely overlooked in studies on eighteenth-century erotica. Peter Wagner makes this point and comments briefly on botanical–biological allegory in his chapter on extended metaphor in *Eros Revived: Erotica of the Enlightenment in England and America* (London: Paladin Books, 1990), pp. 192–4. Much has been written on the geographical or topographical allegory in eighteenth-century erotica, notably by David Foxon, *Libertine Literature in England 1660–1745* (London: Book Collector: 1955); Peter Fryer, *Mrs Grundy: Studies in English Prudery* (London: Dennis Dobson, 1963) and Roger Thompson, *Unfit For Modest Ears* (London: Macmillan, 1979). More recently, Paul-Gabriel Boucé has analysed sexual puns in a selection of scientific/philosophic satires in his essay 'Chthonic and Pelagic Metaphorization in Eighteenth-Century English Erotica', in Robert Purks MacCubbin (ed.), *'Tis Nature's Fault: Unauthorised Sexuality During*

the Enlightenment (New York: Press Syndicate of the University of Cambridge, 1987), pp. 202–17. A number of examples of British erotica from this period have been reprinted in Alexander Pettit and Patrick Spedding (eds), *Eighteenth-Century British Erotica*, 5 vols (London: Pickering and Chatto, 2001).

48 Vincent Miller, *The Man Plant: Or, Scheme for Increasing and Improving the British Breed* (London: M. Cooper, 1752), p. 19.

49 *Ibid.*, p. 9.

50 *Ibid.*, p. 25.

51 *Ibid.*, p. 29.

52 Rose, *Elements of Botany*, p. 151.

53 Charles Alston, 'A Dissertation on the Sexes of Plants', in *Essays and Observations …*, 5 vols, 2nd edn (Edinburgh: Printed for John Balfour, 1771), I, pp. 308–9.

54 For women in scientific societies, see Colin A. Russell, *Science and Social Change 1700–1900* (London: Macmillan, 1983), p. 195.

1
'The sweet flowers that smile in the walk of man': floral femininity and female education

Cultivation of the mind

THE INTERPLAY between the culture of botany and the cultivation of female minds during the Enlightenment in Britain is my wider theme; it provides the context for my unravelling of the dynamics of the encounter between Linnaeus's Sexual System and the lives of British women. Rousseau proves crucial to this discussion as an educationalist and botanist, and Wollstonecraft, much influenced by him, also enters the debate, launching an attack on flowery diction in works for the education of women. The traditional metaphoric association of women with flowers was frequently employed in books which sought to engage women in the different areas of floriculture; Wollstonecraft was to unmask the false sentiment behind these tropes.

Henry Fuseli's frontispiece to Erasmus Darwin's long poem *The Botanic Garden* (1791) depicts Flora as the goddess of botany, being attired by the elements (Fig. 1). Flora gazes into a mirror held before her by the nymph of fire while the other elements, air, earth, and water, adorn her with flowers. An allegorical reading of Fuseli's design suggests that botany is a mirror in which femininity can be examined: similarly, women's relationship to Enlightenment culture can be illuminated through an analysis of literary comparisons between women and cultivated flowers.[1] This chapter investigates the relationship between images of cultivation and growth and those of luxuriant decay in texts by Enlightenment figures such as John Millar and Rousseau, alongside Mary Wollstonecraft's more subversive practice. Many works of this period demonstrate that, while cultivation is connected with Enlightenment progress, femininity is either located within a discourse of luxury and consequent degeneration (i.e. over-cultivation) or in a realm of minimal cultivation, close to a state of nature.

Images of husbandry and cultivation in Enlightenment literature indicate the close relationship that exists between 'culture' and 'cultivation'. In Johnson's *Dictionary* (1755) to 'cultivate' is 'to forward or improve', while 'culture' is 'the act of cultivation' or 'the art of improvement and melioration'.[2] Raymond Williams shows the derivation of 'culture' and 'cultivation' from the Latin, *cultura* and *colere*. *Colere* had a range of overlapping meanings such as 'cultivate' and 'inhabit' which developed through *colonus* to colony. *Cultura* became assimilated with 'cultivation', entering the English language as 'culture' with its primary

1 Henry Fuseli, 'Flora Attired by the Elements' (frontispiece to *The Botanic Garden*)

meaning of husbandry or the tending of natural growth. In its early uses 'culture' had been a noun of process – the tending of something; by the eighteenth century this was extended metaphorically to a process of human development.[3] The interchangeability of 'culture' and 'cultivation' in eighteenth-century literature is common: Johnson, for example, exclaims, 'she neglected the *culture* of her understanding'[4] (1759), while George Colman advises parents to censor their daughter's reading and not to trust 'the *cultivation* of her mind to a circulating library' (1760) [my emphases].[5]

The process of cultivation can itself embody the progressive spirit of enlightenment. Christopher Smart's *Jubilate Agno* (1758–63) rejoices in horticultural advancement:

> Let Hizkijah rejoice with the Dwarf American Sunflower.
> For the art of Agriculture is improving.
>
> Let Azzur rejoice with the Globe-thistle.
> For this is evident in flowers.
>
> Let Hariph rejoice with Summer Savoury.
> For it is more especially manifest in double flowers.[6]

The rearing of unusual flowers, such as Smart's double blooms, shows humanity's ability constantly to improve on the old and to exult over the new, modern or exotic. Thomson's 'Spring', from *The Seasons* (1730), celebrates the successful cultivation of the 'tulip-race' where experimentation has led to the discovery of more exotic varieties:

> The varied Colours run; and, while they break
> On the charmed eye, the exulting florist marks
> With secret pride the wonders of his hand.[7]

Species of cultivated flowers available in England had escalated in numbers from approximately 200 types in 1500 to 18,000 by the 1830s.[8] A desire for novelty instigated a frivolous vogue for new flowers in which unusual varieties were often introduced only to be replaced by newer, more exotic ones. Tulips were one of the first cultivated flowers to command large sums of money – the tulip trade had gained notoriety due to 'tulipomania', the reckless craze over tulip bulbs in seventeenth-century Holland.[9]

Cultivated flowers, particularly the tulip, appear frequently in eighteenth-century satires on women.[10] In Pope's epistle 'To A Lady' (1735), the flamboyant tulip is compared to the richly adorned female figure:

> Ladies, like variegated Tulips, show,
> 'Tis to their Changes that their charms they owe;
> Their happy Spots the nice admirer take,
> Fine by defect, and delicately weak.[11]

Variegated tulips such as feathered or flamed varieties were show flowers, grown solely for competition.[12] During cultivation, a virus sometimes caused the colours of the tulip to 'break' and tulip 'freaks' to appear. The curious streaks of such tulips fascinated the florists who, remaining unaware of their true cause, saw an element of unpredictability or 'sport' in the flower.[13] Pope, however, an experienced gardener,[14] appears to have understood that such flowers were in fact diseased and specifically chose the unique colour changes of variegated tulips to depict the contrarieties that he saw in the female character. Pope's tulips are novel and attract attention but they are also defective; like his women, who are equally charming, they are 'fine by defect' and essentially corrupt.

The fashion for cultivated flowers has obvious associations with fashions in adorning the female body. Swift, in 'The Lady's Dressing Room', compares Celia's ablutions, the artifice by which the corrupt nature of the female body is concealed, to the cultivation of exotics: 'Such order from confusion sprung | Such gaudy *tulips* raised from *dung*'.[15] Rotting plaster or pigeon dung applied to tulip bulbs during cultivation was thought to bring about their coveted colour changes.[16] Celia, who 'rose from stinking ooze', is represented as unnatural, putrescent and infected like the cultivated tulip. The vibrant tulip delights the eye while the unclean practices used to rear them remain hidden; Celia, too, is colourfully adorned but Swift discovers the stinking corruption, the foul decaying body, which lies beneath her paint and powder. Swift's association of luxury with infection and decay recalls Forster's account of the new consumerism in England in 1767: 'In such a state as this fashion must have uncontrolled sway.

And a fashionable luxury must spread through it like a contagion'.[17] Swift saw eighteenth-century consumerism as the trading of unnecessary commodities, particularly for female consumption, and depicted capitalist society as an attempt to 'gratify the vanity and pride and luxury of women'.[18] In 1711, Addison made an ironic quip about man's cultivation of the female sex, stating that 'the whole sex is now dwarfed and shrunk into a race of beauties that seems almost another species'; subsequent analogies between women and cultivated flowers illustrate the specific way in which botany became a discourse on luxurious femininity.[19]

By 1792, Wollstonecraft's *A Vindication of the Rights of Woman* would appropriate and invert conventional cultivation metaphors, substituting images of enlightened growth for those of luxuriant decay in order to demonstrate society's neglect of women's educational potential. Wollstonecraft illustrates how society cultivates women like exotic flowering plants or 'luxuriants', where 'strength of body and mind are sacrificed to libertine notions of beauty'.[20] Her rationalist antipastoralism enables her to unmask the false sentiment behind the traditional metaphoric association of women and flowers and explode the familiar tropes, revealing them as embodiments of male desire, indicative of women's problematic relationship to culture. To understand Wollstonecraft's strategy we must examine the ways cultivation has been linked with progress in mainstream Enlightenment thought. We should also look at how even Enlightenment thinkers still embraced earlier conventions about women, particularly Rousseau who did, however, provide the foundations for much of Wollstonecraft's own philosophy.

Enlightened growth

John Millar's *The Origin of the Distinction of Ranks* (1771) follows the four-stage theory of human progress in which the changing position of women in society is central.[21] Despite the harsh treatment and low status to which women were subject in the early stage of human history, Millar placed considerable faith in the course of human progress, arguing that:

> it ought, at the same time to be remembered, that, how poor and wretched soever the aspect of human nature in this early state, it contains the seeds of improvement, which, by long care and culture, are capable of being brought to maturity.[22]

Such Enlightenment optimism over mankind's progress was often voiced in terms of botanical growth. For agriculturists such as Arthur Young (1741–1820), cultivation of the land was itself a civilising process that might bring 'the waste-lands of the kingdom into culture'.[23] In France, Enlightenment *philosophes* believed that mankind was advancing in a similar fashion from primitive barbarism to reason, virtue and civilisation. The contemporary stress in educational debates on the cultivation of the mind paralleled this Enlightenment faith in a reason that had a potential for open development: French *philosophes* such as Condillac, Turgot and Condorcet all emphasised cultivation as the beginning of the enlightenment process.[24]

The motif of the cultivation of the mind in James Thomson's *Spring* (1728) illustrates the Enlightenment celebration of social progress:

Delightful Task! to rear the tender Thought,
To teach the young Idea how to shoot,
To pour the fresh Instruction o'er the Mind,
To breathe th' inspiring Spirit, and to plant
The generous Purpose in the glowing Breast.[25]

Already a common trope in early to mid-eighteenth-century poetry, this theme appeared widely in educational writing in the 1780s and 1790s. A variant of Thomson's lines appears as a frontispiece to Erasmus Darwin's *A Plan For The Conduct of Female Education in Boarding Schools* (1797): 'Plant with nice hand reflection's tender root / And teach the young Ideas how to shoot',[26] while an extended metaphor of tending natural growth by 'careful cultivation' forms the euphoric epilogue to Dr Aikin and Anna Laetitia Barbauld's educational work, *Evenings At Home* (1792–96):

May wisdom's seeds in every mind
Fit soil and careful culture find;
Each generous plant with vigour shoot,
And kindly ripen into fruit!
Hope of the world, the *rising race*,
May heav'n with fostering love embrace,
And turning to a whiter page,
Commence with them a *better age*!
An Age of light and joy, which we
Alas! in promise only see.[27]

Here an investment in the 'careful culture' of 'wisdom's seeds' is shown to have its returns in the fruit of 'generous' plants. As vigorous young plants, Barbauld's youthful readers represent the promise of the next generation; they are members of 'the rising race' who, with their new-found knowledge, carry with them the 'hope of the world'. Like seeds or plantlets, all children, regardless of sex, have an equal capacity for growth. It is this universal potential which Barbauld's plant imagery celebrates.[28]

Barbauld, writing for the juvenile market, stresses the importance of education as a means to start society afresh by 'turning to a whiter page' in order to begin again, an image reminiscent of John Locke's tabula rasa.[29] In principle, due to its universalism, Enlightenment theories of human learning such as Locke's applied equally to women. However, the utopian drive for social progress during the Enlightenment encountered such barriers to female development as inadequate education and doubts about women's capacity for reason.[30] Women were regarded as being closer to nature, more emotional, incapable of objective reasoning and guided by different principles than men.[31] Gendered assertions such as these challenged those strands in Enlightenment thought that emphasised a universal human nature and human history.

Hegel's account of difference contains a memorable analogy between woman and plant. In attributing a plant-like fixity to women, Hegel is a major example of how universal humanism still managed to exclude women:

> Women may well be educated, but they are not made for higher sciences, for philosophy and certain artistic productions *which require a universal element.* Women may have insights [Einfalle], taste, and delicacy, but they do not possess the ideal. The difference between man and woman is the difference between animal and plant; the animal is closer in character to man, the plant to woman, for the latter is a more peaceful [process of] unfolding whose principle is the more indeterminate unity of feeling [Empfindung].[32]

The male mind, therefore, is active and acquires knowledge through struggle and exertion; the female mind is more placid and plant-like, being rooted and fixed in its immediate surroundings. Thus for Hegel, women's behaviour is prompted by instinct and local knowledge, by the particular and private rather than the universal. Notions of sexual difference of this kind are not in accord with Enlightenment universalism as elaborated by Condorcet, for instance, who argued that women be given the rights of citizenship and proposed the principle of their equality before the law.[33] Hegel's comparison between woman and plant is particularly striking in this context.

Other contemporary discussions of cultivation illustrate women's relationship to culture. For example, education and cultivation become gender-specific terms in Rousseau's *Emile* (1762). The task of early nurturing, of tending natural growth, belongs to the mother while the father is assigned the role of educator: 'The real nurse is the mother and the real teacher the father'.[34] Rousseau declares that 'Plants are fashioned by cultivation, man by education' (6) while simultaneously appealing to the 'tender anxious mother' using images of husbandry and cultivation: 'You can remove this young tree from the highway and shield it from the crushing force of social conventions. Tend and water it ere it dies. One day its fruit will reward your care' (6).

'Cultivation' is an appropriate term for the type of home learning available to women where they are reared to be good wives and mothers. It indicates Rousseau's emphasis on a mother's responsibility for the moral growth of her children: 'The earliest education is most important and it undoubtedly is woman's work' (5). That Rousseau recommends the exercise of careful cultivation is apparent in his enthusiastic description of Sophy, Emile's 'helpmeet': 'Her mind knows little but it is trained to learn, it is well-tilled soil ready for the sower' (373). This hint of authoritarianism is at odds with his earlier critique of the type of education in which 'man must learn his paces like a saddle-horse and be shaped to his master's hand like the trees in his garden' (5).

According to Rousseau, men's education leads them to be 'imprisoned by our institutions' while women undergo a process of cultivation within the home. Sophy's cultivation, however, does not involve the freedom which Rousseau values elsewhere. Emile's radical style of education is carefully planned by Rousseau so as not to stifle 'nature' in him; hitherto, he could have expected his adult life to be a struggle against control, compulsion and constraint.[35] In contrast, we learn that Sophy and her sex 'should early be accustomed to restraint' as 'their childish faults, unchecked and unheeded, may easily lead to dissipation, frivolity, and inconstancy' (322). The cultivation of the mind was thought to bring enlightenment;[36] the cultivation which Rousseau advocates for Sophy, however, reveals a need for order and containment akin to that symmetry and regularity which husbandry imposed on crops and where flowers and herbs were planted in uniform ranks.

Sensualised stasis

Mary Wollstonecraft's *A Vindication on the Rights of Woman* of 1792 turned Rousseau's own rhetoric of cultivation against his gendered view of education. Wollstonecraft confronted the contradictions implicit in Enlightenment ideas of gender by drawing attention to the ill effects suffered by women through inadequate education. Woman who are denied the opportunity to develop rationally become bound to stasis and sensuality, becoming 'insignificant objects of desire' who 'are made ridiculous and useless when the short-lived bloom of beauty is over' (11). According to Wollstonecraft's theory, society has cultivated women, rearing them as if they were exotic flowering plants or 'luxuriants' where 'strength of body and mind are sacrificed to libertine notions of beauty, to the desire of establishing themselves, – the only way women can rise in the world, – by marriage' (10).

The extended metaphor of the cultivation of the mind found in both Rousseau and Millar is taken a stage further by Wollstonecraft and is transformed in the process. She inverts its meaning, with images of sterility and decay replacing those of growth and maturity. By pushing the analogy further, she demonstrates how the limited nature of women's education has resulted in a 'barren blooming' and attributes the blame to those who consider 'females rather as women than human creatures' (7). Women's unenlightened state is described thus:

> The conduct and manners of women, in fact, evidently prove that their minds are not in a healthy state; for, like flowers which are planted in too rich a soil, strength and usefulness are sacrificed to beauty; and the flaunting leaves, after having pleased a fastidious eye, fade, disregarded on the stalk, long after the season when they ought to have arrived at maturity. (7)

'Maturity' is used here in Millar's sense of a potential for human progress that has become realised.[37] Wollstonecraft assumes an anti-pastoral rationalist stance, simultaneously using floral imagery to mimic the 'sickly delicacy' of taste that she abhors.[38] Her aim is to unmask the false sentiment behind the traditional metaphoric association of women and flowers by identifying such fanciful embellishment in educational writing as 'the language of men' whereby male desire conspires to make women 'alluring mistresses' rather than 'affectionate and rational mothers'. She calls for a return to 'the language of simple unadorned truth' in place of 'that flowery diction which has slided from essays into novels, and from novels into familiar letters and conversations' (10).

Linguistic conventions were already in place whereby flowers were emblems of purity, beauty and fragility – the so-called female virtues – and their ephemeral beauty was associated with the female body. By the eighteenth century, such floral imagery proliferated not only in poetry, essays, novels and letters but had extended to philosophic and scientific writing.[39] Linnaeus's description of the bog rosemary (*Andromeda polifolia*) recalls Ovid's *Metamorphoses;* the affinity between woman and plant is so keenly felt by Linnaeus that the marshy shrub is transformed into a beautiful virgin evoking the Andromeda myth:

> As I looked at her I was reminded of Andromeda as described by the poets, and the more I thought about her the more affinity she seemed to have with the plant ... Her beauty is preserved only so long as she remains a virgin (as often happens with women also)—i.e. until she is fertilized, which will not now be long as she is a bride. She is anchored far out in the water, set always on a little tuft in the marsh and fast tied as if on a rock in the midst of the sea. The water comes up to her knees, above her roots; and she is always surrounded by poisonous dragons and beasts—i.e. evil toads and frogs—which drench her with water when they mate in the spring. She stands and bows her head in grief. Then her little clusters of flowers with their rosy cheeks droop and grow ever paler and paler.[40]

Linnaeus's observation of the plant is informed by an idealised conception of passive femininity, of virtue in distress.

Elsewhere, in Burke's *A Philosophical Enquiry* (1757), the 'fair sex' are associated with 'the flowery species so remarkable for its weakness'. According to Burke's aesthetic theory, delicacy is as much a prerequisite for beauty in women as it is in 'the vegetable creation':

> It is not the oak, the ash, or the elm, or any of the robust trees of the forest, which we consider as beautiful ... It is the delicate myrtle, ... it is the jessamine, it is the vine, which we look on as vegetable beauties. It is the flowery species, so remarkable for its weakness and momentary duration, that gives us the liveliest idea of beauty, and elegance. ... The beauty of women is considerably owing to their weakness, or delicacy, and is even enhanced by their timidity, a quality of mind analogous to it.[41]

These sentimental analogies between women and flowers perpetuate notions of the feminine in which women are not only defined by, but are assumed to identify with, the beautiful, innocent and delicate. Fanciful language of this kind permeates treatises on female education. Wollstonecraft called for a return to 'unadorned' language to ensure that women's reading would become a 'rational pursuit', developing a femininity based on utility rather than luxury. She challenges Kant's assumption that the fair sex will always 'prefer the beautiful to the useful',[42] borne out by their supposed penchant for adornment: 'Women have a strong inborn feeling for all that is beautiful, elegant and decorated. Even in childhood they like to be dressed up and take pleasure when they are adorned'.[43]

Rousseau, too, characterised pleasure in adornment and delight in the visual and decorative as feminine, asserting that it is through things 'which appeal to the eye' that 'the art of pleasing finds its physical basis in personal adornment' (*Emile*, 330–1);[44] the use of flowers as adornment, from the wreath to the flower garland, is commonplace. Rousseau's assumption that women are 'using their knowledge for their own adornment' shares the general prejudice that a woman's senses and instincts determine her behaviour more than her reasoning powers.[45] Wollstonecraft fiercely disputed 'prevailing opinions' which claimed that women 'were created rather to feel than to reason' (*Vindication*, 62), exclaiming: 'Understanding, strictly speaking, has been denied to women; and instinct, sublimated into wit and cunning, for the purposes of life, has been substituted in its stead' (69).

Women have 'fallen prey to their senses' as a consequence of sentimental education, their passions and sensations heightened in a 'hotbed of luxurious indolence' and their understandings consequently neglected.[46] Wollstonecraft uses hackneyed floral epithets ironically – 'the sweet flowers that smile in the walk of man' – to illustrate what women are reared to (62). It is through this sensibility that they 'obtain present power' (69).

Luxuriant decay

That discourse on luxuriant femininity expressed through floral language, which we saw in the poetry of Pope and Swift, resurfaces in the work of Anna Laetitia Barbauld; Wollstonecraft will mimic this to further her progressive feminism. Barbauld's 'To a Lady With Some Painted Flowers' contains a sentimental analogy between flowers, 'the sole luxury which nature knew', and the 'fair' sex, nature's 'soft family':

> Flowers to the fair: to you these flowers I bring,
> And strive to greet you with an earlier spring.
> *Flowers* SWEET, *and gay, and* DELICATE LIKE YOU;
> Emblems of innocence, and beauty too.
> With flowers the Graces bind their yellow hair,
> And flowery wreaths consenting lovers wear.
> Flowers, the sole luxury which nature knew,
> In Eden's pure and guiltless garden grew.
> To loftier forms are rougher tasks assign'd;
> The sheltering oak resists the stormy wind,
> The tougher yew repels invading foes,
> And the tall pine for future navies grows;
> But this soft family, to cares unknown,
> Were born for pleasure and delight ALONE.
> Gay without toil, and lovely without art,
> They spring to CHEER the sense, and GLAD the heart.
> Nor blush, my fair, to own you copy these;
> *Your* BEST, *your* SWEETEST *empire is* – TO PLEASE.[47]

Barbauld's 'pretty superlatives' (Wollstonecraft) imply that women have a decorative function and should display all the female virtues by which they can prove themselves 'delicate', 'innocent' and 'sweet' (unlike the masculine trees who are allotted nationalistic roles in 'future navies'). A leisured existence is deemed appropriate for those 'born for pleasure and delight alone'. Utilitarian principles are not suitable for women who are 'Gay without toil' (evoking the 'lilies of the field' who 'toil not, neither do they spin').[48] Like Man before the Fall, women exist in a state of luxuriant innocence; they do not labour and yet they are provided for. Wollstonecraft cites Barbauld's poem to demonstrate that: 'This has ever been the language of men, and fear of departing from a supposed sexual character has made even women of a superior sense adopt the same sentiments'.[49]

By ingeniously incorporating metaphors of cultivation and horticulture into her text Wollstonecraft exposes this construction of femininity through language as a 'sensual error' which 'robs the whole sex of its dignity, and classes the brown and fair with the smiling flowers which only adorn the land'.[50] Drawing an analogy between fashionably educated women (regarded as mere 'beautiful flaws of nature') and over-cultivated flowers or luxuriants, she portrays the stasis and sterility wherein women 'languish like exotics' when they ought to be developing towards enlightened maturity. Like Barbauld, Wollstonecraft explores women's relation to luxury through botanical metaphor, suggesting that society has reared women as luxuriants. She departs from the sentiments of Barbauld by indicating that luxuriants do not create delight – they spread corruption. Her imagery is a further engagement with those debates around luxury in which Swift and Pope participated.

The associations that had grown up concerning women and flowers, luxury and adornment, can be traced in publications such as Augustin Heckle's *Bowles's Drawing Book For Ladies; or Complete Florist ... Adapted for the Improvement of Ladies in Needle-Work* (c. 1785) and G. Brown's *A New Treatise on Flower Painting; or, Every Lady Her Own Drawing Master* (1799–1803) which appealed to 'feminine' attributes, to the decorative and visual and to aspects of leisure rather than utility.[51] Periodical literature also provided instruction in floral pursuits such as painting, drawing or embroidering flowers, and particularly flower gardening, to the growing number of leisured women. *The Lady's Monthly Museum* ran features on making artificial or 'gum' flowers and forming flowers from shells, which were interspersed with moral fables on botanical themes such as 'The Rose Bud and Tulips, A Fable for Young Ladies' and 'The Acorn and Pine: A Tale for the Ladies'.[52] *The Lady's Magazine* offered directions on cultivating flowers in 'The Lady Gardener's Calendar' and 'The English Flower Garden Displayed.'[53]

Female disciples of eighteenth-century floriculture readily embraced sensual 'feminine' qualities. Maria Jacson, author of *A Florist's Manual* (1816), recommended flower gardening to her 'sister florists' as an aesthetic (in the literal, or earlier, sense of the word as pertaining to the senses) exercise, emphasising the olfactory and visual experience.[54] Jacson, an unmarried provincial gentlewoman, was forced to capitalise on her passion for floriculture when the family home was given over to the eldest son after the death of her father.[55] Shunning marriage, Maria and her elder sister embarked on an orphaned existence, eventually settling at Somersal Hall in Derbyshire where both women began writing. Maria's sister, Frances, published five novels whilst Maria published four books; three on botany and vegetable physiology and one on flower gardening.[56]

Lady Charlotte Murray, a woman of some distinction who was living in Bath, was writing from a more privileged position when she published *The British Garden* in 1799.[57] Murray celebrates the feminine art of flower gardening for its ability to elevate the sentiments: 'the ardent and active powers of imagination are constantly gratified by the acquisition of knowledge, and it is a delight to roam in the flowery paths of vegetable luxuriance'.[58] The flower garden was commonly perceived to be a feminine locale; its sensual appeal being ideally suited to satisfy the senses, curiosities and inclinations of women.[59] The idea of a 'garden of delight' as opposed to the utility of a vegetable or herb garden can be traced back to the Elizabethan period. Here, the flower garden was a luxury created in contrast to the herb or vegetable garden. To cultivate such a garden was appropriate for those born for pleasure.[60] The design of a flower garden was on a relatively small scale, focusing on specific areas, plots or borders within a larger estate and fell more within a woman's sphere than did the more ambitious landscape gardening. The vogue for botany which developed among leisured women is clearly related to this idea of flower gardening as a genteel feminine pursuit. Maria Jacson combined botany and flower gardening but like many botanists who gardened she disapproved of florist flowers.

Florist flowers (hyacinths, tulips, *Ranunculi*, anemones, auriculas, narcissi, carnations and pinks) were luxuriants which had been constantly improved by new cultivation techniques. Luxuriants were highly susceptible to disease due to the special conditions needed to rear them and, although exceedingly beautiful, were barren, sickly and short-lived. Their over-refinement through cultivation resulted in artificial hybrids, double blooms, freakish colours and out-of-season flowering. While Christopher Smart interpreted a florist's ability to produce double blooms as a sign that 'the art of agriculture is improving', Rousseau, writing in his capacity as a botanist, mistrusts double flowers reared in luxury. He advises his botanising ladies not to examine luxuriants because:

> nature will no longer be found among them; she refuses to reproduce anything from monsters thus mutilated: for if the most brilliant part of the flower, namely the corol, be multiplied, it is at the expense of the more essential parts, which disappear under this addition of brilliancy.[61]

According to the British botanist, James Lee, 'A flower is said to be luxuriant, when some of the parts of fructification are augmented in number, and others thereby excluded ... the part multiplied is usually the corolla, but sometimes the calyx also'.[62] Lee details luxuriants which, like Wollstonecraft's fashionably educated women, are weakened and corrupted by over-cultivation: 'the parts essential to Generation being thus destroyed in full flower it is evident they must be barren; wherefore no good seed is to be expected from them'.[63] In the wild flower or natural species, which represented health and vitality, an unmodified, essential character could be observed. In comparison, the luxuriant was a gaudy, sickly product of society whose true lineage was disguised. If the wild or native species embodied purity or the unadorned, the luxuriant was a painted courtesan, a degenerate, signifying wantonness and moral decay (as we have seen in the poetry of Pope and Swift where fashionable women are seen to resemble cultivated exotics).

Rousseau's contempt for the artistry of the florist, distaste for luxuriants and preference for pure or native species are symptomatic of anxieties concerning the effects of luxury. Elsewhere, he claimed that cultural and social progress had only led to moral degeneration, attributing the blame to the cultivation of the arts and sciences which had been nourished by luxury. Flowers – luxuriant or otherwise – conceal the true nature of a decadent civilisation which suffocates authenticity:

> the Sciences, Letters, and Arts ... spread garlands of flowers over the iron chains with which men are burdened, stifle in them the sentiment of that original liberty for which they seemed to have been born, make them love their slavery, and turn them into what is called civilized peoples.[64]

For Wollstonecraft, luxury is a false refinement of which monarchy and the corruption of the court are a part. In this 'unnatural state', inequality of rank arrests progress. Women who exist in a state of luxuriance, or are raised in a 'premature unnatural manner' like exotics, 'undermine the very foundation of virtue and spread corruption through the whole mass of society' (9). Corruption, according to Wollstonecraft, is 'most quickly spread by luxury and superstition' which rapidly grows from a 'baneful lurking gangrene' into a 'contagion' (18). The delineation of barrenness and ill health which Wollstonecraft takes from botanical descriptions of cultivated flowers is emblematic of the thwarted progress which all 'weak artificial beings raised above the common wants and affectations of their race represent' (18). Luxury will hinder the expansion of the intellect and prevent the establishment of true civilisation.

John Millar felt that the improved status of women which the introduction of commerce had brought had subsequently been reversed by the continued accumulation of wealth. A deterioration in women's status had occurred in Rome at a time when great wealth had corrupted the manners of the ancients and produced a 'great revolution in their tastes and sentiments'.[65] Similarly, Europe was now affected by 'rapid advances of luxury and refinement' just as changes were occurring in the social position of women. Despite its ideologies of progress, the commercial stage of human history had failed women. In drawing attention to luxuriant femininity, Wollstonecraft had exposed the contradictions implicit in Enlightenment universalism; educators may claim to want to improve women but, in fact:

> the minds of women are enfeebled by false refinement ... the books of instruction, written by men of genius, have had the same tendency as more frivolous productions; and that, in the true style of Mahometanism, they are treated as a kind of subordinate beings, and not as a part of the human species, when improvable reason is allowed to be the dignified distinction which raises men above the brute creation, and puts a natural sceptre in a feeble hand. (*Vindication*, 7–8)

Pope and Swift impugn women as disseminators of luxury, comparing them to exotic tulips; Rousseau instead seems intent on shielding women from any taint of luxury, instructing lady botanists not to meddle with double blooms. In *Julie: ou La Nouvelle Héloïse*, we see a fusion of Rousseau's ideas concerning women, cultivation and luxury, most notably in the account of the community at Clarens and the description of Elysium. Julie lives a life of duty, never yielding to her passion for St Preux, her former lover. The locked, uncultivated garden she has created is emblematic of her new morality; it is a wild and solitary place which she has named 'Elysium' for its soothing, feminine properties. This maternal haven is the only part of the estate over which Julie has authority, it has undergone much care and culture, yet St Preux sees no trace of cultivation: 'The gardener's hand is not to be seen: nothing belies the idea of a desert island which came to my mind as I entered, and I see no human footprints'.[66] All is planted so as to look 'natural', without luxury or ornament:

> I began to roam ecstatically through this orchard thus metamorphosed; and although I did not find exotic plants and products of the Indies, I found the local ones arranged and combined in a manner that yielded a cheerier and pleasanter effect. The verdant grass, lush, but short and thick was mingled with wild thyme, balsam ... and other aromatic herbs. A thousand wild flowers shone there, among which the eye was surprised to detect a few garden varieties, which seemed to grow naturally with the others. (*Julie*, 388)

The alluring effect of the garden has in fact been skilfully contrived; the affected irregularity of the winding paths prolongs the walks, hides the boundaries of the island and appears to enlarge it, while the rivulet has been made to flow in meanders to keep the grounds refreshed so that it may continually yield fresh flowers. The apparent contradictions in Rousseau's description of this uncultivated garden surround his ambiguous discussions on femininity. For Rousseau, Julie's wild garden suggests an ideal femininity; thick foliage renders it impervious to the eye and yet 'it is always carefully locked' (387). This garden wilderness hidden from view but kept under lock and key resembles Rousseau's model female, Sophy, who was brought up 'by nature'; uncultivated yet constantly in need of containment.

Life at Clarens offers an antidote to the ills uncovered in Rousseau's two discourses. Julie's Arcadia provides a delightful asylum from the 'masculine' world of labour and commerce; humanity's lost 'state of nature' can be recaptured in its uncultivated Elysian landscape. The setting for St Preux's conversion from pleasure seeker to virtuous citizen resembles a former, more desirable stage of human history, a pre-civilized golden age: 'I thought I was looking at the wildest, most solitary place in nature, and it seemed to me I was the first mortal who ever had set foot in this wilderness' (387). He experiences Elysium as a traveller who had stumbled upon a precultural island in the South Seas.[67] This sanctuary where no marks of human labour can be detected has been created by Julie, a woman.

Rousseau sees the uncultivated woman as a survival from the second stage of human society as it emerges from the state of nature, found 'at an equal distance from the stupidity of brutes, and the fatal ingenuity of civilised man'.[68] The exalted femininity of Julie and Sophy is an immature, pre-enlightenment state, existing prior to the cultivation of 'all those arts which are exercised in the shade of the study'[69] – hence his attacks on the typical learned lady who 'is always trying to make a man of herself'.[70] Sophy is 'without deep study', lacking 'art' or 'learning': 'Her mind has been formed not by reading but by conversation with her father and mother, by her own reflections, and by her own observations in the little world in which she has lived'.[71] The value of this ideal femininity lies in its stasis.

Wollstonecraft opposed these regressive inclinations of Rousseau and his desire to keep women in sensualised ignorance. Instead, she vehemently advocated the cultivation of the female mind, drawing attention to society's neglect of female potential. Once women acquire rationality through the proper cultivation of the mind, enlightened maturity will supplant luxuriant decay and they will achieve the equality that Millar had foreseen – that true civilisation in which:

> women become neither the slaves, nor the idols of the other sex, but the friends or companions. The wife obtains that rank and station which appears most agreeable to reason, being suited to her character and talents.[72]

Thus Wollstonecraft, by extending rationality and sociality to women, adheres more purely to the Enlightenment ideals of progress, cultivation and universality. She counters the primitivism of Rousseau's prescriptions, Barbauld's exclusion of women from the public sphere and the accusations of decayed luxury from Pope and Swift. In Wollstonecraft's work, Enlightenment femininity, like Fuseli's Flora, examines itself in botany's mirror in order to correct the distorted reflections of those who would keep the female mind barren.

In Chapter 2 the focus shifts to botany and female education, and certain key texts draw our attention. Rousseau's ideal of femininity emerges in significant ways in his botanical letters; and Patricia Wakefield's epistolary text on the instruction of women in botany lies in an instructive relationship with them. It is the feminisation of botany that occurs in these texts and others, and the ambiguous attempts within them to cultivate the botanical woman to which we now turn.

Notes

1 I am indebted to Alan Bewell's analysis here. He argues that this engraving 'provides an allegory of female sexuality, for the woman is in the act of seeing herself in a mirror, ostensibly the one being provided by *The Botanic Garden*', 'Jacobin Plants: Botany As Social Theory in the 1790s', *Wordsworth Circle*, 20 (1989), 132–9 (p. 135). Caroline Jackson-Houlston has taken up this theme in a recent article, tracing the image of the female flower-gatherer back to Milton's Proserpine. She reads Fuseli's Flora as representing 'a process of self-definition' akin to 'Lacan's mirror stage', '"Queen Lilies"? The Interpretation of Scientific, Religious and Gender Discourses in Victorian Representations of Plants', *Journal of Victorian Culture*, 12:1 (2006), 84–110, (p. 100). We can certainly make a connection with Milton's Eve here: Eve is the fairest flower in the Garden of Eden and she is engaged in the act of gazing upon her own reflection.

2 Samuel Johnson, 'Culture', *A Dictionary of the English Language*, 2 vols (London:

printed for J. Knapton; C. Hitch and L. Hawes; A. Millar, R. and J. Dodsley; and M. and T. Longman, 1756).

3 In 1665, Frances Bacon referred to 'the culture and manurance of minds', providing an earlier example of this metaphorical usage. 'Culture' later referred to different nations and periods and also to specific social and economic groups within a nation; the idea of a national culture had emerged by the nineteenth century (Raymond Williams, *Keywords*, rev. edn (London: Fontana, 1983), pp. 87–93).

4 Johnson, cited in Williams, *Keywords*, p. 87.

5 'A man might as well turn his daughter lose in Covent Garden, as trust the cultivation of her mind to a circulating library' (George Colman, *Polly Honeycombe*, in *Eighteenth-Century Afterpieces*, ed. Richard Bevis (London: OUP, 1970), IV, 194–6, p. 159).

6 Christopher Smart, 'Jubilate Agno: Fragment C', in *Selected Poems*, ed. Karina Williamson and Marcus Walsh (Harmondsworth: Penguin, 1990), lines 157–59, pp. 122–3.

7 James Thomson, 'Spring', *The Seasons*, in *The Poems of James Thomson*, ed. J. Logie Robertson (Oxford: Oxford University Press, 1963), lines 542–54, p. 23. This is the expanded version of 1730, which emphasises the active role in cultivation of the florist. The original version of 1728 read:

> The varied Colours run; and while they break
> On the charm'd *Florist*'s Eye, he wondering stands,
> And new-flushed glories all ecstatic marks.
> (*Spring, A Poem* (London: A. Millar & G. Straham), lines 498–500, p. 27)

8 See Keith Thomas, *Man and the Natural World: Changing Attitudes in England 1500–1800* (Harmondsworth: Penguin, 1983), p. 226.

9 Tulipomania was at its greatest height between about 1633–37. Wilfrid Blunt states that 'The highest prices paid for by tulip speculators bore no possible relation to the beauty of the flower' (*Tulips and Tulipomania* (London: Basilisk Press, 1977), pp. 15–16). Comparisons can be made between tulipomania and the South Sea Bubble as many bankrupted themselves due to their mania for tulips. Also the tulip trade offered endless possibilities for fraud because it was impossible to tell from the appearance of a bulb that it would yield the promised variegated specimen. Tulipomania inspired many satires such as *The Fool's Wagon*, a satirical print by Hendrik Pot (Blunt, *Tulipomania,* p. 17), and dialogues between tulipophobes which appeared in *The Tatler*, no. 218, 31 August 1710.

For further reading, see Blunt, *Tulipomania*, and Anna Pavord, *The Tulip* (London: Bloomsbury, 1999). The exemplary work on the tulip in the eighteenth century was J. P. Rome d'Ardène, *Traité des Tulipes ... par l'auteur du Traité des Renoncules* (Avignon: [n. pub], 1760).

10 For such satires, see Felicity Nussbaum, *The Brink of All We Hate: English Satires On Women 1660–1750* (Lexington, KY: Kentucky University Press, 1984); for Swift, pp. 94–116, and Pope, pp. 137–58.

11 Alexander Pope, 'Moral Essays: Epistle II. To a Lady. Of The Characters of Women', *The Poems of Alexander Pope*, ed. John Butt (London: Routledge, 1968), lines 41–4, p. 561.

12 Pavord, *The Tulip*, p. 213.

13 The tulip's habit of breaking into variegated forms is noted by Gerard in his famous *Herball* (1597). Gerard states that nature seems to sport or 'play' with this flower above all others (Blunt, *Tulipomania*, p. 12). An eighteenth-century meaning of 'to

sport' was 'to vary abnormally from the parent stock or specific type, to exhibit or undergo spontaneous mutilation' (*OED*). Tulip 'sports' are streaky or 'broken' flowers.

14 See Peter Martin, *Pursuing Innocent Pleasures: The Gardening World of Alexander Pope* (Hamden: Archon, 1984), and Morris R. Brownell, *Alexander Pope and the Arts of Georgian England* (Oxford: Clarendon, 1978). Most of the seminal studies on landscape and garden history refer to Pope's estates.

15 Jonathan Swift, 'The Lady's Dressing Room', in *The Complete Poems*, ed. Pat Rogers (Harmondsworth: Penguin, 1983), lines 143–4, p. 452. For a discussion of the way Swift uses female dress to exemplify commodification, see Laura Brown's 'Reading Race and Gender: Jonathan Swift', *Eighteenth-Century Studies*, 23 (1990), 425–43. For a similar reading of Pope, see her *The Ends of Empire: Women and Ideology in Early Eighteenth-Century English Literature* (Ithaca, NY and London: Cornell University Press, 1993). The commercialisation of fashion is discussed in Neil McKendrick, John Brewer, and J. H. Plumb, *The Birth of a Consumer Society: The Commercialisation of Eighteenth-Century England* (London: Hutchinson, 1983), pp. 34–99.

16 Pavord, *The Tulip*, p. 11.

17 Nathaniel Forster, *An Enquiry Into the Causes of the Present High Price of Provisions* (London: printed for J. Fletcher & Co; and sold by J. Fletcher in Oxford, 1767), p. 41.

18 Jonathan Swift, 'A Proposal that All the Ladies and Women of Ireland Should Appear Constantly In Irish Manufactures', in *Prose Works*, ed. H. Davies (Oxford: Oxford University Press, 1951), pp. 126–7.

19 Addison, cited in McKendrick, Brewer and Plumb, *Birth of a Consumer Society*, p. 11.

20 Mary Wollstonecraft, *A Vindication of the Rights of Woman*, ed. Carol H. Poston, 2nd edn (1792; New York and London: W. W. Norton, 1988), p. 10. All further references are to this edition.

21 John Millar, *The Origin of the Distinction of Ranks*, 4th edn (1771; Edinburgh and London: William Blackwood and Longman, Hurst, Rees & Orme, 1806). For a discussion of the four stages theory and the Scottish Enlightenment, see David Spadafora, *The Idea of Progress in Eighteenth-Century Britain* (New Haven, CT and London: Yale University Press, 1990), pp. 271–73. For Millar's analysis of women's status, see Paul Bowles's 'John Millar, The Four Stages Theory and Women's Position in Society', *The History of Political Economy*, 16:4 (1984), 619–38.

22 Millar, *Origin of the Distinction of Ranks*, p. 198.

23 Arthur Young, *Observations on the Present State of the Waste Lands of Great Britain* (London: Printed for W. Nicoll, 1773), p. 38, cited in Thomas, *Man and the Natural World*, p. 255. The works of Arthur Young are discussed in Raymond Williams, *The Country and the City* (New York: Oxford University Press, 1973), pp. 66–7, and in Thomas, *Man and the Natural World*, pp. 221, 248 and 255. For a discussion of Young's theories of improvement and their practical application, see Stephen Bending, 'The Improvement of Arthur Young: Agricultural Technology and the Production of Landscape in Eighteenth-Century England', in David Nye (ed.), *Technologies of Landscape: Reaping to Recycling* (Amherst, MA: University of Massachusetts Press, 2000), pp. 241–53.

24 A useful general survey on Enlightenment ideas of progress can be found in Sidney Pollard's *The Idea of Progress* (London: C. A. Watts, 1968), pp. 18–95; and, more

recently, Spadafora, *The Idea of Progress in Eighteenth-Century Britain.*

25 James Thomson, *Spring*, lines 1152–56, p. 57.

26 Erasmus Darwin, A Plan for The Conduct of Female Education In Boarding School (Derby: Printed for J. Johnson, 1797).

27 Anna Laetitia Barbauld, 'Epilogue', in John Aikin and Anna Laetitia Barbauld, *Evenings At Home*, 6 vols (1792–6; London: J. Johnson, 1796), VI, p. 152.

28 Although Barbauld was an educationalist she had limited views on female education. She saw no reason for women to learn foreign languages, for example, and appears fairly conservative compared to radicals such as Wollstonecraft and Catherine Macaulay. For images of progress and educational ideas, see Lucy Aikin's 'Memoir', prefixed to *The Works of Anna Laetitia Barbauld*, ed. Lucy Aikin, 2 vols (London: Longman, Hurst, Rees, Orme, Brown & Green, 1825), and Penny Bradshaw, 'Gendering the Enlightenment: Conflicting Images of Progress in the Poetry of Anna Laetitia Barbauld', *Women's Writing*, 5:3 (1998), 353–71.

29 It is in *An Essay Concerning Human Understanding* (1690) that John Locke challenges the hypothesis shared by ancient Stoics and modern Cartesians that certain notions are innate in the mind. In its place he puts forward the theory advanced earlier by Aristotle and Bacon (Aristotle's *De Anima*, Book III; Bacon's *Novum Organum,* aphorism I), that the mind at birth is a tabula rasa or blank slate and acquires all ideas by experience.

30 The answer to the question of what the heritage of Enlightenment has meant for feminism is highly contentious. Ludmilla Jordanova has pointed to the exclusion of women from a rational life in the philosophies of the key intellectual figures of the Enlightenment (Jordanova, 'Natural Facts: A Historical Perspective on Science and Sexuality', in Carol MacCormack and Marilyn Srathern (eds), *Nature, Culture, Gender* (Cambridge: Cambridge University Press, 1980), pp. 42–70).

Sabina Lovibond, however, claims that modern feminism needs to take stock of its deep indebtedness to the 'emancipatory metanarratives' of Enlightenment ('Feminism and Postmodernism', *New Left Review*, 178 (November–December 1989), 5–28). Katherine B. Clinton and Pauline Johnson also investigate the relationship between contemporary feminism and the so-called project of Enlightenment (Clinton, 'Femme et Philosophe: Enlightenment Origins of Feminism', *Eighteenth-Century Studies*, 8:3 (1975), 283–99; Johnson, 'Feminism and the Enlightenment', *Radical Philosophy*, 63 (1993), 3–12). Useful general surveys of gender in the Enlightenment can be found in Sylvana Tomaselli, 'The Enlightenment Debate on Women', *History Workshop Journal*, 20 (1985), 101–24; Dorinda Outram, *The Enlightenment* (Cambridge: Cambridge University Press, 1995), pp. 80–95; Jane Rendall, 'The Enlightenment and the nature of women', in *The Origins of Modern Feminism: Women in Britain, France and the United States, 1780–1860* (London: Macmillan, 1985), pp. 7–32; and Phylis Mack, 'Women and the Enlightenment', *Women and History*, 9 (1984), 1–11.

31 Religious, medical and philosophical discourses linked women both to the life-giving forces of nature as instruments of moral regeneration and to the forces of anarchy and disorder. See Maurice Bloch and Jean H. Bloch, 'Women and the Dialectics of Nature in Eighteenth-Century French Thought', in MacCormack and Strathern (eds), *Nature, Culture, Gender*, pp. 25–42. See also Jordanova's 'Natural Facts', and the many satires on the female sex from this period show that women were still regarded as differently principled – coquettish, deceitful and vain.

32 G. W. F. Hegel, *Elements of the Philosophy of Right*, ed. Allen W. Wood, trans. H.

B. Nisbet (1821; Cambridge and New York: Cambridge University Press, 1991), p. 207. My emphasis.

33 Jean-Antoine-Nicolas de Caritat, Marquis de Condorcet, 'On the Admission of Women to the Rights of Citizenship' (1790), in *Condorcet: Selected Writings*, ed. K. M. Baker (Indianapolis, IN: Bobbs-Merrill, 1976), pp. 97–104.

34 Jean-Jacques Rousseau, *Emile, or Education*, trans. Barbara Foxley (1762; London: J. M. Dent, 1950), p. 16. All further references are to this edition and page numbers are given in parentheses after quotations in the text.

35 'The infant is bound up in swaddling clothes, the corpse is nailed down in his coffin. All his life long man is imprisoned by our institutions' (Rousseau, *Emile*, p. 10).

36 In Kant's essay on Enlightenment of 1784, the cultivation of the mind is the first step towards maturity; 'immaturity is the inability to use one's own understanding without the guidance of another'. Kant, somewhat ambivalently, appeared aware of the obstacles women would encounter on the way to enlightenment: 'The guardians who have kindly taken upon themselves the work of supervision will soon see to it that by far the largest part of mankind (including the entire female sex) should consider the step forward to maturity not only as difficult but as highly dangerous' ('An Answer to the Question: "What is Enlightenment?"', Immanuel Kant, in *Political Writings*, ed. Hans Reiss, trans. H. B. Nisbet, 2nd edn (Cambridge: Cambridge University Press, 1996), pp. 54–5).

37 See note 21 above. For a discussion of Wollstonecraft's debt to contemporary historical writing, particularly that of the Scottish Enlightenment and her interest in histories of 'civilisation', see Jane Rendall, '"The grand causes which combine to carry mankind forward": Wollstonecraft, History and Revolution', *Women's Writing*, 4:2 (1997), 155–72.

38 Alan Bewell has stated that Wollstonecraft's anti-pastoralism 'is a direct expression of the way that gender differences become cultural differences, and it seeks to provide women with a gender-neutral language' (Bewell, 'Jacobin Plants', p. 13).

39 For a discussion of how buddings and blooms permeate the late eighteenth-century novel of courtship in the light of the newly sexualised botany of Linnaeus, see Amy M. King, 'Linnaeus's Blooms: Botany and the Novel of Courtship', *The Eighteenth-Century Novel*, 1 (2001), 127–60.

40 From the account of Linnaeus's Lapland journey, *Lachesis Lapponica, or, A Tour in Lapland*, 2 vols (London: Printed for White & Cochcrane by Richard Taylor, 1811), cited in Wilfrid Blunt, *The Compleat Naturalist: A Life of Linnaeus* (London: William Collins, 1971), p. 56.

41 Edmund Burke, *A Philosophical Enquiry into the Origin of our Ideas of the Sublime and Beautiful*, ed. Adam Phillips (1756; Oxford: Oxford University Press, 1990), pp. 105–6.

42 Immanuel Kant, 'Of the Distinction of the Beautiful and Sublime in the Interrelations of the Two Sexes', in *Observations on the Feeling of the Beautiful and Sublime*, trans. John T. Goldthwait (1763; Berkeley, CA and Los Angeles: California University Press, 1991), p. 77.

43 *Ibid.* Kant sets up a gendered juxtaposition of beauty and sublimity whereby the fair sex identify with, and are identified by, 'the mark of the beautiful' while the sublime is promoted as a masculine quality befitting the 'noble sex'. All 'judgement', 'education' and 'instruction' must, according to Kant's theory, refer to these criteria since: 'The fair sex has just as much understanding as the male, but it is a *beautiful*

understanding whereas ours should be a *deep understanding*, an expression that signifies an identity with the sublime'(*ibid.*, p. 78). Original emphasis.

44 '[G]irls prefer things which appeal to the eye, and can be used for dressing up – mirrors, jewellery, finery, and specially dolls' (Rousseau, *Emile*, p. 330). From this Rousseau goes on to conclude that 'little girls always dislike learning to read and write, but they are always ready to learn to sew. They think they are grown up, and in imagination they are using their knowledge for their own adornment' (p. 331).

45 Compare, for instance, Rousseau's 'woman has more wit, man more genius, woman observes, man reasons' (*Emile*, p. 350) with Kant's 'her philosophy is not to reason, but to sense' (*Observations*, p. 79). Kant had stated that female understanding is sensuous, avoiding 'abstract speculations' or 'useful' knowledge', since 'Deep meditation and a long sustained reflection are noble but difficult, and do not well befit a person in whom unconstrained charms should show nothing else than a beautiful nature' (p. 78).

46 Wollstonecraft, *Vindication*, p. 69. Hotbeds were used for 'forcing' plants, i.e. accelerating growth or causing premature flowering.

47 Cited with these emphases in Wollstonecraft's notes, *Vindication*, p. 53.

48 Matthew 6. 28.

49 Wollstonecraft, *Vindication*, p. 53. The gendered character of Barbauld's writing was frequently referred to, but ambiguously. Harriet Guest declares that Wollstonecraft accuses Barbauld of 'adopting a masquerade of femininity; a disguise that conforms to the "supposed sexual character" that the language of men creates', but Walpole characterised Barbauld's published support for political causes of the 1790s, such as the 1791 bill for abolishing the slave trade, as unfeminine. Guest also remarks that a reviewer of Barbauld's poems of 1773 was 'disappointed by the absence of feminine sensibility and passion; by Barbauld's failure to display something very close to the "sexual character" that Wollstonecraft deplored in her poetry' (Harriet Guest, 'Eighteenth-Century Femininity: "A Supposed Sexual Character"', in Vivien Jones (ed.), *Women and Literature in Britain 1700–1800* (Cambridge: Cambridge University Press, 2000), pp. 46–68 (pp. 48–9)).

50 *Ibid.*, p. 53.

51 Drawing, already a conventional accomplishment for upper-class girls, became more specifically feminised in works which taught young women the skills needed to draw flowers; many of these manuals also offered instruction in other floral pursuits such as embroidering or fashioning flowers from paper or shells. For a discussion of such manuals designed for women, see Ann Bermingham, *Learning to Draw: Studies in the Cultural History of a Polite and Useful Art* (New Haven, CT and London: Yale University Press, 2000), pp. 202–27. Female members of the Royal family were trained in flower painting, which further boosted its popularity. Francis Bauer gave lessons in botanical drawing to Queen Charlotte and Princess Elizabeth. It must be noted that George III was also instructed in flower painting by a female artist who exhibited at the Society of Arts and specialised in flower painting, Mary Moser. See the account of Mary Moser (1744–1819) in David Scrase, *Flower Drawings* (Cambridge: Cambridge University Press, 1997), p. 70. A general survey of floral femininity in the eighteenth and nineteenth centuries can be found in Jennifer Bennett, *Lilies of the Hearth: The Historical Relationship Between Women and Plants* (Willowdale, Ontario: Camden House, 1991), pp. 93–102.

52 'Methods of Making Artificial, or, Gum Flowers', *The Lady's Monthly Museum, or Polite Repository*, September 1799; 'Various Sorts of Flowers ... Form'd From Shells',

Lady's Monthly Museum, November 1799; 'Rose Bud and Tulips, A Fable For Young Ladies', *Lady's Monthly Museum*, October 1798; 'The Acorn and Pine. A Tale for Ladies', *Lady's Monthly Museum*, May 1799.

53 Flower gardening features appeared regularly in *The Lady's Magazine* from 1784–85.

54 Maria Jacson, *A Florist's Manual* (London: Henry Colburn, 1816). For Maria Jacson, see Joan Percy, 'Maria Elizabetha Jacson and Her Florist's Manual', *Garden History*, 20:1 (1992), 45–56, and G. E. Fussell, 'Some Lady Botanists of the Nineteenth Century', *The Gardener's Chronicle*, 130 (1951), 63–4.

55 Maria Elizabetha Jacson was born in Bebington, Cheshire in 1755, one of eight children of the Reverend Simon Jacson and Anne Fitzherbert of Somersal, Derbyshire. When Maria was 22, the family moved out of the rectory in Cheshire and settled first at Stockport and then Tarporley. After the death of her parents (father d. 1808, mother d. 1795), Maria's life changed forever. Unmarried, she was forced to live at the mercy of relatives. Maria and her sister Frances eventually settled at Somersal Hall in Derbyshire, a house belonging to William Fitzherbert. It was here that both sisters embarked on writing careers and where Maria remained until her death in 1829 while visiting friends in Chelford. I am indebted to Joan Percy's biographical study here. For further details, see Percy, 'Maria Elizabetha Jacson and her Florist's Manual'. Joan Percy writes of the confusion that had arisen over Maria's identity. The second edition of the *Florist's Manual* was the only work to contain her name. *Botanical Dialogues* carried her initials, 'M. E. J', on its advertisement. The publisher Henry Colburn had given her name on the last page of the manuscript as 'Maria Elizabeth Jackson'. Percy was only able to trace Maria's family history once the correct spelling of Jacson had been restored (Percy, 'Maria Elizabetha Jacson', p. 45).

56 Jacson's published works are as follows: Maria Elizabetha Jacson, *Botanical Dialogues Between Hortensia and Her Four Children* (London: J. Johnson, 1797); *Botanical Lectures By A Lady* (London: J. Johnson, 1804); *Sketches of the Physiology of Vegetable Life* (London: John Hatchard, 1811); *A Florists Manual* (London: Henry Colburn, 1816).

57 I offer a much fuller discussion of Murray and her work in Chapter 3.

58 *The British Garden*, 2 vols (Bath: S. Hazard, 1799). For brief discussions of this work, see G. E. Fussell, 'The Rt. Hon. Lady Charlotte Murray', *Gardener's Chronicle*, 128 (1950), 238–9, and Ann Shteir, *Cultivating Women, Cultivating Science* (Baltimore, MD and London: Johns Hopkins University Press, 1996), p. 120.

59 On the subject of women and gardens in the seventeenth-century, the French gardener Nicholas de Bonnefons wrote:

> However differently each [woman] follows her inclinations, all are praiseworthy in their curiosities, but since they seek these things only to satisfy their senses, that which I have is applicable to only one: the garden has this prerogative above all others, that it gives satisfaction to all their five senses (Nicholas de Bonnefons, *Le Jardinier françois qui enseigne à cultiver les arbres et herbes potagères* (Paris: P. Des-Hayes: 1651), as quoted in June Taboroff, '"Wife Unto Thy Garden": The First Gardening Books For Women', *Garden History*, 11:7 (Spring 1983) 1–5 (p. 3)).

60 Wollstonecraft angrily remarked that 'pleasure is the business of women's life, according to the present modification of society' (*Vindication*, p. 55).

61 In Jean-Jacques Rousseau, *Letters on the Elements of Botany* (London: B. White &

Son, 1787), p. 28 (Letter II).

62 James Lee, *An Introduction to Botany*, 5th edn (1760; London: S. Crowder, 1794), p. 58.

63 *Ibid.*, p. 59. Lee's *Introduction*, first published in 1760, had reached its fifth printing by 1794. A sixth edition followed in 1796; hereafter, it was revised and corrected by Charles Stewart in 1799 and 1806, and by the author's son, James Lee Junior, in 1810.

64 Rousseau, 'Discourse on the Sciences and Arts' (1750), in *The Collected Writings of Rousseau*, 7 vols, ed. Roger D. Masters and Christopher Kelly (Hanover, NH and London: University Press of New England, 1990–98), II, trans. Judith R. Bush, Roger D. Masters and Christopher Kelly (1992), p. 5. See also 'Luxury, Commerce and the Arts', in *Collected Writings*, IV, ed. Roger D. Masters and Christopher Kelly, trans. Judith R. Bush, Roger D. Masters and Christopher Kelly (1994), pp. 44–51.

65 Millar, *Origin of the Distinction of Ranks*, p. 223.

66 Jean-Jacques Rousseau, *Julie, or the New Héloïse: Letters of Two Lovers Who Live in a Small Town at the Foot of the Alps* (1761), in *Collected Writings*, VI, trans. and annotated by Philip Stewart and Jean Vaché (1997), p. 393. All further references are to this edition and are given in parentheses after quotations in the text.

67 He is reminded of the Juan Fernandez Islands made famous by Anson's account of his voyage. On arriving at these islands, the crew observe that 'It is in this place … that the simple productions of unassisted nature may be said to excel all the fictitious descriptions of the most animated imagination' (Lord Anson, *A Voyage Round the World in the Years 1740–4* (London: J. M. Dent, 1911), p. 115).

68 Jean-Jacques Rousseau, 'A Discourse on the Origin of Inequality' (1755), in *The Social Contract and Discourses*, trans. G. D. H. Cole, new edn (London: Everyman, 1973), pp. 31–126 (p. 91).

69 Rousseau, 'Discourse on the Arts and the Sciences', *Collected Writings*, II (p. 16).

70 Rousseau, *Emile*, pp. 371–2.

71 Rousseau, *Emile*, p. 358.

72 Millar, *Origin of the Distinction of Ranks*, p. 219.

2
'Unveiling the mysteries of vegetation': botany and the feminine

Cultivating the botanical woman

IN THE EIGHTEENTH CENTURY many botanical texts were specifically addressed to the female sex. The language and arguments of botany, centring on reproduction and sexuality, experience and science, classification and order, introspective solitude and public debate became implicated in arguments about women's intellectual and moral faculties and their general social status. This trend was to continue well into the nineteenth century as gender-specific titles such as John Lindley's *Ladies' Botany* (1834–37) and *Botany for Ladies* by Jane Loudon (1842) illustrate, but significant changes occurred along the way. This chapter will attempt to unveil some of the underlying processes whereby the discourse of botany becomes implicated in concerns over women's education – and cultivation in general – and becomes itself feminised.

Among the most popular of the eighteenth-century texts – though not well-known today even among those quite familiar with Rousseau – was Rousseau's *Lettres elementaires sur la botanique* (1771–74), in which a young woman is instructed in botany in a series of letters.[1] I explained in the introduction that Rousseau wrote his botanical letters for Madame Étienne Delessert, a keen botanist who was the owner of a famous herbarium and botanical library.[2] The letters offer guidance to a young mother over the instruction in botany of her daughter. Thomas Martyn, Professor of Botany at Cambridge, translated Rousseau's epistolary botany into English in 1785 as *Letters on the Elements of Botany Addressed to a Lady*, adding twenty-four letters of his own, 'Fully explaining the system of Linnaeus'. Martyn's Preface suggested that the work 'might be of use to such of my fair countrywomen and unlearned countrymen as wished to amuse themselves with natural history'.[3] His translation of the Letters was inscribed on the title-page to 'THE LADIES of GREAT BRITAIN / No Less Eminent for Their Elegant and Useful Accomplishments; Than Admired for the Beauty of Their Persons'. Martyn openly courted female readers, capitalising on Rousseau's address to a young mother, significantly escalating a demand for botany books written for a particular class of enlightened British women and promoting botany as an elegant pursuit for 'Ladies'.

Priscilla Wakefield's *An Introduction to Botany; in a Series of Familiar Letters* (1796), arguably the first book of botany written by a woman, describes the

TO
THE LADIES
OF
GREAT BRITAIN:
NO LESS EMINENT
FOR THEIR ELEGANT AND USEFUL
ACCOMPLISHMENTS,
THAN ADMIRED
FOR THE BEAUTY OF THEIR PERSONS:
THIS FIFTH EDITION OF THE FOLLOWING
LETTERS
IS, WITH ALL HUMILITY,
INSCRIBED
BY
THE TRANSLATOR AND EDITOR.

2 Title page. Reproduced from Jean-Jacques Rousseau, *Letters on the Elements of Botany Addressed To A Lady*, trans. Thomas Martyn

breakthrough that had taken place as, for the first time, literate but unlearned women gained access to botanical science:

> Till of late years, [botany] has been confined to the circle of the learned, which may be attributed to those books that treated of it, being principally written in Latin: a difficulty that deterred many, particularly the female sex, from attempting to obtain the knowledge of a science, thus defended, as it were, from their approach.[4]

In her *Reflections on the Present Condition of the Female Sex* (1798), Wakefield argued for women's education and vocational opportunities to be extended to include science:

> There are many branches of science, as well as useful occupations, in which women may employ their time and their talents, beneficially to themselves and to the community, without destroying the peculiar characteristic of their sex, or exceeding the most exact limits of modesty and decorum.[5]

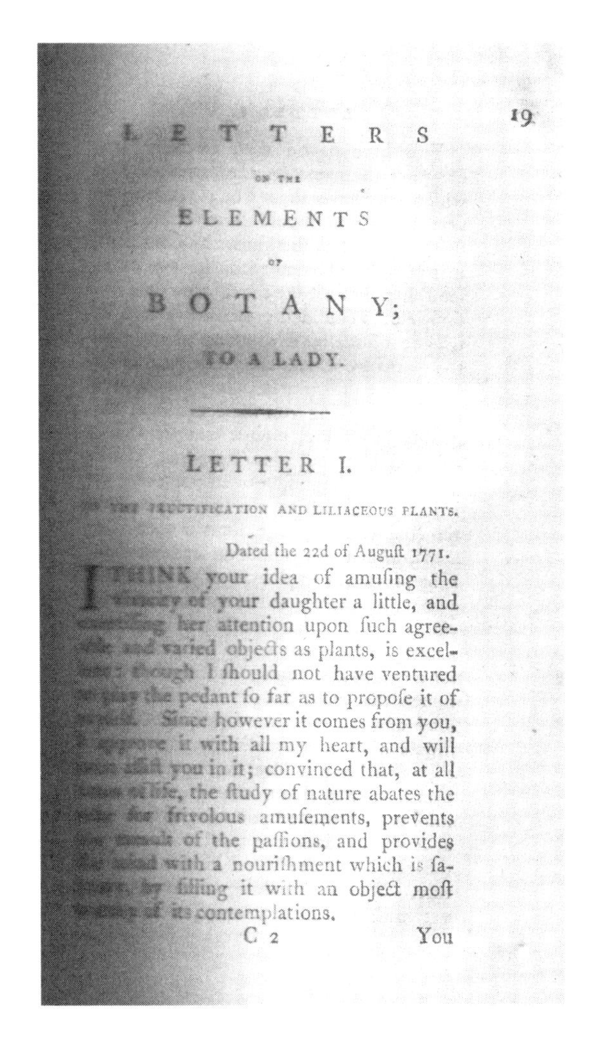

19

LETTERS
ON THE
ELEMENTS
OF
BOTANY;
TO A LADY.

LETTER I.

[illegible] THE [illegible]FICATION AND LILIACEOUS PLANTS.

Dated the 22d of Auguſt 1771.

I THINK your idea of amuſing the [illegible] of your daughter a little, and [illegible] her attention upon ſuch agree-[illegible] and varied objects as plants, is excel-[illegible] though I ſhould not have ventured [illegible] the pedant ſo far as to propoſe it of [illegible]. Since however it comes from you, I [illegible] it with all my heart, and will [illegible] aſſiſt you in it; convinced that, at all [illegible] of life, the ſtudy of nature abates the [illegible] for frivolous amuſements, prevents [illegible] of the paſſions, and provides [illegible] with a nouriſhment which is ſa-[illegible] by filling it with an object moſt [illegible] of its contemplations.

C 2 You

3 Letter I. Reproduced from Rousseau, *Letters on the Elements of Botany Addressed To A Lady*

'Science' here has the contemporary meaning of theoretical knowledge in general (as opposed to the practical arts) rather than just the natural sciences. However, Wakefield does make the natural sciences a central concern throughout the educational dialogues.

By the 1790s, when Wakefield's *An Introduction to Botany* appeared, the botanical dialogue as a genre was enjoying a minor vogue amongst British women as examples from periodical literature show. For example, the *New Ladies Magazine* of 1786 carried a botanical conversation between two women who discussed the properties of the common snowdrop:

> *Ingeana*: What elegant simplicity and innocence in this flower! It belongs, I believe, to the sixth class of the Linnaean system, called Hexandria, and by our botanical society Six Males, and to the first order of that class: but it seems to me to be two flowers, a less within a greater.
> *Flora*: The whole is but one flower; this part, which you suppose to be a lesser flower, is called by our ingenious translators of the immortal Linnaeus, the nectary; and indeed emphatically; for if the bee were now stirring, you would see him drink his honey out of it.[6]

Ingeana and Flora are not engaging in frivolous pursuits such as gathering flowers for a nosegay or admiring exotic garden varieties; they are classifying indigenous plants and using the language of Linnaean nomenclature.[7]

This botanic dialogue is indicative of the developing role of women in botanical culture. Wakefield alludes to the dialogic in *An Introduction to Botany*: speaking of her governess, Felicia writes, 'botany supplied us with subjects for conversation' (II, 3). Ann Murray's *Mentoria: or The Young Ladies Instructor* (1778) offers an insight into the use of the dialogue form in women's education. Murray states that a dialogue acts in the same way as a fable to 'lure the mind into knowledge, and imperceptibly conduct it to the goal of wisdom'.[8] The 'familiar' format is widely adopted by women in the culture of botany; the conversational tone and the dialogic, informal style of texts such as Maria Jacson's *Botanical Dialogues* (1797) and Sarah Fitton's *Conversations On Botany* (1818) suggest that knowledge of botany is feminised and polite.

Botanists wooed female readers, drawing on familiar analogies between women and flowers to celebrate the virtues of the 'British fair' in the prefatory material of their works; many of those addressed were from the highest registers of society. Arabella Rowden, for example, dedicated her introduction to botany to the Duchess of Devonshire, 'who blooms the sweetest flow'r in Britain's Isle'.[9] Robert Thornton's lavish florilegium the *Temple of Flora, or Garden of Nature* (1799–1807) was inscribed to 'Her Gracious Majesty, Queen Charlotte'. [10] A regal rose, this 'Queen of flowers', heads the procession of vegetable beauties displayed in the 'picturesque botanical plates'. The Reverend Charles Abbot's *Flora bedfordiensis* (1798) was designed for the 'amusement and instruction' of 'the fair daughters of Albion';[11] he, too, dedicated his flora to Queen Charlotte 'whose scientific researches have justly obtained for her the character of the first female botanist in the wide circle of the British Dominions'.[12] Charlotte's botanising clearly contributed to the fashion for floral pursuits amongst leisured women.

Fair sexing botany: women and the sexual system

Traditional pastoralism, looking nostalgically to some lost Eden, employed flowers as symbols of innocence; this was dramatically disturbed when the Swedish botanist and classifier of all living things, Carl Linnaeus, focused on the flower in botanical research in order to detail the sexuality of plants by offering precise descriptions of their organs of generation. Linnaeus insisted that the classification of plants must be based on the fructification as comprising the flower and fruit together, consisting in all of seven parts: the calyx, corolla, stamen and pistil of the flower, and the pericarpium, receptacle and seed of the fruit. For Linnaeus, the essence of the plant is in the fructification, because the fructification is dedicated to generation. In the *Systema naturae* of 1735, Linnaeus abandoned Tournefort's purely formal system of classification and founded the Sexual System based on the number, form and position of the stamens, together with the pistils.[13]

In Linnaeus's system, classes are distinguished by the number or proportion of male parts, or stamens in each flower; these are subdivided into orders, which in many of the classes are distinguished by the number of female parts, or pistils. The first eleven classes consist of plants in whose flowers both sexes reside and are distinguished from one another simply by the number of male parts in each flower. For example, *Monandria* are plants with only two stamens in each flower while *Decandria* have ten males or stamens. Later classes are distinguished not by the number of male stamens, but by their union by anthers or filaments to each other or to the female pistil. 'Confederate males' are classes in which many male stamens are united by their anthers, while those in which many stamens are attached to the female pistil are 'feminine males'. Plants whose flowers contain different numbers of male stamens and female pistils are described in terms of 'houses' or 'marriages'. Two male flowers, for example, with separate female pistils residing on the same plant are 'one house'; the presence of male and female flowers on one or more plants with flowers of both sexes is called 'polygamy'. The final class contains plants whose flowers are not discernible and is called *cryptogamia* or 'clandestine marriage'.

James Lee's *Introduction to Botany* (1760), a loose translation of Linnaeus's *Philosophia botanica* of 1751, was the first work to present the Sexual System of classification to British readers.[14] Linnaeus developed a humanised imagery for flowers which is borne out in English adaptations of his Latin works where 'male' stamens are 'husbands', 'female' pistils 'wives', and sexual union a 'marriage'. Flowers lacking stamens or anthers were termed 'eunuchs' and, not surprisingly, the removal of anthers was 'castration'. In Hugh Rose's *Elements of Botany*, a 1775 translation of Linnaeus's *Philosophia botanica*, the union of stamens and pistils during fertilisation is likened to 'husbands and wives on their nuptial bed ... the *calyx* then is the marriage bed, the *corolla* the curtains'.[15] This boudoir version of botany unleashed onto the public imagination the idea that plant reproduction was analogous to human sexuality.

The Sexual System teems with respectable marriage metaphors but Linnaeus had made explicit the indiscriminate sexuality of plant reproduction, devoid of modesty, with little or no degree of selection over sexual unions. In this period the order of society was assumed to rest on the order of nature. Controversies surrounding the Sexual System in England intensified due to the number of women who were practising the modern system of botany. The outraged moralist, Charles Alston, former King's Botanist and Keeper of the Royal Garden,[16] famously remarked that even Linnaeus's description of a pansy, its female parts white and gaping wantonly below the stamens, was 'too smutty for British ears', fuelling debates about whether women might be instructed in Linnaean botany without offending female delicacy.[17] In the 1790s, the reactionary poet, topographer and naturalist, the Reverend Richard Polwhele, was unable to comprehend how an examination of a plant's organs of generation could be conducive to female modesty. He warned that botanising girls anatomising the sexual parts of the flower were indulging in acts of wanton titillation.[18]

Botanical knowledge, then, was simultaneously concealed from and unveiled to women in varying degrees during the mid- to late eighteenth century. James Lee's coeval, William Withering (1749–1801), anticipated that his botanical work would attract a large number of female readers: his *Botanical Arrangement of All the Vegetables Naturally Growing in Great Britain* appeared in 1776 and he attempted to 'fair sex' it by purposefully omitting

> the sexual distinctions in the titles to the classes and orders ... From an apprehension that Botany in an English dress would become a favourite amusement with the ladies, many of whom are very considerable proficients in the study, in spite of difficulty.[19]

Withering's text was the main source of botanical knowledge for many women. It upheld notions of female propriety and came to be regarded as the most authoritative introduction to botany. A handbook with notes on Linnaean classification, 'Withering's Botany', as it became known through several reprints, included directions for the drying and preservation of specimens of plants, a dictionary of botanical terms and a catalogue of useful botanical books. His readers ranged from the novice, including women and young people, to fellow members of the Lunar Society in Birmingham.

One such member, Erasmus Darwin, published a poetic rendering of the Linnaean sexual system in 1789 – *The Loves of the Plants*, which formed part of the epic poem, *The Botanic Garden*, eventually published in 1791. Darwin cast himself in the role of a flower painter, displaying the 'Beaux and Beauties' of the vegetable world before the eyes of his female readers as if they were 'diverse little pictures suspended over the chimney of a Lady's dressing-room, *connected only by a slight festoon of ribbons*'.[20] Darwin restored the sexualised nomenclature which Withering had deliberately erased, initiating female readers into the secret world of 'vegetable loves'[21] and encouraging women to engage with their own sexuality through botany.

Many 'literary ladies' were inspired to write on botany after reading *The Botanic Garden* which had been skilfully directed at female readers.[22] Poetical studies came into vogue, such as Frances Arabella Rowden's *A Poetical Introduction to The Study of Botany* (1801) and Charlotte Smith's 'Flora,' a re-writing of Darwin's poem for young readers. Her *Conversations Introducing Poetry Chiefly on the Subject of Natural History* (1804) enlarged on the theme. Another post-Darwinian study was Sarah Hoare's *Poem on the Pleasures and Advantages of Botanical Pursuits* which was appended to the eighth edition of Wakefield's *Introduction to Botany* in 1818 and published separately in 1826.

Darwin's work was profoundly influential in exciting women's interest in botany and this helped increase the anxieties surrounding the figure of the female botanist. In 1790, the philosopher and naturalist John Berkenhout wrote to his son:

> The lady who asked the question whether women may be instructed in the modern system of botany consistently with female delicacy? was accused of ridiculous prudery; nevertheless, if she had proposed the question to me, I should have answered—they cannot.[23]

Botany was suddenly at the forefront of debates on female education. Mary Wollstonecraft, in *A Vindication of the Rights of Woman* (1792), opposed the threat by Berkenhout and his followers to limit women's access to botanical knowledge. Wollstonecraft argued that, contrary to Berkenhout's 'gross idea of modesty', female reserve was 'far from being incompatible with knowledge'.[24]

Fortunately, the 'fair book' of botanical knowledge was not to be 'shut with an everlasting seal' as Wollstonecraft feared. In Darwin's *A Plan For The Conduct of Female Education In Boarding Schools* (1797) there was a catalogue of books for the improvement of young women which contained a number of titles on botany. Alongside popular texts such as James Lee's *Introduction to Botany* (1760) and Martyn's translation of Rousseau's botanical letters (1785), Darwin recommended *Botanical Dialogues For the Use of Schools* (1797) by Maria Jacson, Curtis's *Botanical Magazine* (1787), and the Botanical Society at Lichfield's translations from Linnaeus, *Families of Plants* (1787) and *System of Vegetables* (1782). Darwin, then, advocated that women acquire a broad botanical knowledge and apparently saw this knowledge as compatible with his opinion that:

> The female character should possess the mild and retiring virtues rather than the bold and dazzling ones; great eminence in almost anything is sometimes injurious to a young lady whose temper and disposition should appear to be pliant rather than robust; to be ready to take impressions rather than to be decidedly mark'd; as great apparent strength of character, however excellent, is liable to alarm both her own and the other sex; and to create admiration rather than affection.[25]

Though threats to female modesty were discerned in Darwin's *Loves of the Plants*, his educational 'plan' was unlikely to 'decidedly mark' or make bold any young woman's character. His views on women's education were not remarkably liberal although he is unusual in suggesting that women should receive training in physical education and science.

Linnaeus in letters

My discussion of botany and the feminine will now focus on two of the most widely-read introductions to botany in the eighteenth century. I introduced these earlier: *Letters on the Elements of Botany Addressed to a Lady*, translated from Rousseau by Thomas Martyn in 1785, and Priscilla Wakefield's *An Introduction to Botany; in a Series of Familiar Letters* which appeared in 1796. There has been little written on Rousseau the botanist, particularly in English, and none of the existing studies examine Martyn's translation of Rousseau's *Letters on Botany* nor do they discuss gender issues in relation to Rousseau and botany[26] Thomas Martyn succeeded his father, John, to the Chair of Botany in Cambridge in 1762. He gave a course of public lectures on the Linnaean Sexual System in 1763 and his flora, *Plantae cantabrigienses*, was published in the same year. After translating Rousseau's *Letters on Botany* in 1785, Martyn was elected a Fellow of the Royal Society in 1786. His final work, a dictionary of Linnaean terms entitled *The Language of Botany*, appeared in 1793.[27]

The educationalist, Priscilla Wakefield (1751–1832), married the Quaker merchant Edward Wakefield in 1771. Wakefield came from a distinguished Quaker lineage; her aunt was Elizabeth Fry and she was related to the Barclay family of bankers and was one of the earliest promoters of the savings banks known as 'frugality banks'. She began writing to support her family and specialised in educational dialogues on the subject of travel and science.[28] Wakefield's *An Introduction to Botany* went through eleven editions and was last reprinted in 1841. It was also translated into French in 1801. The Martyn/Rousseau *Letters* were read extensively and reprinted eight times over the next thirty years.

In the first of the Martyn/Rousseau letters we learn that 'maternal zeal' has driven a young woman to embark on a course in botany so that she may teach her daughter about plants:

> I THINK your idea of amusing the vivacity of your daughter a little, and exercising her attention upon such agreeable and varied objects as plants, is excellent, though I should not have ventured to play the pedant so far as to propose it of myself. (I, 19)

The tone is one of mutual improvement brought about by the intimate exchange of knowledge between a mother and daughter. In this passage, the relationship between the mother and her male instructor is understated but in the succeeding letters it is played out in a flirtatious botanical dialogue: 'I fancy to myself a charming picture of my beautiful cousin busy with her glass examining heaps of flowers, a hundred times less flourishing, less fresh, and less agreeable than herself' (II, 32). The letters have intimate undertones:

> I am jealous, dear cousin, of being your only guide in this part of Botany. When it is the proper time I will point out to you the books that you may consult. In the mean time have patience to read nothing but in that of nature, and to keep wholly to my letters. (III, 34)

The botanical instructions begin to have a latent meaning which conceals the onset of romance: 'Take breath, dear cousin, for this is an unconscionable letter; and yet I dare not promise you more discretion in the next; after that however we shall have nothing before us but a path bordered with flowers' (V, 58).

Rousseau was influenced by popular science dialogues such as Bernard le Bovier Fontenelle's *Entretiens sur la pluralité des mondes,* where during the course of six evenings a cultured Parisian philosopher instructs the 'most amiable creature in the universe', the Marchioness of G., in the mysteries of Cartesian 'Vortexes, Planets and New Worlds'.[29] Fontenelle published the *Entretiens* in

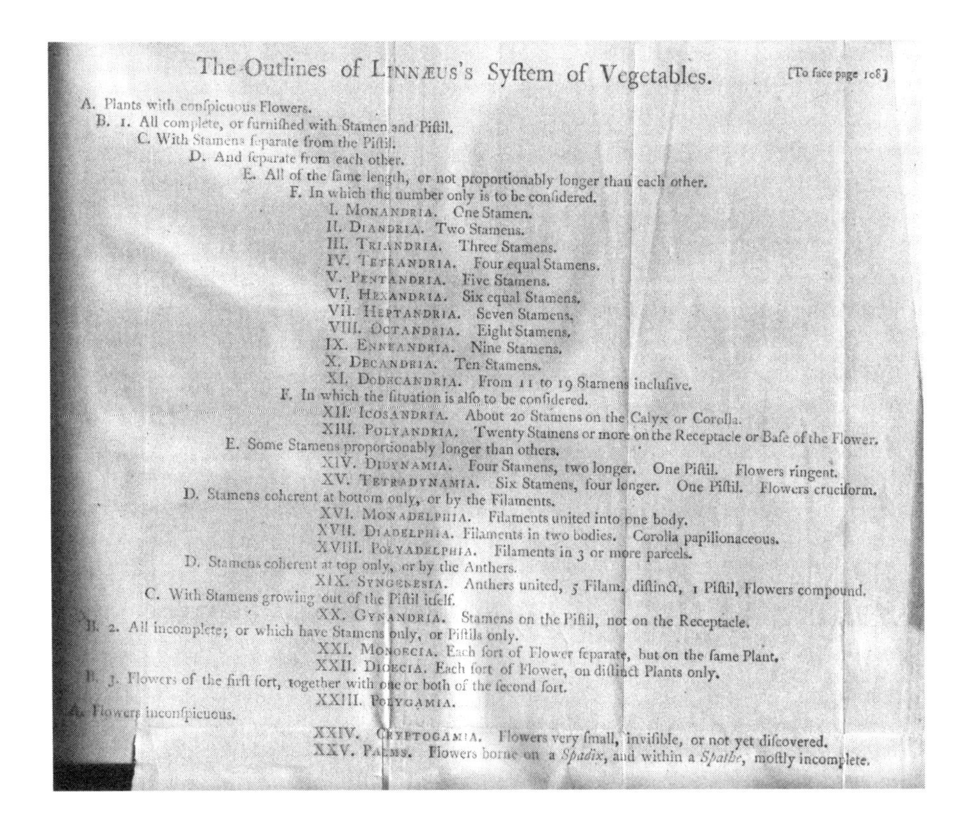

The Outlines of LINNÆUS's Syftem of Vegetables. [To face page 108]

A. Plants with confpicuous Flowers.
B. 1. All complete, or furnifhed with Stamen and Piftil.
C. With Stamens feparate from the Piftil.
D. And feparate from each other.
E. All of the fame length, or not proportionably longer than each other.
F. In which the number only is to be confidered.
I. MONANDRIA. One Stamen.
II. DIANDRIA. Two Stamens.
III. TRIANDRIA. Three Stamens.
IV. TETRANDRIA. Four equal Stamens.
V. PENTANDRIA. Five Stamens.
VI. HEXANDRIA. Six equal Stamens.
VII. HEPTANDRIA. Seven Stamens.
VIII. OCTANDRIA. Eight Stamens.
IX. ENNEANDRIA. Nine Stamens.
X. DECANDRIA. Ten Stamens.
XI. DODECANDRIA. From 11 to 19 Stamens inclufive.
F. In which the fituation is alfo to be confidered.
XII. ICOSANDRIA. About 20 Stamens on the Calyx or Corolla.
XIII. POLYANDRIA. Twenty Stamens or more on the Receptacle or Bafe of the Flower.
E. Some Stamens proportionably longer than others.
XIV. DIDYNAMIA. Four Stamens, two longer. One Piftil. Flowers ringent.
XV. TETRADYNAMIA. Six Stamens, four longer. One Piftil. Flowers cruciform.
D. Stamens coherent at bottom only, or by the Filaments.
XVI. MONADELPHIA. Filaments united into one body.
XVII. DIADELPHIA. Filaments in two bodies. Corolla papilionaceous.
XVIII. POLYADELPHIA. Filaments in 3 or more parcels.
D. Stamens coherent at top only, or by the Anthers.
XIX. SYNGENESIA. Anthers united, 5 Filam. diftinct, 1 Piftil, Flowers compound.
C. With Stamens growing out of the Piftil itfelf.
XX. GYNANDRIA. Stamens on the Piftil, not on the Receptacle.
B. 2. All incomplete; or which have Stamens only, or Piftils only.
XXI. MONOECIA. Each fort of Flower feparate, but on the fame Plant.
XXII. DIOECIA. Each fort of Flower, on diftinct Plants only.
B. 3. Flowers of the firft fort, together with one or both of the fecond fort.
XXIII. POLYGAMIA.
A. Flowers inconfpicuous.
XXIV. CRYPTOGAMIA. Flowers very fmall, invifible, or not yet difcovered.
XXV. PALMS. Flowers borne on a *Spadix*, and within a *Spathe*, moftly incomplete.

4 The Outlines of Linnaeus's System of Vegetables. Reproduced from Rousseau, *Letters on the Elements of Botany Addressed To A Lady*

1686; in England it became a widely read and influential text for women through Aphra Behn's English rendering of it in 1688.[30] Fontenelle strove to make astronomers of the fair sex while Rousseau attempted to instruct them in Linnaean botany. Fontenelle gives an engaging account of the secrets of astronomy being unveiled to an enlightened French lady; Rousseau similarly describes a young woman being 'initiated in the mysteries of vegetation':

> When you have well examined this petal, draw it gently downwards, pinching it lightly by the keel or thin edge, for fear of tearing away what it contains. I am certain you will be pleased with the mystery it reveals when the veil is removed. (III, 36)

The young woman is instructed to proceed with caution when it comes to her daughter and to 'unveil to her by degrees no more than is suitable to her age and sex' (III, 26). In Rousseau's Linnaean-inspired unveiling of the 'mysteries of vegetation' botanical knowledge is compared to something difficult – or even illicit – which can only be revealed 'by degrees'. He alludes to the sexuality of plants while recommending botany as a 'useful' scientific pursuit which is 'amusing' and agreeable to female delicacy. This element of erotic pleasure is understandably missing from Wakefield's text.[31] The spectacle of nature was both concealed from and unveiled to women in varying degrees during the eighteenth century; few, however, considered a study of plant sexuality to be quite so conducive to female character building as Rousseau.

Wakefield and Rousseau's botanical texts are exemplary in that they indicate the ambivalence in the process of the feminisation of botany: while they are open to a liberationist reading, offering women access to scientific knowledge for the first time, they also have a conservative function in that they can be seen to reaffirm conduct-book constructions of femininity. Gender-coded representations of botany often depicted it as a genteel amusement for 'ladies' within a familial setting. Rousseau, for example, was concerned that his botanical 'ladies' did not consider botany to be a 'great undertaking':

> You must not, my dear friend, give more importance to Botany than it really has; it is a study of pure curiosity, and has no other real use than that, which a thinking sensible being may deduce from the observation of nature and the wonders of the universe. (VII, 71)

Botany was thought highly beneficial to female minds since it was a rational, industrious study that discouraged superficial, even sinful behaviour. Thus, Wakefield promoted botany as

> a substitute for some of the trifling, and not to say pernicious objects, that too frequently occupy the leisure of young ladies of fashionable manners, and, by employing their faculties rationally, act as an antidote to levity and idleness. (Preface, iii)

Botany and no other natural science has thus been singled out to act as an antidote to 'feminine' faults such as idleness and frivolity. It is these traits, along with insubordination, which Rousseau warned are 'most dangerous' and 'very hard to cure once established' in girls.[32] He reassures the young mother who features in *Letters on the Elements of Botany* that botany can supply an alternative focus for these wayward urges:

> at all times of life, the study of nature abates the taste for frivolous amusements, prevents the tumult of passions, and provides the mind with a nourishment which is salutary, by filling it with an object most worthy of its contemplations. (I, 19)

It is worth exploring the specific way in which Wakefield and Rousseau promote botany as a feminine pursuit. This chapter discusses the use of Linnaean methodology in these texts, demonstrating how it became a means of encouraging women (who were imagined to lack discipline) to engage with order and regularity, then looks at how both Wakefield and Rousseau insist that book learning in itself is inadequate and substitute lessons in outdoor exploration and direct observation; methods which, it can be argued, discouraged women from the solitary pursuit of scientific knowledge – though this is ambiguous. A discussion of the feminisation of botany in relation to the gendered dichotomy of the public and private spheres follows.

Wakefield's *An Introduction to Botany* describes the Linnaean system of plant classification in a series of letters. In the first of these, Felicia explains how she will impart the botanical knowledge she has learnt in formal lessons from her governess, Mrs Snelgrove,[33] to her sister Constance so that 'by mutually pursuing the same subject, we may reciprocally improve each other':

> How should I enjoy this pursuit in your company, my dear sister! but as that is impossible at present, I will adopt the nearest substitute I can obtain, by communicating to you the result of every lesson. (I, 2)

Felicia has been encouraged to take up botany by her mother in her sister's absence. Wakefield hoped her letters would 'be sought rather as indulgences, than avoided as laborious toils' (Preface, ii). Felicia expresses similar concerns in the text: 'I am fearful, lest by this time you are wearied with the minute descriptions of the separate parts of flowers and plants, and that you begin to wish for something more amusing' (VI, 28). Rousseau's epistolary text had similarly acted as a substitute for formal lessons; his eight letters instruct a young mother about botany so that she can teach her own daughter in turn. As translator, Martyn declares that Rousseau's intention is to reveal knowledge through a gradual process.[34] Like Wakefield's Felicia, Rousseau's botanist/tutor is also afraid of tiring his pupil with long descriptions and frequently apologises for 'fatiguing [her] attention upon atoms' (VI, 61). Both texts share the Enlightenment ideal of rational amusement.[35]

Wakefield discusses plant structure and fructification; subsequent letters take the reader through each Linnaean class in turn and emphasise the importance of classification. Rousseau's letters expound what he believed to be the proper methodology of botany: the entry on the contents page, for example, begins with 'The true use of Botany ... not mere names, but the vegetable structure – component parts of a plant' and ends with 'Botany a study of observation and facts' (xiii), while that for Letter III begins 'Botany not to be studied by books, but by nature' (xiii). In Martyn's translation, the text is given a more Linnaean emphasis by the translator's own appended letters; in Martyn's words: 'the system I propose to you is not the French one of Tournefort, which is very beautiful and has great merit; but the Swedish one by Linnaeus. I prefer this because it is most complete, and most in fashion' (IX, 86).

Ann Shtier incorrectly states that Rousseau had been 'antipathetic to systemizing and to any focus on names of plants'.[36] It is an understandable misconception that Rousseau, the man who famously linked the advancement of the arts and sciences to the spread of luxury and the corruption of morals, was antipathetic to the scientific frame of mind. Rousseau's antagonism towards the sciences surfaces in the 'Discourse on the Sciences and Arts':

> Astronomy was born from superstition ... Geometry from Avarice; physics from vain curiosity; all even moral philosophy, from human pride. Thus the Sciences and Arts owe their birth to our vices; we would be less doubtful of their advantages if they owed it to our virtues.[37]

In fact, Rousseau was driven to study plants systematically and on a Linnaean basis in spite of his hostility to academic science (Fig. 5). Threatened with imprisonment due to the Archbishop of Paris's condemnation of *Emile*, Rousseau

TABLE OF THE CLASSES, referring to PLATE VIII.

a distinguishes the Stamens; *b* the Pistils.

Classes.			*Familiar British Examples.*	
Monandria,	*fig.* 141.	One Stamen	Marestail and Water Starwort	*Class* 1
Diandria,	142.	Two Stamens	Speedwell and Brooklime	2
Triandria,	143.	Three Stamens	Grasses and Crocuses	3
Tetrandria,	144.	Four Stamens (All of the same length)	Teasel and Plantain	4
Pentandria,	145.	Five Stamens	Honeysuckle and Primrose	5
Hexandria,	146.	Six Stamens (All of the same length.)	Harebell and Snowdrop	6
Heptandria,	147.	Seven Stamens	Wintergreen	7
Octandria,	148.	Eight Stamens	Mezereon and Willowherb	8
Enneandria,	149.	Nine Stamens	Flowering Rush	9
Decandria,	150.	Ten Stamens	Pink and Stitchwort	10
Dodecandria,	151.	Twelve Stamens, or more (fixed to the Receptacle.)	Houseleek	11
Icosandria,	152.	Twenty Stamens (fixed upon the Calyx.)	Strawberry, and Black and White Thorn	12
Polyandria,	153.	Many Stamens (fixed to the Receptacle.)	Poppy and Buttercups	13
Didynamia,	154.	Four Stamens, two of them longer. One Pistil. Flowers ringent	Foxglove and Deadnettle	14
Tetradynamia,	155.	Six Stamens, four of them longer. One Pistil. Flowers cruciform	Stock Gillifiower and Wallflower	15
Monadelphia,	156.	Threads united at bottom, but separate at top	Mallow and Cranesbill	16
Diadelphia,	157.	Threads in two sets. Flowers Butterfly-shaped.	Pea and Clover	17
Polyadelphia,	158.	Threads in three or more sets	St. John's Wort	18
Syngenesia,	159.	Anthers united. Five Stamens. One Pistil. Flowers Compound.	Dandelion, Daisey, and Thistle	19
Gynandria,	160.	Stamens upon the Pistil	Orchis	20
Monoecia,	161.	Stamens and Pistils in separate Flowers, upon the same Plant	Bryony and Hasel	21
Dioecia,	162.	Stamens and Pistils distinct, upon different Plants	Hop and Willow	22
Polygamia,	163.	Stamens only, others with Pistils only, others with both	Orach	23
Cryptogamia,	164.	Flowers inconspicuous	Ferns, Mosses, Liverworts, Flags, Mushrooms	24

*** The first twenty-three Classes are denominated *Phanerogamia* or *Phaenogamia*, a term opposed to Cryptogamia, and implying that the flowers are conspicuous. The first fifteen are called *Apandrous*, because their stamens are distinct; and the next five, *Synandrous*, because their stamens are united. The three penultimate classes, viz. the 21st, 22d, and 23d, are united by Pursh into one called *Diclisia*, because they have stamens and pistils in separate flowers; and the first twenty classes having their stamens and pistils together, are called *Monoclinous*.

To face page 36.

5 Wakefield's Table of Linnaean Classes. Reproduced from Priscilla Wakefield, *An Introduction to Botany*

fled to Switzerland, moved north to Môtiers and took to botanising. He began notes towards a dictionary of botanical terms in the year 1764. The dictionary was finally abandoned but the completed introduction to it remained. It was a lengthy history of the 'rise and progress of botany' which celebrated Linnaeus's contribution to the advancement of botanical science. Martyn translated this essay as an introduction to the *Letters on the Elements of Botany Addressed to a Lady* when it appeared in 1785. What is striking about Rousseau's essay on botany is that, contrary to the usual expectations already described, it shows a typical man of the Enlightenment concerned with methodology and systematic thought:

> distant voyages were incessantly enriching Botany with new treasures; and, whilst the old names already overloaded the memory, it was necessary to invent new ones incessantly for the new plants that were discovered. Lost in this immense labyrinth, the botanists were obliged to seek a thread to extricate themselves from it; they attached themselves therefore at last seriously to method. (Introduction, 9)

Rousseau lionises Linnaeus for supplying the Ariadne thread in botany, a universal system which led botanists out of the labyrinth of local knowledge and instigated botany's departure from herbalism and superstition. Botany's subsequent break with apothecaries, herbalists, infusions and poultices was celebrated by Rousseau in *Rêveries du promeneur solitaire* (1777).[38] According to Rousseau, Linnaeus's simple binomial nomenclature had created a new language for botany 'which is as convenient and necessary for Botanists as that of algebra is to mathematicians' (Introduction, 12).

Wakefield is also indebted to Linnaeus, 'the great master of method and arrangement' (44), for making the acquisition of botanical knowledge easier for the novice: 'he has divided the orders, when numerous, into several divisions, each including one or more genera, which is a means of diminishing the pupil's labour' (VIII, 44). She urged her readers to embrace Linnaean systematics, 'for it is by method only, that it is possible to obtain a knowledge of so many particulars' (V, 26) and endeavoured to explain the importance of the new system of botany:

> Botany was in an imperfect state, when he [Linnaeus] undertook to form a new system, which he effected so excellently, that it has immortalised his name, and although it may probably receive improvement from some future naturalist, it is never likely to be superseded. (V, 27)

Linnaean classes are illustrated in a table in Wakefield's book which shows familiar British plants of each class, emphasising the easy application of the Linnaean system to British flora (Fig. 6). An illustration showing the position and number of the stamens and pistils in each class appears later in Wakefield's book (see Fig. 7). A list of orders is also included and illustrations of each of the orders (Figs 8 and 9). Wakefield thus instructs women how to classify native plants according to Linnaeus.

Martyn added a number of letters to Rousseau's original eight, describing each Linnaean class in turn, but fearing that the introduction of method would lose him the attention of his female readers, he made the following plea:

> Do not suffer yourself to be terrified at the word *system*. I promise you there shall be little difficulty in it to you who have patience and attention; and as little parade of hard words as possible, only allowing me to name my classes and orders. (IX, 86)

Passages such as this point to the patronising way some women were perceived as consumers of science.

However, the authors of these introductory texts encouraged radically different levels of engagement for their female readers, from gentle exercise and plant collecting in Rousseau, to active involvement with proper scientific instruments in Wakefield: 'WHENEVER you set out on a botanical excursion, remember to put your magnifying glass and dissecting instruments into your pocket, that you may not be obliged to neglect those flowers that are small, for want of this precaution' (VIII, 43). Wakefield instructs her botanising ladies to 'confirm your knowledge by practice, and do not suffer a day to pass without amusing yourself in dissecting some flower or other' (V, 25).

Withering advocated the use of instruments such as the magnifying glass, dissecting knife and needle. Later editions of the *Arrangement* even carried an advertisement for a portable botanical microscope invented by Withering himself

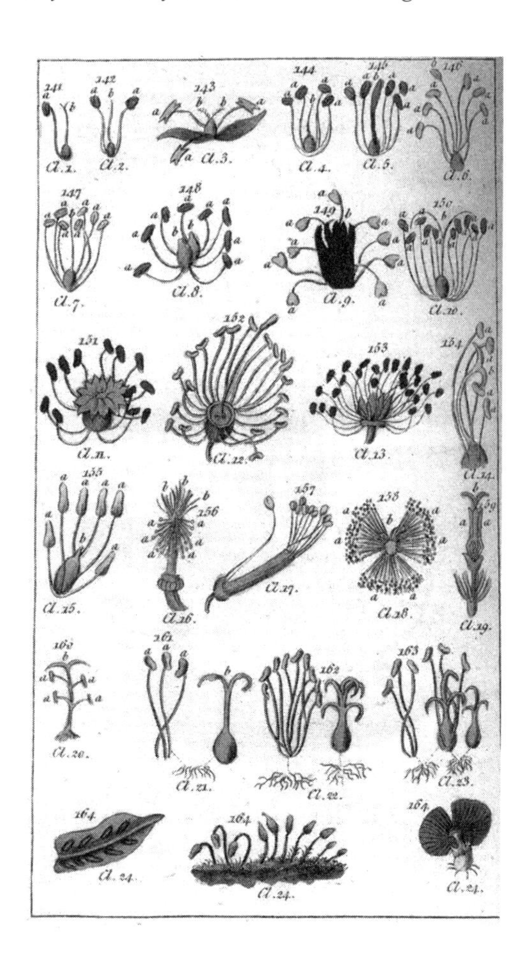

6 Illustration of Wakefield's Table of Classes.
Reproduced from Wakefield, *An Introduction to Botany*

which was sold along with the text by his publishers (see Figs 10 and 11).[39] The microscopic world had already been made more accessible to the amateur and the portable microscope had become fashionable with many British women; Swift is known to have purchased one for Stella.[40] Rousseau listed the glass, needle, lancet and 'a pair of good scissars [*sic*]' as the tools of the botanist (II, 32); Wakefield takes the recommended method of observation one step further than Rousseau by encouraging the use of a microscope when observing small flowers like the daisy: 'apply your microscope, and you will be pleased with the beauty and variety discernible in this little disregarded flower' (XXIII,136).

Lessons on the use of the microscope were often directed towards women:

> Investigations of this kind particularly recommend themselves to the attention of the ladies, as being congenial with that refinement of taste and sentiment, and that

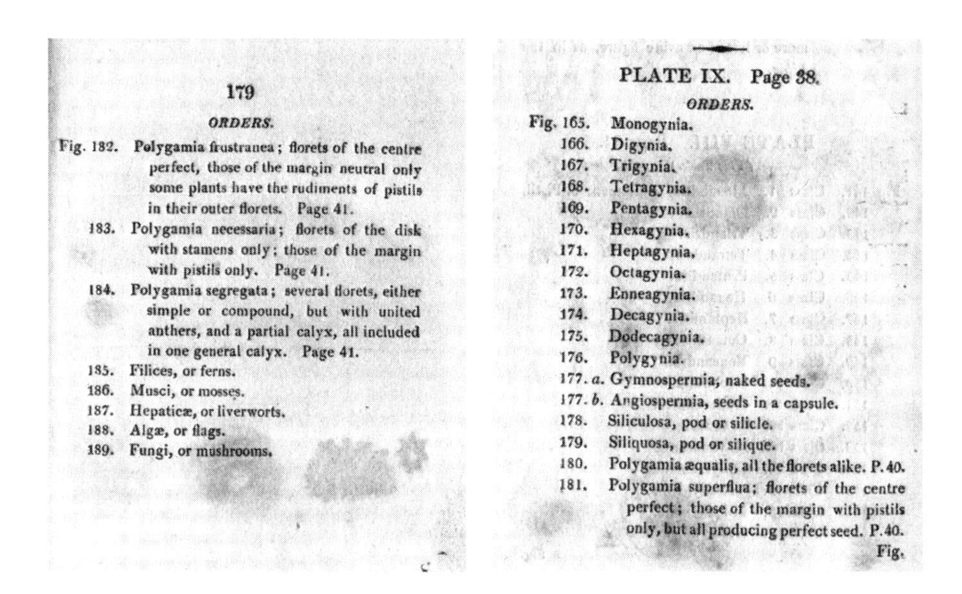

179

ORDERS.

Fig. 182. Polygamia frustranea; florets of the centre perfect, those of the margin neutral only some plants have the rudiments of pistils in their outer florets. Page 41.
183. Polygamia necessaria; florets of the disk with stamens only; those of the margin with pistils only. Page 41.
184. Polygamia segregata; several florets, either simple or compound, but with united anthers, and a partial calyx, all included in one general calyx. Page 41.
185. Filices, or ferns.
186. Musci, or mosses.
187. Hepaticæ, or liverworts.
188. Algæ, or flags.
189. Fungi, or mushrooms.

PLATE IX. Page 38.

ORDERS.

Fig. 165. Monogynia.
166. Digynia.
167. Trigynia.
168. Tetragynia.
169. Pentagynia.
170. Hexagynia.
171. Heptagynia.
172. Octagynia.
173. Enneagynia.
174. Decagynia.
175. Dodecagynia.
176. Polygynia.
177. *a.* Gymnospermia, naked seeds.
177. *b.* Angiospermia, seeds in a capsule.
178. Siliculosa, pod or silicle.
179. Siliquosa, pod or silique.
180. Polygamia æqualis, all the florets alike. P. 40.
181. Polygamia superflua; florets of the centre perfect; those of the margin with pistils only, but all producing perfect seed. P. 40.

Fig.

7 Wakefield's Table of Linnaean Orders. Reproduced from Wakefield, *An Introduction to Botany*

> pure and placid consistency of conduct which so eminently distinguish and adorn those of this happy isle

George Adams wrote in a popular text on microscopy.[41] However, despite Wakefield's enthusiasm for the microscope, both Rousseau and Wakefield's texts gave botany a familial setting and discouraged an engagement with scientific theory beyond simple classification and plant collecting. Wakefield introduces the female reader to scientific classification but avoids using scientific terms in the body of the text, substituting common plant names such as 'Lungwort', 'Houndstongue', 'Goosefoot', and 'Henbane' where possible, and placing botanical nomenclature, '*Pulmonaria*', '*Cynoglossum*', '*Chenopodium*', '*Hyoscyamus*', in footnotes.

While she is committed to the cultivation of female minds and the development of female reason, Wakefield delimits this with many gender- and class-specific boundaries. In *Reflections on the Present Condition of the Female Sex*, for example, she warns against women moving into 'masculine' spheres and straying too far outside the domestic home. She also advocates that a woman should be educated according to her social position in society, claiming that 'the different orders or conditions of mankind require the performance of duties, and the cultivation of talents, peculiar to each'.[42] In a similar way, she derives social implications from the Linnaean hierarchy of orders and classes. We learn that the class *Cryptogamia* is made up of vegetables 'of the lowest kinds, whose parts of fructification have hitherto escaped the most attentive researches of learned botanists' (XXVII, 162). Her fictional governess, Mrs Snelgrove, considers the members of this class – mushrooms, lichens and mosses – to be 'uncouth'

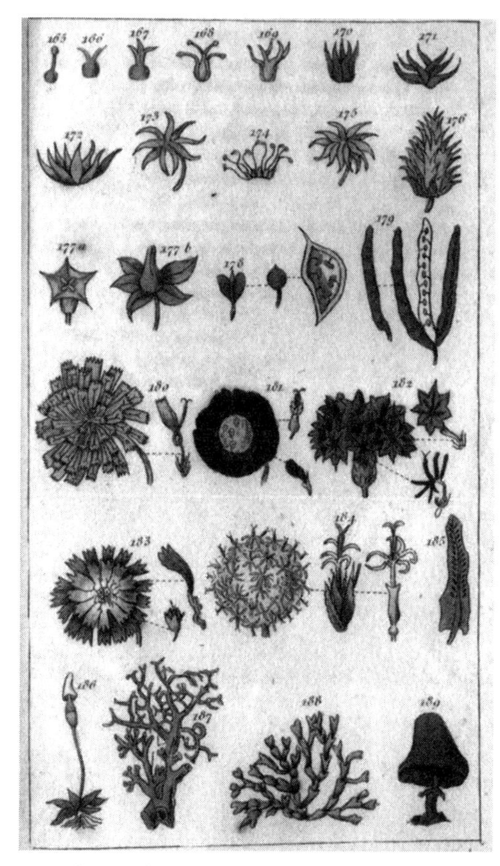

8 *(above)* Illustration of Wakefield's Table of Orders. Reproduced from Wakefield, *An Introduction to Botany*

9 *(below)* Withering's Portable Botanical Microscope. Reproduced from William Withering, *An Arrangement of British Plants*

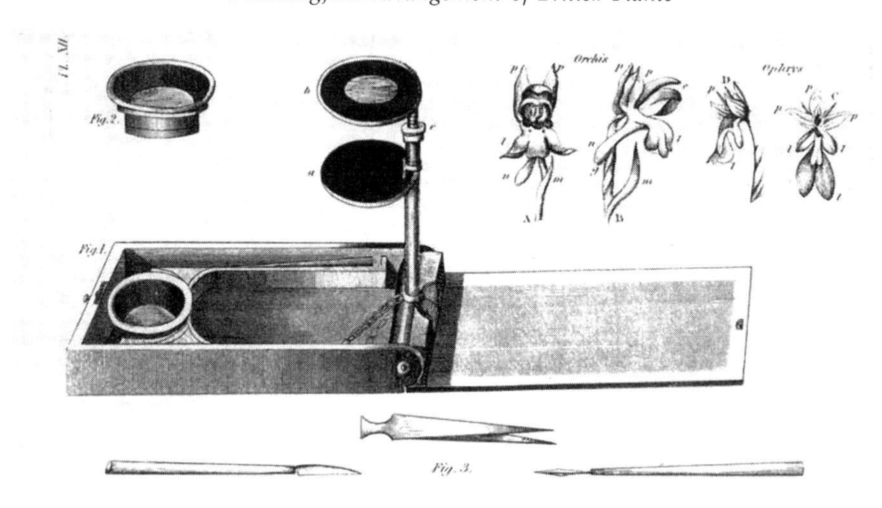

PLATE XII.

BOTANICAL MICROSCOPE.

FIG. 1. Represents the Botanical Microscope in its present improved state.

FIG. 2. Is a Magnifying Glass, to be held in the hand, and applied close to the eye, whilst the object to be examined is brought immediately under it, at such a distance as shall be found to give the most distinct vision.

FIG. 3. Shews the Dissecting Knife, the Triangular Needle, and a pair of small steel Plyers. These instruments are useful in the dissection of flowers, even when the plants are so large as not to require magnifying.

When the parts in question are very minute, and require a nice and careful dissection, place the microscope upon a table, and raise it, if necessary, on a book or two, so that the eye may be applied with ease immediately over and close to the glass (*b.*) Lay the object to be examined on the dark stage (*a.*) and turn the screw at (*c.*) until you see the object upon the stage perfectly distinct. With the needle in the left, and the knife in the right hand, the elbows resting on the table, proceed in the dissection at the same time that the eye is applied to the glass (*b.*)

When the microscope is shut up, the instruments and the hand-glass are to be put into the cells destined to receive them, and the whole forms a shape and size convenient to carry in the pocket.

10 Withering's Microscope – Description.
Reproduced from Withering, *An Arrangement of British Plants*

and unworthy of attention. She is equally quick to dismiss non-native plants and even those which are used for culinary purposes such as cinnamon or bay are treated dismissively. Rhubarb, she explains, is successfully cultivated in Britain, 'but as its extraction is foreign, it does not come within my plan to give a further account of it' (XV, 88). Preference must be given to 'genus natural to this country' (XXII, 129).

Richardson's *Clarissa* had dramatised the often minute regulation of young women's letter writing; similarly, we learn from Felicia that the botanising governess 'superintends my letters, and points out what I should write', that she is 'incapable of methodising so accurately' without her assistance, for she 'will not allow me to do anything without some degree of regularity' (XXII, 29). This regularity can be authorised by botany: Felicia encourages Constance to observe the 'beautiful regularity in most of Nature's works' (VI, 32). Methodical and systematic, Linnaean botany was a paradigm of order and was recommended to women for this very reason. For Rousseau, too, botany was a means by which women could become acquainted with – and implicitly, socialised into – an ordered system: 'you must go forth into the garden or the fields, and there become

The backwardness of the Spring accounted
for 1772
+May Day
Last + Wednesday when Jupiter rose to survey
The annual return & procession of May
Concluding the Lady with Venus and Flora
Would come in full dress in the Coach of Aurora
That a string of attendants as usual would follow
And the rear of the Show be brought up by Appollo
He looked & enquired and gave order in vain
Time seemed to stand still and to wait for the train
Aurora was sulky and loath to appear
And the Devil an Hour, Flower or Sunshine was there
May came it is true but in strange dishabille
Was wrapp'd up in flannels & looked very ill
The God shook his Curls for he little expected
To see an old favorite of his so neglected
Besides he was vexed to see things out of Season
And Mercury straight was dispatch'd for a reason
From his Mother a full information he got
And importantly thought he discover'd a plot
On Flora he seiz'd as the cause & contriver
And up to Jove's throne he determined to drive her
The God who rules all things but home & his wife
And was ne'er contradicted elsewhere in his life
Bounc'd about in a passion as soon as he saw her
And swore thro' the Kennel his servants should draw her

11 Manuscript of [Anna Seward (?)], 'The Backwardness of Spring Accounted for'. Reproduced from Linnaeus, *A System of Vegetables*, trans. by a Botanical Society at Lichfield

familiar with Nature herself; with that beauty, order, regularity, and inexhaustible variety which is to be found in the structure of vegetables'.[43] This concern with order enables that familiar slide from the natural to the social,[44] making botany, as an exemplification of regularity, an ideal discipline for women and children.

Not only social order was involved: studying botany was also a means of observing divine order; the divine order was, in turn, obviously an ideological projection of concerns about the social once more. Some prominent botanists sought to avoid the subversive aspects of materialistic science by linking the religious faith of Newton and Boyle with the new scientific attitude:

> Following the Restoration of Charles II, Boyle and his followers used their synthesis of science and religion to uphold the idea of a constitutional monarchy that allowed freedom for commercial activity ... Newtonian science upheld a view of the universe that provided the model for an orderly society.[45]

This became an institutionalised practice through the Boyle lectures and was taken up into botany from there.[46] Newton's conception of a dynamic universe, initially deriving its movement from God, but thereafter moving according to strict internal law without divine intervention to sustain it, was admirably fitted to include and rationalise the study of the world of living things. It was a point of view closely allied to that of the naturalist John Ray.[47] Boyle and Newton were anxious that the compatibility between science and religion be promulgated as widely as possible. Most of the Boyle lecturers were Newtonians, including William Derham (1657–1735), whose *Physico-Theology* gave its name to the whole programme by which the natural philosophers sought to demonstrate the wisdom and goodness of God through the study of his creation. Derham's study drew heavily on the 'argument from design' in living Nature expressed in Ray's *Wisdom of God Manifested in the Works of the Creation* (1691).[48] Here, Ray uses the trope of discussing all of nature as evidence of 'God's handiwork': 'My Text warrants me to run over all the visible Works of God in particular, and to trace the Footsteps of his Wisdom in the Composition, Order, Harmony, and Uses of every one of them'.[49]

There were innumerable clergymen and theologians who observed and recorded flora and fauna, from John Ray and the Hampshire curate, Gilbert White, to the poet/vicar George Crabbe; this indicates that a close relationship existed between botany and religious contemplation.[50] Natural history texts for the instruction of women or young persons seldom neglected to provide religious – and hence, moral guidance.[51] Quakers, in particular, thought that, since Nature was God's creation, truth could be revealed through the direct observation of it; Wakefield urges her female botanists to 'perceive and admire the proofs of Divine Wisdom exhibited in every leaf, and in every flower' (IV, 17).[52] Felicia concludes one letter to Constance by declaring that

> The finger of the Divine Artist is visible in the most minute of his works, let us be excited to observe them with the greatest attention, they will not only supply us with present amusement and wonder, but will serve as a hidden treasure to alleviate the solitude and wearisomeness of old age. May a similarity of taste and sentiment continue to unite us in the same pursuits, to the end of our days. (XXI, 122)

Writing for the educational market, Wakefield is keen to define the advantages of botanical study for the guidance of supposedly impressionable young women by ending the letter on this note of piety.

The Quaker pioneer, William Penn, had stated that, 'It were Happy if we studied Nature more in natural Things; and acted according to Nature; whose Rules are few, plain & most reasonable.'[53] The study of botany was in accord with Quaker principles since it encouraged the profitable employment of leisure time, diverting energies which might otherwise be misapplied and, at the same time, promoting health through mental and bodily exercise.

In Wakefield's text, for example, botany acts as 'an inducement to take air and exercise' (Preface, ii), whereby girls are encouraged to search far afield for plants: 'you must seek for them growing wild in their native fields; nor confine your walks within the limits of a garden wall' (VIII, 44). A Quakerly commitment to simplicity and utility and a rejection of ornament and luxury informs Wakefield's botany. The 'much-neglected' grasses are perceived to be finer and of greater worth than 'a bouquet of the gayest flowers'; each is

> perfect in all its parts; nay, more complete than the fragrant Lily or the gaudy Tulip, and only requires to be nicely viewed, to excite our value and admiration. This humble tribe, is extremely numerous, and, like modest merit in other situations, of most extensive utility. (VIII, 47)

Wakefield extended her utilitarian values to people, and to women as much as men. In *Reflections on the Present Condition of the Female Sex*, she cites Adam Smith: 'every individual is a burthen upon the society to which he belongs, who does not contribute his share of productive labour for the good of the whole'.[54] She noted that this idea applied equally to women:

> he speaks in general terms of man as being capable of forming a social compact for mutual defence, and the advantages of the community at large. He does not absolutely specify, that both sexes in order to render themselves beneficial members of society are equally required to comply with these terms; but since the female sex is included in the idea of the species, and as women possess the same qualities as men though perhaps in a different degree, their sex cannot free them from the claim of the public for the proportion of usefulness.[55]

Wakefield's professional writing exemplifies this idea of usefulness. The profits from her numerous books gave financial support to her family, including her husband and brother, who proved unsuccessful in business.

A poem by Sarah Hoare entitled 'The Pleasures of Botanical Pursuits' was appended to the eighth edition of Wakefield's *Introduction to Botany* in 1818. Sarah Hoare, identified in Wakefield as 'S.H.', taught the daughters of Quakers in Ireland for many years before returning to Bristol where she published her poetical works on botany and continued to teach the daughters of Friends.[56] For Hoare, as much as Wakefield, botany was connected with the ideas of personal and social usefulness. Hoare published *A Poem on the Pleasures and Advantages of Botanical Pursuits, with Notes, and Other Poems*, independently of Wakefield in 1826. Here she confesses to being 'obliged to make every exertion in my power for a subsistence, and to secure the means of preserving myself from indigence, or becoming a burden to my friends, should I live to experience the helplessness of old age'.[57]

Wakefield and Hoare both offer a teacherly, maternal discourse. Wakefield's text features a governess who, like Mrs Harcourt in *Mental Improvement*, is 'never better pleased than when she has an opportunity of improving young people'.[58] The 1826 edition of Hoare's botanical poems was attributed to '*A*

Friend To Youth Addressed to Her Pupils'. Hoare delivers a Quakerly address to her former pupils who had become mothers:

> at home, and with its concerns, are your primary duties. If those duties be neglected, I cannot believe that any of your ever benevolent exertions, however laudable in themselves, can be acceptable in the Divine right ... It must be obvious to you, and to everyone who has thought upon the subject, that the good of society in general, principally depends upon the judicious management of mothers.[59]

This text tells mothers how to 'direct their [daughters'] pursuits', 'regulate their conduct' and 'form the character' to 'lasting benefit ... for the good of society' through the study of botany.[60]

Hoare, like Wakefield, is unconcerned with the emblematic and non-functional traditions associated with plants, preferring to consider their utility for humankind. However, Wakefield, who is more of a true Linnaean, appears to support the new botany's lack of interest in medical practice, emphasising taxonomic description, whereas Hoare retains an interest in the medicinal properties of plants such as the poppy and foxglove:

> For not alone to please the eye,
> Nor deck our fields, this rich supply
> Of ornaments profuse;
> Medicinal their juices flow;
> Nor void of use their colours glow;
> And He who dress'd the beauteous show,
> Assign'd to each its use.
>
> They who with scientific eye,
> Explore the vast variety,
> To find the hidden charm;
> 'Tis to allay the fever's rage,
> The pang arthritic to assuage,
> To aid the visual nerve of age,
> And fell disease disarm.[61]

In 'On the Pleasures of Botanical Pursuits', Hoare celebrates botanical pursuits as 'the happiest employ / of praise to Deity';[62] but there is a more secular aspect:

> SCIENCE, illuminating ray,
> Pure wisdom's beam, extend thy sway,
> And shine from pole to pole;
> From thy accumulated store,
> O'er ev'ry mind thy riches pour,
> Excite from low pursuits to soar,
> And dignify the soul.
>
> Science, thy charms have ne'er deceiv'd,
> Are safely trusted and believ'd,
> Will strengthen and refine;
> Nor ever leave on mem'ry's page,
> A pang repentance would assuage,

> But purest, happiest thoughts engage,
> To sweeten life's decline.[63]

These opening verses show that this is a hymn to empirical science.

Speaking of the formulation of Quaker principles, George Fox stated that religion came to him experimentally by direct experience and not filtered through any human authority; a distrust of ancient authority and belief in the importance of empirical evidence also lay at the heart of enlightenment science.[64] In the same way as new ideas in science were put to the test of observation and experiment, Quakers' approach to religion was to be one of personal experience: 'The attitude of mind which scientists put to the exploration of the outer, phenomenal world, the Quakers put to the inner world of their religion'.[65] Quakers such as Priscilla Wakefield and Sarah Hoare preferred to teach factual lessons in natural history and science to young girls because they conformed to Quaker views on utility and truthfulness.[66] Camilla Leach and Joyce Goodman state that 'many Quakers' rejected the arts

> on the grounds that emotions engendered by music, a play, or the reading of a novel were second hand emotions, created by the imagination and hence not 'true' feelings. This was reflected in Priscilla Wakefield's antipathy to novel reading, and her caution in respect of both the stage and music, which she termed one of the seductive arts.[67]

Opposed to this notion of art as deception and seduction, Sarah Hoare's poem on botany posits a trustworthy science reliant on Quakerly practices of proof and honesty: 'Science, thy charms have ne'er deceiv'd / Are safely trusted and believ'd'.[68]

Recreation for the eyes

> I came to enjoy this recreation of the eyes, which relaxes and amuses the mind, taking it off our misfortunes and making us forget our sufferings.[69]

Wakefield and Rousseau insist that book learning in itself is inadequate and substitute lessons in outdoor exploration and direct observation; methods which, it can be argued, discouraged women from the solitary pursuit of scientific knowledge – though this is ambiguous. Rousseau is famously antagonistic towards book learning, a contradiction, given his role as an educationalist and writer.[70] Books, he argues 'lead us to neglect the book of the world' (*Emile*, 414) and book learning comes into conflict with the idea of 'an education according to nature' (147) in *Emile*. Given Rousseau's hostility to books it comes as no surprise to find that his botanising ladies are encouraged to study botany in nature herself and not from the pages of a book.

As we have seen, Wakefield's approach to the study of nature is informed by those dissenting notions of immediacy, utility and fidelity to observed facts; it is similarly closely connected with that tradition of fieldwork in natural history which emphasised direct observation and visual perception: 'Remember to use your eyes', writes Wakefield, 'and let none of Flora's beauties escape your observation' (77).[71] The Martyn/Rousseau letters present botany for women as a lesson in outdoor observation, warning that 'Botany is not to be learned in the closet' (Preface, xi). Wakefield demonstrated that botany also 'contributes to health of body and cheerfulness of disposition, by presenting an inducement to take air and exercise' (Preface, ii). Outdoor botanical activity, she implies, is more beneficial to the female mind and body than book learning:

> my fondness for flowers has induced my mother to propose Botany, as she thinks it will be beneficial to my health, as well as agreeable, by exciting me to use more air and exercise than I should do, without such a motive; because books should not be depended upon alone. (I, 2)

In his 'Reflections On a Flower Garden in a Letter To A Lady' (1746) James Hervey depicts a distinctly feminine locale to illustrate the spiritual benefits of encountering the beauties of nature first-hand. The education of women, it is suggested, should emerge not from the dry pages of a book but through contemplation among the beauties of the flower garden where

> the instructive lessons are found, not on the leaves of some formidable Folio, but stand legible on the fine sarcenet of a Narcissus; when they savour not of the Lamp and Recluse, but come breathing from the fragrant Bosom of a Jonquil.[72]

Surprisingly, this idea is still evident in the Linnaean texts of Wakefield and Rousseau, written some forty years later. It seems that a woman's knowledge of the natural world is not to be learned from scholarly reclusive study but from observing a nearby field or flower garden. Women are dissuaded from the solitary pursuit of scientific knowledge and from closeting themselves away with books and specimens to pursue academic study. This can be seen as a way of diverting women away from masculine knowledge, embodied in books and 'learned languages' in the botanical texts; at the same time, however, Enlightenment modernists tended to see the way forward for science as being precisely this turning away from books towards experience. Thus, Bacon had argued against the scholastic method of deducing particular facts about nature from the general truths held in canonised texts such as those of Aristotle and had proposed a new, inductive science that gathered particulars in order to derive general laws. Newton had applied this method with spectacular success in his experimental science in the fields of optics and mechanics. Locke had provided Newton with an empiricist underpinning that again stressed the derivation of knowledge from experience rather than written authority. Hence, to encourage women actively to derive botanical knowledge from observation and experience was, in some way, to invite them to participate in the whole modernist project of experimental science. This must be qualified somewhat as men could, and did, conduct scientific experiments or study specimens in isolation but, nevertheless, there remained the emphasis on experience over book-learning.

Wakefield's Felicia does retire from company and indulge in some private botanising ('suppose me seated in our dressing room, with many specimens before me of the class *Tetradynamia*') (XX, 113), but perhaps somewhat subversively, she is able to 'devote an hour to [this] agreeable employment' (XX, 112) because it is assumed that she is writing letters at her desk. The Martyn/ Rousseau *Letters* are clearly an introduction to a subject more concerned with observation and plant description than scientific theory or academic study; at this stage, botany had not yet developed the theoretical backing that, in particular, physics had. Despite Linnaeus's monumental system of classification, no Newton had emerged to supply botany with a quantitive, mathematical foundation. As Peter J. Bowler says, summing up the orthodox view of the history of science at this time:

> Newton's theory was seen as a triumph of the human mind, a clear indication that the application of rational methods would lead to the uncovering of all Nature's secrets. In fact, though, the development of a scientific account of the origins of the earth and its inhabitants was delayed until the nineteenth century. Natural history seems to have been left behind in an age of description and classification.[73]

This is not the full story. Eighteenth-century naturalists, inspired by Newton, 'certainly thought they were engaged in a revolutionary activity' but, nevertheless, 'the search for a mechanistic biology made only limited advances in the seventeenth and eighteenth centuries'.[74]

This contention between botany as a highly observational practice or as bookish theory continues. Martyn's 'Ladies of Great Britain' are again encouraged to learn from the direct experience of plants in the nearby field or garden rather than from the pages of a book:

> I beg leave to protect against these letters being read in the easy chair at home; they can be of no use but to such as have a plant in their hand; nor do they pretend to anything more, than to initiate such as, from their ignorance of the learned languages, are unable to profit by the works of the learned, in the first principles of vegetable nature. (Preface, x)

Again, this is double-edged, for women are, in fact, barred from book-learning in any case since they are ignorant of 'the learned languages'. Still, however, Martyn asserts the value of empirical knowledge. The table of contents entry for Rousseau's third letter states that 'botany is not to be studied by books but by nature' (xiii). Observation of the natural world, it is suggested, is a source of self-regulation for the unlearned – notably, women excluded from formal education, but also the labouring classes.[75] Wakefield implied that botany is accessible to the inexperienced and unlearned because 'it is adapted to the simplest capacity, and the objects of its investigation offer themselves without expense or difficulty, which renders them attainable to every rank in life' (Preface, ii).

'Botany is not a Science of Parade'.

However, despite being enticed out of studious isolation into the fields and gardens, women who were encouraged to engage with botany were not expected to 'parade' their scientific knowledge in public. Sarah and Elizabeth Fitton sought to justify botany's suitability as a scientific pursuit for women by announcing in the preface to their *Conversations on Botany* (1817) that 'botany is not a science of parade'.[76] Rousseau advocated that botany remain in the feminine private sphere, shielded from the vanity of authors and professors; when self-interest comes into play, Rousseau argues, 'the woods become for us merely a public stage where we seek applause'.[77] Fitton and Rousseau are in agreement that botany is conducive to 'the mild and retiring virtues' and can be pursued in private. Propriety dictated that women should use their botanical knowledge with discretion, to guard against provocatively parading any knowledge of Latin, or scientific terms in conversation.[78] Rousseau endorsed Linnaeus's binomial system of assigning universal Latin names to all known species of plant, and yet he obviously felt that women were not an appropriate audience for this scientific language:

> Nothing is more pedantic or ridiculous, when a woman, or one of those men who resemble women, are asking you the name of an herb or a flower in a garden, than to be under the necessity of answering by a long file of Latin words that have the appearance of a magical incantation; an inconvenience sufficient to deter such frivolous persons from a charming study offered with so pedantic an apparatus. (Introduction, 13)

A female audience, it seemed, called for a more familiar, domestic approach to scientific study. Rousseau's theory of gendered complementarity is notoriously articulated in the final section of *Emile* (1762).[79] There, discussing women's acquisition of scientific knowledge, Rousseau writes: 'The search for abstract and speculative truths, for principals and axioms in science, for all that tends to wide generalisation is beyond a woman's grasp: their studies should be thoroughly practical'.[80]

Why then does Rousseau recommend botany to women so vehemently and what is the reason for this apparent contradiction in his thought? As a nascent science, botany had not yet achieved the status of other disciplines but this is not the reason for thinking it suitable for the female sex. It is in the *Reveries of the Solitary Walker* and the *Confessions* that Rousseau's more intimate style offers an insight into how he reconciles his belief in the limitations of a woman's ability to 'grasp' science with his advocacy of botanical study for girls. Women represent a desired closeness to nature: they are also, through this closeness to nature, objects of adulation and an inspiration to virtue. To Rousseau, the 'true' study of botany was 'understanding plants in their natural state, before they had been cultivated and denatured by the hands of men'.[81] Unlearned women, closer to a state of nature, had a special affinity for this kind of exploration, which even Linnaeus lacked: he was criticised by Rousseau for studying botany 'too much in herbaria and in gardens and not enough in nature herself'.[82]

In Rousseau's complex dialectic of the relationship between reason and nature, femininity is close to nature but it is also a potential source of disorder which needs to be tamed by reason.[83] The study of botany, therefore, is ideally suited to undisciplined women; it employs their faculties rationally and acts as an antidote to feminine faults ('dissipation, frivolity and inconstancy') which need to be held in check.[84] Botany can also act as a form of self-regulation whereby, according to Martyn, who endorses Rousseau's ideas, young women are urged to 'go forth into the garden or the fields and there become familiar with ... beauty, order, regularity'.[85]

Rousseau's renewed enthusiasm for botany came in the wake of his exile and persecution, his isolation from books and authorship. His dialogue with plants came only after he lost his dialogue with humanity. In a letter to Malesherbes, Rousseau writes: 'botany is the only occupation left to a wandering machine such as me to indulge in, after having been warned off from thinking again and again'.[86] Botany's main virtue is that it takes place outside of public life.

In *Strictures on Female Education* (1799), Hannah More wrote that women

> excel in details; but they do not so much generalise their ideas as men, nor do their minds seize a great subject with so large a grasp. They are acute observers, and accurate judges of life and manners, as far as their own sphere of education extends; but they describe a smaller circle. A woman sees the world as it were, from a little elevation in her own garden.[87]

As a botanist, Rousseau is a feminine figure in this sense; on a plant-collecting expedition in *Reveries*, for example, he exclaims 'my understanding cannot transcend the objects which form my immediate surroundings'.[88] Attached to the local, he 'excels in details', rejoicing in the minutiae of grasses and wild flowers growing on the island of St Pierre and fantasising about compiling a flora of the island which would occupy his entire life:

> The diverse soils into which the island was divided in spite of its smallness offered me a sufficient variety of plants for my whole life's study and amusement. I did not want to leave a leaf of grass without analysis, and I was already settling down to write the *Flora Petrinsularis* with an immense collection of curious observations.[89]

Rousseau no longer has any affinity with the 'masculine' sublime and relies solely on empirical knowledge:[90] 'My soul, being dead to all sublime impulses, can no longer be touched by anything except through the senses; only sensation is left to me, and it alone can now bring me pleasure or pain in this world'.[91]

Where previously he acquired knowledge of the world from books and men, now, in his exile, he relies only on his own senses. In this feminised state he can virtuously enjoy the study of botany as a science of observation:

> Attracted by the charming objects that surround me, I look at them, observe them carefully, compare them, and eventually learn to classify them, and lo and behold, I am as much a botanist as anyone needs to be who only wants to study nature in order to discover ever new reasons for loving her.[92]

Botany is a pastime which can educate via the experience of a series of 'pleasant impressions' in a state of 'pure' contemplation. This passive impressionism seems to indicate how botany can be accommodated with the feminine (and this positive valuation suggests a certain ambivalence about Rousseau's apparently uncompromising attitude to the feminine and to women). As a form of study that relies primarily on the senses, it is immediately accessible to the unschooled and, of equal importance, it is a science that thrives in the feminine private sphere outside of public life.

Many of the books which recommend botany for women also made gestures towards certain categories of men – effeminate, perhaps, or uncultured. Rousseau addressed women or 'one of those men who resemble women' (Introduction, 13) when discussing the names of plants, while Thomas Martyn, in his translation from Rousseau, made passing references to a small circle of men ('unlearned countrymen')[93] who he thought might also benefit from the *Letters* which are primarily addressed to a young lady. Rousseau discerned a trend towards effeminisation in men, blaming the decay of French arts and letters on the strong influence of women in the salons which had left men stripped of their strength and scholarly style of its vigour. For Rousseau, the salons are symptomatic of 'this indolent and soft life to which our dependence on women reduces us'.[94] Rousseau claims that Linnaean classification is as essential to botany as algebra was to mathematics. Yet though Rousseau calls for system and method as a means to shake off effeminate 'soft' influences, he also celebrates botany as a leisure activity for women within the private sphere, seeking to defend it from the influence of 'professors' and from 'towns and academies', which only serve to rob it 'of its true nature', and 'where it degenerates no less than exotic plants in the garden of collectors'.[95] Rousseau attempts a precarious reconciliation between the 'feminine' truthfulness of non-academic, direct observation, free from the distortions of the public sphere, and the 'masculine', algebraic rigour that marks a true science.

Thus, no longer confined to those who could read the principal texts in Latin, botany came to be seen as an elegant pursuit for 'young ladies and effeminate youths'.[96] By the nineteenth century, botany was feminised to such an extent it was thought 'unmanly'; Wakefield and Rousseau's letters on botany, addressed primarily to women, mark the beginning of this feminisation process. Projects to cultivate the botanical woman were ambiguous – outdoor plant collecting and botanising diverted women away from solitary reclusive study, from 'masculine' knowledge embodied in books and learned languages; at the same time, however, the stress on experiment was a progressive, Enlightenment tenet. For Rousseau, the virtuous study of botany was ideally suited to the private domestic sphere, to the nearby hedgerow or meadow and to the breakfast room, where it remained free from the corrupting influence of academies and institutions.

Rousseau sought to protect botany from the taint of ambition, and yet it was botany which gave women such as Wakefield and Hoare entry into professional writing. In publishing and allowing her name to appear on the title page instead of the more usual 'by a Lady', Wakefield paraded her botanical knowledge on the 'public stage'. Sensitive to criticism, aware of breaching decorum, she apologised in her preface for 'obtruding' her work 'upon the public' even after having channelled her botanical knowledge into an educational work which offered moral guidance for girls. The emphasis on 'proper' feminine roles in botanical texts demonstrates that, while popular translations from Linnaeus such as those by Wakefield and Rousseau led women out of the labyrinth of ignorance and local knowledge, they were still bound by the cords of propriety.

Young women were not encouraged to 'parade' their knowledge of botanical Latin in public. Furthermore, Linnaean botany acted as a form of containment, regulating and ordering supposedly undisciplined women.

Despite these limitations and contradictions, Wakefield and Rousseau's botanical letters were unique in giving women access to botanical knowledge for the first time. They demonstrate sociability and the desire for self-education, declare the advantages of the new language of botany, engage in current debates on the ancients and moderns and extol the new reliance on empirical evidence in science.[97] What is more, they epitomise Enlightenment botany, moving on from the local and particularised knowledge of plants commonly found in seventeenth-century herbals and embracing the universal systematising of Linnaeus. Botany, here, is dialogic and exploratory; the medium of familiar conversation lures women into deriving botanical knowledge from their own observations – allowing them to participate in the modernist project of experimental science.

Given that botany grew out of an alliance of herbals, healing and gardening, areas in which women had long been active,[98] it does not seem surprising that botany was thought to be an appropriate study for women.[99] Evidence suggests that local knowledge about plants was often gleaned from women and written up in herbals, while physicians and apothecaries had long depended for their supplies upon herb-women.[100] These associations alone, however, do not sufficiently account for the feminisation of botany in the eighteenth century, when advocates of women's botany seldom referred to those areas of knowledge. In this chapter I have identified some of the other determinants in this process.

The different ways in which botany now becomes feminised need to be traced through Linnaean texts. I focus on Darwin and Withering's adaptations of Linnaeus and explore how they address women through botanical discourse. Debates around sexuality and nationality are opened up. In other texts, by Lady Charlotte and Arabella Rowden, Linnaean systematics become appropriated for the promotion of a local, indigenous botany and the universalist Linnaeus is sidelined. Rowden's genteel reworking of Darwin's interpretation of Linnaeus proves to be important in demonstrating the interlinking themes of nationality and sexuality in women's botanical writing. Nation and class are prominent issues in such texts and the dialectic between social order and, particularly, anarchic sexuality reveals itself, as we will now see.

Notes

1 I should mention that there are four modern editions of the letters: Jean-Jacques Rousseau, *Lettres sur la botanique*, ed. Ernest J. Bonnet and Bernard Gagnebin (Paris: Saverne, 1962); Jean-Jacques Rousseau, *Oeuvres completes* (Paris: Bibliothèque de la Pléiade, 1969), IV: *Lettres sur la botanique et fragments pour un dictionnaire de botanique*, intr. Roger de Vilmorin; Jean-Jacques Rousseau, *Pure Curiosity: Botanical Letters and Notes Towards a Dictionary of Botanical Terms*, ed. Roy McMullen, trans. Kate Ottevanger (New York and London: Paddington Press, 1979).

2 Madame Delessert (1747–1816) was married to a prosperous Swiss banker. Rousseau

had known her family in Switzerland and had won her friendship by saving her from a marriage of convenience when she was just fifteen. He referred to her affectionately as *cousine* like the archaic English term of endearment 'coz'. She had written to him throughout his wanderings and in 1771 asked for his help in introducing her daughter, Marguerite-Madeleine, to botany. See Roy McMullen's introduction to Rousseau, *Pure Curiosity*, pp. 15–18, and Robert Wokler, *Rousseau* (Oxford and New York: Oxford University Press, 1995), pp. 110–14.

3 Thomas Martyn, 'Preface', in Jean-Jacques Rousseau, *Letters on the Elements of Botany, Addressed to A Lady*, 2nd edn (London: B. White & Son, 1787), p. v. All further references are to this edition and are given in parentheses after quotations in the text, with the letter number followed by the page number.

4 Priscilla Wakefield, 'Preface', *An Introduction to Botany in a Series of Familiar Letters* (Dublin: Printed by Thomas Burnside. For Messrs P. Wogan, P. Byrne, J. Milliken, J. Rice, B. Dugdale, J. Gough, P. Moore and George Johnston, 1796), p. ii. All further references are to this edition and are given in parentheses after quotations in the text, with the letter number followed by the page number.

5 Priscilla Wakefield, *Reflections on the Present Condition of the Female Sex* (London: J. Johnson, 1798), p. 6.

6 *New Lady's Magazine; or, Polite and Entertaining Companion for the Fair Sex*, May 1786, p. 177.

7 Ingeana and Flora are briefly discussed by Ann B. Shteir, '*Flora Feministica*: Reflections on the Culture of Botany', *Lumen*, 12 (1993), 167–76 (pp. 167–8), and in *Cultivating Women, Cultivating Science*, p. 1.

8 Ann Murray, 'Preface', *Mentoria, or The Young Ladies Instructor* (London: C. Dilly, 1778), p. xi.

9 Frances Arabella Rowden, *A Poetical Introduction to the Study of Botany* (London: T. Bensley, 1801), title-page.

10 Robert John Thornton, 'Dedication', *New Illustrations of the Sexual System of Carolus Von Linnaeus ... And the Temple of Flora, or Garden of Nature* (London: T. Bensley, 1807), unpag.

11 Abbot, 'Preface', *Flora bedfordiensis*, p. vi. For a discussion of local floras, including Abbot's and Curtis's, see Henrey, *British Botanical and Horticultural Literature*, II, pp. 47–77. For Abbot in particular, see II, pp. 73–5, and for Curtis, II, pp. 65–74.

12 Abbot, 'Epistle Dedicatory', *Flora*.

13 Tournefort's system of classification as expounded in *Institutiones rei Herbariae*, 3 vols (Paris: [n. pub.], 1700) was essentialist and artificial compared to English naturalist John Ray's natural system in *Methodus Plantarum* (London: [n. pub.], 1703). Tournefort divided flowering plants into twenty-two classes based primarily on the general form of the corolla, with subclasses depending on the position of the ovary. See Morton, *History of Botanical Science*, p. 257. For a description of Linnaean classification based on the fructification of plants, see Morton, *History of Botanical Science*, p. 263.

14 James Lee, *An Introduction to Botany* (London: J. and R. Tonson, 1760). This publication brought notoriety to Lee and his Vineland nursery in Hammersmith. The second edition (London: J. and R. Tonson, 1765) was dedicated to Linnaeus. The work proved very popular, staying in print in numerous further editions until 1806. For James Lee (1715–95), see Henrey, *British Botanical and Horticultural Literature*, II, pp. 355–6.

15 Rose, *The Elements of Botany*, p. 151.

16 Charles Alston was appointed King's Botanist in 1716; he succeeded George Preston as Professor of Botany at the University of Edinburgh in 1738. Alston had studied under the botanist and physician, Hermann Boerhaave, at the University of Leyden and favoured Tournefort's system of classification. When Linnaeus introduced his sexual system of classification, Alston argued against it in a paper entitled 'A Dissertation on the Sexes of Plants' which was read before the Edinburgh Medical Society and published in 1754.

17 Alston, 'A Dissertation on the Sexes of Plants', I, p. 266.

18 See my discussion of Polwhele's *Unsex'd Females* (1798) in Chapter 4.

19 William Withering, 'The Design', *A Botanical Arrangement of All Vegetables Naturally Growing in Great Britain*, 2 vols (Birmingham: T. Cadell and P. Elmsley, and G. Robinson, 1776), I, p. v.

20 Erasmus Darwin, 'Proem', *The Loves of the Plants*, in *The Botanic Garden* (London: J. Johnson, 1791; repr. Menston: Scolar Press, 1973), p. vi. All further references are to this edition and are given in parentheses after quotations in the text. Darwin writes: 'I am only a flower painter, or occasionally attempt a landskip; and leave the human figure with the portraits of history to abler artists' ('Interlude', p. 40). In her biography of Darwin, Anna Seward claimed that this remark 'is neither true, nor did Dr Darwin desire that it should be considered as veritable' (*Memoirs of the Life of Dr Darwin*, p. 302).

21 'What Beaux and Beauties croud the gaudy groves / And woo and win their vegetable Loves' (I. 9–10).

22 For a discussion of Darwin's influence on women's poetry, see Judith Pascoe, 'Female Botanists and the Poetry of Charlotte Smith', in Carol Shiner Wilson and Joel Haefner (eds), *Re-visioning Romanticism: British Women Writers, 1776–1837* (Philadelphia: University of Pennsylvania Press, 1994), pp. 193–209.

23 John Berkenhout, *A Volume of Letters from Dr Berkenhout to his Son at the University* (Cambridge: for T. Cadell; London: J. Archdeacon, 1790), p. 307.

24 Wollstonecraft, *Vindication of the Rights of Woman*, p. 123.

25 Darwin, *A Plan For the Conduct of Female Education*, p. 10.

26 Albert Jansen undertook a study of Rousseau's plant-collecting expeditions, *Jean-Jacques Rousseau als Botaniker* (Berlin 1885). This work was never translated into English and is now very scarce. A free translation of some of the passages appears in Sir Gavin De Beer's article 'Jean-Jacques Rousseau: Botanist', *Annals of Science*, 10:3 (September 1954), 189–223. Paul Cantor has written on botany in the *Reveries*: 'The Metaphysics of Botany: Rousseau and the New Criticism of Plants,' *South West Review*, 70 (Summer 1985), 362–80. Jane Walling's 'The Imagination of Plants: Botany in Rousseau and Goethe', *Comparative Critical Studies*, 2:2 (2005) 211–25 is essentially a study in ecocriticism, though Walling, too, is concerned with the interstices between literary and scientific writing. David Scott is also concerned with the ambivalence of Rousseau's attitude towards botany as both a science and a source of imaginative reverie ('Rousseau and Flowers: the Poetry of Botany', *Studies on Voltaire in the Eighteenth Century*, 182 (1979), 73–86). The comparison between Rousseau and Goethe as botanists, discussed by Walling, is an area formerly explored by Lisbet Koerner. Koerner does explore Goethe's female students in 'Goethe's Botany: Lessons of a Feminine Science', *ISIS*, 84:3 (1993), 470–95. Marc Oliver has explored the collaborative use of botany in the botanical letters as a means to both construct and preserve childhood in 'Lessons for the Four-Year Old

Botanist: Rousseau's "Forgotten Science" of Childhood', in Norman Buford (ed.), *The Child in French Francophone Literature* (New York: Rodopi Editions, 2004), pp. 161–9.

27 For Martyn's published works, which are extensive, see Henrey, *British Botanical and Horticultural Literature*, I, pp. 54–57.

28 Biographical details of Priscilla Wakefield can be found in 'Wakefield, Priscilla', *DNB*; Joan Shattock, *The Oxford Guide to British Women Writers* (Oxford: Oxford University Press, 1993), pp. 443–4; and Ray Desmond, *Dictionary of British and Irish Botanists and Horticulturists* (London: Taylor and Francis, 1977), p. 633. For a general discussion of Wakefield's educational works, see Bridget Hill, 'Priscilla Wakefield as a Writer of Children's Educational Books', *Women's Writing*, 4:1 (1997), 3–13.

For Wakefield's botany, see Henrey, *British Botanical and Horticultural Literature*, II, pp. 581–2; Shteir, *Cultivating Women*, pp. 83–9; Shteir, 'Priscilla Wakefield's Natural History Books', in Alwynne Wheeler and James H. Price (eds), *From Linnaeus to Darwin*, Papers from the fifth Easter Meeting of the Society for the History of Natural History (March 1983), 3 (London: Society for the History of Natural History, 1985), pp. 29–35; and Pascoe, 'Female Botanists and the Poetry of Charlotte Smith', pp. 199, 207.

A selection of Wakefield's published works is listed in the Bibliography. *A Catechism of Botany* (1817) was attributed to her in the *DNB* (1899 edn) and the entry has not been amended in the current edition, but it seems an unlikely work for her; she tended to produce texts that were genuinely dialogic rather than the one-sided form of the catechism. A thorough search of library catalogues such as COPAC and those of the British Library and the Library of Congress fails to uncover this work under her name.

29 The 'worlds of Fontenelle' was one of the few books that Rousseau carried into his father's workshop and read to him every day during his work (Jean-Jacques Rousseau, *Confessions*, in *The Collected Writings of Rousseau*, 7 vols, ed. Roger D. Masters and Christopher Kelly (Hanover, NH and London: University Press of New England, 1990–98), V, ed. Christopher Kelly, Roger D. Masters & Peter G. Stillman, trans. Christopher Kelly (1995), p. 8. All further references are to this edition and are given in parentheses after quotations in the text). For the influence of Fontenelle and the familiar way of dialogue in the scientific education of women, see Gerald Dennis Myer, *The Scientific Lady in England 1650–1760* (Berkeley and Los Angeles: University of California Press, 1955). Literary representations of the scientific lady, such as Fontenelle's Marchioness, are discussed in Myra Reynold's *The Learned Lady in England 1650–1760* (Massachusetts: Peter Smith, 1964), pp. 372–419.

30 Behn's *A Discovery of New Worlds* appeared just two years after the French original (Bernard le Bovier de Fontenelle, *A Discovery of New Worlds*, trans. Aphra Behn (London: William Ganning, 1688)). Other translations were: *A Discourse of the Plurality of Worlds*, trans. Sir W. D. Knight (Dublin: William Norman, 1687); *A Plurality of Worlds*, trans. Mr Glanville (London: R. Bentley & S. Magnes, 1688); *Conversations on the Plurality of Worlds*, trans. William Gardiner (London: A. Bettesworth, 1715); *Conversations on the Plurality of Worlds*, trans. Elizabeth Gunning (London: T. Hurst, 1803).

31 It is not difficult to see how Rousseau's botanising activities in *Reveries* are in some sense related to the kind of illicit pleasures hinted at in the *Letters*. Rousseau seems determined to use botany as an illustration of his own errant pleasures. I am indebted

here to the eminent Rousseauvian, Professor Robin Howells, who has kindly offered his comments on Rousseau's sexuality in response to this research.

32 'Idleness and insubordination are two very dangerous faults, and very hard to cure once established. Girls should be attentive and industrious, but this is not enough in itself; they should early be accustomed to restraint ... Their childish faults, unchecked and unheeded, may easily lead to dissipation, frivolity and inconstancy. To guard against this, teach them above all things self-control' (Rousseau, *Emile*, p. 332).

33 In later editions Wakefield changes the name of her governess to Mrs Woodbine which has more of a botanical feel to it.

34 'A language must be acquired; but then it may be done gradually; and the *tædium* of it may, in some measure, be relieved by carrying on at the same time a study of facts and the philosophy of nature. This seems to have been Rousseau's idea, and I have endeavored not to loose sight of it in my continuation of his eight ingenious letters' (Thomas Martyn, 'Translator's Preface', in Rousseau, *Letters*, p. ix).

35 The ideal of rational amusement or pleasurable instruction is exemplified in the work of educationalists Richard Lovell Edgeworth and his daughter Maria Edgeworth. For an account of their influence on eighteenth-century education through books and toys, see F. J. Darton Harvey, *Children's Books in England* (Cambridge: Cambridge University Press, 1960), pp. 141–57.

36 Shteir, *Cultivating Women, Cultivating Science*, p. 20.

37 Rousseau, 'Discourse on the Arts and Sciences', p. 12.

38 Botany, explains Rousseau in his *Reveries of the Solitary Walker*, involves 'pure and disinterested contemplation' and could not be further removed from medicine and anatomy, from 'stinking corpses, livid running flesh, blood, repellent intestines, horrible skeletons, pestilential vapours'. Rousseau turns to botany to cleanse him of this barbarous science: 'Bright flowers, adornment of the meadows, cool shades, streams, woods and green glades, come and purify my imagination of all these hideous images' (Rousseau, *Reveries of the Solitary Walker*, trans. Peter France (1782; Harmondsworth: Penguin, 1979), p. 114).

39 Later editions of his work carried an advertisement which read: 'The Botanical Microscope invented by Dr Withering, which is more portable and convenient than any other, is now manufactured by Mr Beilby, Optician, Clare Street Bristol, and may be likewise had of the publishers of this work, and other booksellers' ('Advertisement', *An Arrangement of British Plants*, I, 6th edn (London: Cadell and Davies, 1818)).

For eighteenth-century microscopy, see Barbara Stafford, 'Images of Ambiguity: Eighteenth-Century Microscopy and the Neither/Nor', in David Philip Miller and Peter Hanns Reill (eds), *Visions of Empire: Voyages, Botany, and Representations of Nature* (Cambridge: Cambridge University Press, 1996), pp. 230–57); 'Voyeur or Observer? Enlightenment Thoughts on the Dilemmas of Display', *Configurations: A Journal for Literature, Science and Technology*, 1 (1993), 95–128; and Joanna Piccioto, 'Optical Instruments and the Eighteenth-Century Observer', *Studies in Eighteenth-Century Culture*, 29 (2000), 123–53. An earlier study is the aforementioned work by Meyer, *The Scientific Lady in England*. For a more general study of the influence of scientific treatises on eighteenth-century poets, see Marjorie Hope Nicholson's pioneering work, *Newton Demands the Muse*.

40 See Marjorie Hope Nicholson, *Science and Imagination* (Ithaca and New York: Great Seal Books, 1956), p. 157. Elsewhere in this study, Nicholson discusses the

new interest in scientific instruments in relation to the ongoing controversy between ancients and moderns. Neophiles paraded their interest in the new science by flaunting the latest scientific instruments but this penchant for modernity amongst scholars could not compete with the common man's desire to explore nature with his own eyes. See *Science and Imagination*, pp. 200–20.

41 George Adams, *Essays on the Microscope*, 2nd edn, 3 vols (1787; London: Dillon and Keating, W. & S. Jones, 1798), II, p. 666.

42 Wakefield, *Reflections*, p. 67. Wakefield divides society into four classes. The first class is comprised of the nobility, the second those who 'procure a respectable subsistence approaching to opulence', the third class is 'those whose honest and useful industry raises them above want' and the fourth class is comprised of the labouring poor (pp. 56–7). She proceeds to discuss the duties, employments and attainments of women according to their social class.

43 Martyn, 'Translators Preface', in Rousseau, *Letters*, p. xi.

44 Such as the age-old use of the social system of the bee to justify monarchy and a hierarchical class structure (ironically, the queen bee was for a long time thought to be male and this was used to justify patriarchy in addition). Terry Eagleton succinctly discusses the problems of naturalism, where 'there can be a direct inference from fact to value, or from nature to culture', in 'Culture and Nature', in his *The Idea of Culture* (Oxford: Blackwell, 2000), pp. 87–109 (p. 103).

45 Peter J. Bowler, *The Fontana History of the Environmental Sciences*, The Fontana History of Science (London: Fontana, 1992), p. 95. However, Newton's own views on religion were complex and controversial.

46 For a discussion of how and why the lectureship was created, and what role Newton himself played in this first popular exposition of his philosophy, see Margaret C. Jacob, *The Newtonians and the English Revolution 1689–1720* (Sussex: Harvester Press, 1976), pp. 162–201. Jacob cites Boyle's will which stated that the lectures should be 'for proving the Christian Religion, against notorious Infidel, *viz.* Atheists, Theists, Pagans, Jews, and Mohometans' (p. 144).

47 For a discussion of the relationship between Newton's *Principia* (1687) and Ray's *Historia Plantarum* (1686), see Morton, *History of Botanical Science*, pp. 232–4.

48 See Bowler, *History of Environmental Science*, pp. 96–7.

49 The words Ray chooses to introduce his work 'How manifold are thy works, O Lord! In wisdom hast thou made all' indicate the recurring theme throughout the two-volume work. The first volume celebrates the multitude of God's works, from insects, fishes, quadrupeds, birds and animals to species of plant, and the second, his wisdom in the creation of them (John Ray, 'Preface', *The Wisdom of God Manifested in the Works of the Creation: In Two Parts*, 4th edn (1691; London: Printed by J. B. for Sam Smith, 1704), I, pp. i, viii.

50 Patrick Armstrong provides a general survey of this in *The English Parson-Naturalist: A Companion Between Science and Religion* (Leominster: Gracewing, 2000). For local floras, see pp. 54–63, and for natural history societies run by the country clergy, pp. 143–9.

For John Ray and botany, see C. E. Raven, *John Ray: Naturalist* (Cambridge: Cambridge University Press, 1942; repr. 1986). Raven documents Ray's botany from the structure and classification of plants to his last work in botany (pp. 181–306). For an eighteenth-century account of Ray and his works, see Richard Pulteney's *Historical and Biographical Sketches of the Progress of Botany in England From Its Origin to the Introduction of the Linnaean System*, 2 vols (London: T. Cadell, 1790), pp. 189–281 (Chs. 15–20). For Gilbert White, see Allen, *The Naturalist in Britain*, pp. 20–6, 49–54, 228–9, and Richard Mabey's introduction to White's *The Natural History of Selborne* (1788–89; Harmondsworth: Penguin, 1977).

George Crabbe had a lifelong passion for botany and entomology and even compiled a treatise on English botany which he showed to Dodsley with a view to publishing, but the manuscript was never published and was eventually burnt. Crabbe's botanising, including his supposed fascination for 'the rarer weeds of Britain', is documented in the biography of George Crabbe written by his son, George Crabbe the younger: *The Life of George Crabbe by his Son*, intr. Edmund Blunden (London: Cresset Press, 1948).

51 Charlotte Smith's *Conversations Introducing Poetry* was specifically designed 'for the use of Children and Young Persons'. In this text the children's governess, Mrs Talbot, teaches children 'to look thro' Nature up to Nature's God', referring to Pope (Pope, 'An Essay on Man', *The Poems of Alexander Pope*, ed. John Butt (London: Routledge, 1968), Epistle IV, line 332, p. 546).

52 For Wakefield's Quakerism, see Joseph Smith, *A Descriptive Catalogue of Friends' Books*, 2 vols (London: J. Smith, 1867), II, pp. 848–51, and Camilla Leach and Joyce Goodman, 'Educating the Women of the Nation: Priscilla Wakefield and the Construction of National Identity', *Quaker Studies*, 5:2 (2001), 165–82. A general discussion of women dissenters of this period, including educationalists such as Wakefield, can be found in Kathryn Gleadle, *The Early Feminists: Radical Unitarians and the Emergence of the Women's Rights Movement 1831–57* (New York: St Martin's Press; London: Macmillan, 1995). The *DNB* (1899 edn) attributes a *Memoir of the Life of William Penn* to Wakefield but, as with the *Catechism on Botany* (see note 28 above), this cannot be found under her name on library catalogues.

53 William Penn, *Some Fruits of Solitude in Reflections and Maxims Relating to Conduct* (1693; London: Edward Arnold, 1901), p. 4 (Maxim 4).

54 Wakefield, *Reflections*, p. 1.

55 *Ibid.*, p. 2.

56 Sarah Hoare, teacher and author, was born in Bristol (*c.* 1767) and died in Bath in 1855. Her published works are as follows: 'The Pleasures of Botanical Pursuits, A Poem', appended to Priscilla Wakefield, *An Introduction to Botany*, 8th edn (London: Darton Harvey & Co., 1818); *Poem on the Pleasures and Advantages of Botanical Pursuits*; *Poems on Conchology and Botany with Plates and Notes by Sarah Hoare* (London: Simkin & Marshall; Bristol: Wright & Bagnall, 1831). See the entry for Hoare in Desmond, *Dictionary of British and Irish Botanists*, p. 312. For a discussion of these works, see Ann Shteir, *Cultivating Women*, pp. 74–7. For biographical details, including membership of the Society of Friends, see Smith, *A Descriptive Catalogue*, I, pp. 955–6.

57 Hoare, 'Preface', *A Poem on the Pleasures and Advantages of Botanical Pursuits*, p. i.

58 Wakefield, *Mental Improvement; or the Beauties and Wonders of Nature and Art*, I, p. 6 (Conversation I).

59 Hoare, 'Preface', *A Poem on the Pleasures and Advantages of Botanical Pursuits*, p. vi.

60 *Ibid.*, p. v.

61 Hoare, 'The Pleasures of Botanical Pursuits, A Poem', lines 41–54, pp. 181–7, (p. 183).

62 *Ibid.*, lines 34–5, p. 182.

63 *Ibid.*, lines 1–14, p. 181.

64 For Quakers and science, see Maurice J. Whigham, *Quakers in Natural History and Medicine in Ireland and Britain* (Dublin: National Botanic Gardens, 1996).

65 *Ibid.*, p. 2.

66 Natural history was to become an important part of the curriculum in Friends' schools in the nineteenth century. The Friends' School in Akworth in Yorkshire has a Juvenile Natural History Society which was founded in 1834 and is still in existence today and the Friends' School at Bootham in York established a *Natural History Journal* in 1878. An exceptionally large number of naturalists of distinction are amongst its old scholars. The Grubb family, makers of telescopes, were Quakers and presented telescopes and microscopes to all Friends schools in 1868. For the teaching of natural history and science in Friends' schools, see Whigham, *Quakers in Natural History*, pp. 1–3, 8.

67 Leach and Goodman, 'Educating the Women of the Nation', 165–82 (p. 176).

68 Hoare, 'The Pleasures of Botanical Pursuits: A Poem', lines 8–9, p. 181.

69 Rousseau, *Reveries*, pp. 108–9.

70 In *Emile*, Rousseau asserts that 'when I thus get rid of children's lessons, I get rid of the chief cause of their sorrows, namely their books' (*Emile*, p. 80) and boasts that 'Emile, at twelve years old, will hardly know what a book is' (p. 80). However, he does allow Emile to read *Robinson Crusoe* because it is the one book which 'supplies the best treatise on an education according to nature' (p. 147). Sophy when she is older is offered *Telemachus* and selections from *The Spectator*, though she is advised to 'study the duties of good wives in it' (p. 413). The sections on Sophy in *Emile* allow us to see that Rousseau is clearly repulsed by the idea of a 'learned lady' ('a female wit is a scourge to her husband … from the lofty height of her genius she scorns every womanly duty, and she is always trying to make a man of herself after the fashion of Mlle. L'Enclos' (p. 371)). For his own part he states 'I hate books; they only teach us to talk about things we know nothing about' (*Emile*, p. 147).

71 In *Mental Improvement*, Wakefield claims that, although many authors have the ability to encourage their readers to exercise the faculties of thinking and reflection, 'it requires the skill of a master's hand, to lead the minds of youth to the habit of observation'. By declaring this in her preface, Wakefield indulges in a clever piece of self-promotion by implying that as an author she possesses the rare skill of encouraging children to observe the world around them ('Preface', *Mental Improvement*, I, p. i). For a discussion of visual education and the open book or 'spectacle of nature', see Barbara Stafford, *Artful Science: Enlightenment, Entertainment and the Eclipse of Visual Education* (Cambridge, MA: MIT Press, 1994), pp. 217–38.

72 James Hervey, 'Reflections On a Flower Garden in a Letter To A Lady', *Meditations and Contemplations*, 25th edn, 2 vols (1746; London: J. F. & C. Rivington, 1791), I, p. 237.

73 Bowler, *History of the Environmental Sciences*, pp. 85–6.

74 *Ibid.*, p. 86.

75 Thomas Martyn, addressing his audience of 'fair countrywomen and unlearned countrymen', claimed that a reading of the Letters will save the 'unlearned' student of botany from becoming 'bewildered in an inextricable labyrinth of unintelligent terms', as he imagines might have happened if they had gone straight to the works of Linnaeus ('Translator's Preface', p. vii).

76 [Sarah Mary Fitton and Elizabeth Fitton?], 'Preface', *Conversations on Botany* (London: Longman, Hurst, Rees and Orme, 1817), p. iv. Much of the Fittons' work is derivative and this description of the virtues of botany is taken directly from Maria

Edgeworth's *Letters for Literary Ladies*. Edgeworth is, in fact, discussing chemistry in these terms:

> Chemistry will follow botany. Chemistry is a science well suited to the talents and situations of women; it is not a science of parade; it affords occupation and infinite variety; it demands no bodily strength; it can be pursued in retirement. (Maria Edgeworth, *Letters for Literary Ladies*, ed. Claire Connolly (2nd edn, 1798; London: J. M. Dent, 1993), p. 21.)

77 Rousseau, *Reveries*, p. 116 (Seventh Walk). Rousseau advocated that botany should remain untainted by the 'public stage' of authorship, and yet it was botany which gave many women entrance into professional writing.

78 In Wakefield's *Mental Improvement*, Sophie is encouraged to develop an interest in science: she uses a microscope to study bees and is particularly adept at botany. In a subsequent conversation, however, she is informed that:

> A young lady of your age is not expected to be deeply skilled in philosophy; much less to display her knowledge, should she possess a small share; but a general acquaintance with the uses of the most common philosophical instruments is not only ornamental, but also a very useful accomplishment, and should form part of every liberal education. (Wakefield, *Mental Improvement*, II, pp. 172–3.

79 Rousseau introduces Emile to Sophy, who is to be his 'helpmeet'. He states 'man and woman are unlike; and each is the complement of the other' (*Emile*, p. 321 (Book V)). Once this fact has been established we learn as they are unlike in constitution and in temperament 'it follows their education must be different' (p. 326). Separate spheres are prescribed: 'Women's reign is a reign of gentleness, tact and kindness; her commands are caresses, her threats are tears. She should reign in the home as a minister reigns in the state' (p. 370).

80 Rousseau, *Emile*, p. 370.

81 Rousseau, *Confessions*, p. 539.

82 *Ibid.*, p. 538.

83 For a discussion of reason/nature in relation to femininity in Rousseau, see Genevieve Lloyd, *The Man of Reason: 'Male' and 'Female' in Western Philosophy* (London: Routledge, 1994), pp. 57–64, and Lieselotte Steinbrügge, *The Moral Sex: Women's Nature in the French Enlightenment*, trans. Pamela E. Selwyn (Oxford, Oxford University Press, 1995), pp. 54–83.

84 For Rousseau's discussion of these feminine traits, see note 32 above.

85 Martyn, 'Translator's Preface', in Rousseau, *Letters*, p. xi.

86 Rousseau to Malesherbes, 11th November, 1964, cited in de Beer, 'Jean-Jacques Rousseau, Botanist', 189–223 (p. 208).

87 Hannah More, 'Practical Use of Female Knowledge – A Comparative of Both Sexes', in *Strictures on the Modern System of Female Education*, 3rd edn, 2 vols (London: T. Cadell & W. Davies, 1799), II, p. 25. A preoccupation with minute detail was also considered feminine in contemporary aesthetics. Naomi Schor argues this point in *Reading in Detail: Aesthetics and the Feminine* (London: Methuen, 1987).

88 Rousseau, *Reveries*, p. 112. Mary Louise Pratt claims that 'The naturalist's production of knowledge has some decidedly non-phallic aspects, perhaps alluded to by Linnaeus' own image of Ariadne following her thread out of the labyrinth of the Minotaur' (*Imperial Eyes*, p. 56). She implies that the Rousseau of *Reveries* is feminine ('Rousseau's *Memoirs of a Solitary Walker* includes a famous portrait of the

author herborizing in a long Turkish robe') but she fails to develop this argument or offer any analysis of Rousseau as a botanist. Rousseau's well-documented (by himself, especially in the *Confessions*) masochism and his fear of, and feelings of inferiority towards, women could be used to characterise him as, in some way, feminine. For an analysis of Rousseau's gynophobia, see Victor G. Wexler, '"Made for Man's Delight": Rousseau as Antifeminist', *American Historical Review*, 81:2 (April 1976), 266–91.

89 Rousseau, *Confessions*, p. 537.

90 Edward Burke's *A Philosophical Enquiry into the Origin of Our Ideas of the Sublime and Beautiful* was published by Robert and James Dodsley in London in 1757; reviving the original discussion by Longinus, it had an enormous influence on eighteenth-century aesthetics. Despite the great influence Burke's enquiry was to have on Kant, it appears that Burke himself did not have a strongly gendered notion of the *reception* of the beautiful and sublime. It is true that, for Burke, the feminine is often the cause of the beautiful and the masculine that of the sublime but, unlike Kant, he makes no explicit distinction between the abilities of men and women to respond to these qualities.

In *Observations on the Feeling of the Beautiful and Sublime*, Kant offered a gendered reading of the distinction of the beautiful and sublime in terms of men and women's capacity to respond to the two qualities. A woman's knowledge of the world is gained primarily from the senses: 'her philosophy is not to reason but to sense'; 'the fair sex has just as much understanding as the male but it is a *beautiful understanding*', whereas 'ours' should be 'a *deep understanding*, an expression that signifies identity with the sublime' (Kant, *Observations On the Feeling of the Beautiful and Sublime*, pp. 78–9). For a discussion of Kant as a distinguished eighteenth-century reader and admirer of Rousseau, see Ernst Cassirer, *Rousseau, Kant and Goethe*, trans. by James Gutmann, Paul Oskar Kristeller and John Herman Randall Jr (New York: Harper and Row, 1963).

General discussions of the sublime in the eighteenth century can be found in Samuel Holt Monk, *The Sublime: A Study of Critical Theories in Eighteenth-Century England* (Ann Arbor, MI: University of Michigan Press, 1960), and Peter De Bolla, *The Discourse of the Sublime: Readings in History, Aesthetics and the Subject* (Oxford: Basil Blackwell, 1989).

91 Rousseau, *Reveries*, p. 114. For Rousseau, elsewhere in his political theory, the sublime is again universal rather than particular; the general will is a '*sublime* reason, which rises above the grasp of common men' (*On the Social Contract, with Geneva Manuscript and Political Economy*, ed. Roger D. Masters, trans. Judith R. Masters (New York: St Martin's Press, 1978), pp. 69–70 (emphasis added), cited in Marie-Hélène Huet, 'The Revolutionary Sublime', *Eighteenth-Century Studies*, 28:1 (Autumn, 1994), 51–64 (p. 60)).

92 Rousseau, *Reveries*, p. 115.

93 Martyn, 'Translator's Preface', in Rousseau, *Letters*, p. v.

94 Rousseau, 'Lettre à M. d'Alembert sur les spectacles' (1758), quoted in Schiebinger, *The Mind Has No Sex*, p. 157.

95 Rousseau, *Reveries*, p. 116.

96 J. F. A. Adams, 'Is Botany A Suitable Study for Young Men?', *Science: An Illustrated Journal*, 9 (1887), 116–17 (p. 116).

97 Rousseau, for example, asserted that, prior to the introduction of method, botanical science failed to advance because 'instead of searching for plants where they

grew, men studied them only in Pliny or Dioscorides' (Rousseau, 'Introduction', *Letters*, p. 3).

98 The gardener, John Parkinson, author of *Paradisi in Sole Paradisus Terrestris* (London: Printed by Humfrey Lownes and Robert Young, 1629), often addressed gentlewomen in his writings, adding that their husbands might also share the joys of flower gardening. William Lawson's *A New Orchard and Garden* (London: R. Aesop for R. Jackson, 1618) was the earliest gardening book written specifically for women, but it had many successors such as Charles Evelyn's *The Lady's Recreation* (London: [n. pub.], [c.1718]). For a discussion of such works, see Taboroff, '"Wife, Unto Thy Garden".

99 A claim made by Schiebinger, *The Mind Has No Sex*, p. 241.

100 The herbalist John Gerard (1545–1607) attributed the naming of plants to local women (*The Herball, or Generall Histoire of Plantes* (London: J. Norton, 1597)): herbalists in general thought women were responsible for most common names of plants. Joseph Banks, the future president of the Royal Society and the botanist who accompanied Captain James Cook on his *Endeavour* voyage, began to learn about botany from knowledge passed on to him from a herb-woman during his time at Eton. His confidant in old age, Sir Everard Home, claimed that 'for want of more able tutors', Banks 'submitted to be instructed by the women, employed in culling simples, as it is termed, to supply the druggists and apothecaries shops, paying sixpence for every material piece of information' (Sir Everard Homes, 'The Hunterian Oration', pp. 10–11; quoted in John Gascoigne, *Joseph Banks and the English Enlightenment: Useful Knowledge and Polite Culture* (Cambridge: Cambridge University Press, 1994), p. 83).

3
Sex, class and order in Flora's army

Model and metaphor in botanical taxonomy

IN LATE EIGHTEENTH-CENTURY Britain, in a climate rife with anxieties over disorder and the threat of foreign invasion, botany became bound up with concerns over order and national identity. An anonymous poem – there are good reasons to attribute it to Anna Seward – written to commemorate the Lichfield Botanical Society's translation of Linnaeus's *A System of Vegetables* (1783) indicates that, during this period, botany was lauded as a panacea for both moral and social disorder (see Fig. 12).[1] Jupiter here is represented as descending to earth on May Day to look for signs of spring; he finds instead 'a confusion of manners and morals'[2] and earth's vegetation 'o'errun with disorder' (line 45). Flora laments that Linnaean classification – 'her system' – has not yet been introduced in Great Britain:

She spoke much in praise of good order & laws
She went round the globe, called on every nation
Haranguing at large upon civilisation
Her own reputation in Sweden she hit on
And that brought her home to it's state in Great Britain
Where an ignorant treatment of her & her System
Encouraged her subjects she said to resist them
Vegetation of course was o'er run with disorder
From the wood & the wall to the bank & the border. (lines 37–46)

Rebellion, then, is rife; vegetables openly consort with those of other tribes and refuse to honour their proper place in the plant kingdom; the 'Vagabond Fungus' is treading 'on the toes of his highness the oak' (lines 50–1). The poem then conflates class disorder with sexual instability; this aspect of the poem will be analysed in Chapter 4.

'The Backwardness of Spring Accounted For' was most probably inspired by *Deliciae Naturae*, or 'The Delights of Nature', the famous oration delivered by Linnaeus when his office as Rector at the University of Uppsala came to an end in December 1772.[3] Here, as in the poem, botanical taxonomy is rendered homologous with a hierarchical model of human society and all its social classes and military ranks: grass is likened to downtrodden peasantry, the herbs to nobility in gaudy dress and the fungi or mushrooms to a disorderly mob.

12 John Russell and John Opie, 'Aesculapius, Ceres, Flora, and Cupid, Honouring the Bust of Linnaeus'. Reproduced from Robert Thornton, *Temple of Flora*

In 1780, the Gordon Riots occurred. The first phase saw a revolutionary crowd marching to present a petition against Catholic toleration to the Houses of Parliament. The refusal of the House of Commons to debate the petition led to the second stage of the riot where angry scenes ended in mob violence on the streets of London.[4] The anonymous poem, written in honour of the first literal translation – rather than an adaptation – of Linnaeus into English in 1783, uses botany to illustrate the necessity for hierarchy and order amid rising fear of the mob in Britain. The discord of the plant kingdom parallels the disorder of civil society; luckily, help is at hand in the guise of the Botanical Society at Lichfield and Linnaean classification. Flora informs Jupiter:

"But Sir I have lately adopted a measure
"The prospect of which gives me infinite pleasure
"Some Scholars of Litchfield that came recommended
"By the Muses who there on their *Seward* attended
"Now constitute wholly my administration
"Indeed they are men of no small reputation
"And they are compiling my Classification. (83–9)

The poet elevates the achievements of the Lichfield scholars:

"These great legislators will shortly prescribe
"The Laws rules & habits of every tribe
"Thus their manners no longer each other will shock
"What is wrong in a rose may be right in a dock
"Rejoice then my Children the hour is at hand
"When Botanical knowledge shall govern the land. (96–101)

The capricious tone of the poem should not detract from the weight of its social meaning: that in this period of social upheaval, Linnaean botany will help restore Britain's order, hierarchy and decorum.

Robert Thornton commissioned a 'British trophy in honour of Linnaeus' during the turbulent period between 1797 and 1807. The 1807 edition was comprised of *A New Illustration of the Sexual System of Carolus Von Linnaeus,* 'Comprehending An Elucidation of the Several Parts of Fructification, A Prize Dissertation on the Sexes of Plants [and] A full Explanation of the Classes and Orders of the Sexual System'; and *Temple of Flora, or Garden of Nature,* 'Being Picturesque Botanical Coloured Plates of Select Plants, Illustrative of [the Linnaean system] With Descriptions by Robert John Thornton'.[5] Thornton had a fierce regard for hierarchy and order. Volume 3 of his philosophical work, *A Politician's Creed* (1795), is 'by a lover of social order' and contains a lengthy condemnation of 'the mob'. Elsewhere in this text, he warns of the dangers of 'levelling ideas' and encourages us to 'honour the stay of monarchy'.[6] There are obvious affinities between this work and his botanical enterprise which was no less polemical or patriotic.

The *Temple of Flora* promoted 'national honour' by attempting to surpass in lavishness all previous foreign works of a similar nature. Thornton was particularly driven by a patriotic urge to challenge French supremacy in 'public works'; Britain had been at war with France since 1793. The following lines from Thomson's 'On Liberty' (1735–36; 1738) are defiantly displayed on Thornton's title page:

Shall Britons, in the field
Unconquered still, the better laurel lose?
In finer arts, and public works, shall they
To Gallia yield?[7]

The science of botany, Thornton informs us, has enlisted 'the fine arts into her service'; British superiority in painting and engraving is to be demonstrated. A catalogue accompanying an exhibition of the specially commissioned botanical prints is informed by the same nationalistic fervour:

> The British Empire ... at the same time that she crowns the brow of the conqueror with the laurel expressive of victory, respects and cherishes the Liberal Arts, which add no less to the glory of a nation. Thus, whilst her thunders are hurled in the North, and South and East, the labours of Art are encouraged at home, and under BRITANNIA'S auspices, even during a period of a ten years warfare, supported with

> the firmness and dignity of a great nation, *Stupendous Works* have been undertaken, which prove the great advancement of the Imitative Arts.[8]

Here, Thornton appropriates botany in order to celebrate English pre-eminence in the Arts.

13 Emma Crewe, 'Flora at Play with Cupid' (frontispiece to *The Loves of the Plants*). Reproduced from Erasmus Darwin, *The Botanic Garden*

Linnaeus is commemorated in one of the *Temple*'s most striking plates; this depicts him being honoured by Flora, Aesculapius, Ceres and Cupid (see Fig. 13). Thornton said of this plate:

> The introduction of Flora, Ceres and Aesculapius, is emblematic of the advantages derived from the study of the science of Botany, as in the works of Linnaeus, to *physic, agriculture*, and as an *elegant pursuit* for ladies. Cupid is represented in allusion to the sexual system, invented by Linnaeus. The Zephyr above denotes *spring*, the season most favourable to the study of Botany.[9]

Linnaeus is honoured here and yet he is largely overlooked in the preceding pages where Thornton is more intent on lionising the British botanist, Joseph Banks:

> Long may he shine the bright ornament of cultivated society, and diffuse that genial warmth to a science, which may be compared to a tender plant, requiring the fostering hand of rich individuals, who employ their substance, not in pomp and vain enjoyments, but in the better pursuit of knowledge and an eternal fame.[10]

Banks is likened to a collector's item himself: a prize 'ornament' (in Queen Charlotte's cabinet, perhaps), an emblem of 'cultivated society'; the science of botany is itself a 'tender plant' to be adopted and cultivated by 'rich individuals'. These patrons, we are told, are not motivated by 'vain enjoyments' (as were the florists) but honour the 'pursuit of knowledge' and enlightenment civilisation and progress.

Gill Saunders asserts that, 'whilst purporting to be a serious botanical treatise [*The Temple of Flora*] was in fact closer to the florilegium tradition, and was of little value to the scientific enterprise of its time despite its impressive folio-sized colour printed plates'.[11] Thornton's botanical work was essentially a luxurious piece of propaganda through which he embraced the monarchy and asserted the superiority of the British in the arts and sciences.

Linnaeus regarded new species of plant as 'new recruits' in Flora's army; English adaptations from the works of Linnaeus were greatly inspired by these military analogies.[12] William Withering's *A Botanical Arrangement of all Vegetables Naturally Growing in Great Britain* (1776), the first of these adaptations, described and catalogued all known indigenous species of flora using Linnaean classification. Withering informs his readers that Linnaeus has 'aptly' compared

> A CLASS .... to an ARMY;
> An ORDER .... to a REGIMENT;
> A GENUS .... to a COMPANY;
> and a SPECIES .... to a SOLDIER.[13]

For Withering, however, 'no comparison can be more in point than that which considers the vegetables upon the face of the Globe, as … analogous to the inhabitants' thus:

> VEGETABLES resemble the INHABITANTS in general;
> CLASSES resemble NATIONS;
> ORDERS resemble TRIBES
> GENERA resemble FAMILIES
> SPECIES resemble INDIVIDUALS.
> And VARIETIES are the same *Individuals* in different circumstances.[14]

Withering's adaptation from the works of Linnaeus first appeared in the era of the American Revolution and was updated and reprinted during the events leading up to the war with France; these militaristic metaphors and territorial analogies demonstrate how botany could take on a nationalistic, ordering role in eighteenth-century Britain.

Withering claimed to present Linnaeus in 'an English dress', but his botanical terminology was not a literal translation from Linnaeus. Terms such as 'stamen' and 'pistil' were introduced by Tournefort and taken up in the Latin works of

Linnaeus.[15] 'Pistil' signified the ovary and its parts, but Withering's anglicised version of these terms, where 'pistil' was transcribed as 'pointal', and 'stamen' as 'chive', masked any reference to the organs of generation and disguised the sexual character of the Linnaean classes and orders. Elsewhere in the text, Linnaeus's risqué sexual metaphors were replaced by innocuous comparisons which were deemed more appropriate for female readers and served to strengthen notions of family, nationality and order. The table above compares all 'the vegetables on the face of the Globe' to all 'the inhabitants'; Withering now narrows his focus to a more local analogy where readers should compare 'The vegetable kingdom to the kingdom of England' thus:

CLASSES	to the COUNTIES
ORDERS	to the HUNDREDS
GENERA	to the PARISHES
SPECIES	to the VILLAGES
VARIETIES	to the HOUSES [16]

Withering's botany shifts away from sexuality towards nationality and is characterised by an emphasis on country of origin and lineage, together with extended analogies between the human and vegetable inhabitants of Britain.

For English Linnaeans, Withering's failure to acknowledge the sexual distinctions of the classes and orders ignored the greatest advance in botanical science. By 1783, the Botanical Society at Lichfield, headed by Darwin, had issued an accurate and literal translation of Linnaeus's *Systema Vegabilium*. The 'Preface of the Translators' deliberately undermined Withering, ruthlessly promoting the new translation:

> Dr Withering ... has intirely omitted the sexual distinctions, which are essential to the philosophy of the system; and has introduced a number of english generic names, which ... bear no analogy to those of Linneus [*sic*] ... and has thus rendered many parts of his work unintelligible to the latin Botanist; equally difficult to the english scholar, and loaded the science with an addition of new words.[17]

Thus the Linnaean system has not only been desexualised but its universalism has been replaced by English parochialism – even losing clarity in the process. The third enlarged and revised edition of Withering's flora appeared in 1796. As a result of earlier hostility, Withering made an attempt to use Linnaean names for classes and even included some Latin terminology. 'The English reader will perceive,' he wrote, 'that considerable changes have made in the *Terms*, by a nearer approach to the Linnaean language'.[18] Withering had re-Latinised nomenclature according to established versions of Linnaeus and yet what is striking about this later version is its nationalism: 'descriptions taken from foreign Authors have been discarded, to make room for others made by the Author or his friends from recent examination of the plants as they grow in this island'.[19] The true nature of Withering's 'improvements' becomes apparent if we compare the names of those who assisted with the first edition to those in the third. By the 1796 version, a notable list of British botanists has superseded the smattering of 'foreign Authors' listed in earlier editions; with the exception of two botanists from the University of Uppsala in Sweden, the remaining thirty-two names are all British.[20]

Withering, as already stated, anglicised Linnaean botany from a conviction that 'botany in an English dress would become a favourite amusement with the ladies'.[21] His British flora, then, was a popularisation or, more specifically, feminisation of botany for the general reader. The number of botanising women influenced by Withering from Charlotte Smith to Dorothy Wordsworth testifies to the commercial success of this venture.[22] One of the female botanists heavily indebted to Withering was Lady Charlotte Murray.[23] She compiled *The British Garden: A Descriptive Catalogue of Hardy Plants, Indigenous, Or Cultivated in the Climate of Great Britain* (1799), aided by the works of Withering, Berkenhout, and the Lichfield translation of Linnaeus, all of which are acknowledged in her preface. *The British Garden* is a flora in the manner of Withering's, prefixed by a few short extracts from the Linnaean system.

Murray rejects the epistolary, conversational or poetical styles widely adopted by women in favour of a somewhat drier catalogue format. Surprisingly, *The British Garden* was printed without the usual letter of recommendation or lengthy advertisement praising the work, as was customary for botanical works by women.[24] However, despite her 'Honourable' status, the self-deprecating tone of her preface indicates that she was not exempt from the anxieties surrounding publication which were common among women botanists of this period. She urges readers to consider her work

> rather as a Direction Post, which without any merit of its own, points out to the passenger the road he is desirous to travel, than the Guide who particularly describes the country through which he is to pass, or the various beauties he is about to meet in his journey.[25]

This expensive two-volume work could be used by cultivated ladies on a visit to botanic gardens.

While Withering had 'given a very full elucidation of the plants of these tribes which are natives of Great Britain', Murray states that she has undertaken her flora 'at the request of a Friend, who wished to see those plants which are described in the *Hortus kewensis* as adapted to the British climate, *in an English dress*'.[26] *Hortus kewensis* contained engravings of the choicest plants brought to Kew from 'every climate of the globe'; it was undertaken and executed under the immediate direction of Sir Joseph Banks.[27] Inspired by Banks's empire of flora as documented in *Hortus kewensis,* Murray enthusiastically catalogues non-native species which have been successfully transplanted to Great Britain. The names of British cultivators follow the description of the plant itself. For example, *B. capitum* (Berry-Headed Strawberry Blite), a native of Austria, was cultivated in 1633 by Mr J. Parkinson, while *C. squarrosum* (Rough-Spiked Tick Feed), a native of Russia, was cultivated in Great Britain in 1757 by Mr Philip Miller.[28] The British origin of indigenous plants is triumphantly proclaimed; for example, the entry for *Cerastium aquaticum* from the class *Decandria Pentagnia* reads

> Leaves heart-shaped, fitting; flowers solitary;
> fruit pendent. Flowers in July. *Native of Britain*.[29]

Some highly esteemed species are cited as 'Native of England' such as *C. hispida*, or 'Prickly Chard'.[30]

Murray explicitly cites Withering's comparisons between botanical class and nation, taxonomy and social hierarchy. Murray's debt to Withering is evident from those passages which refer to genera or classes in which she extends his analogy between the vegetable and human populations 'of the globe': 'the *Generic* name of the plant may be considered as the family surname, and the *Specific* one as the proper name of the individual'.[31] While Murray includes exotic species which have been cultivated in English soil, she is careful to inform her readers that hybrids, or those types which deviate from their true character such as 'double flowers', have not been selected for the purpose of investigation because their class (i.e. nation) cannot be so easily ascertained. A plant's true lineage must be proven for it to be verified as wholly British. Erasmus Darwin had drawn attention to the 'waning lineage' of cultivated varieties of carnation which were thought to be barren: 'Canker taints the vegetable blood ... Till *curled leaves* or *barren flowers* betray / A waning lineage, verging to decay'.[32] Luxuriants of this kind symbolise a decaying line of descent; by cataloguing distinct tribes with easily identifiable characteristics, Murray is able to prevent 'nature's bastards'[33] such as Darwin's carnation or other 'varietals' from infiltrating her British flora.

Charlotte Murray's *The British Garden* is one of a number of Linnaean floras where habitat and country of origin are central: here, localism, though sometimes in the form of nationalism, and universalism appear to coexist. The subtitle to the first edition most accurately describes her project which was to collate a 'descriptive catalogue of hardy plants, indigenous, or cultivated in the climate of Great Britain with their generic and specific characters, Latin and English names, native country, and time of flowering'.[34] Murray learnt Linnaean systematics from Withering's *Arrangement of British Plants*; her system of classification was informed by Withering's emphasis on lineage and nationality.

Murray and Withering's endeavours to anglicise botany were also commercial bids to court women readers. Withering simultaneously dropped the 'sexual distinctions in the titles to the classes and orders' when he clothed botany in 'English dress' in order to make it more agreeable to female delicacy. Botanical texts in Latin might contain 'illicit' references to the sex life of plants and, whilst they were suitable for private consumption by gentlemen, a sociable botany, in 'an English dress', would be deemed more appropriate for women.[35] Withering included a 'Dictionary of Botanical Terms' for the use of 'the learner', adding 'the Ladies too, who, in spite of the obstacles attendant on a dead language, often have recourse to Linnaeus in the original Latin, will find their researches facilitated by it'.[36] However, Withering's notes explain that 'the plants referred to in this Dictionary, for the sake of illustrating the different *Terms*, are, for the most part, natives of this island, and are quoted by their most common English names'.[37] Murray also strove to be accessible:

> It has been endeavoured, by avoiding as much as possible every term not to be found in an English Dictionary, to render the following catalogue easy to be understood without the necessity of constant recurrence to a Glossary.[38]

She hoped to encourage women without a classical education to engage with her text by omitting the token dictionary of Latin terms.

Maria Jacson's *Botanical Lectures by a Lady* (1804) was marketed specifically for use with the Lichfield translation of Linnaeus which Jacson had praised as 'the only English work from which the pupil can become a Linnaean or universal botanist'.[39] However, while Murray and Withering simultaneously Anglicise and feminise botany, Jacson has difficulty reconciling these two tendencies. In an earlier version of this work, her *Botanical Dialogues*, she raises a number of objections against English nomenclature, claiming that English generic names were merely arbitrary when they 'ought to be equally familiar to botanists of every nation', and, while her botanical thought is clearly universalist, she discourages women from using Linnaean Latin names in public.[40] In *Botanical Dialogues Between Hortensia and Her Four Children* (1797), for example, Harriet is warned by her mother, Hortensia, not to make 'a display' of her scientific knowledge who insists that if she is heard 'officiously using' botanical names in public, she will 'deservedly be ridiculed both by the ignorant and well informed.'[41] Elsewhere, Harriet is afraid of 'speaking' botanical Latin lest she should appear vain or precocious:

> *Harriet*: I would rather all plants had English names. I shall be afraid of speaking the botanical names though they are accented, lest I should be thought conceited.
> *Hortensia*: You may avoid that evil by a discreet use of them.[42]

Similar passages occur in Charlotte Smith. While Smith is not afraid to indulge in a little false modesty, using her knowledge of natural history to promote novels such as *The Young Philosopher*, her work is everywhere fraught with anxieties over how to make public one's botanical knowledge.[43] In *Conversations Introducing Poetry* Mrs Talbot's daughter Emily invites criticism when, instead of merely admiring flowers for a nosegay, she ascribes them botanical names verbally:

> 'Lord,' cried one of them, 'what signifies what the name of this plant and that plant is?', 'What nonsense and affectation, my dear creature!' said another, in a half whisper, 'what an amazingly conceited little thing is Emily Talbot! I am sure I should never know one flower from another if I was to live an hundred years, and I wonder what good it does?' 'O 'tis the fashion, you know', cried a Miss, a cousin of theirs, in a drawling tone—'but if *my* existence depended upon it, I'm sure I could never make anything of remembering these hard names'.[44]

These passages indicate that a bold display of the botanical Latin which had enabled Linnaeus to universalise his science (which he could not have achieved in his native Swedish) was still considered to be at odds with femininity.[45] Anglicised versions of Linnaeus, therefore, continued to be prepared for women during this period.

Sex, class and order

Linnaean metaphors tended to fall into two categories, either sexual or military. While military analogies enabled botany to take on an ordering nationalistic role, Linnaean sexual metaphors could be interpreted as subversive, undermining moral and social order. These opposing aspects of Linnaean botany are represented by the separate adaptations of Linnaeus by Withering and Erasmus Darwin. Withering had been inspired by analogies with military rank but Darwin took the botanical/social analogy in a new direction, shifting away from order and discipline towards promiscuity and sexual anarchy. Darwin's work illustrates the dialectical ambivalence of Linnaean botany as applied to society. For, just as Withering was able to justify a hierarchical society from botany's taxonomical order, Darwin could as easily legitimate an anarchic, emancipated sexuality.

Withering had omitted the sexual distinctions that defined Linnaeus's classes and orders, producing a decorous, indigenous botany that young women could be exposed to with safety, whereas his arch rival, Erasmus Darwin, specifically focused on the Linnaean sexual content to create a provocative poetic account of the sex life of plants.[46] 'The Loves of the Plants,' Part II of the epic poem *The Botanic Garden*, was published in 1789 and composed with the aid of the translations of Linnaeus by the Botanical Society at Lichfield, whose preface, as we have seen, publicly belittled Withering's work.

Darwin's *The Loves of the Plants* disturbed morality by inviting women to view the vegetable harems as if through a Camera Obscura for their own amusement:

> Lo, here a CAMERA OBSCURA is presented to thy view, in which are lights and shades dancing on a whited canvas, and magnified into apparent life! if thou art perfectly at leasure for such trivial amusement, walk in and view the wonders of my INCHANTED GARDEN.[47]

A series of 'diverse little pictures' revealed that polygamous unions were not uncommon in the plant world. *Maedia*, the American Cowslip, for example, has five male stamens and one female pistil; Darwin describes the moment of fertilisation as the female stigma bends downwards to receive the fecundating dust from the anthers of the male stamens. The 'Fair Lychnis' has ten males and five females residing on the same plant. According to Darwin's notes, 'when the females arrive at their maturity, they rise above the petals, as if looking abroad for their distant husbands'.[48] In his poetic account of these processes, 'wanton' females compete to be fertilised by the males:

> Each Wanton beauty, Tricked in all her grace
> Shakes the bright dewdrops from her blushing face;
> In gay undress displays her rival charms
> And calls her wondering lovers to her arms.[49]

Darwin's depiction of vegetable harlotry undermined the conventional justification of social order through analogies with the laws of nature; the disciplinary role that botany had taken on with the advent of Linnaean classification now seems to have collapsed. The plant kingdom, it was now evident, showed practically no modesty in sexual matters and little or no degree of discrimination regarding sexual unions. Darwin was regarded as a dangerous sceptic and revolutionary; the houses of Lunar Society members were ransacked in anti-Jacobin Birmingham riots in the same year.[50] He was subject to a sustained satirical attack in the reactionary journal, *The Anti-Jacobin*, through a parody of 'Loves of Plants' entitled 'The Loves of the Triangles. A Mathematical and Philosophical Poem. Inscribed to Dr. Darwin', which ran for several weeks.[51] These incidents indicate how significant botany had become; Anti-Jacobin propaganda warned the public that toleration of Darwin's ideas would contribute to the collapse of civil order.[52]

Frances Arabella Rowden's *A Poetical Introduction To The Study of Botany* (1801) was a reworking of Darwin's poetic account of Linnaean classes and orders for the young female market. Acting in her capacity as an educator of girls (she worked as a governess and teacher before becoming a headmistress at a fashionable school in Chelsea between 1801–20), she openly criticised Darwin, claiming to find his language 'frequently too luxuriant for the simplicity of female education'.[53] Ironically, she took Darwin as her model and endeavoured to imitate his classical versification while purging his botanical description of the sexualised analogies which threatened female modesty.[54]

Rowden discusses plant structure before illustrating Linnaean classification in a sequence of verses. In 'Horse-Chestnut, or *Æsculus* (Class vii, *Heptandria Monogymia*)', Rowden depicts the seven stamens, or 'males', as gallant soldiers in ardent pursuit of the solitary female pistil:

> Arm'd with strong mail the proud Æscula stands,
> And sounds her thunders through the distant lands;
> Shakes her dread lances o'er her valiant tribe,
> And calls the conqu'ring heroes to her side,
> Quick, at the sound, sev'n gallant soldiers wield
> The pointed jav'lin or the burnish'd shield:
> At Beauty's shrine with ardent suit they sigh
> And bravely swear to conquer or to die.[55]

Rowden's plants exhibit none of the wantonness of Darwin's; the females, or pistils, though constantly under threat from ardent male stamens, remain chaste and intact. The moment of fertilisation is never written into the poem. While her chivalric images of endangered female virtue are not that far removed from Darwin's courtship scenes, there are none of his vegetable harems: Rowden prefers to portray virtuous plants which appear almost to resist fertilisation. The *Mimosa pudica* folds up its leaves in reaction to touch and is known as 'the sensitive plant'.[56] It is of the Class xxiii, *Polygamia Monoecia*, in which there are many stamens (males) and only one pistil (female). *Pudica* means 'modest; chaste'; Darwin orientalised the Mimosa as 'an eastern bride' entering a harem:

> Veil'd with gay decency and modest pride,

Slow to the mosque she moves, an eastern bride;
There her soft vows unceasing love record,
Queen of the bright seraglio of her Lord.[57]

Rowden's Mimosa, in contrast, is compared to a virginal English maid whom one could not imagine entering into anything but a strictly monogamous union:

As some young maid, to modest feeling true,
Shrinks from the world, and veils her charms from view,
At each slight touch her timid form receives,
The fair Mimosa folds her silken leaves.[58]

Following Withering, Rowden's depiction of Linnaean botany is morally unthreatening: she draws on a method of classification based on the sex life of plants but does not admit any description relating to sexual union (male anthers and stamens fertilising female pistils).

Promoting virtue, Rowden focuses on indigenous plants such as the British Oak (Class XXI, *Quercus*, *Monoecia Polyandria*) which is championed as the saviour of the British monarchy. 'Distress'd Britannia' appeals to the 'venerable Quercus' during the war with France because it had saved the British monarchy in a previous rebellion (Charles II after his defeat at Worcester by Cromwell escaped his pursuers by hiding in an oak tree).[59] A weeping Britannia throws her arms around the heroic oak's 'aged neck' and pleads for England's safety:

Oh! let our navy still triumphant reign,
And rule the mighty monarch of the main;
From Heav'n and thee alone success can spring,
Then save thy Country, as thou sav'dst thy King.[60]

This image of a British fleet serves to remind us that the oak provides the raw material for shipbuilding, playing a vital part in the triumphs of the British navy. Charlotte Smith also alludes to this: 'On the rough Oak are buds minute unfurl'd / Whose giant produce may command the world'.[61] Burke had famously compared the state to an oak, with the people portrayed as cattle, contentedly sheltering beneath it;[62] for Rowden, the oak is essential to every aspect of English life, from architecture to agriculture (its acorns provide food for swine and its leaves make hotbeds for forcing plants).

It is not just the stately oak which is upheld as a symbol of order and liberty: Rowden also invests such lowly plants as *Trientalis*, or the Chick Weed, with heroic virtue. Sadly, for Rowden, in the current moral climate this humble native plant is neglected as was 'Belisarius in degen'rate Rome [who] / Seem'd like a stranger in his native home'.[63] Like Jacson, Rowden sees the humble British flower as a symbol of the blessings of our native land: 'Where native freedom, peace and plenty smile / For George and Charlotte guard Britannia's Isle'.[64] Rowden and Thornton are notable here for their deliberate attempts to appropriate botany for the cause of monarchy and order after the controversy surrounding Darwin's Jacobin plants.

Robert Thornton's elaborate plates are humbly dedicated to Queen Charlotte who is hailed as the 'Patroness of Botany and the finer Arts', she 'has long shone the brightest example of conjugal fidelity and maternal tenderness'.[65] Thornton compares her to the red rose which 'is styled the queen of flowers by the poets', embarking on this conceit:

> She moves at the head of this long procession of vegetable beauties, pouring out her incense to FLORA, with all the grace and dignity of majesty. Nature has given her a vest of purest white, and also imperial robes of the brightest scarlet; and that no rude hand should tear her from her rich domain she is protected by myriads of soldiers, who present on every side their naked and sharp thorns against the daring invader.[66]

The 'rude hand' threatening to tear this 'Queen of flowers' from her floral throne is suggestive of the threat to the monarchy posed by revolution. Thornton enlists femininity and botany in defence of royalty. He informs us that the Queen is proficient in botany while the princesses are particularly adept in botanical drawing:

> There is not a plant in the Garden of Kew (which contains all the choicest productions of the habitable globe) but has been either drawn by her gracious Majesty, or by some of the princesses, with a grace and skill which reflect on these personages the highest honour.[67]

Thornton selects the Poet Laureate, James Henry Pye, to celebrate the royal dignity of *Strelitzia reginae*, or the Bird of Paradise Flower, which had been imported from the Cape of Good Hope and renamed 'Queen Plant' by Banks:[68]

> Crown of his labours! this imperial flower
> Wafted from burning Afric's rugged scene,
> 'Neath Britain's better skies, in happier hour,
> Enjoys the patronage of Britain's QUEEN!
>
> Grac'd by *her Name*, its shining petals boast
> Above the rest to charm her favouring eyes,
> Though Flora brings from every clime her host
> Of various Odours and of varied dyes.[69]

The Royal princesses appear in the closing stanza as botanising nymphs who preserve the beauty of the plant for posterity:

> While Royal Nymphs, fair as the Oreade race
> Who trod Eurota's brink, or Cynthus' brow,
> Snatch from the wreck of time each fleeting grace,
> And bid its leaves with bloom *perennial* glow![70]

In this poem the plant-collecting expeditions of Joseph Banks are seen to be executed under the auspices of the patroness of botany, Queen Charlotte. The newly transplanted flower flourishes in British soil under the protection of 'Britain's Queen'. The poem represents Britain's taming of the exotic: 'Afric's' unrefined and 'rugged scene' has been replaced by a cultivated British garden.

As an emblem of civilisation, the British garden underlines the close relationship that has always existed between culture and cultivation. Exotic flowers usually signify the pernicious effects of luxury: here, however, having been transplanted to Britain, the Bird of Paradise flower is admired for being highly cultivated and luxurious and becomes a highly charged symbol of British botany.

The later verses in Rowden's *Poetical Introduction* also describe non-native species encountered on the voyages of discovery. In '*Thea*, or Tea Tree (Class XII, *Polyandria Monosygnia*)' 'gay sylphs' act as agents of the British botanic empire: 'Bear on your silver plumes, across the sea / To British Beauty, the *Imperial Tea*' (77). Some of the supernatural machinery of Darwin surfaces here. '*Musa*, or Banana Tree (Class XXIII, *Polygamia Monoecia*)' recounts 'Brave Cookes' voyage to the Sandwich Islands. While the ship's crew find a 'cool retreat' under the thick foliage of the exotic banana palm 'their gallant chief' is 'By a *rude race* of savage Indians slain / E'en where he bade fair Arts and Science reign' (144). Rowden also depicts Oberea, the 'Queen of Otaheite', mourning the loss of her idol Banks under the shade of the banana. These poems by Rowden indicate the extent to which the voyages of discovery had excited the imagination of the British public and initiated a vogue for the study of natural history.

A number of the poems in Thornton's *Temple of Flora* draw attention to the botanising activities of Joseph Banks on Cook's *Endeavour* voyage where he was accompanied by the Linnaean, Daniel Solander.[71] Maurice's closing verses in this collection underscore the specific way that Thornton's literary and artistic appropriation of the world's flora mirrors the actual plant-collecting practice of Joseph Banks. Surprisingly, 'Thy' refers to Thornton here and not to Banks as we might have assumed.

> From orient regions where the tropic ray
> Lights beauty's beams, and pours the glowing day,
> To where th' *eternal snows* of *winter* spread,
> And ice-clad mountains rear their lofty head,
> *Thy* daring hand hath cull'd the loveliest flow'rs
> To deck delighted ALBION'S happier bow'rs
>
> *Thy Mighty Work complete*, through ALBION'S bounds,
> *Thy* name is echoed, and *thy* fame resounds;
> Exalting Science weaves the deathless bays,
> And rival Monarchs swell the note of Praise.[72]

Thornton's compendium is celebrated with the patriotic fervour that was already surrounding Banks's enterprise.

The plates in Thornton's *Temple of Flora* are eye-catching portraits of plants rather than accurate botanical illustrations. The plants are set in elaborate picturesque landscapes where 'each scenery is appropriated to the subject'; for example:

> In the *large flowering* MIMOSA, first discovered on the mountains of Jamaica, you have the Humming birds of that country, and one of the aborigines struck with astonishment at the peculiarities of the plant.[73]

Thornton makes an apology to 'the rigid botanist' for endeavouring to unite 'beauties of the vegetable race' from every corner of the globe. While a plant's country of origin is implied by features in the landscape, this 'universal appropriation' suggests they are being celebrated as fruits of the British botanic empire.

The Linnaean-inspired botanical works of Murray and Rowden incorporate plants which have been successfully transplanted to British soil in the manner of *Hortus kewensis* and the *Temple of Flora,* whereas Jacson and Wakefield's exemplify 'Botany in an English dress', combining the emblematic tradition which associated women and flowers with a patriotic celebration of native species. Jacson and Wakefield elevate simple native plants whereas Rowden and Murray also celebrate 'exotics' which are seen to thrive 'Neath Britain's better skies'.[74] Thus the depiction of English culture wanders uneasily between a natural puritan simplicity that shuns feminine ornament and artifice to a civilisation that promises a luxuriousness that is denied to more barbaric sorts.

Indigenous plants were given preferential treatment by female Linnaeans: the planting schemes in Jacson's *A Florist's Manual* were specifically designed to display humble British flowers and to prevent her 'sister florists' from introducing foreign luxuriants into their British gardens. This debate is developed in Chapter 5 in my discussion of Charlotte Smith and the little-known poet Cordelia Skeeles's contributions to the *Temple of Flora*. Here, British flora denotes private virtue in contrast to the suspiciously alien exhibitionism of cultivated florist flowers or 'exotics', which signify a kind of harlotry. Florist flowers were sometimes called 'exotics' by Jacson but she was usually referring to French or Dutch varieties which had been reared in conditions of luxury and not to pure species which had been imported by British botanists.

Shifting attitudes to 'exotics' or 'luxuriants' and the subsequent promotion of indigenous botany form part of a more general campaign to ward off moral decay which could be spread by French or Dutch influences; British flowers are upheld as symbols of virtue, free from any taint of luxury. Wakefield thought that women who received a defective education would contribute to 'national decay'. She was antipathetic to the French, fearing the effects of imported French teachers on young British women, and emphasised the importance of women's reformed education in reconstructing national life.[75] Her indigenous botany, therefore, specifically instructs women about the harmful effects of luxury; luxuriants are regarded as 'improper' for their investigation and they are advised to seek out 'worthy' plants 'of our own growth' or those flowers 'growing wild, without culture' which are equated with virtue and utility. Horace Walpole maintained that the new gardening style followed nature and liberty and was, therefore, unmistakably English. Women botanists participated in this patriotic opposition to artifice and luxury as my discussion has shown.

These women's texts offered, in various ways and degrees, an emancipated space for women, allowing them access to the public sphere of debate. For instance, women could contribute to the formation of national identity via botany and the privileging of native plants therein. Murray promoted the study of botany as a pursuit which was immediately accessible to women: chemistry and astronomy were 'confined to a few' because they required the 'apparatus of the conservatory' whereas the 'pleasing science of botany' was 'open to every curious mind'.[76]

An engagement with Linnaean botany proved liberating for these British women botanists in a different sense. Maria Jacson actively encouraged women to depart from the local and particularised knowledge of the florist and embrace universal botany. The ability to grasp the relations of general and particular that were fundamental to correct taste was earlier considered to be outside a woman's grasp and hence women were everywhere excluded from the republic of taste.[77]

However, those such as Rousseau who decreed that women lacked the ability to abstract or generalise continued to promote botany as a feminine pursuit. My discussion in Chapter 2 of Rousseau and Wakefield's botanical letters demonstrated that it was not always the universal aspect of Linnaean botany which made it conducive to the female character but its method.[78] The emphasis on systematic method in the teachings of Linnaeus encouraged women to engage with order and regularity and was perceived to contribute to what Rowden referred to as that 'regulation of their minds' on which 'the foundation of their future happiness is laid'.[79]

There is, therefore, a contrasting tendency in these texts to reposition women back into the domestic sphere. Gendered notions of privacy can be mediated through Linnaean botanical texts: Rowden, for example, recommends botany as a means by which women can 'learn to concentrate their pleasures within a narrow circle', embracing the prevailing domestic ideology which dictated that women be devoted to 'a retired and domestic life'.[80] Rousseau, who himself sought refuge from persecution away from the public realm in the solitude and privacy of plant collecting, explicitly feminised botany as a study ideally suited to virtuous women who do not 'seek applause' on a 'public stage'.[81] The anonymity of works such as *Botanical Dialogues for the use in Schools and Adapted to the use of Persons of all Ages by A Lady* and *Botanical Lectures*, also attributed to 'A Lady', indicate that botanists like Jacson were shielded from public life whereas women such as Lady Charlotte Murray, who were writing from a position of privilege, were more likely to make public their true identity.

A number of Charlotte Smith's poems are supplied with copious references to Rousseau – most notably the solitary botanising figure of *Reveries du Promenade Solitaire*. Having retreated from public life, from the society of men and books, Rousseau turns to botany with renewed avidity.[82] Smith confesses to feeling a strong affinity to Rousseau; she is similarly seeking refuge in the innocent pleasures of botany:

> Without any pretensions to those talents which were in him so heavily taxed with that excessive irritability, too often, if not always attendant upon genius, it has been my misfortune to endure real calamities that have disqualified me for finding any enjoyment in the pleasures and pursuits which occupy the generality of the world. I have been engaged in contending with persons whose cruelty has left so painful an impression on my mind, that I may well say … 'Brilliant flowers, adornment of meadows, cool shades … arbours, foliage, come purify my imagination sullied by these hideous objects'.[83]

Shunning those pleasures which occupied the 'generality of the world', Smith fixed her attentions on the minutiae of wild flowers growing in hedgerows and meadows in the surrounding area.

Smith's poems are informed and animated by her use of the portable botanical microscope designed by Withering and sold by his publishers along with his text. Her access to minute worlds through the botanical microscope points to the emancipating potential of particularity as against the doctrines of Reynolds and others. The particular or specific, therefore, is as liberating for Smith as it was for Blake who saw 'a World in a Grain of Sand / and a Heaven in a Wild Flower'.[84] Her descriptions of the minute parts of the flower are influenced by a need to identify plants according to the Linnaean system; she writes as a universalising botanist, yet she simultaneously resists the erasure of the particular.

As botany became increasingly tied up with the voyages of discovery, women's botanical study was largely confined to the drawing-room, garden and hedgerow. As a private activity shielded from the corruptions of public life, botany mirrored the confinement of the feminine domestic sphere and yet, through Linnaeus and his English followers, these female botanists contributed to the formation of national identity. Barred from academies, universities and learned societies, British women entered into aesthetic, philosophic and scientific debate through botany. The principal medium for this was the Anglicization of the Linnaean Sexual System but this, in turn, conjured up its own attendant anxieties.

Notes

1 The poem is most probably by Anna Seward; I discuss the authorship in Chapter 4. The Botanical Society at Lichfield consisted of Erasmus Darwin, Sir Brooke Boothby and a proctor in the cathedral jurisdiction whose name was Jackson. Anna Seward recalls that observations were often sent to journals signed 'Lichfield Botanical Society'; no one knew there were only three members (Seward, *Memoirs of the Life of Dr Darwin*, p. 99). See also Jenny Uglow, *The Lunar Men: The Friends Who Made the Future* (London: Faber and Faber, 2002), pp. 379, 381–3, 389. For a discussion of eighteenth-century natural history societies, see Allen, *The Naturalist in Britain*, and for the Botanical Society at Lichfield, see pp. 45–6.

2 [Anna Seward (?),] 'The Backwardness of Spring Accounted For', line 58. All further references to this poem are cited in the text in parentheses. This anonymous poem appears in manuscript on the endpapers of the second volume of a British Library copy of Linnaeus, *A System of Vegetables*, 2 vols (Lichfield: printed by John Jackson for Leigh and Sotherby ... London, 1783). Ann Shteir refers to the poem's 'implicit argument about the value of the Linnaean system' yet she does not make any reference to its important social/political context (*Cultivating Women*, pp. 15–16).

3 The striking imagery which Linnaeus employed to describe the natural world in *Deliciae Naturae* captured the public imagination. The oration was delivered in Latin and proved so popular with students at the university that they made a special trip to Linnaeus's house to ask for a Swedish translation to be published (see Blunt, *The Compleat Naturalist*, pp. 229–30). From there it passed into English. Knut Hagberg quotes widely from *Deliciae Naturae* citing passages which demonstrate the hierarchical, military imagery: birds are 'cavalry, light nimble, resplendently clad' and amphibians 'an ugly horrible, naked pack on foot' (*Carl Linnaeus*, trans.

Alan Blair (London: Jonathan Cape, 1952), p. 151). Linnaeus suffered a stroke in 1774 and his health continued to fail until his death in 1778. Delivered in December 1772, this oration was one of the last public addresses by the famous Swede. The type of analogies Linnaeus used in his important oration would be known to English Linnaeans. Hagberg states that by the time D. H. Stoever's biography appeared 'the English public was already familiar with Linnaeus and his life's work' (Hagberg, *Carl Linnaeus*, p. 262. Stoever's work was *Life of Sir Charles Linnaeus* (London: B and J. White, 1794)).

4 E. P. Thompson identifies three different stages of the riot, culminating in an attack on the Bank itself. Those involved are described as 'something of a mixture of manipulated mob and revolutionary crowd' (*The Making of the English Working Class*, new edn (Harmondsworth: Penguin Books, 1980), pp. 77–8. The second, more violent phase of the riot, is described as

> one of licensed spontaneity, leading onto mob violence informed by 'a groping desire to settle accounts with the rich, if only for a day'; some of the 'better sort of tradesmen' faded away, while journeymen, apprentices, and servants – and some criminals – thronged the streets (Thompson, p. 77).

5 The *Temple of Flora* is the most lavish section of a larger work entitled *A New Illustration of the Sexual System of Linnaeus*. As Blunt and Stearn explain, 'the work was advertised in 1797 and issued in parts, first at a guinea and then at twenty-five shillings each, between 1799 and 1807. The elucidation of the various editions and issues of this work is a tangle for bibliographers' (Blunt and Stearn, *The Art of Botanical Illustration*, p. 26).

My references are to the full 1807 edition, *New Illustration of the Sexual System of Carolus von Linnaeus ... And The Temple of Flora, or Garden of Nature* (London: T. Bensley, 1807).

6 Thornton venerates the British constitution in the manner of classic liberal thought (after Montesquieu) as that which is: 'nicely poized between the extremes of too much liberty, and too much power; the *several parts of it* having a proper check upon each other' (Robert Thornton, *The Politician's Creed* (London: T. Cox, 1795), p. 101).

7 Thornton here transposes lines v. 456–7, placing them before lines v. 444–5 (James Thomson, *Liberty: A Poem*, in *The Poems of James Thomson*, ed. J. Logie Robertson (Oxford: Oxford University Press, 1963), p. 319.

8 The reader also learns that 'the English have likewise carried the manufacture of *Paper* to the utmost pitch of perfection, and our *Type* has risen superior to that of any other civilised nation on the globe' (Robert Thornton, *An Account of Dr Thornton's Exhibition of Botanical Paintings*, 4th edn (London: C. Whittingham, 1804), unpag.).

9 The painting is by John Russell and John Opie and was engraved by Ridley in 1799. In 1806, however, Thornton had the painting re-engraved by Caldwall and published it in colour.

10 Thornton, 'An Explanation of the Picturesque Plates', *Temple of Flora*, unpag.

11 Gill Saunders, *Picturing Plants: An Analytical History of Botanical Illustration* (Berkeley, CA: University of California Press, 1995), p. 92. The term 'florilegium' is derived from the Latin adjective *florilegus*, flower-gathering. 'Florilegium' is often simply defined as 'anthology', which in turn was described by Dr Johnson in 1755 as both a collection of flowers and a collection of poems. For a fuller explanation, see Blunt and Stearn, *The Art of Botanical Illustration*, pp. 13–14.

12 Sten Lindroth writes that 'Linnaeus was inspired above all by military ranks' and traces martial imagery in a number of his works. Many of these examples are light-hearted; Linnaeus, for example, is reputed to have referred to himself as the commander-in-chief of all botanists and to his arch enemy Siegesbeck as a mere corporal. See Sten Lindroth, 'The Two Faces of Linnaeus', in Frängsmyr (ed.), *Linnaeus: the Man and the Work*, pp. 1–62 (p. 23).
13 William Withering, 'Introduction to the Study of Botany', *An Arrangement of British Plants*, 3rd edn, 4 vols (Birmingham: Printed by M. Swinney for G. G. & J. Robinson, and B. & J. White, London, 1796), I, p. 6. All further references are to this third edition unless otherwise stated.
14 *Ibid.*, I, p. 6.
15 A fuller Latin version of Tournefort's *Elements de Botanique* (1694), entitled *Institutiones rei Herbariae*, was published in 1700. It is in this Latin text that Tournefort introduced these terms. See Morton, *A History of Botanical Science*, note 43, p. 281.
16 Withering, *An Arrangement of British Plants*, I, p. 6.
17 A Botanical Society at Lichfield, 'Preface of the Translators', in Linnaeus, *A System of Vegetables*, I, p. ii. The project was organised by Erasmus Darwin; Joseph Banks and Samuel Johnson were consulted and Carl Linnaeus the Younger personally sent over an early version of *Supplementum Plantarum* for their use prior to its publication.
18 Withering, 'Preface', *An Arrangement of British Plants*, I, p. vii.
19 *Ibid.*, I, p. vi.
20 Names include English botanists such as Mr Thomas Milne, the late curator of the Botanic Gardens at Oxford; Dr Thomas Arnold, Fellow of the Royal College of Physicians, and of the Royal Medical Society of Edinburgh; John Stackhouse, Esq. F.L.S., author of the *Nereis Britannica*; and Mr James Dickson, F.L.S., author of the *Plant Cryptogam Britanniae*.
21 Withering, 'The Design', *A Botanical Arrangement of All the Vegetables Naturally Growing in Great Britain*, 2 vols, (Birmingham: T. Cadell and P. Elmsley, and G. G. & J. Robinson, 1776), I, p. v. While working as a medical doctor, Withering had collected botanical specimens for a female patient to sketch; he later married his former patient, the sister of Dr Brooke Hector at Lichfield, in 1772. This exercise may have given him the idea of writing a botanical textbook for women as he had already begun a book on botany arranged in the system of Linnaeus. For biographies of Withering, see 'Memoir of his Life Character and Writings' by William Withering Jnr., prefixed to *Miscellaneous Tracts of the Late William Withering, M.D., F.R.S.* (London: Longman, Hurst, Rees, Orme and Brown, 1822), and T. W. Peck and K. D. Wilkinson, *William Withering of Birmingham M.D., F.R.S., F.L.S.* (Bristol: John Wright and Sons, 1950).
22 See D. E. Coombe, 'The Wordsworths and Botany', *Notes and Queries*, 197 (1952), 298–9.
23 Blanche Henrey states that Lady Charlotte Murray was the eighth child of John, third Duke of Atholl and died unmarried at Bath in 1808. Her father made extensive plantations, especially of larches, at his Perthshire estates of Dunkeld and Blair. Her brother John was also an enthusiastic planter of larches and the author of a pamphlet entitled *Observations on Larch*, published in 1819. According to Henrey, in Volume 6 of the 1797 edition of Sowerby's *English Botany*, James Edward Smith records that a double variety of *Geranium Pratense* was discovered by Lady Charlotte

Murray in 1793 and sent to Lady Banks (Henrey, *British Botanical and Horticultural Literature*, II, p. 584).

Murray is mentioned briefly by Ann Shteir where she is described as 'a noblewoman living in Bath' (Shteir, *Cultivating Women*, p. 68). *The British Garden* was first published in 1799; a further edition followed in 1805. The work seems to have been a success as a third edition was printed by Thomas Wilson in London in 1880. These details are documented in Fussell's 'The Rt. Hon. Lady Charlotte Murray'. No further biographical material is given.

24 Jacson's *Botanical Dialogues*, for example, was printed with an advertisement congratulating the author on such a splendid work, which was in turn prefixed by a letter from Erasmus Darwin and Brooke Boothby, praising Jacson for having explained a difficult science in 'an easy and familiar manner'.

25 Lady Charlotte Murray, 'Preface', *The British Garden* (Bath: S. Hazard, 1799), p. vi. All further references are to this first edition.

26 *Ibid.*, p. vi. Original emphasis.

27 William Aiton's *Hortus kewensis*, 3 vols (London: George Nicol, 1789) was published while Banks was the honorary director of Kew. It gives brief descriptions of plants in Latin according to the Linnaean style, not only of plants grown at Kew, but of almost all the species then cultivated in England. In addition, it records the native country of all species, date of introduction, and who introduced them. See Henrey, *British Botanical and Horticultural Literature*, II, p. 246.

28 Murray, *British Garden*, p. 4.

29 *Ibid.*, p. 377. Original emphasis.

30 *Ibid.*, p. 3.

31 *Ibid.*, p. xx.

32 Extract from Darwin, *The Botanic Garden*, cited in text accompanying the illustration of the carnation, Thornton, *Temple of Flora*, unpag.

33 A phrase used by Thornton to describe carnations which have been improved by florists (text accompanying plate of the carnation, *Temple of Flora*, unpag.).

34 The subtitle to the first edition of *The British Garden*. See above, note 25.

35 Richard Polwhele described female botanists as being 'eager for illicit knowledge': notes to lines 33–6, *The Unsex'd Females* (London: Cadell and Davies, 1798; repr. New York: Garland Press, 1974), p. 9.

36 Withering, *An Arrangement of British Plants*, I, p. 40.

37 *Ibid.*, footnotes, p. 40

38 Murray, 'Preface', *British Garden*, p. xxv.

39 Jacson, 'Advertisement', *Botanical Lectures by a Lady*.

40 Jacson, *Botanical Dialogues*, p. 63.

41 Jacson, *Botanical Dialogues*, p. 63.

42 *Ibid.*, p. 62.

43 In the preface to *The Young Philosopher*, Smith writes of her story, 'it is relieved with such ornaments as a very slight knowledge of natural history and a minor talent for short pieces of poetry, have enabled me to give it' (Charlotte Smith, 'Preface', *The Young Philosopher: A Novel, in Four Volumes By Charlotte Smith*, 4 vols (London: T. Cadell & W. Davies, 1798), I, p. vii).

44 Smith, *Conversations Introducing Poetry*, II, p. 174.

45 In her recent study of Linnaeus, Lisbet Koerner states that Linnaeus 'mourned the decline of Latin' and points out that he had limited language skills despite his wealth of botanical knowledge. Quoting a passage from the autobiographical *Vita Caroli*

Linnaei (1720s–1770s; Stockholm: Almqvist & Wiksell, 1957), she demonstrates that Linnaeus 'learnt neither English nor French nor German nor Lapp, yes not even Dutch, even though he stayed a full three years in Holland'. The majority of his correspondents wrote to him in Latin although he did receive some letters in English and French (Koerner, *Linnaeus: Nature and Nation*, p. 47).

Wilfrid Blunt notes that Linnaeus's botanical Latin was not 'classical Latin but a technical language derived from Renaissance and medieval Latin' (*The Compleat Naturalist*, p. 247). Botanical Latin, which can largely be attributed to Linnaeus, is still a means of internationalising botanical science.

46 While Darwin and Withering were both medical doctors and botanists, and fellow members of the Lunar Society, there was a rivalry between them resulting in a feud which lasted many years. Withering had replaced Darwin's esteemed friend Dr Small, a mathematician in the Lunar Society and was soon being criticised by Darwin in a review in the *Monthly Magazine* of 1799. Darwin expressed disappointment at Withering's work on British plants which, in Darwin's opinion, had become little more than a loose translation from Linnaeus.

In 1778 Darwin competed with Withering over a cure for scarlet fever. Darwin later edited an essay for publication which was written by his son, Charles, who had died while at medical college in Edinburgh. The essay included a discussion of the medicinal properties of the *Digitalis* or Foxglove. However, Withering had been the first to prescribe digitalis in a medical context but had not been acknowledged in the essay which attributed the important work on the digitalis to Darwin's son, Charles. Withering and Darwin were never reconciled although they kept up appearances at Society gatherings. See G. C. Cook, *Erasmus Darwin and the Foxglove Controversy* (London: Royal Society of Medicine, 1993). Darwin later worked on the Lichfield translation of Linnaeus's *A System of Vegetables*, the preface of which publicly undermined Withering. Further details of Lunar Society members can be found in Robert Schofield, *The Lunar Society at Birmingham: A Social History of Provincial Science and Industry in Eighteenth-Century England* (Oxford: Clarendon Press, 1962) and Uglow, *The Lunar Men.*

47 Darwin, 'Proem', *The Botanic Garden*, pp. v–vi.

48 Darwin, 'Lychinis', *The Loves of the Plants*, *The Botanic Garden*, I, note 1, p. 12.

49 Darwin, *The Loves of the Plants*, *The Botanic Garden*, I. 113–16.

50 For a general background to the anti-Jacobin sentiments that erupted in the Birmingham (and other) riots of the 1790s, see Thompson, *The Making of the English Working Class*, pp. 111–30.

51 'The Loves of the Triangles' first appeared in *The Anti-Jacobin or, Weekly Examiner* on 16 April 1798, continuing on 23 April 1798 and 7 May 1798. The poem is written in mock-Darwinian verse, complete with scientific notes elaborating on the terms cited in the poem. In Canto I, for example, the nymphs and deities of mathematical mythology gather, 'Divine NONSENSIA' is invoked in place of Flora, to tell 'How Loves and Graces in an *Angle* dwell' ('Loves of the Triangles', I. 38, *The Anti-Jacobin*, 16 April 1798, p. 181). The marriage of Euclid and Algebra is described and 'licentious' Optics with her telescope. The theory of Fluxions is explained and a Rectangle, a magician, educated by Plato and Menecmus in love with three curves, Parabola, Hyperbola and Ellipsis, is served by Genii and transforms himself into a cone. The final sequence of the poem ends with images of revolution, as 'sylphs of death' and 'imps of murder' gather where 'the tall Guillotine is rais'd for PITT' and 'FREEDOM hails the happy blow' ('Loves of the Triangles', I. 105 and 111, *The Anti-*

Jacobin, 7 May 1798, p. 206).

52 Works by Darwin were selected for censure by the *Anti-Jacobin* up until 1798 when *Zoonomia* was placed in the same category as 'atheistic' works such as Godwin's *Political Justice* (1791).

53 Frances Arabella Rowden, Advertisement, *A Poetical Introduction to the Study of Botany* (London: T. Bensley, 1801). All further references are to this edition.

54 Her relationship to Darwin is ambivalent; she wished to distance herself from his radicalism and potentially inflaming sexual metaphors, yet the very fact that she chose him as a model caused her own book to be slated in the *Anti-Jacobin Review* (no. 10, December 1801, p. 356).

55 Rowden, *Poetical Introduction*, p. 39.

56 The plant mimosa was central to the question of analogy between animal and plant because it appeared to have the elements of a nervous system. It became a symbol of human sensibility in Cowper's 'The Poet, The Oyster and the Sensitive Plant' (1782) and was used to explore sentiency in nature and human feeling in Shelley's 'The Sensitive Plant' (1820). The sensitive plant was also a metaphor for male and female genitalia in bawdy works: James Perry's *Mimosa: or, The Sensitive Plant* (London: Printed for W. Sandwich, 1779) contains phallic imagery. For a broad discussion of the mimosa as a literary emblem, see Robert M. Maniquis, 'The Puzzling *Mimosa*: Sensitivity and Plant Symbols in Romanticism', *Studies in Romanticism*, 8:3 (Spring 1969), 129–55. Maniquis observes that 'the sensitive plant' appears three times in Darwin's *The Botanic Garden* (1791) but he does not offer any reading of the poem, commenting instead on Darwin's description of organs of sense in flowers in *Zoonomia* (1794–1801). He does not appear to be familiar with Rowden's poem on the mimosa.

57 Darwin, *The Loves of the Plants*, I. 225–8.

58 Rowden, *Poetical Introduction*, p. 153.

59 Rowden's notes to the 'Class xxi, Quercus (Oak)' describe Charles II's adventures thus: 'To conceal himself he was obliged to climb a spreading oak, among the thick branches of which he passed a whole day, and saw the soldiers of the enemy pass underneath in pursuit of him' (*Poetical Introduction*, p. 132.)

60 Rowden, 'Quercus', *Poetical Introduction*, p. 131.

61 Charlotte Smith, 'Flora', *The Poems of Charlotte Smith*, ed. S. Curran (Oxford: Oxford University Press, 1993), lines 33–4, p. 284.

62 Edmund Burke, *Reflections on the Revolution in France*, ed. and intr. Connor Cruise O'Brien (1790; Harmondsworth: Penguin, 1969), p. 181.

63 Rowden, 'Trientalis', *Poetical Introduction*, p. 41.

64 *Ibid.*, p. 41.

65 Thornton, 'Dedication', *Temple of Flora*, unpag.

66 Text accompanying the plate 'A Group of Roses', Thornton, *Temple of Flora*, unpag.

67 Thornton, notes to Pye's poem on Strelitzia Reginae, or the Bird of Paradise Flower, *Temple of Flora*, unpag. The artist Mary Moser (1744–1819) was appointed flower painter to Queen Charlotte. She decorated a room at Frogmore in Windsor Park for Queen Charlotte, which came to be known as 'Miss Moser's room'. It is likely that she helped the Queen and princesses with their studies of plants. Queen Charlotte and the Princess Elizabeth also received lessons in botanical drawing from the Viennese artist and botanist Francis Bauer (1758–1840).

For a discussion of women flower painters, see Jack Kramer, *Women of Flowers: A Tribute to Victorian Women Illustrators*, ed. by Linda Sunshine (New York:

Stewart, Tabori & Chang, 1996). Despite its title, this text covers women botanical artists of the eighteenth and nineteenth centuries. For Mary Moser, see Bermingham, *Learning to Draw*, p. 205; For Bauer and Moser, see David Scarse, *Flower Drawings* (Cambridge: Cambridge University Press, 1997), pp. 94–6, 70–2. The seminal study on botanical illustration remains Blunt and Stearn's *The Art of Botanical Illustration*.

68 The *Strelitzia* (Bird of Paradise) was named in honour of Queen Charlotte, who came from Mecklenburg-Strelitz.

69 James Henry Pye, 'Strelitzia Reginae', in Thornton, *Temple of Flora*, lines 1–8, unpag.

70 Pye, 'Strelitzia Reginae', in Thornton, *Temple of Flora*, lines 9–12, unpag.

71 The Swedish naturalist Daniel Carl Solander (1733–82) came to England in 1760 after studying under Linnaeus at the University of Uppsala. He was secretary and librarian to Joseph Banks from 1771 until his death. He was engaged by Banks to accompany him on Cook's *Endeavour* voyage (1768–71) and visited Iceland with Banks in 1772.

72 Reverend Mr Maurice, 'Verses Addressed to Dr Thornton on the Completion of His Temple of Flora, or Garden of Nature', in *Temple of Flora*, lines 1–6, 13–16, unpag.

73 Thornton, 'An Explanation of the Picturesque Plates', *Temple of Flora*, unpag.

74 Pye, 'Strelitzia Reginae', in Thornton, *Temple of Flora*, line 3, unpag.

75 Wakefield launches an attack on French teachers in British boarding schools in *Reflections on the Present Condition of the Female Sex*, p. 47. A discussion of these ideas can be found in Leach and Goodman, 'Educating the Women of the Nation', pp. 176–8. For French women as seen by Britons, see Linda Colley, *Britons Forging the Nation 1707–1837* (New York: Vintage Books, 1996), pp. 263–6.

76 Murray, *British Garden*, p. vi

77 See John Barrell on the 1770s in *The Political Theory of Painting From Reynolds to Hazlitt: The Body of the Public* (New Haven, CT and London: Yale University Press, 1986), pp. 65–8.

78 See my exploration in Chapter 2 above of the influence of Linnaeus on Rousseau's and Wakefield's letters on botany.

79 Rowden, 'Advertisement', *A Poetical Introduction to the Study of Botany*, 2nd edn (London: Printed by A. J. Valpy; sold by Longman, Hurst, Rees, Orme, and Browne; J. White and Cochrane; J. Murray and J. Harris, 1812), p. ix.

80 Rowden, 'Advertisement', *A Poetical Introduction*, 2nd edn, p. ix.

81 See my discussion in Chapter 2. In his *Reveries*, Rousseau writes:

> as soon as our self interest or vanity are brought into play and we are concerned to obtain positions or write book ... and devote ourselves to botany merely for the sake of becoming authors or professors, all this sweet charm vanishes, we see plants simply as the instruments of our passions, we take no real pleasure in studying them, we do not want to know, but to show that we know, and the woods become merely for us a public stage where we seek applause. (Rousseau, *Reveries*, p. 116).

82 'The pleasure of going to some lonely spot in search of new plants is combined with that of escaping from my persecutors, and when I reach traces where there is no trace of men I breathe freely, as if I were in a refuge where their hate could no longer pursue me' (Rousseau, *Reveries*, p. 117).

83 From Smith's notes to 'To the Goddess of Botany', in *Poems*, pp. 68–9. Jacqueline

Labbe has argued that Smith used the footnote as a 'navigating tool':

> For her, the marginal nature of footnotes proved an opportunity to explore spaces not thought proper for a woman to visit, and in the footnotes she created a marginal persona whose grasp of history, botany, science and culture was unfettered by convention. (Jacqueline Labbe, "Transplanted into More Congenial Soil': Footnoting the Self in the Poetry of Charlotte Smith', in Joe Bray, Miriam Handley and Anne C. Henry (eds), *Ma(r)king the Text: The Presentation of Meaning on the Literary Page* (Aldershot: Ashgate, 2000), pp. 71–86 (pp. 72–3)).

84 William Blake, 'Auguries of Innocence', *The Complete Poems*, ed. Alicia Ostriker (Harmondsworth: Penguin, 1977), lines 1–2, p. 506.

4

Forward plants and wanton women: botany and sexual anxiety in the late eighteenth century

CHAPTER 3 DEMONSTRATED how one of the earliest proponents of women's botany, William Withering, attempted to censor Linnaeus by disguising the sexual distinctions in the titles to the classes and orders, replacing gendered sexualised terms such as 'pistil' and 'stamen' with 'chive' and 'pointal'.[1] Moreover, as the fashion for 'ladies botany' became more prevalent in the later eighteenth century, moralists would again hold that the Sexual System of classification was not conducive to female delicacy. Women's botany comes under attack in Richard Polwhele's *The Unsex'd Females* (1798):

> Botany has lately become a fashionable amusement with the ladies. But how the study of the sexual system of plants can accord with female modesty, I am not able to comprehend.[2]

Opposition to women practising the modern system of botany intensified in the years leading up to the French Revolution and the wars with France when a backlash against the Sexual System occurred, fuelled by anxieties over moral and social disorder and the increasing fluidity of gender differences. Linda Colley has charted the deepening anxieties surrounding these shifting gender roles in late eighteenth-century Britain. By this time, 'the boundaries supposedly separating men and women were, in fact, unstable, *and becoming more so*' (my emphasis).[3]

Alongside the female botanist, Polwhele selected for censure those literary women who had transgressed into the political sphere and followed the example of the 'Arch-priestess of female Libertinism', Mary Wollstonecraft, by giving their support to French revolutionary politics.[4] Anna Laetitia Barbauld, once regarded as a 'chaste and elegant' writer, was deemed the most 'conspicuous figure' in a group of women poets who no longer hide 'the smile of complacency, the glow of self-congratulation'.[5] Barbauld published her 'Epistle to William Wilberforce' on the evils of the slave trade under her own name in 1791; she also published three political tracts anonymously between 1790 and 1793.[6] This pamphleteering coincided with her new interest in botany. Samuel Rogers remarked that 'in spite of her correct taste, Mrs. Barbauld was quite fascinated with Darwin's *Botanic Garden* when it first appeared and talked of it with rapture; for which I scolded her heartily'.[7] Unease about Linnaean botany posing a threat to female modesty was spreading due to the publication of Darwin's *Loves of the Plants*. For Polwhele, Barbauld's preoccupation with Darwin's botany was indicative of her dissenting religion and liberal political views; it contributed to his attack on her in the *Unsex'd Females*.[8]

In writing *The Botanic Garden*, Darwin was reworking themes and material from the poems of Anna Seward. She had written verses on Darwin's botanic garden at Lichfield where plants were grouped according to the Linnaean scheme. Darwin sent Seward's verses to the *Gentleman's Magazine* for publication without informing her that he had substituted eight lines of his own composition for her last six, causing a disagreement between them. Darwin thought Seward's verse should 'form the exordium of a great work' and began to develop the idea of committing the Linnaean system to verse:[9]

> The Linnaean system is unexplored poetic ground, and an happy subject for the muse. It affords fine scope for poetic landscape; it suggests metamorphoses of the Ovidian kind, though reversed. Ovid made men and women into flowers, plants, and trees. You should make flowers, plants, trees into men and women. I, continued he, will write the notes, which must be scientific; and you shall write the verse.[10]

Seward declined to write the Linnaean verses for Darwin because 'the plan was not strictly proper for a female pen'.[11] When she published her *Memoirs of the Life of Dr Darwin* in 1804, however, she defended Darwin's account of the floral harems because they came from Linnaeus and were grounded in fact: 'let it never be forgotten that the sexual nature of plants has a demonstrated existence'.[12]

Seward was not alone in this fraught textual relationship with Darwin: a new genre of women's writing, the botanical poem with scientific notes, was emerging, developing directly out of *The Botanic Garden*. Elizabeth Moody's 'To Dr. Darwin, On Reading His Loves of the Plants' appeared in 1798. Arabella Rowden's ambiguous alliance with Darwin is discussed in Chapter 3 (she took the *Botanic Garden* as the model for her *Poetical Introduction to the Study of Botany* in 1801), and Charlotte Smith's 'Flora' (1804) was essentially a re-working of Darwin's poem for young female readers. Sarah Hoare's *A Poem on the Pleasures and Advantages of Botanical Pursuits* (1818; 1825) also drew on Darwin's *Botanic Garden*. However, these literary women remained silent on the issue of plant sexuality, and downplayed Darwin's colourful descriptions of the sex life of plants. This chapter explores all of these poems in relation to Darwin, beginning with a detailed look at Darwin's *Loves of the Plants*. The controversy surrounding this work changed the course of women's botany in England and ushered in a new, less enlightened age, dominated by works on 'ladies' botany' which rejected Linnaeus's Sexual System in favour of a 'natural system' of classification.

The Loves of the Plants

Linnaeus's classification of the natural world in *Systema Naturae* (1735) was inspired by Ovidian metamorphoses between plant and human and the language of the Book of Psalms.[13] Significantly, Linnaeus also referred to his wife as 'my *monandrian* lily'. The lily symbolised her purity and *monandrian*, referring to the first Linnaean class *Monandria*, which is named from the Greek *μσνανδροζ* – 'having one husband' – affirmed her chastity.[14] These Ovidian comparisons and gendered analogies between women and flowers were taken up into Darwin's poem through the Sexual System. Formerly Ovid had transformed men, women – even gods and goddesses – into trees and flowers; Darwin, 'by similar art', restored them to 'their original animality, after having remained prisoners so long in their respective vegetable mansions'.[15]

Darwin's poem functions as a 'Camera Obscura' through which pictures of plants are presented to our view and 'magnified into apparent life' for our amusement (Proem, v). Darwin begins by projecting an image of blissful monogamy illustrative of the class *Monoecia,* which has one male stamen and one female pistil, and ends with tableaux of polygamy and sexual freedom. The transposed images become increasingly erotic, detailing the descent into sexual anarchy, symbolised by the appearance of the plant named after Adonis (*Adonis vernalis*) in Tahiti.

Darwin's reversal of Ovidian metamorphosis commences with *Canna*, the virtuous Indian Reed, in which one male stamen and one female pistil inhabit each flower. His description is steeped in the language of epic heroism, with the reed depicting male virility:

> First the tall CANNA lifts his curled brow
> Erect to heaven, and plights his nuptial vow;
> The virtuous pair, in milder regions born,
> Dread the rude blast of Autumn's icy morn;
> Round the chill fair he folds his crimson vest,
> And clasps the timorous beauty to his breast.
> (I. 39–44)

At first this appears to be a safe image of monogamous love in which the 'virtuous pair' delay their embrace until the heroic male has plighted his 'nuptial vow'. The fair female satisfies ideals of female modesty: 'chill' and 'timorous' in the protective arms of her 'husband'. Even the fruit of this union exemplifies virtue and propriety; the seeds 'are strung for prayer-beads in catholic countries' (note to I. 39). However, a closer reading indicates that the image of heroic virtue cannot suppress the underlying eroticism in the image of the male, 'Erect to heaven', as he 'plights his nuptial vow'(I. 40).

As the poem continues, the descriptions of plant reproduction become increasingly improper until just about every form of sexual union (sisters with brothers, mothers with sons) has been identified in the plant kingdom. In the following extract, a number of promiscuous plants are united to maximum effect. *Genista,* or Dyer's Broom, has ten males wooing one female, and *Melissa*, or Balm, has four males and one female residing on the same plant. The suggestion of promiscuity is heightened by the appearance of 'laughing belle', *Meadia* (American Cowslip) – a golden-haired harlot wantonly flirting with her five 'beaux':

> Sweet blooms GENISTA in the myrtle shade,
> And *ten* fond brothers woo the haughty maid.
> *Two* knights before thy fragrant alter bend,
> Adored MELISSA! and *two* squires attend.
> MEADIA'S soft chains *five* suppliant beaux confess,
> And hand in hand the laughing belle address;
> Alike to all, she bows with wanton air,
> Rolls her dark eye, and waves her golden hair.
> (IV. 57–64)

The poem's finale gives us some indication of how Darwin intended his poetic description of the sex life of plants to be received. Here Darwin unites the 'vegetable loves' in one promiscuous union, transferring them to a South Sea island setting where they take part in the nuptials of a Tahitian marriage ceremony: 'the society called the Areoi in the island of Otaheite', consists 'of about a hundred males and a hundred females who form one promiscuous marriage' (note to IV. 388). Polygamy descends into orgiastic chaos with the appearance of plants in which

> A *hundred* virgins join a *hundred* swains,
> And fond ADONIS leads the sprightly trains;
> Pair after pair, along his sacred groves
> To Hymen's fane the bright procession moves;
> Each smiling youth a myrtle garland shades,
> And wreaths of roses veil the blushing maids;
> Light joys on twinkling feet attend the throng,
> Weave the gay dance, or raise the frolic song;
> Thick, as they pass, exulting cupids sling
> Promiscuous arrows from the sounding string;
> On wings of gossamer soft whispers fly,
> And the sly Glance steals side-long from the eye.
> As round his shrine the gaudy circles bow,
> And seal with muttering lips the faithless vow,
> Licentious Hymen joins their mingled hands,
> And loosely twines the meretricious bands.
> Thus where pleased VENUS, in the southern main,
> Sheds all her smiles on Otaheite's plain,
> Wide o'er the isle her silken net she draws,
> And the Loves laugh at all, but Nature's laws.
> (IV. 387–406)

Darwin's bold descriptions of Tahiti featuring the promiscuous society of Areoi are likely to be based on John Hawkesworth's account of Cook's voyage to the South Pacific in the *Endeavour* in 1768. Hawkesworth collated Banks's and Cook's journals from the voyages, rewriting the two accounts as one, re-imagining some events and interspersing speculations and pronouncements of his own.[16] He wrote of the Areoi:

> A very considerable number of the principle people of Otaheite, of both sexes, have formed themselves into a society in which every woman is common to every man;

> thus securing a perpetual variety as often as their inclination prompts them to seek it, which is so frequent, that the same man and woman seldom cohabit together more than two or three days. These societies are distinguished by the name of *Arreoy*.[17]

Elsewhere, a number of passages dwell on Hawkesworth's envisaging of more erotic Tahitian customs and uninhibited sexual displays: 'A young man, near six feet high, performed the rites of Venus with a little girl about eleven or twelve years of age, before several of our people' (128).[18] Hawkesworth also describes the dance called the *Timorodee*, 'consisting of motions and gestures beyond imagination wanton' (206), performed by young girls 'as an incitement to desires which it is said are frequently gratified upon the spot' (207–8). Darwin's plants imitate the rituals of the *Arreoy* and participate in a nuptial dance. Adonis and 'Licentious Hymen' appear in the closing lines of the poem and take part in this fitting finale of rampant sexuality, culminating in the provocative image of Venus smiling over the plains of Tahiti, the land of free love.[19]

Hawkesworth unwittingly provided rich source material for satirists who revived the form of those botanical satires employed in *The Man Plant*, but now targeted at the Linnaean, Joseph Banks – or the Banks depicted in the *Account*.[20] In *An Epistle From Mr Banks, Voyager, Monster Hunter and Amoroso To Oberea, Queen of Otaheite* (1773), Banks is lampooned for having more experience of exotic women than exotic plants and for his supposed liaisons with Oberea, which gave license to many sexual puns: 'I own the plants thy love has given to me, / But what a plant did I produce to thee!'.[21] Oberea is featured dancing the *Timorodee* for Banks who is caught inspecting the tattooed buttocks of Tahitian women. The coupling of Banks and Oberea became a common motif.[22] Women botanists also took up this theme: Arabella Rowden depicted the 'Sad Queen of Otaheite Mourning her Idol Banks' under the shade of a banana tree.[23] Rowden's poem, appearing in *A Poetical Introduction to the Study of Botany* in 1801, indicates that public interest in Banks's supposed sexual encounters with exotic women was sustained over a long period. However, Rowden, rather than participating in the satirical mood against Banks, instead empathises with the mourning queen.

Banks became the object of bawdy humour in *Mimosa; or, The Sensitive Plant* (1779), a poem attributed to James Perry. Here, the mimosa, which is sensitive to touch, represents both the male and female sexual organs. Banks the plant hunter is constantly in search of new varieties of the 'sensitive plant' (that is, the vagina) and the females he encounters are equally fascinated by the amazing qualities of his English mimosa, his 'sensitive plant' (the penis): 'various and many are the kinds, / The botanist, and female finds / of this luxuriant plant'.[24]

Linnaean botany, it seems, could not now dissociate itself from sexual connotation due to Hawkesworth's account of the Linnaean, Joseph Banks, in Tahiti, and to Darwin's florid account of the Sexual System, both of which featured images of sexual promiscuity. Darwin transferred his plants to the non-Christian world of Tahiti in order to address human sexuality more freely. He used the overt artificiality of pastoral convention with its gendered images of happy swains and blushing maids in order to comment on the artificiality of all modes of sexual behaviour. It is likely that the sexual customs of Tahiti were misinterpreted in accounts of the voyages; despite this, Hawkesworth's descriptions of the sexual relations of the 'Arreoy' led to the recognition that the patriarchal family and monogamous marriage were not universal human institutions – different societies had developed other arrangements.[25] Darwin's *Loves of the Plants* reinforced these ideas: his plants 'laugh at all, but Nature's laws' (IV. 406) and emphasise the artificiality of monogamy.[26]

In contrast, Linnaean terminology suggests that plant sexuality remains within the confines of marriage. The names of the Linnaean classes and orders are derived from the Greek, formed from the roots *andros* (ανηρ, ανδρσξ; man or husband) and *gynae* (γυνη; woman or wife).[27] In *Systema Naturae* the marriages are divided into public or clandestine (plants whose flowers are not discernible), which reflects social custom, being the two types of marriage in law.[28] Until Darwin, the vegetable world appeared to mirror the mores of eighteenth-century European society; Darwin demonstrated that plants were more analogous to so-called primitive South Sea Islanders like the Arreoy who thrived on what seemed to be sexual anarchy, rather than monogamy and order.[29]

The Botanic Garden and the female botanist

Darwin showed an awareness of his prospective readers, capturing the female market for both introductory books on botany and the feminised form of romance. The floral harems are central to his poem and he addresses his descriptions of vegetable courtship to women. His plants amuse like elegant, cultivated women 'by the beauty of their persons, their graceful attitudes, or the brilliancy of their dress' (Proem, vii). Darwin's suggestion that Seward should compose the verse while he compiled the scientific notes implied that different classes of readers might be involved: those who would confine themselves to the poetry and those educated in science and philosophy who would engage with the scientific notes. Women with an interest in botany, however, might well be awakened to an enthusiasm for both.[30]

Judith Pascoe describes the *Loves of the Plants* as 'a curious hybrid of detailed scientific tract and cheap romance, in which anthropomorphized plants engage in languid scenes of courtship'.[31] However, this is a somewhat reductive and unsatisfactory description of Darwin's use of analogy. The Linnaean classes and orders provide the structure for the poem but it is the plant's human analogues that engage the reader, direct the poem and ultimately shape its meaning. In this section I aim to bring out the radical aspects of the poem, demonstrating how Darwin explores the social and sexual behaviour of women through the sexual system of botany. What is subversive about *The Loves of Plants* is the active part females play in these processes; the female pistils are assigned a central role in courtship and reproduction whereas each male, or stamen, is represented merely as the 'swain' or 'beau' of the females. Throughout the poem foreign plants give licence to more overt images of female sexuality and desire than do their English counterparts.

Darwin's plant-women are archetypal females: angel, virgin, whore, sorceress, Amazon, good and bad mother. In the index to the floral vignettes, which Darwin calls the 'Catalogue of the Poetic Exhibition', female subjects range from 'Harlots', 'Lady and cauldron', 'Coquet', and 'Turkish lady in an undress', to 'Angel bathing', 'Forlorn nymph', and 'Lady burying her child in the plague'. All are subject to stereotyping. Plants in which the female pistil has four or more stamen-suitors are characterised as wanton. The first of these vegetable harlots is *Meadia dodecatheon*, or American cowslip, where the female 'in gay undress' is fertilised by five male stamens. *Lychnis*, another 'wanton', has ten male stamens to five female pistils and appears in the catalogue to the poetic exhibition under the title 'Coquet'.

The females of the climbing plant *Cuscuta*, or Dodder (four males/stamens, two females/pistils) are 'Harlot-Nymphs' who entrap the males with their 'dangerous charms'. Half harlot, half nymph, the females are both wanton and chaste, seductresses disguised as modest virgins. The unsuspecting males fall victim to the predatory behaviour of the females:

In the meek garb of modest worth disguised,
The eye averted, and the smile chastised,
With sly approach they spread their dangerous charms,
And round their victim wind their wiry arms.
(III. 261–4)

Darwin interprets the behaviour of *Cuscuta,* entwining itself around a tree or shrub which it finally smothers, as sexual.

Gloriosa (six males/stamens, one female/pistil) is the most striking of Darwin's vegetable harlots. The male stamens develop at different rates and half reach maturity a few days before the others. The female pistil is fertilised by both groups of males. Darwin personifies *Gloriosa* as the celebrated female voluptuary, Ninon de L'Enclos. Contemporary readers would be familiar with Madame de L'Enclos, whose memoirs were translated from the French and published by Dodsley in 1761. Banks unkindly remarked that Oberea seemed

> to us to act in the character of a Ninon d'Enclos [sic] who satiated with her lover resolves to change him at all Events ... I am offered if I please to supply his place, but I am at present otherwise engag'd; indeed was I free as air her majesties person is not the most desireable.[32]

Darwin's Ninon not only entertains lovers of many different ages (stamens at varying stages of maturity), she wantonly seduces her own son:

So NINON pruned her wither'd charms, and won
With Harlot-smiles her gay unconscious son;—
Clasp'd in his arms she own'd a mother's name,
Shook her grey locks, and tittering mock'd his flame;
With mad despair he plunged the guilty dart,
And life and love gush'd mingled from his heart!
(I. 125–30)

Seward argued that Ninon's intentions towards her son were 'purely maternal': 'the declaration by which she repulses his impious suit, entirely acquits her of the least design to inspire him with passion'.[33] She implied that Darwin's portrait of Ninon as an ageing harlot and unnatural mother was unjust:

> In the first edition of *Loves of the Plants* this extraordinary woman received both personal and mental injustice from the prelude to that story. She is there represented by the poet, as wrinkled, grey and paralytic; circumstances incompatible with the possibility of the attachment, and contrary to the representation of her biographers. Upon their testimony we learn that Ninon retained a large portion of her personal beauty and graces to an almost incredible period; that it was considerable enough to procure her young lovers at the age of eighty.[34]

In later editions of *Loves of the Plants*, Darwin softened his approach to Ninon, replacing 'harlot smiles' with 'fatal smiles', but he is still unwilling to portray a woman such as Ninon, with a sexual history, as anything other than a dangerous harlot.

The *Hedysarum movens*, or moving plant ('two brotherhoods, ten males'), is the Turkish 'maid', Chunda.[35] The rising and falling of the plant's leaves, which are 'continually in spontaneous motion', are transformed into the 'rising bosom' of a 'panting' Turkish maid:

> Fair CHUNDA smiles amid the burning waste,
> Her brow unturban'd, and her zone unbrac'd;
> *Ten* brother-youths with light umbrellas shade,
> Or fan with busy hands the panting maid;
> Loose wave her locks, disclosing, as they break,
> The rising bosom and averted cheek;
> Clasp'd round her ivory neck with studs of gold
> Flows her thin vest in many a silky fold;
> O'er her light limbs the dim transparence plays,
> And the fair form, it seems to hide, betrays.
> (IV. 237–46)

'Unturban'd' and 'unbrac'd', her hair hanging 'loose', Chunda represents unbridled female sexuality; her thin transparent dress simultaneously hides and reveals her shapely form.[36] She is the brazen Other to such chaste English maids as *Galantha* the snowdrop, who displays her modesty by blushing sweetly when she is pursued by 'six rival swains'.[37]

Gentle pastoral conventions are used to evoke commonplace native plants whereas 'exotics' such as *Hedysarum movens* are described in the extravagant language of contemporary travel narratives. Women such as Lady Mary Wortley Montagu and Elizabeth Craven, who had travelled to Constantinople, observed that, in spite of their confinement, Turkish women seemed to exercise greater liberty than English women, who lacked autonomy and freedom in marriage and were confined to the private sphere.[38] ''Tis very easy to see,' wrote Montagu, 'they have, in reality more liberty than we have'.[39] The custom and dress of Turkish women provided anonymity (no woman of whatever rank was allowed to go into the streets without a headdress or *murlin*, which covered all but the eyes, and a *ferigee* which wrapped around the body and head like a riding hood), freeing them from any distinction of rank:

> there is no distinguishing the great lady from her slave. 'Tis impossible for the most jealous husband to know his wife, when he meets her, and no man may touch or follow a woman in the street. This perpetual masquerade gives them entire liberty of following their inclinations without danger of discovery.[40]

Darwin appears to have been influenced by these accounts of Turkish women. Montagu recounts how Turkish women would often recline on sofas with their slaves seated behind them. They were sometimes attended by black eunuchs but their slaves were usually girls of about seventeen or eighteen. Fanned by ten 'brother-youths', Chunda enjoys even greater liberty than was customary. Orientalising the *Hedysarum movens*, or moving plant, as a 'Turkish lady in an undress', Darwin transfers female eroticism onto the exotic Other, upholding notions of English virtue.

Alongside the harlots, another female group to emerge are the witches or enchantresses. *Rubia madder* (four males/stamens, one female/pistil), used for making red dye, is depicted bending over her cauldron like Medea who restored Æson, Jason's father, to the full vigour of youth – an apt allusion to the faded beauty who restores her lost youth with rouge.[41] The poppy ('many males, many females' (note to II. 268)) is *Papavar*, a drowsy sorceress who freezes the 'vital currents' (II. 284) of the nymphs with one wave of her 'ebon wand' (II. 276). Her feminine charms are as dangerous as opium: 'In small quantities it exhilarates the mind, raises the passions, and invigorates the body; in large ones it is succeeded by intoxication, languor, stupor and death' (note to II. 268). *Circea*, Enchanter's Nightshade ('two males, one female'), is used for 'raising the devil' (note to I. 7); Darwin's *Circea* 'waves her dread wand' over tombs of the dead (III. 10). *Prunus laurocerasus* (twenty males/stamens, one female/pistil) is a furious priestess with foaming lips and 'wild dishevel'd hair' (III. 39–50).[42]

The most sentimental of the vignettes are those depicting mothers. The parent root of the *Orchis morio*, which shrivels up and dies as the young shoot increases, is likened to a doting mother nursing her infant at the expense of her own life. The tulip bulb was thought to contain next year's flower in miniature;[43] the embryo tulip inspired Darwin's depiction of the tulip mother sheltering her infant in an underground cave:

> Quick flies fair TULIPA the loud alarms,
> And folds her infant closer in her arms;
> In some lone cave, secure pavillion, lies,
> And waits the courtship of serener skies.
> (I. 177–80)

The parent plant of the cyclamen evokes female sensibility and emphasises the bond between mother and child. The reproduction process in this plant is described in full: 'when the seeds are ripe, the stalk of the flower gradually twists itself spirally downwards, until it touches the ground, and forcibly penetrating the earth lodges its seeds; which are thought to receive nourishment from the parent root' (note to III. 311). The burying process explicitly refers to a grieving mother in plague-ridden London resigning her departed infants to the grave and piously willing their resurrection.[44] Seward referred to this vignette as 'perhaps the sublimest passage in the whole work':[45]

Long with wide eye-lids on her Child she gazed,
And long to heaven their tearless orbs she raised;
Then with quick foot and throbbing heart she found
Where Chartreuse open'd deep his holy ground;
Bore her last treasure through the midnight gloom,
And kneeling drop'd it in the mighty tomb;
'I follow next!' the frantic mourner said,
And living plunged amid the festering dead. (III. 335–42)

Such sentimental portraits of nurturing plant-mothers contrast with untypical females such as *Arum*, or cuckoo-pint, which is of the Linnaean class XX, *Gynandria*, or 'masculine ladies'. Arum appears in the poetic catalogue as 'Lady in regimentals'. The pistil or female part of the flower is enlarged, rising 'like a club' or lance, covered or clothed by male stamens; because of the phallic appearance of the female it is metamorphosised into an Amazon in military attire:

With net-wove sash and glittering gorget dress'd,
and scarlet robe lapell'd upon her breast,
Stern ARA frowns, the measured march assumes,
Trails her long lance, and nods her shadowy plumes;
With Love's soft beams illume her treacherous eyes,
And Beauty lightens through the thin disguise.
(IV. 187–92)

Dryden's imitation of Juvenal's sixth satire provided a model for the use of the Amazon trope in the eighteenth century.[46] Dryden's Amazons assume the role of men by dressing in military garb and fighting as gladiators.[47] Amazonian women reputedly cut off one of their breasts in order to use their weapons more efficiently; hence the stern look, military attire and 'measured march' of Darwin's Ara. Attacks on masculine women of this kind fitted with wider cultural concerns around gender, especially in the 1790s where, as Linda Colley has noted, 'separate sexual spheres were being increasingly prescribed in theory, yet increasingly broken through in practice'.[48] 'Amazon' had undergone a degeneration of meaning and was extended to radical feminists and prominent literary women such as Wollstonecraft and Mary Hays. 'Amazonian' is the term Polwhele uses in 1790 to describe his 'Unsex'd Females' – bold unruly women who have abandoned their 'softer charms' in pursuit of reason and invoked a 'gallic frenzy' which has 'unsex'd' them.[49] Darwin's scarlet-robed, treacherous-eyed, 'masculine lady', Ara, has a fictional counterpart in Defoe's *Roxana*, another '*Man-Woman*' whose very name means 'whore'.[50] Arum was thought to be an aphrodisiac due to its phallic-shaped spadix.[51]

Callitriche or fine-hair stargrass, where 'one male and two females inhabit each flower', is unusual in that it is the only plant where there are more females

14 Philip Reinagle, 'Cupid Inspiring Plants with Love'. Reproduced from Thornton, *Temple of Flora*

than males. Here '*two* virgins share' one beautiful 'youth'. The solitary male is uninterested in the females and self-absorbed. Living solely in the company of women, he has become feminised (symbolised by his 'floating train of tresses') and Narcissus-like, admiring his 'fair features' in 'the watery glass'. Darwin's note informs us that in this plant 'the male sometimes lives in a separate flower'; the females are said to be 'smit' with the starry-eyed youth but Darwin avoids an erotic image of troilism, opting instead to depict a feminine male who abstains from sexual union with the females (I. 45).

Darwin seems intent on proving that the female role in courtship and reproduction was far from passive, depicting females actively pursuing males, but the succession of blushing maids and wanton harlots leads one to question just how liberal his views on the social and sexual behaviour of women were. Chapter 1 shows how such analogies between women and flowers embody male desire and are indicative of the problematic representation of women in culture. These linguistic conventions epitomise Wollstonecraft's 'language of men'[52] and point to a 'botany for gentlemen', rather than 'ladies'.[53] And yet Darwin perceives botany as a specifically feminine occupation. Flora, the goddess of botany and Darwin's muse, acts as a female botanist, guiding the reader through the Linnaean schemes of Darwin's botanic garden (see Fig. 14). Darwin addresses his poem to women and celebrates women in the culture of botany. Female Linnaeans such as Linnaeus's daughter, Elisabeth, and Mary Delany appear in floral vignettes, together with a number of women who have excelled in the botanical arts such as Emma Crewe (1768–1850) and Angelica Kauffman (1741–1807): 'So with waving pencil CREWE commands / The realms of Taste, and Fancy's Fairy Lands' (II. 291–2). Crewe was responsible for the elegant frontispiece to the *Loves of the Plants*, 'Flora at Play with Cupid' (see Fig. 14). Alluding to the marriage of plants, Flora is dressed in a bridal gown adorned with flowers while, in the foreground, Cupid has donned a labourer's apron and hat. In a comic reversal, Flora mischievously inspires the plants with love using Cupid's bow and arrow, while Cupid, commonly represented at play, is busy with his gardening tools. Darwin openly celebrates Crewe's interpretation of the sexual system, whereas Polwhele considered this representation of licentiousness as unbefitting a woman. He complained in the *Unsex'd Females* that Crewe 'rather overstepped the modesty of nature, by giving the portrait an air of voluptuousness too luxuriously melting' (note to line 106). The iconography of Cupid as a personification of the sexual system recurs in Philip Reinagle's similar plate of 'Cupid Inspiring the Plants with Love' from Robert Thornton's *Temple of Flora* (see Fig. 15).

Darwin continues to address women who have cultivated a knowledge of botany. Mary Delany designed and sculptured a *Hortus Siccus*, or paper garden, consisting of some nine hundred and seventy accurate representations of flowers according to the classification of Linnaeus;[54] Darwin celebrates her in a simile relating her to the plant *Papyra*:

—So now DELANEY [*sic*] forms her mimic bowers,
Her paper foliage, and her silken flowers;
Her virgin train the tender scissors ply,
Vein the green leaf, the purple petal dye:
Round wiry stems the flaxen tendril bends,
Moss creeps below, and waxen fruit impends.
Cold Winter views amid his realms of snow
DELANEY'S vegetable statues blow;
Smoothes his stern brow, delays his hoary wing,
And eyes with wonder all the blooms of spring.
(II. 153–62)

Linnaeus's daughter was remarkable in publishing a short botanical report in the *Transactions of the Royal Swedish Academy of Sciences* in 1762 on the electrical or phosphorescent effects in nasturtiums, observed in her garden at Uppsala.[55] Darwin exalts Elisabeth Linnaeus, depicting her as the 'chaste tropæo' or garden nasturtium, a virtuous female pistil courted by eight 'watchful swains', or male stamens. He dramatises her acting out the curious phenomena of sparks emitted around the flower – the nasturtium's electric flashes that she herself had

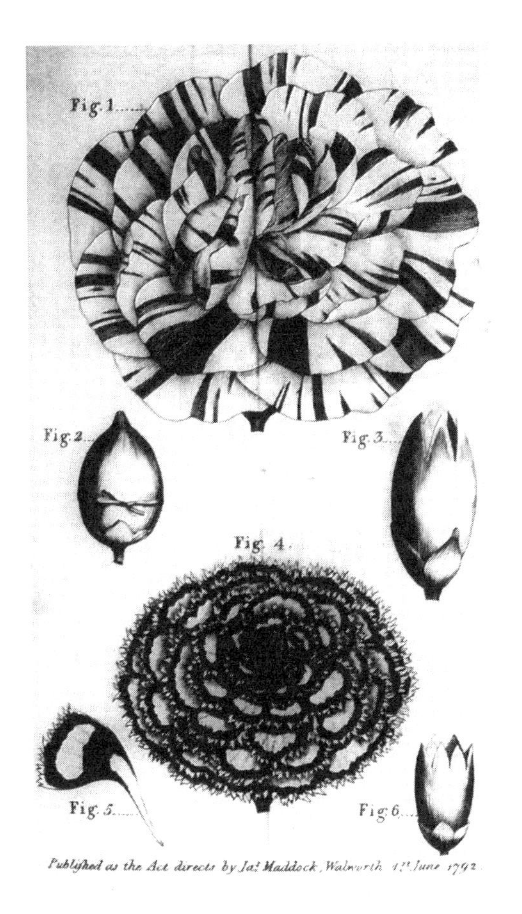

15 The Variegated Double Carnation. Reproduced from James Maddock, *The Florist's Directory*

observed. She appears as a 'virgin light' and a 'saint like glory trembles round her head' (IV. 45–50). Having looked in detail at Darwin's plants we can now see that Darwin has feminised botany to such an extent that it has become a discourse on the social and sexual behaviour of women.

A number of texts published in the last decade of the eighteenth century draw directly on Darwinian botany in their discussions of female sexuality. James Plumptre's *The Lakers* (1798), which I touched on in my introduction, is one such text. Veronica, the heroine of Plumptre's play is 'a great botanist' (I.1.2) who is on a picturesque tour of the lakes. Veronica is also in search of a titled husband. She sets her sights on Sir Charles Portinscale, a would-be suitor to her niece Lydia. Sir Charles disguises himself as a botanist and guide to escape the unwelcome attentions of Veronica, Lydia's aunt. In this guise he is able to amuse the ladies with his knowledge of plants, poetry and the picturesque. He is often seen engaging in a flirtatious dialogue around botany:

> *Sir Charles*: The *touch me not*! It is found in great plenty near Windermere. It is a pity that your Ladyship is so entirely unacquainted with it, as it is a curious plant, and well worthy your attention – This, Madam is the delightful village of Grange, celebrated for its hospitality to Mr. Gray; and this the gorge of Borrowdale, whose terrible appearance intimidated him from exploring further these finest of scenes.[56]

Sir Charles is an obvious caricature of Erasmus Darwin, and Veronica makes no secret of her admiration of his botanical/sexual knowledge: 'Oh Sir Charles! I am no stranger to your perfect knowledge of the Linnaean system' (I.3.17). Throughout the text botanical conversation is made to substitute for discussions around courtship and to refer to possible marriages or sexual unions. 'Pray, Sir Charles, could you be contented to be a *monogynia* all your life?' (I.1.11), asks Veronica. The footnotes inform the reader that '*monogynia,* in botanic language, signifies possessing one female' (I.1.11). Lydia is rather naïve when it comes to men and Veronica is keen for her to learn botany: 'Do Mr Botanist instruct her a little; show her a *cryptogamy* or two' (I.3.12). This is, of course, a reference to clandestine marriage in Linnaean terms.

In a comic twist Sir Charles orders his servant Speedwell to impersonate him and to pursue Veronica, so that he might woo Lydia. During this unlikely courtship Veronica often speaks of herself in botanical terms, as a female plant, and this allows Plumptre to orchestrate a number of comic Darwinian dialogues. For example, she declares 'I am not a *mesembryanthemum crystallium*, I could not forbear now and then showing a little spontaneity of scintillation: I am certainly phosphorescent like the *Trepoeolum*' (II.1.30). When she is pursued by Sample and Speedwell, who are both pretending to be Sir Charles, she exclaims, 'I remind myself of *Collinsonia*', before reciting Darwin's account of this adulterous female plant from *The Botanic Garden* (I.51–6):

> *Two brother swains, of* Collin's *gentle name,*
> *The same their features, and their forms the same,*
> *With rival love for fair* Collinia *sigh,*
> *Knit the dark brow, and roll th' unsteady eye:*
> *With sweet concern the pitying beauty mourns;*
> And soothes with simpering smiles, the pair by turns. (II.1.31)

Veronica is a disciple of Darwin and Linnaeus, and Plumptre suggests in his preface that *The Botanic Garden* might act as a key to his play. Plumptre is clearly lampooning Darwin throughout in the figure of Sir Charles who speaks in mock Darwinian verse and is seen advocating botany as a means of seduction:

> *Sir Charles*: I question whether your knowledge does not exceed Veronica's. I have often explained to you the outlines of Linnaeus's System of Vegetables; you therefore can very well
>
> In filmy, gawsy, gossamery lines,
> With lucid language and conceal'd designs,
> In sweet monandrian monogynian strains
> Pant for your mistress in botanic pains. (II.1.24)

Plumptre points to the dangerous allure of Darwin's poetry here and Speedwell is advised to adopt a similarly poetic approach when attempting to seduce Veronica, who is 'deeply versed in the mysteries of the loves of the plants' (II.3.52).

As to Plumptre's stance towards women botanists themselves in the play, it is significant that it is the deluded, predatory aunt and not the sensible, modest, more desirable niece, who practises botany (the only other female who displays an interest in botany is Veronica's incorrigible maid, Anna). Veronica's botanising is symptomatic of her lack of decorum and her wantonness. Speedwell wonders whether such a woman would ever make a suitable wife:

> she is a botanist, and deeply versed in the mysteries of the loves of the plants; and she who is bawd to a blossom, may not be very nice in the intercourse of her own species. (II.3.52)

Veronica's artfully dishevelled appearance when out botanising is a further indication of her precocity 'her hair partly done up in a silk net, partly hanging lose, a straw hat and green veil, her gown fantastically drawn up' (II.1.27). Self-deluded and foolish, Veronica is eventually undone by botany: 'blinded by vanity folly and botanic nuptials' (II.1.23), she makes an unlikely match and agrees to marry Speedwell, Sir Charles's servant, because 'the incident would be picturesque; and it would be perfectly botanic for Veronica and Speedwell to marry' (II.3.58).

Plumptre is humorous in his portrayal of Veronica, the forward female botanist, throughout the main action of the play but his preface has a darker, more serious, tone:

> The Author assures himself he is not singular in thinking the study of Botany not altogether a proper amusement for the more polished sex; and the false taste of a licentious age, which is gaining ground, and corrupting the soft and elegant manners of the otherwise loveliest part of creation, requires every discouragement which can be given. (xii)

The Lakers is one of a number of texts that purposefully attack Darwin and his female disciples. Plumptre was a Church of England clergyman as well as a playwright. Many of the clergy (Polwhele, for example) did not like the direction botany had taken since Linnaeus. Plumptre's involvement with drama was as a moral educator; he wished to improve its tone.[57]

After the publication of *The Botanic Garden*, Darwin was seen as an advocate of free love, whose views threatened to undermine English society.[58] The debate around taste and propriety in relation to botany continued and Darwin came under attack again in Thomas James Mathias's satirical poem *The Pursuits of Literature* (1798), published in the same year as *The Lakers*, for inciting wanton or immodest behaviour in young women in the guise of expounding Linnaean botany. Parodying the *Botanic Garden*, Mathias portrays Darwin enticing young girls to 'Pant for a *pystill* in botanick pains'.[59] A variation of this line – '*Pant for your mistress in botanic pains*' – appears in *The Lakers*. Mathias suggests that Darwin's poem produces the conditions for unnatural, premature growth, acting like a hotbed for forcing florist flowers. James Lee claimed 'no luxuriant flowers are natural, but all [are] monsters'.[60] Darwin's forward plants are monstrous girls, female botanists who 'Raise lust in pinks; and with unhallow'd fire / Bid the soft virgin violet expire'.[61] The premature development of flowers unnaturally forced in a hotbed is an appropriate metaphor for forward botanising girls: 'Precocity' originally referred to the early flowering or ripeness of plants.[62] 'Forward' in Johnson's *Dictionary* has obvious sexual connotations, meaning 'Ardent; eager; hot; violent', as well as 'Ready; confident; presumptuous' and it is also defined as 'premature or early ripe'.

Mathias critiques literary taste by attacking those who prefer Darwin's 'exotick poetry', his 'distortion' of 'sentiment' and 'harlotry' of 'ornament', to the poetry of Dryden and Pope. Darwin is exposed as a poet/florist who has reared exotics by 'artificial heat' whereas the flowers of Mathias's own rhetoric have been produced by 'the common sun'. 'Modern ears are absolutely *debauched* by such poetry as Dr Darwin's', rants Mathias, who feels that *The Botanic Garden* 'marks the decline of simplicity and of true taste in this country'.[63] Botany for ladies is shown to have contributed to this degeneration of morals and continues to pose a threat to decorum and taste: 'it is a matter of some curiosity to me, to conceive how young ladies are instructed in the terms of botany which are *very significant*'.[64]

Richard Polwhele's *The Unsex'd Females* (1798) is addressed to 'the author of the pursuits of literature' and takes up the latter's theme of women and botany. However, Polwhele departs from Mathias by uncharacteristically defending the literary merits of *The Botanic Garden*.[65] In Polwhele's poem, botany is likened to sexual instruction because of its 'unreserved discussion' of the 'organs of generation'. Polwhele portrays 'unblushing' female botanists, 'eager for illicit knowledge', as 'disciples' of Wollstonecraft, who 'does not blush to say' that

> it would be proper to familiarize the sexes to an unreserved discussion of those topics, which are generally avoided in conversation from a principle of false delicacy; and that it would be right to speak of the organs of generation as freely as we mention our eyes and hands.' *To such language our botanizing girls are doubtless familiarized*: and, they are in a fair way of becoming worthy disciples of Miss W. If they do not take heed to their ways, they will soon exchange the blush of modesty for the bronze of impudence. (notes to lines 33–6, p. 9; my emphasis)

According to Polwhele, impudent botanising girls are following Wollstonecraft's revolution in female manners by replacing modesty with boldness and ambition: Wollstonecraft is 'a sworn enemy to blushes'.[66] In the following extract, female botanists are engaged in a Linnaean exploration of the sexual organs of plants: Polwhele describes this activity as compulsive and orgiastic:

> With bliss botanic as their bosoms heave,
> Still pluck forbidden fruit, with mother Eve,
> For puberty in sighing florets pant,
> Or point the prostitution of a plant;
> Dissect its organ of unhallow'd lust,
> And fondly gaze the titillating dust. (29–34)

These sighing, panting girls are indulging in something akin to sexual experimentation: 'I have several times seen boys and girls botanizing together', exclaims the outraged Polwhele. Women who 'anatomise a plant ... Dissect its organ of unhallow'd lust' and gaze upon the 'prolific dust of the botanist' (note to line 34) have fallen prey to immodest curiosity. Polwhele characterises botanic exploration as an uneasy blend of science and voyeurism; the scrutinising gaze of the female botanist penetrates a microscopic world in order to expose the 'organs of generation'.[67]

The Linnaean project is often figured in the image of Adam in the Garden of Eden.[68] Polwhele's female botanists, instructed in the Sexual System of classification, 'still pluck forbidden fruit with Mother Eve' – the implication being that 'they who are so fond of handling the leaves will long for the fruit at last'.[69] As daughters of Eve they are open to temptation, inhabiting 'A wild, where flowers and weeds promiscuous shoot; a garden tempting with forbidden fruit'.[70] Linnaean botany again poses a threat to female virtue.

Fearing that botanising girls are fast becoming Wollstonecraft's 'disciples', Polwhele cites a passage from *The Botanic Garden* emphasising Wollstonecraft's supposed promiscuity, underscoring the relationship between her own sexuality and her sanctioning of women who practise the sexual system of botany. *Collinsonia* has two male stamens and one female pistil: 'I have lately observed,' wrote Darwin, 'a very singular circumstance in this flower; the two males stand widely diverging from each other, and the female bends herself into contact first with one of them, and after some time leaves this, and applies herself to the other'.[71] Polwhele appropriates this image of the promiscuous female to allude to Wollstonecraft's sexuality, drawing on forward plants in Darwin and Mathias:

> Thrill'd with fine ardors *Collinsonias* glow,
> And, bending, breathe their loose desires below.
> Each gentle air a swelling anther heaves,
> Wafts its full sweets, and shivers thro' the leaves.
> Bath'd in new bliss, the fair one greets the bower,
> And ravishes a flame from every flower;
> Low at her feet inhales the master's sighs,
> And darts voluptuous poison from her eyes.
> Yet, while each heart-pulse, in the Paphian grove,
> Beats quick to IMLAY and licentious love,
> A sudden gloom the gathering tempest spreads;
> The floral arch-work withers o'er their heads;
> Whirlwinds the paramours asunder tear;
> And wisdom falls, the victim of despair.[72] (146–59)

Godwin's *Memoirs* had made public the fact that Wollstonecraft had fled to France to escape her passion for Fuseli, a married man, and had there begun a relationship with Gilbert Imlay with whom she had borne a child.[73] Darwin's description of 'the manifest adultery of several females of the plant *Collinsonia*, who had bent themselves into contact with the males of other flowers of the same plant' (note to line 99), inspired Polwhele's satire on Wollstonecraft. She is classified according to the sexual system of botany, using the ratio of the number of males to females. I have noted above that Darwin's verses on the Collinsonia are cited by Veronica in Plumptre's *The Lakers* when she is simultaneously pursued by two men.

The painters Angelica Kauffman and Emma Crewe were celebrated by Darwin and satirised by Polwhele who included them in his band of 'female quixotes'. Crewe is derided for her immodest portrait of Flora, the frontispiece to 'The Loves of the Plants', and Kauffman for her depiction of Priapus, a phallic deity who presided over gardens and the parts of generation in the sexes. Polwhele mockingly suggests that Kauffman's Priapus 'accompany Miss Wollstonecraft's Instructions in Priapism, already noticed by way of illustration. This, and a little plant-adultery, would go great lengths, in producing among girls, the consummation so devoutly wished' (note to line 106, p. 21). He is also responding to Wollstonecraft's defence of women's botany in *A Vindication of the Rights of Woman* by forging a connection between her sanctioning of the Sexual System and her liberal views on sex education for women.[74]

The Unsex'd Females registers anxieties over a new bolder femininity which ultimately threatens to overturn social order. The female botanist is closely allied to 'female Quixotes of the new philosophy'[75] (women who have failed to observe the 'natural,' intellectual and qualitative difference between the genders) who are set to imitate the 'Amazons' of republican France and introduce into England the disorder that has swept through that country. *The Botanic Garden* was considered to be a hotbed for such forward plants because it combined botany with liberal politics.[76] Women writers, as will be demonstrated, would be influenced by Darwin but would tend to avoid these more disturbing implications.

'Not strictly proper for a female pen': women, writing and the sexuality of plants

Darwin's *Botanic Garden* was extremely influential in popularising botany as a female pursuit; as already noted, it held a particular fascination for women. Maria Edgeworth, novelist and writer of moral tales for children, was acquainted with Darwin through her father, Richard Lovell Edgeworth, a member of the Lunar Society.[77] She introduced botanical themes into *Early Lessons* (1801) after reading *The Botanic Garden.*[78] Her subsequent enthusiasm for botany was such that the botanical textbook, *Dialogues on Botany for the use of Young Persons* (1819), has sometimes been attributed to her.[79] The poet and educator Anna Laetitia Barbauld was also, as already mentioned, seduced by the charms of *The Botanic Garden.* A number of botanical dialogues ('The Leguminous Plants', 'The Umbelliferous Plants', 'The Cruciform-flowered Plants', 'The Compound-Flowered Plants') were incorporated into the educational work *Evenings at Home,* on which she collaborated with her brother John Aikin.[80] The influence of *The Botanic Garden* is easily identified in this six-volume work published between 1792 and 1796.[81] It is commonly assumed that it was John and not Anna who wrote the botanical dialogues. John had studied botany and medicine and Lucy Aikin, Barbauld's niece and editor, does not list these pieces amongst her contributions to the work.[82] However, Barbauld, an admirer of Darwin, was certainly knowledgeable enough about botany to have written these dialogues. The author, like many women discussed here, was cautious about transcribing Linnaean/Darwinian terms in her own work and adopted the non-sexual terminology of Withering when discussing the fructification, referring to stamens as 'chives'.[83]

Maria Elizabetha Jacson was in the unique position of having her botanical writing approved by Darwin, whom she met through her cousin, Sir Brooke Boothby, a member of the Botanical Society of Lichfield.[84] Darwin singled out *Botanical Dialogues* (1797), by 'a lady well-skilled in botany', for special commendation in *A Plan for the Conduct of Female Education* (1797).[85] Jacson's venture into print was aided by her associations with Darwin. The publisher of *Botanical Dialogues*, Joseph Johnson, exploited her connections with the Botanical Society at Lichfield, printing a letter by Darwin and Sir Brooke Boothby among the prefatory material to the first edition, which praised her work for 'explaining a difficult science in an easy and familiar manner'.[86] Jacson was still writing under the auspices of Darwin and Boothby in *Botanical Lectures* (1804). She informed her readers that the work was specifically for use with the Botanical Society at Lichfield's *A System of Vegetables* (1782–83), a new translation of Linnaeus's *Systema vegetabilium.*[87] She contributed to the Lichfield project of popularising the universal system of Linnaeus, and was bold in criticising those such as Withering who had attempted to substitute English generic names, but despite this she shied away from confronting the issue of plant sexuality. There are no descriptions of the vegetable harems and, while the stamens and pistils are identified as male or female, they are not analogous to the human reproductive organs:

> The system of Linnaeus is called the sexual system of botany, because it is founded on observations, which seem to prove, that there are males and females in the vegetable world, as well as in the animal.[88]

Hortensia, the botanising mother of *Botanical Dialogues*, does not permit herself any conversation relating to the sexual parts of the flower; Jacson prefers to leave the subject of fertilisation to Darwin. We learn that Hortensia has acquired a 'variety of knowledge' about plants from the *Botanic Garden* and her children are initiated into botanical/sexual knowledge in a similar fashion; Harriet and Charles are encouraged to read aloud from Darwin during their botanical rambles:

> *Hortensia*: Charles shall read to us … out of the botanic garden [*sic*].
> *Harriet*: We shall all like that vastly; you have treated us with some things out of that poem before ma'am.
> *Hortensia*: I shall have frequent occasion to recur to it, as we proceed in our botanical studies: I do not know a book, which contains more variety of knowledge on the subject, or any one where that knowledge is so clearly and agreeably given: I have learnt much from it.[89]

Jacson brings in Darwin to substitute for Hortensia in an attempt to guard against accusations of immodesty resulting from her learnedness and her instruction of young people in the Sexual System of classification. She knew that she would be criticised by some for 'obtruding [her] knowledge upon the public' and she was sensitive to this gendering of knowledge: 'the world has agreed to condemn women to the exercise of their fingers, in preference to that of their heads; and a woman rarely does herself credit by coming forward as a literary character'.[90]

The Botanic Garden was influential in inspiring other literary women such as Charlotte Smith, Sarah Hoare and Arabella Rowden, all of whom wrote botanical poems with scientific notes in the manner of the *Loves of the Plants*.[91] However, while Charlotte Smith's 'Flora', Sarah Hoare's 'On the Pleasures of Botanical Pursuits', and Arabella Rowden's *Poetical Introduction to the Study of Botany* (1801) drew heavily on Darwin's poem, they deliberately downplayed his 'extravagant' descriptions of promiscuous plants and failed to address his central theme, the sexuality of plants/women. Therefore, given these moral re-writings of *The Botanic Garden* by women poets, and the fact that Anna Seward refused to collaborate with Darwin on this work, this chapter will conclude by ascertaining how far the sexual system was deemed 'not strictly proper for a female pen' and by investigating why women writers remained silent about plant sexuality.[92]

Charlotte Smith's 'Flora' first appeared in *Conversations Introducing Poetry, Chiefly on the Subject of Natural History*, in 1804, and was republished posthumously with 'Studies by the Sea' in *Beachy Head and Other Poems* in 1807. Augustan and epic in form, written in heroic couplets, and with detailed scientific notes, 'Flora' imitated the subject matter and versification of Darwin's *Loves of the Plants*. The preface to *Conversations* states that Smith composed the poem for a young girl who had just moved to England from abroad.[93] Smith attempts a virtuous re-writing of the *Loves of the Plants* for such young people. There is an emphasis on mnemonics and moral instruction in this collection as the mentor and mother figure, Mrs Talbot, instructs the children, George and Emily, simultaneously on natural history and poetic form.

The unsophisticated nature of her audience may in part explain Smith's fraught relationship to the scientific throughout the poem. She takes a national pride in English plant names and is inconsistent in her use of Linnaean names: 'Adders-tongue' is referred to by its local name in the poem, and its botanical name (*Asplenium scolopendrium*) in the footnotes; on the other hand, in the section on seaweeds, the opposite occurs: *Chelidonium* and *Eryngium* appear in the text while their common names, 'sea poppy' and 'sea holly', are confined to footnotes. Here, Smith parades her botanical knowledge before the reader in the main body of the poem. Smith's scientific footnotes may be inconsistent but she is original in adopting a device that would not be thought proper for women; scholarly footnotes could substantiate a writer's claims to originality and allow them to demonstrate their learnedness. She composed with Withering's *Botanical Arrangement of British Plants* and Miller's *Gardener's Dictionary* close at hand, and her use of terminology such as 'hybernacle' and 'spatha' suggests that she intended her young readers to refer to such works as Withering's, which contained a glossary of botanical terms.[94]

Smith addresses the subject of botanical illustration as a feminine accomplishment at the beginning of the poem and instead of championing the fanciful productions of artists such as Emma Crewe (active 1787–1818), who depicted the Linnaean marriages in the frontispiece to the *Loves of the Plants,* she lauds the amateur naturalist who botanises in private and remains true to the observable characteristics of the plant. Botanising in the open air can restore the 'bloom' of youth and the botanical sketch can similarly preserve the beauty and freshness of flowers for posterity:

> Come then Fancy! deign,
> Queen of ideal pleasure, once again
> To lend thy magic pencil, and to bring
> Such lovely forms, as in life's happier spring
> On the green margin of my native Wey,
> Before mine infant eyes were wont to play,
> And with that pencil, teach me to describe
> The enchanting Goddess of the flowery tribe,
> Whose first prerogative is to chase
> The clouds that hang on languid beauty's face;
> And while advancing Suns, and tepid showers,
> Lead on the laughing Spring's delicious hours,
> Bid the wan maid the hues of health assume,
> Charm with new grace, and blush with fresher bloom. (7–20)

Unlike Darwin, Smith juxtaposes feminine accomplishment – botanical drawing – with actual female experience; the reader's easy association between women and flowers is abruptly displaced by the image of a woman whose beauty has been blighted by unhappiness and loss. Elsewhere, in 'Reflections on Some Drawings of Plants' from *Elegiac Sonnets and Other Poems* (1784–97), artistic pleasures cannot compensate for a mother's loss. The portrait of the flower cannot supplant the daughter's image, forever enshrined in the mother's 'bleeding breast'.[95] Flora is a benevolent force in Smith, restoring beauty and softening grief in the manner of Cowper's *The Task* (1785). Line 10 of the poem contains a footnote to the following lines from Cowper:

> The spleen is seldom felt where Flora reigns;
> The low'ring eye, the petulance, the frown,
> And sullen sadness, that o'ershade, distort,
> And mar the face of beauty, when no cause
> For such immeasurable woe appears,
> These Flora banishes, and gives the fair
> Sweet smiles, and bloom less transient than her own.[96]

The theme of a benevolent Flora is given a more literal interpretation in Smith's novel, *The Young Philosopher* (1798). When Smith's heroine Medora, who has been taught botanical drawing by her mother Laura and is a competent botanist, is imprisoned on the top floor of a house, she escapes her persecutors by climbing down a vine. Botany is prominent in this novel, significantly in the many emblematic dwelling places of the heroine Medora and her mother Laura. Vegetation and plant life offer a realm of freedom and discovery to these women in contrast to the castles and houses of their imprisonment. Laura, for example, seeks refuge from the Lady of Kilbrodie's Gothic castle in a hermitage or cave covered with wild flowers, lichens and moss. She is able to find solace after undertaking a minute examination of this plant life: 'amidst the many sad hours I have passed, I have never failed to feel my spirits soothed by the contemplation of vegetable nature'.[97] Veronica, in Plumptre's *The Lakers*, fantasises about writing a romance, 'The Horrors of the Hermitage', which features a female botanist:

> I believe Lydia, I shall draw my heroine from either you or myself, and make her passionately fond of drawing and botany; she shall be mistress of the Linnaean system, and then, if I should make her stop, in the midst of her distress, to admire the scenery, or gather a plant, it will be perfectly natural. (I. 2. 18)

We can only speculate as to whether Plumptre has Smith's novel in mind here. It is probable, given that both works were published in the same year, that Plumptre was responding satirically to Smith. There are many connections that can be teased out in this small group of interrelated and contemporaneous texts.

Smith's benevolent muse descends to earth to awaken vegetation in spring and to 'dress' and adorn the earth with flowers: 'Thro' the deep woodland's wild uncultured scene, / Spreads the soft influence of the floral Queen' (127–8). She observes wild herbs and forest flowers newly blown, woodland trees in bud and the marshy shrubs around the mountain stream before a Naiad escorts her to the sea, allowing Smith to demonstrate her specialist knowledge of marine plants; these also feature in *Beachy Head*.[98] Sporting a crown of rush, a robe of floating thistle's down, and a wand of *Athoxanthum,* or meadow grass, this 'enchanting goddess of the flowery tribe' (14) is not luxuriously adorned. Her humble dress is comprised of 'uncultured' wild flowers; her 'leafy car' of 'forest foliage', oak, beech, ash, and moss (lines 29–32). Smith's native woodland plants display none of the promiscuity of Darwin's exotics and Flora herself is virtuous and simply attired. In comparison, Darwin's muse is a voluptuous procuress who wantonly seduces Linnaeus and encourages him to speak of the secret sexuality of plants:

> BOTANIC MUSE! who in this latter age
> Led by your airy hand the Swedish Sage
> Bad his keen eye your secret haunts explore
> On dewy dell, high wood and winding shore;
> Say on each leaf how tiny Graces dwell;
> How laugh the pleasures in a blossoms bell
> How insect loves arise on cobweb wings'
> Aim their light shafts and point their little stings. (II.31–8)

Given the supposition that Flora was originally a common courtesan,[99] this coupling of Flora and Linnaeus alludes to wanton sexuality in the vegetable kingdom. Smith's goddess modestly restores the blush of innocence and the bloom of youth to 'languid' middle-aged ladies, whereas Darwin's muse is a precocious precursor to Polwhele's 'unblushing' botanising girls.

Smith invokes both the fanciful and the scientific, creating a magical microscopic world. Flora's attendant nymphs Floscella, Petalla, Nectarynia and Calyx are named after the parts of a flower:

From the wild bee, whose wondrous labour weaves,
In artful folds the Rose's fragrant leaves,
Was borrow'd fair Petalla's light cymarre;
And the Hypericum, with spangling star,
O'er her fair locks its bloom minute enwreathed;
Then, while voluptuous odours round her breathed,
Came Nectarynia; as the arrowy rays
Of lambent fire round pictured Seryphs blaze,
So did the Passiflora's radii shed
Cerulean glory o'er the Sylphid's head,
While round her form the pliant tendril's twined.
And clasp'd the scarf that floated on the wind. (85–95)

Darwin claimed to have 'inlisted Imagination under the banner of science' ('Proem', v) and some of the supernatural elements of the *Botanic Garden*, such as the sylphs of the air, are taken up by Smith:

Around the Goddess, as the flies that play
In countless myriads in the western ray,
The Sylphs innumerous throng, whose magic powers
Guard the soft buds, and nurse the infant flowers,
Round the sustaining stem weak tendrils bind,
And save the pollen from dispersing wind,
From sun's too ardent shade their transient hues,
And catch in odorous cups translucent dews. (49–56)

However, Smith's sylphs are the purveyors of order and the custodians of virtue, shielding the vulnerable flowers from random pollination by 'dispersing wind', and preventing their 'transient hues' from flushing in the 'sun's too ardent' rays. When the Darwinian theme of courtship surfaces in the description of the rival roses below, it is the paler 'modest beauties' that take the centre stage and are admired, above their bold and glowing rivals:

The yellow rose her golden globe displays;
There, lovelier still, among their spiny sprays
Her blushing Rivals glow with brighter dyes,
Then paints the Summer Sun, on western skies;
And the scarce ting'd, and paler Rose unveil
Their modest beauties to the sighing gale. (121–6)

While Smith refers to Darwin affectionately in the notes – drawing on him to lend authority to her section on marine plants, for example – the influence of Withering is everywhere evident in the poem, from the emphasis on native plants to the lack of concern with the sexualised parts of the flower.[100] Withering adapted

Linnaean botany for women readers by purposefully omitting the sexual distinctions in the titles to the classes and orders, and Smith similarly de-sexed Darwin, re-writing *The Loves of the Plants* for supposedly impressionable young women.

Frances Arabella Rowden sought to distance herself from Darwin and to confirm her commitment to female education. The advertisement to the first edition of *A Poetical Introduction to the Study of Botany* (1801) explains that the author

> intended at first to select a few passages from Dr Darwin's elegant Poem ... and arrange them according to the system of Linnaeus; but finding many of the Classes not treated on in that work, and the language frequently too luxuriant for the simplicity of female education, she attempted the following descriptions, in which she endeavoured to imitate the classical distribution and versification of this elegant writer.[101]

An educator of girls, Rowden strove to win the approval of influential families and did not want to jeopardise her good reputation by strongly associating her own text with that of Darwin.[102] The *Anti-Jacobin Review* of 1801 implied that her poetical debt to Darwin was evidence of a certain lack of judgement on her part:

> We could have wished, indeed, that our author had not taken Dr. Darwin for her model, who, amidst a croud of poetical beauties, exhibits so many meretricious embellishments, as tend to dazzle the eye and to bewilder the understanding.[103]

The reviewer goes on to applaud Rowden for 'avoiding as much as possible, the defects of her master'.[104] *The Monthly Review* of 1813 similarly selected for praise lines which were 'less Darwinian' and 'stamped with the features of simplicity and truth'.[105] The reception of *A Poetical Introduction to the Study of Botany* in periodicals demonstrates that a woman's reputation and character was frequently esteemed above her genius for poetry:

> These excerpts can scarcely fail to impress our readers with a very favourable opinion of the poetical talents, and, which is of much greater consequence, of the religious and moral principles, of the author.[106]

Rowden published her work by subscription and the subscribers to the first edition include such dignitaries as a Lady Mary Parker, Lady Caroline Ponsonby, the Duchess of Devonshire, and the author of pious educational works for young persons, Mrs Sarah Trimmer. Aware of the expectation of her subscribers and the importance of reputation to her position at the school, Rowden appears unable to approve of a woman pursuing botanical knowledge for its own sake: a strict moral agenda comes into play. Plants have been selected 'from which some moral lesson might be derived, that the improvement of the heart might keep pace with the information of the mind' ('Advertisement').[107]

Rowden's representation of the Linnaean Sexual System is curiously devoid of sexuality. The relationship between stamens and pistils is non-sexual, with one or two exceptions. The majority of the males/stamens are 'gallant youths' or 'brother-saints' and pose no sexual threat to the females/pistils. *Hippuris*, or 'mare's tail', is typical in that Rowden allows the female a rational friendship rather than a romantic union with her male companion:

> No velvet mantle, no embroider'd veil,
> Shields poor Hippuris from the northern gale;
> 'Midst the damp meadow, or the oozy bed,
> In lowly modesty she rears her head.
> No gaudy train this simple fair attend,
> No crowd of sycophants before her bend;
> *One* friend alone her hapless fortune cheers;
> He soothes her woes, and dries her pearly tears. (1)

The female plant is an archetypal shrinking violet: 'hapless', 'lowly', tearful and modest to the point of complete passivity. Rowden's females have none of the feistiness of Darwin's coquettes; they exemplify the feminine virtues, being 'modest', 'pure' and 'meek'. Veronica, or Speedwell (Class II, *Diandria Monogynia*), is an innocent wildling 'named after a female saint':

> In clouds of *azure* see the sainted *fair*
> On angel's pinions wafted through the air;
> Humble and modest, meek Religion's child,
> Her pure abode is mid th' Uncultur'd wild;
> Then her blue eye she lifts to heav'n's vast height,
> And hails the God of everlasting light.
> *Two* brother-saints the holy maid attend,
> And to her sage commands obsequious bend. (6)

This class is not monogamous – there are two male stamens and one female pistil – but there is no suggestion of courtship as the males are 'brother saints', and not the suitors of this ethereal 'holy maid'.

Rowden's *Canna* (*Monandria Monogynia*) has none of the eroticism of Darwin's reed. His sexually potent exotic is replaced by a virtuous British variety, a 'gallant youth' that does not display its sexual prowess nor force itself forward for notice but is found tucked way in ditches. Darwin's notes on this plant (I. 39) inform us that the seeds are used as shot by 'Indians' and as prayer beads in Catholic countries. Rowden incorporates these facts, emphasising the utility of the plant for humanity:

> FROM the tall Canna's sable polish'd seeds,
> The pious nun prepares her holy beads;
> While at the shrine she seeks almighty grace,
> The savage Indian shoots the feather'd race:
> Arm'd with those beads that mark her sacred pray'r,
> He hurls destruction through the trackless air,
> *A gallant youth*, in crimson vest array'd,
> Supplies the Indian, and the cloister'd maid. (3)

In the next two classes the males are equally 'gallant' and are attentive and protective of the virtuous females. In Class III, *Triandria Monogynia*, for example, 'three noble youths' administer a 'healing cordial' to *Valeriana*, a 'sinking fair' (13); Rowden's notes inform us that the plant is 'peculiarly efficacious in nervous affections' (13). In Class IV, *Tetrandria Monogynia* (four stamens, one pistil), *Galium* or 'Lady's Bedstraw', 'four gay sylphs' attend the 'modest' Galia.

Lily of the Valley and Mimosa are Rowden's model females. Thwarting male attentions, they display their sensibility like sentimental heroines, trembling and blushing profusely at any indiscretion. In Class VI, *Hexandria Monogynia* (six stamens, one pistil), *Convallaria's* icy virtue cools the fiery passion of her ardent suitors:

The icy virtue of her soul imprest
Mocks the soft accents of his ardent breast:
So the meek lily, void of art's vain aid,
Blooms the sweet emblem of the timid maid.
Attention's gaze her trembling heart alarms,
And in the shade she hides her blushing charms
Round her fair form the light of reason plays,
And each pure image of her mind displays
Six simple brothers, nature's fav'rite care,
In happy innocence the pleasures share;
With fragrant flow'rs her humble cot adorn,
And taste the joys that bloom without a thorn. (36–7)

The Lily is a virginal 'maid' who shuns 'attention's gaze' while Mimosa, the sensitive plant, shrinks from touch. A symbol of exemplary virtue, Mimosa is an emblem of Lady Caroline Ponsonby, Rowden's 'lov'd pupil', who is 'Blest with each virtue Nature could impart, / A soul exalted and a feeling heart'(154). The cultivation of the female mind is viewed through an image of ripening blossom, carefully nurtured by a devoted mother/gardener:

So, my lov'd pupil, may thy op'ning mind,
For virtue's brightest deeds by Heav'n design'd,
In Nature's early, and Youth's tender hour,
Shrink from the blast of Folly's dang'rous pow'r;
And as thy step with modest grace retires
To scenes more suited to thy pure desires,
Maternal Love with rapture may behold
The ripen'd blossoms of her care unfold;
And as she views thy mind, from day to day,
Some artless grace, some winning charms display,
View in those charms, which all her wishes crown,
The true, but fainter, image of her own. (155)

The poem on *Cistus* – the Rock Rose – tells the story of another mother and daughter. The daughter succumbs to madness after being shamefully deflowered, leaving the mother to grieve 'O'er her spoil'd flow'r' (74). She mourns 'The flow'r she rear'd with sweet Affection's care; / And fondly ling'ring where she saw it bloom, / The grave of innocence becomes her tomb' (75). Scorned by society, the daughter/flower sinks into decline, repents and, redeemed through suffering, dies a moral death:

Scorn in her bleeding bosom strikes his dart,
And sad Repentance writhes around her heart.
Remorse her stinging snakes in fury throws,
And Madness heightens her exalted woes.
Poor injur'd suff'rer! bid adieu to peace;
Not in this world of sin thy pangs will cease:
Not kill kind Mercy takes thee to her breast,
And bears thy spirit to the realms of rest. (75)

Darwin, in *The Botanic Garden*, tells of the short duration of the beautiful and fragrant flowers of the *Cistus* and Smith uses this plant as a symbol of mutability in 'A Walk in the Shrubbery'.[108] Rowden, however, derives a moral lesson from her botanical knowledge: the early shedding of the flowers is emblematic of a fallen woman whose loss of virtue brings about the sad demise of mother and daughter. In such descriptions, the characteristics of the plant are obscured by her moralising. Rowden's is the closest of the women's texts to Darwin in its scheme and format but it could not be further removed from his playful exploration of female sexuality. Rowden instead produces a genteel book on botany which uses analogies between women and flowers to persuade women to cultivate the domestic virtues. She appropriates the Linnaean system to teach women about their place in society. *Thea*, or the Tea Tree (Class XII, *Polyandria Monogynia*), has many male stamens and one female pistil residing on the same plant; the female is an emblem of civility and conviviality but also of compliance and submission: 'To her charm'd guests she bows with modest ease, / And shows her dearest pleasure is to please' (78).

The pleasures alluded to in Sarah Hoare's 'Pleasures of Botanical Pursuits, A Poem' are clearly distinct from the illicit pleasures of Darwin's *Botanic Garden*. Hoare recalls innocent pleasures, such as rambling 'along the banks of Froome, searching for plants'.[109] She makes no mention of Darwin in the version which appeared in a collection published around 1826, referring instead to Withering, Boyle's *Gentleman's Magazine*, and the *Encyclopædia Britannica* for botanical knowledge, and to Paley's *Natural Theology* (1802) for evidence of the benevolent 'intelligent author' in all of nature's works.[110] The greatest pleasure botany affords is to 'look thro' Nature up to Nature's God':

Great Source of true felicity!
Father Omnipotent! 'tis thee
We view in grove and mead;
Thy name, thy pow'r, that we revere,
Sublime, intelligent, and clear,
Inscrib'd on all around appear,
That he who runs may read. (172–8)

The joy of motherhood is another heartfelt pleasure she associates with botany, using plants to illustrate the virtues of maternity:

Averse from evening's chilly breeze,
How many close their silken leaves,
To save the embryo flow'rs;

As if ambitious of a name,
They sought to spread around their fame,
And bade the infant buds proclaim
The parent's valu'd pow'rs. (158–64)

These embryo flowers and their protective parent plants are reminiscent of the tulip mother in Darwin's *Botanic Garden.* Women writers, such as Sarah Trimmer and Priscilla Wakefield, frequently used the trope of the moral mother in natural history texts.[111] Mrs Harcourt in Priscilla Wakefield's *Mental Improvement* (1794) draws on examples from the animal kingdom to illustrate the qualities of good and bad mothers. The children learn that fish do not take care of their young once the eggs are laid whereas birds make dutiful parents:

> [fish are] strangers to the pleasing solicitude of parental fondness, they may with propriety be ranked in an inferior scale of existence to the beautiful feathered race, whose tenderness and patient care may serve as models to careless mothers, who neglect their offspring from indolence, or a love of other pursuits.[112]

The 1826 version of Hoare's poem, a Quakerly address to her former pupils who will themselves become mothers, exemplifies this type of maternal discourse. Hoare celebrates the archetypal mother through botany as Darwin had done, but she does not attempt to give voice to female sexuality nor does she describe the sexual parts of the flower. She refers to 'the sexual system' by name but the sexuality of plants is never even alluded to in the poem. Sexual knowledge, it seems, is not to be imparted through botany.

Hoare's views on female education were inspired by the evangelical teachings of Hannah More:

> I call that education which inculcates principles, polishes taste, regulates temper, cultivates reason, subdues the passions, directs the feelings, habituates to reflection, trains self denial, and more especially that which refers all actions and feelings, sentiments, tastes, and passions to the love and fear of God.[113]

In citing the conservative, anti-Jacobin propagandist, Hannah More, in her preface, Hoare distances herself from the apparent atheism of Darwin and the radicalism which Mathias and Polwhele had exposed as thriving in botanical circles. She eventually dropped any reference to the Sexual System from the poem. The following stanza of the 1818 edition of 'Pleasures of Botanical Pursuits' was modified significantly in a later version:

Linné, by thy experience taught,
And ample page so richly fraught
    With scientific lore,
We scan *thy sexual system* clear,
Of plants that court the mountain air,
That bloom o'er hills, o'er meadows fair,
    The forest and the moor. (57–63; my emphasis)

Line 60 was subsequently changed to 'I scann'd *thy curious system* clear' (my emphasis), when the same poem appeared in *Poems on Conchology and Botany* in 1831.[114] By changing these lines, Hoare removed any obvious association between female 'pleasures' and the Linnaean Sexual System from the poem, in a post-Polwhelean attempt to dissociate herself from female libertinism.

Such fears that a Linnaean plan was 'not strictly proper for a female pen' extended beyond the genres of poetry and the botanical dialogue. The botanical artist Henrietta Maria Moriarty struggled to produce an accurate pictorial representation of the Sexual System which would be approved by those who had 'the fashioning of young minds most at heart'.[115] *A Viridarium* (1806) combined illustrations of flowers, arranged alphabetically by their Latin names, with Linnaean descriptions of each plant. Moriarty avoided representing the plants' organs of generation in any detail and chose not to include separate drawings of the stamens and pistils; such illustrations, in the corner of each plate, were conventional for male botanical artists such as Francis and Ferdinand Bauer, George Ehret, or Pierre Redouté.[116] *A Viridarium* was designed for 'the rising generation' ('Preface', v), but her prospective audience became more gender-specific in the second edition which was issued under the title *Fifty Plates of Green-House Plants ... For the Improvement of Young Ladies in the Art of Drawing* (1807). The popularity of the Linnaean system was on the decline in England by this date and Moriarty went one step further than her Linnaean predecessors, publicly rejecting the sexual system and those who had championed it:

> I have taken as little notice as possible of the system of the immortal Linneus [*sic*], and of all the illustrations and comments on it; nay, I have not once named the fanciful doctor Darwin.[117]

Moriarty does, however, classify plants according to Linnaeus and she encourages a scientific engagement with plants which goes beyond feminine accomplishment in drawing.[118]

A guarded sense of propriety is evidenced here, one which leads us to question whether there are any women's texts on botanical themes that deviate from or challenge these conventions. To address this question more fully I want to bring in another example of this genre, Elizabeth Moody's 'To Dr. Darwin, on Reading his Loves of the Plants' (1798). Moody's poem is bolder and more ambiguous than the female responses to Darwin that I have looked at so far and there is a marked difference in tone.

Elizabeth Moody, née Greenly (1737–1814), married the Dissenting clergyman Christopher Lake Moody at the mature age of 40. She was a successful critic, becoming the first regular woman reviewer for the *Monthly Review*. She also published poetry, contributing verses to a number of journals including *The Gentleman's Magazine*, and the *St James's Review*, earning her the title of 'Muse of Surbiton'.[119] *Poetic Trifles* (1798) contains her poem to Darwin and the verses that she had contributed to periodicals as well as some new poems. Mary Waters has written on Moody's literary criticism and she argues that it reveals 'an urbane irony of tone'.[120] This tone is also apparent in her poetry. Many of her poems are satirical. The most notable example is entitled 'Sappho, Tempted by the Prophesy Burns All her Books and Cultivates the Culinary Arts'.[121] Here,

Sappho abandons her literary vocation to salt ham and mix pies. The poem takes on an additional irony if, as Waters suggests, Moody occasionally signed herself 'Sappho'. Moody's satirical impulse is slightly at odds with the rather self-deprecating title of *Trifles*. However, this could act as a ploy, allowing her irony and humour around prominent male figures and conventionally feminine roles to go unnoticed.

'To Dr. Darwin' is presented as a female complaint against Darwin and yet the poet's playful, ironic tone only serves to celebrate him. Darwin is chastised for his gossipy 'tales' of amorous plants and championed as the bard who brought the loves of the plants to life:

No Bard e'er gave his tuneful powers,
Thus to traduce the fame of flowers;
Till Darwin sung his gossip tales,
Of females woo'd by *twenty* males.
Of *plants* so given to amorous pleasure;
Incontinent beyond all measure.
He sings that in botanic schools,
Husbands adopt licentious rules;
Plurality of Wives they wed,
And all they like – they take to bed.[122]

Darwin may have traduce[d] the fame of flowers but it was Linnaeus, Moody argues, who first spoke of the marriage of plants:

Linneus [sic] things, no doubt, reveal'd,
Which prudent *Plants* would wish conceal'd;
So free of *families* he spoke,
As must that modest race provoke.
Till he invaded Flora's bowers
None heard of marriage among flowers;
Sexual distinctions were unknown;
Discover'd by the Swede alone.
He blab'd through all the list'ning groves,
The mystick rites of *flow'ry loves*.
He pry'd in every blossom's fold,
And all he saw unseemly – told. (15–26)

However, a crucial distinction is made between Darwin and Linnaeus in terms of their appeal, which according to Moody, is largely determined by genre:

But then in prose Linneus prattles,
And soon forgot is all he tattles.
While better pleas'd retains,
The frolicks of poetic brains. (35–8)

Darwin adopts an elevated literary form and his poetic rendering of botany is more easily committed to memory than Linneaus's prose. Botany in a poetical format proved popular and Darwin was to inspire a new genre of women's writing, one to which Moody's poem itself belongs. But Darwin is presented as something of an enchanter here, too. His scientific poetry is 'Control'd by Fiction's magic hand' (43), reason is suspended, and readers, enamoured, 'feel each fair delusion true' (45).

The tone of the poem then moves between approval and condemnation but Moody's criticism is never sustained. This is evident in the way she playfully complains that Darwin has changed her perception of plants forever:

> Then, DARWIN! Were it not for thee,
> I sure must venerate this tree.
> But as his boughs hand oe'er my head,
> I recollect from you I read,
> His wife he exiles from his bed. (81–5)

She concludes by acknowledging the power of his 'art' but bids him cease using poetry to 'libel harmless trees and flowers':

> Since thus thy fascinating art,
> So takes possession of the heart,
> Go bid thy Muse a wreath prepare,
> 'To bind some charming Chloe's hair'
> But tune no more thy Lyre's sweet powers,
> To libel harmless trees and flowers. (86–91)

Moody is aware of the powerful influence of the *Loves of the Plants* on enlightened British women. She is astute in distinguishing between the works of Darwin and Linnaeus. Darwin after all could be credited with inventing the Linnaean poem, feminising botany and popularising the Sexual System in England.

In this context it is fascinating to discover the remarkable handwritten poem attributed to Anna Seward, with its ambiguous exploration of sexual impropriety. This poem's engagement with social disorder has already been examined in Chapter 3; it deserves a further reading in the light of this discussion of sexuality and female responses to Darwin. Seward moved, and was actively involved, in the same intellectual circles as Darwin at this time. Roger Lonsdale writes that 'from her headquarters in Lichfield Close, she projected herself for many years as perhaps the most prominent and formidable woman writer of the later century'.[123] Darwin was a regular visitor to Bishop's Palace, Cathedral Close where Seward grew up. It was here that Seward remained until her death in 1809. The palace became the centre of a cultivated circle of Enlightenment thinkers including Darwin, Thomas Day, and Richard Lovell Edgeworth. Seward took a leading role in these intellectual gatherings. Later, in her *Memoir*, she would describe the Enlightenment culture of Lichfield. She had by this time been at the centre of this culture for several decades.[124]

Darwin took an active interest in Seward's education and literary aspirations from an early age. Since she was fifteen, he had been convinced of her talent as a poet and assumed the role of editor and advisor. Seward had always had a close textual relationship to Darwin, one which was often fraught: I have already outlined earlier in this chapter their quarrel over the botanical verses that inspired *The Botanic Garden*, and after Seward's death it was claimed by some that Darwin had written the best part of her *Elegy on Captain Cook* (1780).[125] If the elegy is reminiscent of Darwin's poetic style it is hardly surprising, given that Darwin first encouraged her to write and edited her early poems.[126] Given their joint ventures, it is not far-fetched to suggest that she might attempt a poem on Darwinian botany to mark his translations from Linnaeus. Her residence in Lichfield and her close association with Darwin meant that she would almost certainly be involved with celebrations to mark his latest publication. Moreover, Seward had an involvement with and knowledge of Linnaean botany: she and Darwin were in the habit of discussing science and literature at the intellectual gatherings at the Bishop's Palace. Her botanical knowledge is evident in the verses she wrote in Darwin's botanic garden at Lichfield, which was planted in a Linnaean scheme, and in her detailed discussion of the botanical imagery in *The Botanic Garden* in her posthumous biography of Darwin.

Elsewhere, in 'Sonnet. To the Poppy' (*c.* 1789), written around the same year as *The Loves of the Plants*, Seward attempts something almost Darwinian when she delineates the properties of the poppy and describes the scarlet flower itself as 'a love crazed maid' in the long grass.[127] Her description is reminiscent of one of Darwin's wanton plant women, the scarlet poppy/maid is 'gaudy' and 'wild', her 'flaccid vest', 'as the gale blows high' flaps in folds around her head (lines 6–7). It is important to remember that Darwin credited Seward with botanical knowledge enough to undertake an ambitious project when he solicited her to write the poetry for his own Linnaean scheme; it was after all a venture that had largely been inspired by her. Seward conversed on the subject of botany with other literary women, namely the 'Ladies of Llangollen', Sarah Ponsonby and Lady Eleanor Butler, with whom she struck up a close friendship. Seward's visits to their house at Plas Newydd were spent in the library discussing their favourite topics, namely works on the picturesque, Rousseau, Cook's *Voyages* and botany books.[128] Seward often uses botanical metaphors in her verse. The woman/flower analogy recurs in *Verses Written in Dr Darwin's Botanic Garden* (1778), 'Colebrooke Dale' (1810) and 'Sonnet. To Colebrooke Dale' (1799).

The playful ironic tone of 'The Backwardness of Spring Accounted For ' has led some to question whether it was, in fact, written by a woman.[129] If more proof were needed that women could write satirically in response to Darwin, Moody's similarly ironic poem confirms the possibility. Seward's poetry is stylistically diverse; anyone who is familiar with 'Verses Inviting Stella to Tea on the Public Fast-Day [During the American War]', written in 1781 and published in 1791, will be aware of her comic genius. There are many similarities between this and the manuscript poem – metrically, lexically, and sharing the same flippant tone towards political unease. Seward's poetry embodies Midlands Enlightenment thought, particularly concerning the conjuncture of science and society. Writing on her verses on Colebrook, Roy Porter has noted that, for Seward, 'natural disorder presaged social disorder', and this too is evidenced in the botanical poem.[130] This imagery around order has been discussed in Chapter 3. Seward references herself in the poem ('By the Muses who there on their *Seward* attended' (86)). No doubt Shteir has this line in mind when she remarks that 'internal evidence suggests Anna Seward', whereas others have questioned this.[131]

'The Backwardness of Spring Accounted For 1772' was written into the endpapers of Joseph Banks's copy of *A System of Vegetables* which was published in 1783. It marks the publication of Darwin and the Botanical Society at Lichfield's translation from Linnaeus. We cannot know exactly when this poem was written, though the project it refers to dates from around 1783. It predates *The Loves of the Plants*, a text Seward was to distance herself from because she thought it was 'not strictly proper for a female pen'. Crucially, the evidence of this manuscript poem which was clearly never meant for publication shows – if it is indeed by her – that, in private, she did not remain silent on the issue of sexuality, freely exploring promiscuous plants and polygamous unions. We can now see how one woman explored her interest in Linnaean/Darwinian botany and its remarkable aptness as a mirror for anxieties over social and sexual order.

Seward's poem, written in honour of the first literal translation – rather than an adaptation – of Linnaeus into English in 1783, uses botany to illustrate the necessity for hierarchy and order in Britain, as demonstrated in Chapter 3. The discordance of the plant kingdom parallels the perceived disorder of civil society; classes and sexes overrun their borders; there is a 'want of distinction of sexes and classes' and a 'confusion of manners and morals'.[132] But this is not all; there is a gendered dimension. Promiscuity is a temptation to the continent:

"Ye ladies with Eunuchs, now is it not hard
["]That your virtue should seem to require such a guard
"While your gay painted Cowslip may gad where she will
"Yet her Husband good Creature suspecteth no ill. (71–4)

Those who are already promiscuous can only be encouraged to be more so:

"Ye wives with ten husbands, say will they content ye
"Whilst a neighbour lies by you with no less than twenty
"Ye husbands in wives tho' not stinted to few
"Don't you envy the Flower that has Concubines too. (69–72)

This unbridled sexuality crosses class boundaries:

"Patricians stand forth & say what lady's bosom
"Makes amends for your joining a plebian blossom
"And will you tho' in a laced button hole stoop
"Any longer with Soldiers & Servants to group. (77–80)

And the imminent threat of secession by the American colonists is somehow an added consequence: 'No no my gay empire will sooner dissever / And my Colonists claim independence forever' (81–2).

But Seward's poem is not simply a reactionary complaint. What is interesting is that Seward seems to be proposing a new order that contains dissent by allowing a certain amount of sexual impropriety; it is an enlightened, rationalist and liberal order that tolerates difference to some extent: 'What is wrong in a rose may be right in a dock' (99). The knowledge spread by the dissemination of the

Linnaean system means that people no longer have any reason to be shocked by sexual deviance:

"No tongue can excusably drop a rude word
"Before Flowers that are parted from bed & from board
"Or put to distress those unfortunate Spouses
"Who live from their husbands in separate houses.[133] (92–5)

Rank and hierarchy is still preserved and each person is in their proper place, associated with the appropriate bouquet which contents them somehow with an appropriate pleasure:

Gardener's Girls their boquets shall compose
"Corresponding in rank with their Customers nose
"Yes, yes, I perceive the great moment approaches
"When buds of distinction shall ride in their Coaches
"When family weight shall their blossoms promote
"And titles advance them to noses of note
"My Commoners too whom less honours attend
"From highest to lowest shall each have a friend
"This the Captain's high nostrils shall please with its prickles
"Whilst that with soft wings a fat Alderman tickles. (106–15)

The poem ends with Flora announcing that she will not appear until the Lichfield scholars have popularised Linnaean classification in Britain and with Jove agreeing to delay the onset of spring until this time:

"My subjects will thus be employed with decorum
"And till this is done Sir I'll not march before them
Jove was glad when she finished accepted her reason
So called for the Jordan & put back the Seasons. (148–51)

Seward had distanced herself from the publication of *The Botanic Garden*. However, the evidence of this manuscript poem, which was clearly never intended for publication, shows – if it is indeed by her – that she did not remain silent on the issue of sexuality in private, freely exploring promiscuous plants and polygamous unions.

In the last decade of the eighteenth century, anxieties over the increasing instability of gender roles and over revolutionary politics provoked a moral backlash against those female botanists who had adopted the Sexual System of Linnaeus. One of the leading mouthpieces against radicalism, Polwhele compared radical politics to botany, warning that women botanists were as precocious and unnatural a 'breed' as the 'impious Amazons of Republican France'.[134] Botany was used to reaffirm conceptions of 'the proper lady' at a time when radical women were challenging such social constructions of femininity; female precocity was a prominent subject in poetic exchanges between Mathias and Polwhele where comparisons between forward plants and wanton women were fully exploited.[135]

Contrary to the fears of anti-Linnaeans, women's fascination with Darwin seemed not to be primarily about sexuality but with the space botany afforded them. Botany was a means of gaining entrance into professional writing and women benefited from the feminisation of botany that Darwin had so successfully exploited. Darwin, an eminent man of science, could explore the sexuality of women through the sexual system of Linnaeus but women writers were not at liberty to address such potentially inflammatory issues. Sarah Hoare never married and found herself at a later stage in her life 'obliged to make every exertion in [her] power for a subsistence', and Charlotte Smith, who was separated from her husband, supported herself and her children, while her estranged husband, who eventually expired in a debtors' prison, continually sought to obtain money from her literary ventures.[136] These women were economically dependent on the proceeds of their writing and could not afford to court controversy by explicitly detailing the sexuality of plants.

Conventions of female propriety were such that not even Maria Jacson, writing under the auspices of the Botanical Society at Lichfield and committed to the Linnaean sexual system in England, attempted to give voice to the sexuality of plants. Arabella Rowden was keen to fulfil the moral expectations of her subscribers and aspired to attract the daughters of prominent local families to the school at which she was headmistress. Seward was also extremely mindful of her reputation. Prior to her death, she spent many years preparing her poetry and letters for publication. She went to great lengths to safeguard her reputation and to seize editorial control by writing lengthy letters of instruction to her literary executors. She left Walter Scott very little editorial work to do when she bequeathed him exclusive copyright to her poetry. The letters she bequeathed to Mr Constable the publisher.[137] Fearing her contribution to *The Botanic Garden* was 'not strictly proper', Seward began distancing herself from what was to become the most influential literary and scientific project of the day, despite her earlier involvement with it.

Reputation was extremely important to such women; they were not prudish – merely practical; there is little evidence of the kind of moral repulsion for Linnaeus that we find in the Victorian texts of, for example, Jane Loudon. Seward went on to defend Darwin against charges of corruption in her letters: 'do not suppose that a virtuous girl, or a young married woman, could be induced, by reading the botanic garden, to imitate the involuntary libertinism of a fungus or flower'.[138] Poetical responses to Darwin, with the exception of Moody and Seward, were modest and guarded. Women poets simply remained silent on the issue of sexuality, following in the tradition of educationalists such as Barbauld and Wakefield. Seward's poem, however improper for a female pen, with its playfully ambiguous attitudes to sexuality and its suggestion of a rationalist politics, is a more naked illustration of such women's relation to Enlightenment botany. For a brief time then, before reaction set in, Linnaean botany opened up a space for female radicalism, though not without ambivalence.

By the early nineteenth century, the project to spare the 'innocent fair' the 'blush of injured modesty' in botany books was well and truly under way. Darwin's promiscuous plants had changed the course of women's botany and a new, less enlightened approach emerged, dominated by the works of Jane Loudon and John Lindley, both of whom were fiercely anti-Linnaean. Lindley (1799–1865), the first Professor of Botany at the University of London, lauded the advantages of what was called the 'Natural System', 'to which the method of Linnaeus had universally given way amongst Botanists'.[139] Lindley was active in encouraging women to abandon the 'mistaken' system of Linnaeus in *Ladies' Botany* (1834–7, 1841).[140] Furthermore, Jane Loudon (1807–58) confessed in *Botany For Ladies* (1842) that 'there was something in the Linnaean system ... excessively repugnant to me', and stated that she had rejected Linnaean works designed for women because 'with the exception of Dr Lindley's Lady's Botany they were all sealed books to me'.[141] She endeavoured to rescue women from being initiated in such a method and instructed them instead in the classification of plants 'according to the natural system of Jussieu, as improved by the late Professor De Candolle'.[142]

This was still a radical, enlightened period for women's botany, however, before the appearance of the language of flowers which would dominate Victorian flower books for 'ladies' later in the nineteenth century. Women were encouraged to move away from floriculture and floristry and to embrace scientific botany and Linnaeus. In the following chapter, I will explore further this opposition of botany to floristry in other works by Jacson, and by Charlotte Smith, who mediate these tensions in different ways. The preference for native species in educational texts by women leads me to return to the debates around nationality and patriotism, to the aesthetics of particularity, and the use of native flowers as moral emblems in educational works for young women at this time.

Notes

1 See my discussion of Withering's *A Botanical Arrangement* (1776) in Chapters 2 and 3.

2 Richard Polwhele, *The Unsex'd Females* (London: Cadell and Davies, 1798; repr. New York: Garland Press, 1974), notes to lines 27–32, p. 8. All further references are to this edition.

3 As an example she cites 'the very stridency of the opposition' to Georgiana, the Duchess of Devonshire, resulting from her electioneering activities during the campaign to elect Members of Parliament for the city of Westminster in 1784 (Colley, *Britons: Forging the Nation*, p. 263).

4 Polwhele, *The Unsex'd Females*, note to line 99, p. 20.

5 *Ibid.*, note to line 99, p. 16.

6 These political tracts were: *An Address to the Opposers of the Repeal of the Corporation and Test Acts, signed 'A Dissenter'* (London: J. Johnson, 1790); *Civic Sermons to the People* (London: Printed for J. Johnson, 1792); *Sins of Government, Sins of the Nation. A discourse for the fast, appointed on April 19, 1793, By a Volunteer* (London: J. Johnson, 1793).

Stuart Curran observes that Barbauld had written 'in a style of such commanding vigour that, when the word leaked out that they were written by a woman, it seemed incredible to all' ('Women Readers, Women Writers', in Stuart Curran (ed.), *The Cambridge Companion to British Romanticism* (Cambridge: Cambridge University Press, 1993), pp. 177–95 (p. 189).

7 Samuel Rogers, *Recollections of the Table Talk of Samuel Rogers*, ed. Rev. Alexander Dyce (New Southgate: H. A. Rogers, 1887), p. 182, cited in Judith Pascoe, 'Female Botanists and the Poetry of Charlotte Smith', in Wilson and Haefner (eds), *Re-visioning Romanticism*, pp. 193–209 (p. 201).

8 Polwhele, *The Unsex'd Females*, note to line 91, pp. 15–17.

9 Seward claims that Darwin later made these lines the 'exordium' to the first part of his poem, interweaving them with eighteen lines of his own and that he did not acknowledge this. See Seward, *Memoirs of Dr Darwin*, pp. 131–2.

10 *Ibid.*, p. 131.

11 *Ibid.*, p. 131.

12 *Ibid.*, p. 283.

13 For the influence of Ovid and classical mythology on the work of Linnaeus, see John Heller, 'Classical Mythology in the *Systema Naturae* of Linnaeus', *Transactions and Proceedings of the American Philological Association*, 76 (1945), 333–57. Heller analyses the names Linnaeus gives to 200 species of genus *Papilo* butterflies in his new binominal system, nearly all of which recall persons of classical mythology. Linnaean language was also heavily influenced by Pliny's *Natural History*. For Linnaeus's biblical influences, see Sten Lindroth, 'The Two Faces of Linnaeus', in Frängsmyr (ed.), *Linnaeus: The Man and His Work*, p. 10.

14 See the entry 'Monandria' in the *OED*. A reference to Linnaeus's name for his wife appears in one of the verses addressed to the bride and bridegroom on the occasion of Linnaeus's marriage to Sarah Lisa Moraeus. The couple had a three-year engagement during which time Linnaeus composed many poems addressed to her. For an account of the wedding poems, see Blunt, *The Compleat Naturalist*, p. 134.

15 Erasmus Darwin, 'Proem', *The Botanic Garden* (London: J. Johnson, 1791; facs. repr. Menston: Scolar Press, 1973), p. vi. All further references are to this edition and are given in parentheses in the text.

16 The text of Cook's own journal from this voyage was not published until many years later in 1893. A version of Sir Joseph Bank's *Endeavour* journal was published in 1896, edited by Sir Joseph Dalton Hooker. See *The Endeavour Journal of Joseph Banks, 1768–1771*, ed. J. C. Beaglehole, 2nd edn, 2 vols (Sydney: Angus & Robertson, 1963). See also Beaglehole's textual introduction to the records of the *Endeavour*'s voyage, *The Journals of Captain Cook on His Voyages of Discovery*, 4 vols (Cambridge: Cambridge University Press for the Hakluyt Society, 1955) I: *The Voyage of the Endeavour, 1768–1771*, ed. J. C. Beaglehole, pp. cxciii–cclxiv. For a discussion of Hawkesworth's, Cook's and Banks's accounts, see Lamb, *Preserving the Self in the South Seas*, pp. 94–105; Jonathan Lamb, 'Minute Particulars and the Representation of the South Pacific', *Eighteenth-Century Studies*, 28:3 (Spring 1995), 281–94, and Carol Percy, 'In the Margins: Hawkesworth's Editorial Emendations to the Language of Captain Cook's *Voyages*', *English Studies*, 77:6 (November 1996), 549–78.

17 John Hawkesworth, *An Account of the Voyages*, 3 vols (London: printed for W. Strahan & T. Cadell, 1773), II, p. 207. Further references are given in parentheses in the text.

18 Jonathan Lamb has remarked that Hawkesworth was particularly 'attentive to moments of aesthetic pleasure' (Lamb, *Preserving the Self in the South Seas*, p. 105).

19 One of the objects of the *Endeavour* voyage was to observe the whole of the passage of the planet Venus over the sun's disk.

20 Banks invested much of his scientific reputation in Linnaeus, botanising with Daniel Solander, Linnaeus's favourite pupil, on the *Endeavour* voyage and employing

another prominent Linnaean, Jonas Dryander, as his librarian in Soho Square. He gave his support to the new translations of Linnaeus from the Botanical Society at Lichfield which in turn were dedicated to him. Banks also arranged his herbarium in London according to Linnaean schemes and commissioned a grand portrait of Linnaeus which was given pride of place in his study (*Linnaeus, a portrait in oils by Laurent Pasch after Alexander Roslin*, 1775). For Banks as a Linnaean, see Stafleau, *Linnaeus and the Linnaeans*, pp. 199–240.

21 [Anonymous,] *An Epistle From Mr Banks* (London: sold by J. Swan & Thomas Axiell, 1773), lines 17–18, p. 6.

22 For a discussion of satirical poems inspired by Hawkesworth's *Voyages*, see Bernard Smith, *European Vision and the South Pacific* (New Haven, CT: Yale University Press, 1988), pp. 46–51.

23 Arabella Rowden, *A Poetical Introduction to the Study of Botany* (London: T. Bensley, 1801), p. 147. The notes to the poem state that Oberea 'regretted the departure of Sir Joseph Banks from the Island'. All further references are to this edition and are in parentheses in the text.

24 [James Perry,] *Mimosa: or The Sensitive Plant* (London: Printed for W. Sandwich, 1779), p. 13. Plant imagery was used to describe both male and female sexual organs in John Cleland's *Memoirs of a Woman of Pleasure*, 2 vols (London: G. Fenton, 1749). The most infamous description of the penis as a phallic plant was made by John Wilkes in *An Essay on Woman* (London: [n. pub], 1763). For a brief discussion of James Perry, see Bewell, '"On the Banks of the South Sea", pp. 173–91 (pp. 182–3).

25 Hawkesworth's account was deemed unsuitable for British women because he focused attention on the 'wanton' behaviour of Tahitian women including Oberea who had a young lover named Obadeé. *An Epistle From Mr Banks* implies that Oberea also pursued Banks for sex:

> One page of *Hawkesworth*, in the cool retreat,
> Fires the bright maid with more than mortal heat;
> She sinks at once into the lover's arms,
> Nor deems it vice to prostitute her charms;
> 'I'll do' cries she, 'what Queens have done before'
> And sinks, *from principle*, a common whore
> (Anon., *An Epistle from Mr Banks*, 151–6).

26 Janet Browne has suggested that Darwin, a sceptic and radical with two illegitimate children, may be playfully questioning the state of monogamy. He had two illegitimate daughters between marriages, Susan and Mary Parker, who were raised on equal terms with his other children. Browne also points out that in 1778 Darwin was in love with Elizabeth Pole, a married woman. *The Loves of the Plants* was begun in 1779. The poem itself shows women to be the arbiters of masculine behaviour and Browne argues that it may have been intended as a love poem for Elizabeth Pole. Mrs Pole was soon widowed and married Darwin in 1781. See Browne, 'Botany for Gentleman', pp. 607–8.

27 For a discussion of these terms, see Stearn, 'The Origin of the Male and Female Symbols of Biology'. Londa Schiebinger argues that the notion that plants and animals reproduce within marital relations persisted into the nineteenth century: 'The term "gamete" – adopted by biologists in the 1860s to refer to a germ cell capable of fusing with another cell to form a new individual – derives from the Greek *gamein*, to marry' (Schiebinger, 'The Private Life of Plants', p. 128).

28 Clandestine marriages were only done away with in England in 1753 when Lord Hardwicke's 'Marriage Act' required couples to undergo a public proclamation of banns.

29 François Delaporte writes that 'far from being subversive, sexuality in plants was modelled on permissible human behaviour, respectable marriage' (*Nature's Second Kingdom*, p. 143).

30 Anthony Grafton has written that in the eighteenth century the footnote was 'a high form of literary art'; he is referring in particular to the historical footnote as exemplified in Edward Gibbon's *History of the Rise and Fall of the Roman Empire* (1776–88). The role played by footnotes in the literary culture of Enlightenment Europe was of equal importance:

> For in that age of polite conversation, when philosophers loved to present the most abstruse problems of Newtonian physics at a level accessible to the gentle – especially the gentle female – reader, the footnote enjoyed surprising popularity as a literary device (Anthony Grafton, *The Footnote: A Curious History* (London: Faber and Faber, 1997), p. 110).

Useful studies of the footnote in literature can be found in Bray, Handley and Henry (eds), *Ma(r)king the Text.*

Marilyn Butler has hinted that Darwin's poem was in danger of being upstaged by its footnotes, but that this may have been intended:

> Anyone trained in journal-reading to respect the latest learned intelligence (and the customary sign of its presence, the footnotes' parade of authorities) would begin to read the upstaged poem for its footnotes, rather than the other way round – a reader response Darwin presumably hoped for (Marilyn Butler, 'Cultures Medium, the Role of the Review,' in Curran, *Cambridge Companion to British Romanticism*, pp. 120–47 (p. 129)).

After the publication of *The Botanic Garden* many of the most ambitious poems of the period had footnotes.

31 Pascoe, 'Female Botanists and the Poetry of Charlotte Smith', p. 199.

32 Banks, *Endeavour Journals*, I, p. 279 (May 1769). Beaglehole notes that Ninon de l'Enclos – the correct spelling – was 'the free and dazzling mistress of the most celebrated of seventeenth century salons' (note 1, p. 279). The implication is that Oberea was promiscuous.

33 Seward, *Memoirs of Dr Darwin,* p. 289.

34 *Ibid.*, p. 287.

35 Darwin's female is named Chunda as *Chundali Borrum* is the name 'natives' give to this plant.

36 Contemporary descriptions of Turkish women's dress consisting of a revealing silk smock clasped at the neck could be found in Lady Wortley Montagu's *Letters* (Lady Wortley Montagu, *Letters*, 3 vols (London Printed for T. Becket & P. A. De Hondt, 1763), II, pp. 28–9 (Letter XXIX, 'To the Countess – ', Adrianople, 1 April 1717).

37 'Warm with sweet blushes bright GALANTHA glows' (IV. 103).

38 Montagu wrote:

> I look upon the Turkish women, as the only free people in the Empire; the very Divan pays a respect to them, and the Grand Signior himself, when a *Bassa* is executed, never violates the privileges of the *Haram* (or women's apartment), which remains unsearched and entire to the widow (Montagu, *Letters*, II, p. 35 (Letter XXIX)).

For a discussion of Montagu, and other women travellers such as Elizabeth Craven in relation to the Seraglio, see Felicity Nussbaum, *Torrid Zones: Maternity, Sexuality and Empire in Eighteenth-Century English Narratives* (Baltimore, MD and London: Johns Hopkins University Press, 1995), pp. 137–42.

39 Montagu, *Letters*, II, p. 33 (Letter XXIX).

40 *Ibid.*, II, pp. 33–4 (Letter XXIX).

41 For *Rubia*, see *Ibid.*, I. 321–38.

42 An infusion of laurel leaves leads to intoxication and sometimes death.

43 'By cautiously cutting through the concentric coats of a tulip-root, longitudinally from the top to the base, and taking them off successively, the whole flower of next year's tulip is beautifully seen by the naked eye, with its petals, pistils, and stamens' (Darwin, 'Loves of the Plants', note to I. 177).

44 'One pit to receive the dead was dug in Charter-house, 40 feet long, 16 feet wide, and about 20 feet deep; and in two weeks received 1114 bodies. During this dreadful calamity there were instances of mothers carrying their own children to these public graves, and of people delirious, or in despair from the loss of their friends, who threw themselves alive into the pits' (Darwin's note to III. 338). Darwin's source here is Daniel Defoe, *A Journal of the Plague Year* (London: E. Nutt, J. Roberts, A. Dodd and J. Graves, 1722).

45 Seward, *Memoirs of Dr Darwin*, p. 340.

46 Brown, *The Ends of Empire*, p. 16.

47 Behold the strutting *Amazonian* Whore,
She stands in Guard with her right Foot before:
Her Coats Tuck'd up; and all her Motions just,

She stamps and then Cries hah at every thrust,
But laugh to see her tyr'd with many a bout,
Call for the Pot, and like a Man Piss out.

(John Dryden, *The Sixth Satyr of Juvenal*, 350–70, in *The Poems of John Dryden*, ed. James Kinsley (Oxford: Clarendon Press, 1958)).

48 Colley, *Britons: Forging the Nation*, p. 263.

49 Polwhele associates radical feminism with revolutionary politics; the new breed of literary women, the 'The Amazonian band, the female Quixotes of the new philosophy' were set to imitate the women of republican France – to introduce into England the disorder that had swept through France (Polwhele, *The Unsex'd Females*, notes to line 12).

50 Roxana, a woman with a sexual history, refuses to marry her lover and turns down the respectability that marriage would offer 'seeing Liberty seem'd to be the Men's property, I wou'd be a *Man-Woman;* for as I was born free, I wou'd die so. Sir *Robert* smil'd, and told me, I talk'd a kind of *Amazonian* Language' (Daniel Defoe, *Roxana: The Fortunate Mistress*, ed. John Mullan (1724; Oxford: Oxford University Press, 1996), p. 171).

51 The earliest reference to Cuckoo pint (or 'wake robin') as an aphrodisiac is in John Lyly's play *Loves Metamorphosis*, published in 1601. Cuckoo pint, also known by the name of Lords and Ladies, is still known to have phallic associations in the twentieth century. Roy Vickery, for example, records schoolgirls in Dorset in 1982 being told never to touch the cuckoo pint for fear of becoming pregnant (Roy Vickery, *A Dictionary of Plant Lore* (Oxford: Oxford University Press, 1995), p. 224).

52 Wollstonecraft, *Vindication*, p. 53. For a discussion of this phrase, see Chapter 7 on cultivation.

53 Janet Browne uses this phrase in relation to Darwin in 'Botany For Gentleman', 593–621 (p. 621).

54 In 1788, when Darwin was composing the poem, Delany was in her 89th year and still working on her paper collages. She did not begin working in this medium until the age of 74 when her sight became too poor to continue painting. Darwin describes her method of 'placing the leaves of each plant with the petals, and all the other parts of the flowers on coloured paper, and cutting them with sissers accurately to the natural size and form, and then pasting them on a dark ground; the effect of which is wonderful, and their accuracy less liable to fallacy than drawings' (note to II. 153).

Anna Seward explains that Darwin gave an 'entirely false description' of Delany's art because she used neither 'the wax, moss or wire' that Darwin attributed to her. See Seward, *Memoirs of Dr Darwin*, p. 315. Biographical details of Delany can be found in Hayden, *Mrs Delany and her Flower Collages* and in Verna Linney, 'A Passion for Art, A Passion for Botany: Mary Delany and Her Floral Mosaiks', *Eighteenth-Century Women: Studies in Their Lives, Work and Culture*, 1 (2001), 203–35.

55 Elisabeth Christina Linnea, 'Om Indianska Krassens Blickande,' *Svenska Kongliga Vetenskaps Academiens Handlingar*, 23 (1762), 284–6. Linnaeus appended a description of three varieties of Nasturtium to his daughter's account which no doubt influenced the editor's decision to publish the findings of a woman botanist in a scientific journal. Darwin writes:

> Miss E. C. Linnaeus first observed the tropæolum majus, to emit sparks or flashes in the mornings before sunrise, during the months of June or July … Mr Wilcke, a celebrated electrician, believed them to be electric. (note to I. 45, p. 137).

56 James Plumptre, *The Lakers*, intr. Jonathan Wordsworth (London: W. Clarke, 1798; facs. repr. London: Woodstock Books, 1990), p. 40. All further references are to this edition and are given in parentheses in the text.

57 James Plumptre, 1770–1832, playwright and Church of England clergyman, is listed in the *DNB*. See also Eric Robinson, 'John Clare (1793–1864) and James Plumptre (1771–1832): A Methodistical Parson', *Transactions of the Cambridge Bibliography Society*, 11:1 (1996), 59–88.

58 In 1795 the *British Critic* urged the public not to read Darwin's work. For a discussion of the reception of Darwin in the periodical press, see Norton Garfinkle, 'Science and Religion in England, 1790–1800: The Critical Response to the Work of Erasmus Darwin', *Journal of the History of Ideas*, 16:3 (June 1955), 376–88.

59 Thomas James Mathias, *The Pursuits of Literature: A Satirical Poem in Four Dialogues*, 16th edn, (1798; London, Becket and Porter, 1812), p. 71 ('Dialogue the First'). All further references are to this edition.

60 Lee, *An Introduction to Botany*, p. 152.

61 Mathias, 'Dialogue the First', *The Pursuits of Literature*, line 90.

62 'Precocious: of a plant: Flowering or fruiting early; *spec.* bearing blossom before the leaves, also said of the blossoms or fruit. 1650 Sir T. Browne, *Pseud. Ep.* II. vi. (ed. 2) 79 "Many Precocious trees, and such as have their spring in the winter, may be found in most parts of Europe"' (*OED*).

63 Mathias, 'Dialogue the First', note 22.

64 *Ibid.*, note 23.

65 'I agree with the author of "the Pursuits", both in his praises and censures of the writers of this country, with a few exceptions only. To his eulogia, indeed, I heartily

assent: but, I think his animadversions on Darwin and Hayley in particular, are unmerited. In composing his Botanic Garden, Dr. Darwin was aware, that though imagination refuse to enlist under the banner of science, yet science may sometimes be brought forward, not unhappily under the conduct of imagination: and of the latter ... we are presented with a complete specimen in that admirable poem.' (Polwhele, *The Unsex'd Females,* note to line 5).

66 'That Miss Wollstonecraft was a sworn enemy to blushes, I need not remark' (Polwhele, *The Unsex'd Females*, note to line 66, p. 13). On the subject of women's botany, Polwhele had at first written:

> More eager for illicit knowledge pant,
> With lustful boys anatomise a plant;
> The virtues of its dust prolific speak,
> Or point its pistil with unblushing cheek.
>
> (Polwhele, *The Unsex'd Females*, note to line 29, p. 8).

67 For a discussion of observation, microscopy and voyeurism in the Enlightenment see Stafford, 'Voyeur or Observer?, and *Artful Science*, pp. 217–38.

68 I am thinking of the work of Mary Louise Pratt. She cites Daniel Boorstein, *The Discoverers* (New York: Random house, 1983), p. 25: 'nature was an immense collection of natural objects which he himself walked around as superintendent, sticking on labels. He had a forerunner in this arduous task: Adam in Paradise' (Pratt, *Imperial Eyes*, p. 32).

69 'Madam, a circulating library in a town is as an evergreen tree of diabolical knowledge! It blossoms through the year! – and depend on it, Mrs Malaprop, that they who are so fond of handling the leaves, will long for the fruit at last' (Richard Brinsley Sheridan, *The Rivals,* I. 2, in *The School For Scandal and Other Plays*, ed. Michael Cordner (Oxford: Oxford University Press, 1988), p. 20.)

70 Alexander Pope, cited in Polwhele, *Unsex'd Females*, note to line 52.

71 Darwin, note to 'Collinsonia', 'Loves of the Plants', line 51.

72 Polwhele alludes to Godwin's *Memoirs* which details Wollstonecraft's depression and suicide attempt when she was abandoned by Imlay.

73 William Godwin, *Memoirs of the Author of a Vindication of the Rights of Woman* (London: J. Johnson, 1798), pp. 73–126 (Chapters 6 and 7).

74 See Polwhele, *The Unsex'd Females*, note to lines 33–6, p. 9, cited above. I have argued that Polwhele is elaborating on his theme of women and botany here; however, G. J. Barker-Benfield has suggested that Polwhele could be referring to Wollstonecraft's translations of Salzman's *Elements of Morality*, which offers advice on curbing masturbation (*The Culture of Sensibility: Sex and Society in Eighteenth-Century Britain* (Chicago: Chicago University Press, 1992), p. 379).

75 Polwhele, *The Unsex'd Females*, note to line 13.

76 For botany and Jacobinism, see Bewell, '"Jacobin Plants"'.

77 Darwin is a prominent figure in Maria's letters. In a letter to Mrs Ruxton, for example, Maria expresses her excitement at her father bringing home a copy of Darwin's *Botanic Garden* for the first time. See *Chosen Letters*, ed. F. W. Barry (London, Jonathan Cape, 1931), p. 58 (14 August 1792). For the Edgeworth family's association with Darwin, see Uglow, *The Lunar Men* (for Richard Lovell Edgeworth, see pp. 182–6, and for Maria Edgeworth, see pp. 315, 320, 372, 377, and 460).

78 *Early Lessons* was published in six volumes by J. Johnson in 1801. The parts include 'Harry and Lucy', 'Rosamond' and 'Frank'. 'Rosamond', in particular, treats the botanical themes of 'The Hyacinths' and 'The Thorn'.

79 R. L. Praeger, in *Some Irish Naturalists* (Dundalk: Dundalgan Press, 1949) lists *Dialogues on Botany for the use of Young Persons* (London: R. Hunter, 1819) under the entry for Maria Edgeworth on p. 77. *Dialogues on Botany* was in fact written by Harriet Beaufort (1788–1865) who was related by marriage to Maria Edgeworth. Her older sister, Frances, was the fourth wife of Maria Edgeworth's father, Richard Lovell Edgeworth. For Harriet Beaufort and botany, see Ann Shteir, *Cultivating Women*, pp. 93–5. For a discussion of the authorship of this work, see M. E. Mitchell, 'The Authorship of Dialogues on Botany', *Irish Naturalist's Journal*, 19:11 (1979), 407.

80 See Daniel E. White, 'The "Joineriana": Anna Laetitia Barbauld, The Aikin Family Circle and the Dissenting Public Sphere', *Eighteenth-Century Studies*, 32:4 (Summer 1999), 511–33.

81 Anna Laetitia Barbauld and John Aikin, *Evenings at Home*, 6 vols (London: J. Johnson, 1792–96).

82 Anna Laetitia Barbauld, *The Works of Anna Laetitia Barbauld, with a Memoir by Lucy Aiken*, 2 vols (London: Longman, Hurst, Rees, Orme, Brown & Green, 1825), I, pp. xxxvi–xxxvii.

83 In 'The Umbelliferous Plants', for example, the children are told that the umbelliferous class has 'five chives' (Barbauld and Aikin, *Evenings at Home*, IV, p. 74).

84 Sir Brooke Boothby (1744–1824) of Ashbourne Hall succeeded to the baronetcy on the death of his father in 1789. He published poems and was a member of the literary circle in Lichfield to which Darwin, Anna Seward, Thomas Day and the Edgeworths belonged. The artist Joseph Wright of Derby painted him in 1781, in a botanical scene, holding a manuscript by Jean-Jacques Rousseau. For Sir Brooke Boothby, see Henrey, *British Botanical and Horticultural Literature*, II, p. 132. For the Botanical Society at Lichfield, see Seward, *Memoirs of Dr Darwin*, pp. 98–100.

85 Darwin, *A Plan for the Conduct of Female Education In Boarding Schools*, p. 41.

86 From the letter by Sir Brooke Boothby and Erasmus Darwin, dated 24 August 1795, printed in the prefatory material to Jacson's *Botanical Dialogues*.

87 'I flatter myself that the following work, in *Botanical Lectures*, will be found an early introduction to the use of the Translated System of Vegetables, the only English work from which the pupil can become a Linnaean or Universal Botanist' (Jacson, 'Advertisement,' October 1803, *Botanical Lectures By a Lady*.

88 Jacson, *Botanical Lectures*, pp. 3–4.

89 *Ibid*., p. 26.

90 *Ibid*., p. 238.

91 Clara Reeves's poetry book, *The Flowers at Court* (London: Printed for the author by C & R. Baldwin, 1809) has not been included in the discussion here because it has no scientific content. A moral fable, it has more affinity to those Victorian pocketbooks which feature flowers as moral emblems.

92 Seward, *Memoirs of Dr Darwin*, p. 131.

93 'I wished to find some short and simple pieces on the subject of natural history, for the use of a child of five years old, who on her arrival in England could speak no English, and whose notice was particularly attracted by flowers and insects' (Smith, 'Preface', *Conversations Introducing Poetry*, I, p. i).

94 *The Gardener's Dictionary* was published in 1731; successive editions appeared between 1731 to 1768. For a discussion of the many editions of Miller's *Gardener's Dictionary*, see Henrey, *British Botanical and Horticultural Literature*, II, pp. 213–19. Judith Pascoe claims that Smith was using Martyn's edition of Miller, *The Gardeners*

and Botanists Dictionary (1807) (Pascoe, 'Female Botanists and the Poetry of Charlotte Smith', p. 195); however, this is a little late and I would argue that she was using Miller much earlier in 1804 when 'Flora' first appeared. Another work Smith regularly referred to was John Aikin, *An Essay on the Application of Natural History to Poetry* (London: J. Johnson, 1777).

95 The poem may refer to Smith's daughter, Augusta, who died in April 1795. Loraine Fletcher outlines autobiographical narratives in Smith's works including the prefaces to her various collections of poems in *Charlotte Smith: A Critical Biography*. For her interpretation of 'Reflections on Some Drawing of Plants', see pp. 263–4. For a discussion of how Smith along with Seward 'diverges from the standard romantic model of poetic reflections on painting ... and ... moves towards the depictions of an alternative "feminine accomplishment"', see Jacqueline M. Labbe, 'Every Poet Her Own Drawing Master: Charlotte Smith, Anna Seward and *ut pictura poesis*', in Thomas Woodman (ed.), *Early Romantic Perspectives in British Poetry From Pope to Wordsworth* (London: Macmillan, 1998), pp. 200–14 (p. 201).

96 William Cowper, *The Task*, in *Complete Poetical Works of William Cowper*, ed. H. S. Milford (London: Oxford University Press, 1907), I. 455–61.

97 Smith, *The Young Philosopher*, II, pp. 165–6. For a discussion of botanical motifs in *The Young Philosopher*, see Fletcher, *Charlotte Smith*, pp. 266–74. Fletcher claims that the botanical cave in *The Young Philosopher* was inspired by John Lightfoot's *Flora scotica* (1777), p. 269). I indicated in the introduction that Lightfoot was employed by Margaret Cavendish Bentinck, Duchess of Portland, at Bulstrode in Buckinghamshire to classify her natural history collection and was popular with such ladies (see John Gascoigne, *Joseph Banks and the English Enlightenment: Useful Knowledge and Polite Culture* (Cambridge: Cambridge University Press, 1994), pp. 80–1).

98 'Beachy Head' is concerned with the geological controversy surrounding sea-shell fossils. The poem appears to hold more interest for Smith scholars than 'Flora' which, in comparison, has largely been overlooked. Anne D. Wallace has argued that '*Beachy Head*'s particularized, expert botanical observations stand in instructive contrast to its vague, deliberately ignorant geological observations' ('Picturesque Fossils, Sublime Geology? The Crisis of Authority in Charlotte Smith's *Beachy Head*', p. 85). Contrary to Wallace's view that Smith is always the expert in her botanical notes, I have argued that Smith is inconsistent in her notes and sometimes reverts to using local names of plants. Her preference for English plant names means that she sometimes lacks authority in such notes. Her fraught relationship to the scientific is evident here and she is sensitive to accusations of immodesty arising from her appropriation of a device that is used to demonstrate learnedness in scholarly texts. Donelle R. Ruwe interprets Smith's penchant for botanical detail in *Beachy Head* as a rejection of scientific and literary authority which 'attends to the flower's irreducible alterity and doesn't try to transcend or absorb it' ('Charlotte Smith's Sublime: Feminine Poetics, Botany and *Beachy Head*', p. 123).

99 Flora married Zephyrus and received from him the privilege of presiding over flowers and enjoying perpetual youth. Lemprière's *Classical Dictionary* (1788) suggests that Flora left the riches she gained through prostitution to the Romans who instituted a festival in her honour (J. Lemprière, 'Flora', *A Classical Dictionary*, new edn, ed. F. D. Lemprière (London: T. Cadell, 1839), unpag.

100 Smith only cites Darwin once in 'Flora': in the note to line 192 she refers the reader to note 27 of Darwin's 'Economy of Vegetation' (from Part One of *The Botanic*

Garden). He features more prominently in other works such as *Rural Walks* (1794). 'The 'beautiful little Ode to May from The Botanic Garden of Dr. Darwin' is cited by Mrs Woodfield in Dialogue v, 'The Lily of the Valley' (Smith, *Rural Walks*, 2nd edn, 2 vols (London: T. Cadell & W. Davies, 1795), p. 141) and he is cited again in Dialogue VIII, 'Strawberry Girls': 'What can be finer than these lines of Dr Darwin's, that set before us some of the most striking features of a polar winter: "When leads the northern star his lucid train, / High o'er the snow-clad earth and icy main"' (*Rural Walks*, II, pp. 144–5).

101 Frances Arabella Rowden, from the 'Advertisement', *A Poetical Introduction to the Study of Botany* (London: T. Bensley, 1801) All further references are to this edition and are given in parentheses after quotations in the text.

102 Rowden eventually became headmistress at the Hans Place School in Chelsea where she worked between 1801 and 1820. She also wrote the following educational works: *The Pleasures of Friendship* (London: [n. pub.], 1810), *A Christian Wreath for the Pagan Deities: or An Introduction to Greek and Roman Mythology* (London: A. J. Valpy, 1820) and *A Biographical Sketch of the Most Distinguished Writers of Ancient and Modern Times* (London: Longman, Hatchard & Son. Seely, Laker, Uxbridge, [n.d]).

103 From a review of Rowden's *Poetical Introduction*, *The Anti-Jacobin; or, Weekly Examiner*, no. 10, December 1801, pp. 356–67 (p. 356).

104 *Ibid.*, p. 356.

105 From a review of Rowden's *Poetical Introduction*, *The Monthly Review*, no. 70, January 1813, pp. 98–9.

106 A review of *A Poetical Introduction*, *The Anti-Jacobin*, December 1801, p. 366.

107 Rowden married the French co-proprietor of the Hans Place School, Dominique de St. Quentin. He was a follower of the teachings of Abbé Gaultier (1745–1818). Gaultier developed a method of teaching based on a course of instructive games and conversation. Rowden's 'Advertisement' states that a 'friend' (probably her husband) had suggested that she 'compose a few elementary lessons on Botany, adapted to Abbé Gaultier's plan of instruction'.

108 Smith's 'A Walk in the Shrubbery' is dedicated to 'the cistus or rock rose, a beautiful plant, whose flowers expand and fall off twice in twenty-four hours' (*The Poems of Charlotte Smith*, ed. Curran, p. 303).

109 'The Pleasures of Botanical Pursuits, A Poem', line 19, appended to Priscilla Wakefield, *An Introduction to Botany*, 8th edn (1818), p. 182. All further references are to this edition and are given in parentheses after quotations in the text. Hoare seeks out plants of 'humbler growth' (line 113) in preference to those 'fam'd exotics rich and rare' (line 110) and esteems those plants which are most useful, for 'He who dress'd the beauteous show, / Assign'd to each its use' (lines 48–9). So, the flowers of the pimpernel afford pleasure because they close against impending rain, and 'Warning the swain' (line 118) of approaching showers.

110 Sarah Hoare, *A Poem on the Pleasures and Advantages of Botanical Pursuits* (Bristol: Philip Rose, [1826 (?)]).

111 The mother figure as educator shaped young people's access to the natural world in works for the juvenile market. Mrs Benson in Sarah Trimmer's *Fabulous Histories* (1786) shows Frederick and Harriet 'the sentiments and affections of a good Father and Mother ... possessed by a nest of redbreasts' ('Introduction', *Fabulous Histories* (London: J. Johnson, 1785; repr. New York and London: Garland Publishing, 1977), p. 10). For a general discussion of moral mothers in works for the juvenile

market, see Mitzi Myers, 'Impeccable Governesses, Rational Dames and Moral Mothers: Mary Wollstonecraft and the Female Tradition in Georgian Children's Books', *Children's Literature,* 14 (1986), 31–59.

112 Wakefield, *Mental Improvement*, p. 26 (Conversation 3).

113 Hannah More, cited in Hoare's 'Preface' to *A Poem on the Pleasures and Advantages of Botanical Pursuits*, pp. viii–ix.

114 Hoare, 'Pleasures of Botanical Pursuits', *Poems on Conchology and Botany.*

115 Henrietta Maria Moriarty, 'Preface', *A Viridarium* (London: [n. pub.], 1806), p. v. All further references are to this edition. For a brief discussion of this work, see James Britten, 'Mrs Moriarty's *Viridarium*', *Journal of Botany*, 55 (1917), 52–4. Moriarty also wrote the novels: *Brighton in an Uproar Comprising Anecdotes of Sir Timothy Flight, Mr. Abrahams ... A Novel Founded on Facts* (London: Printed by the Author, 1811) and *Crim. Con. A Novel Founded on Facts* (London: [n. pub.], 1812).

116 Blunt and Stearn describe the work of these artists and their centrality:

> The unsettled state of Europe during the opening years of the eighteenth-century was not propitious for the patronage of art and science; but before the middle of the century, the great names of Linnaeus (b. 1707) in botany and Ehret (b. 1708) in illustration became prominent. Many new plants from America were introduced and recorded at this time. The close of the century inaugurated ... a truly remarkable age when scientific illustration reached aesthetic heights never surpassed before or since. For this Linnaeus's so-called 'Sexual System' of classification with its emphasis on floral details and his binomial nomenclature for species were in no small measure responsible. (Blunt and Stearn, *The Art of Botanical Illustration*, pp. 327–8).

117 Henrietta Maria Moriarty, 'Preface', *Fifty Plates of Green-House Plants* (London: T. Bensley, 1807), p. vi.

118 Linnaeus himself did not think illustrations were particularly useful to botanical study, attributing progress to detailed description rather than pictures (see Karen Reeds, 'When the Botanist Can't Draw: The Case of Linnaeus', *Interdisciplinary Science Reviews*, 29:3 (2004), 248–58). Reeds argues that this disregard for illustration reflects his personal difficulties with drawing. The sketches and drawings from his Lapland journey (published in manuscript form in 1811) are evidence of a lack of skill in this area.

119 For brief biographies of Elizabeth Moody, née Greenly (1737–1814), see Roger Lonsdale (ed.), *Eighteenth-Century Women Poets* (Oxford: Oxford University Press, 1989), pp. 401–2; Mary Waters, 'Elizabeth Moody', *The Literary Encyclopedia*, www.literarydictionary.com/php/speople.php?rec=true&UID=3170 (accessed 24 August 2006).

120 Waters, *The Literary Encyclopedia*, p. 2. For a fuller account of Moody's literary criticism, see Mary Waters, *British Women Writers and the Profession of Literary Criticism 1789–1832* (Basingstoke: Macmillan, 2003).

121 I first came across this poem in Roger Lonsdale's seminal anthology of eighteenth-century women poets. He is unusual in selecting a number of poems by Moody as she is often overlooked. See 'Sappho Burns her books and Cultivates the Culinary Arts', in Lonsdale, *Eighteenth-Century Women Poets,* pp. 406–7.

122 Elizabeth Moody, 'To Dr Darwin, on Reading his Loves of the Plants', in *Poetic Trifles* (London, printed by H. Baldwin and Son for T. Cadell, Jun. and W. Davies, 1798), pp. 8–12; facs. repr. in Judith Hawley and others (eds), *Literature and Science,*

1660–1834, 8 vols (London: Pickering and Chatto, 2003–4), IV: *Flora*, ed. Charlotte Grant (2003), pp. 251–5. All further references are to this edition and are given in parentheses in the text.

123 Lonsdale, *Eighteenth-Century Women Poets,* p. 313. Lonsdale provides a brief biography of Seward on pp. 311–13. There are also long entries on Seward by Sylvia Bowerback in the *DNB*. She has inspired a number of biographies, though none of them are recent: E. V. Lucas, *A Swan and Her Friends* (London: Methuen, 1907); Margaret Ashmun, *The Singing Swan* (New Haven, CT: Yale University Press, 1931); Hesketh Pearson (ed.), *The Swan of Lichfield. Being a selection from the correspondence of Anna Seward, with a short biography and preface* (London: Hamish Hamilton, 1936).

124 Seward's involvement with Midlands Enlightenment culture is discussed by John Brewer in '"Queen Muse of Britain": Anna Seward of Lichfield and the Literary Provinces', in *The Pleasures of the Imagination: English Culture in the Eighteenth Century*, pp. 573–612; and by Jennifer Kelly, 'Introduction', in Gary Kelly and others (eds), *Bluestocking Feminism: Writings of the Bluestocking Circle, 1738–1790*, 6 vols (London: Chatto & Pickering, 1999), IV: *Anna Seward*, ed. Jennifer Kelly, pp. ix–xxi. See also Uglow, *The Lunar Men*. Though, as the title suggests, the author focuses on prominent men.

125 Anna Seward, *Elegy on Captain Cook* (London: J. Dodsley, 1780). The controversy around authorship is detailed in Kelly, *Bluestocking Feminism*, IV, p. xvi.

126 Jennifer Kelly makes this point in her introduction to *Anna Seward*, p. xvi

127 Anna Seward, 'Sonnet. To the Poppy', in Lonsdale, *Eighteenth-Century Women Poets,* line 8, p. 318. All further references are to this edition.

128 See Brewer, *Pleasures of the Imagination*, p. 606. Seward was to publish a volume of verse dedicated to these women in 1796 (*Llangollen Vale with Other Poems* (London: G. Sael. 1796)).

129 Desmond King-Hele, for example, expressed doubts in my conversation with him in July 2004.

130 The poems concerned are 'Colebrooke Dale' (1810) and 'Sonnet. To Colebrooke Dale' (1799). See Roy Porter, *Enlightenment: Britain and the Creation of the Modern World* (London: Penguin, 2000), p. 316.

131 Shtier, *Cultivating Women*, note 4, p. 240. Professor Sally Shuttleworth has questioned whether Seward would refer to herself in this way. Given the fact that the poem is handwritten and anonymous, designed to be read in private, and written to mark a celebration amongst friends, it is possible that she intended to leave a clue to its authorship. I believe the poem to be the work of Seward and am in the process of authenticating this.

132 [Anna Seward (?),] 'The Backwardness of Spring Accounted For', lines 56, 58. This anonymous poem appears in manuscript on the endpapers of the second volume of a British Library copy of Linnaeus, *A System of Vegetables*, 2 vols (Lichfield: printed by John Jackson for Leigh and Sotherby ... London, 1783). All further references to this poem are cited in the text in parentheses.

133 Marion Roberts has suggested that lines 92–5 could relate to John Saville. Seward was reputed to be in love with Saville, who lived apart from his wife during their intense friendship. Despite this, Roberts has written to me to confirm that she does not believe the poem 'to be by Anna'.

134 From the preface to the American edition of *The Unsex'd Females* (New York: W. Cobbett, 1800). It is assumed that Polwhele wrote the preface himself; it is unattributed but contains material found elsewhere in Polwhele's work.

135 For discussion of the 'proper lady', see Mary Poovey, *The Proper Lady and the Woman Writer* (Chicago: University of Chicago Press, 1984).

136 Hoare, 'Preface', *A Poem on the Pleasures of Botanical Pursuits*, p. i. Little is known about Sarah Hoare apart from the details that she gives in her botanical writing and in *Memoirs of Samuel Hoare By His Daughter Sarah and His Widow Hannah* (London: Headley Brothers, 1911), but Smith's remarkable life is well documented in Fletcher, *Charlotte Smith*, and Florence Hilbish, *Charlotte Smith, Poet and Novelist 1749–1806* (Philadelphia: University of Pennsylvania, 1941).

137 Seward had been preparing her poetry and letters for publication some years prior to her death. For her instructions to Scott and Constable see Kelly, *Anna Seward*, p. xx.

138 Seward, *Letters*, VI, pp. 144–5.

139 John Lindley, 'Preface', *Ladies' Botany*, 2 vols (London: Henry G. Bohn, 1841), I, p. v. Lindley was Professor of Botany at the University of London between 1829–60. He launched an attack on Linnaeus in *An Introductory Lecture Delivered to the University of London on April 30th, 1824* (John Taylor: London, 1829). He was a proponent of the 'Natural System' of classification (postulated by Antoine Laurent de Jussieu, *Genera Plantarum* (Paris: Apud viduam Herissant, 1789), and popularised by Professor De Candolle in *Catalogus plantarum* (Montpelier: J. Martel, 1813), and Lindley and Robert Brown in England). Lindley's published works on the natural system included: *An Introduction to the Natural System of Botany* (London: Longman, Rees, Orme, Brown & Green, 1830), *The Vegetable Kingdom* (London: Bradbury and Evans, 1846), *Ladies' Botany* (London, [n. pub.], 1834). For an account of the life and works of John Lindley, see William T. Stearn, *John Lindley 1799–1865, Gardener, Botanist and Pioneer Orchidologist* (Suffolk: Antique Collectors' Club, 1999).

140 'The theoretical simplicity of the Linnaean system is mistaken' (Lindley, *Ladies' Botany*, I, p. 3).

141 Jane Loudon, 'Preface', *Botany For Ladies* (London: John Murray, 1842), I, pp. iii, iv. Jane Wells Loudon (née Webb) (1807–58) married the gardener J. C. Loudon (1783–1843) in 1830. John Loudon pursued Jane after he discovered that she was the author of the novel, *The Mummy, A Tale of the Twenty Second Century* (London: Henry Colburn, 1827), which was published anonymously. After her marriage, she developed an interest in botany and gardening through her husband and is known to have attended the lectures of John Lindley. She founded and edited the *Ladies Magazine of Gardening* (1842) and is now known as one of the most famous women gardeners of the nineteenth century. Loudon's output was prolific; a selection of her published works is listed in the bibliography. See Bea Howe, *Lady With Green Fingers: The Life of Jane Loudon* (London: Country Life, 1961); Geoffrey Taylor, *Some Nineteenth-Century Gardeners* (Essex: Anchor Press, 1951), pp. 1–39; Shteir, *Cultivating Women*, pp. 220–7; Bennett, *Women and Gardens*, pp. 90–100; Deborah Kellaway (ed.), *The Virago Book of Women Gardeners* (London: Virago, 1996), pp. 18–19.

142 Jane Loudon, *Botany for Ladies*, I, p. 1. Antoine Laurent de Jussieu (1748–1836), *Genera plantarum*, 8 vols (Paris: Apud viduam Herissant, 1789); Augustin Pyramus de Candolle (1778–1841), *Catalogus plantarum* (Montpelier: J. Martel, 1813). The 'natural system', pioneered by Jussieu and updated by Candolle, was popularised in Great Britain by Robert Brown and John Lindley; for Lindley, see J. Reynolds Green, *A History of Botany in the United Kingdom* (London: J. M. Dent, 1914), pp. 353–66, and for Robert Brown, pp. 309–35.

5

'Botany in an English dress': British flora and the 'fair daughters of Albion'

The Dutch tulip and the modest English rose

Nor are the plants which Britain calls her own,
Few, Or unlovely.[1]

'EXOTICS' WERE CLEARLY still an object of fascination at the beginning of the nineteenth century, featuring in plant collections, landscape gardens and botanical gardens, but now it was commonplace native flowers that were celebrated by women in the culture of botany: that is, in scientific, literary, and pedagogical texts. Native flowers were invested with greater strength and virtue than their foreign counterparts in women's poetry and were frequently used as moral emblems by women educators in works for the improvement of young women. Comparisons between native British plants and luxuriant foreign varieties similarly occur in periodical literature for women.

The discussion on floriculture in Chapter 1 referred to *The Lady's Monthly Museum*, which carried a number of verse fables on botanical themes between 1798 and 1799, during the war with France. In one such fable, 'The Acorn and Pine, A Tale for Ladies', female readers are called upon to compare, an 'exotic PINE', 'the choicest pride of India's race', with 'a haughty son of British Mould', a 'rugged OAK'.[2] The oak, at first deemed to be uncouth, eventually proves to be more useful and worthy than its exotic rival, the luxuriant but helplessly enfeebled pine. The same wind which tears down the pine sends the oak, 'for nobler purposes design'd' (33) as a British bark 'O'er foaming waves, with rapid course / To shores, perhaps whose hostile force / Views her approach with pale affright' (41–3). As the raw material of shipbuilding the oak is assigned a vital nationalistic role in the British Navy. Readers of the *Lady's Monthly Museum* arrive at the following moral: 'Though Foreign Luxuries obtain / With the voluptuous and vain, / For such, the sober reas'ner will not roam, / Who sees the useful virtues spring at home' (151–4). Such sentiments are in agreement with the teachings of women in the culture of botany: Priscilla Wakefield, Maria Jacson, and Charlotte Smith similarly locate the 'useful virtues' in British plants.

This chapter will discuss the cultivated Englishwoman's preference for indigenous botany and examine the treatment of native species of flower in botanical texts and educational works by women writers. Florist flowers (hyacinths, tulips, *ranunculi*, anemones, auriculas, carnations, pinks, and polyanthus) were often disregarded or dismissed by British botanists, whose systems failed to categorize foreign hybrids or 'varieties' which were not 'pure' species. The separation of the spheres of botany and floristry (of which the latter art had its origins in Dutch and Flemish culture and at which the French excelled) will be accounted for. The opposition of floristry to botany involved notions of class and nation and the tensions between the general and the particular.

The Linnaean revolution in botanical taxonomy involved a shift away from an emphasis on a (flowering) plant's habitat or cycle of growth towards a focus on the minute anatomy of the flower. This concentration on the flower – given the conventional positioning of flowers within the female domain – was to be an important determinant of the new interest in botany that many women were to cultivate. Writing on the subject of flowers, the botanist and florist Maria Jacson confessed that 'from early childhood to an advanced age, [I] possessed, I may almost say, an hereditary liking for this lovely order of creation.'[3]

According to Jacson's *Florist's Manual* (1816), a universal botanist – a 'botanic philosopher' as opposed to a 'fashionable florist' – would award greater value to the commonplace native flower. For Jacson, the florist's superficial observations of cultivated varieties of tulip or carnation pale before the botanist's noble investigation of 'the simplest flower of our meadows'. British flowers had come to be regarded as more appropriate symbols of purity and virtue than their foreign counterparts. Small, sweet-smelling native flowers such as the snowdrop, violet and lily of the valley adorned the cemetery or graveside garden, whereas ornamental and showy florist flowers such as the (Turkish) tulip or the flamboyant African or French marigold would appear immodest in such a spiritual setting. Lilies of the valley and snowdrops were thought particularly appropriate for the graves of children or young women due to their association with innocence and purity; the motif of the broken lily can be found on urns and monuments commemorating young women 'cut off in the flower of their youth'.[4] Women's poetry often draws on these floral traditions. For example, Anna Seward's poem 'Eyam' (written in 1788 and published in 1792) records the custom of hanging garlands of white flowers over the church pews of village maids who 'die in the flower of their age'.[5]

Robert Thornton specifically selected women writers to commemorate British flowers when he united 'beauties of the vegetable race' from every corner of the globe, compiling a poetical empire of flora. His florilegium *Temple of Flora, or Garden of Nature* (1799–1807) boasts a rich array of botanical poetry by such women as Arabella Rowden, Charlotte Smith, Charlotte Lennox and Anna Seward, among others. From this work, Cordelia Skeeles's celebration of the common snowdrop is illustrative of the way indigenous species of flower had come to denote virtue:

Drooping harbinger of flora,
Simply are thy blossoms drest;
Artless as the gentle virtues
Mansioned in the blameless breast.[6]

Elsewhere, in the poetry of the aspiring botanist Arabella Rowden, the 'untainted' beauty of the native wild flower, 'simply ... drest' and 'artless', is set up in opposition to the harlotry of the florists' flower or 'exotic':

Seek not this flower, and its fraternal tribe,
Amid the garden's gay luxuriant pride;
Explore the woods, the meadows, and the wild,
For Sweet Simplicity's Untainted Child.[7]

Charlotte Smith expresses similar sentiments in a sonnet from *Rural Walks: in Dialogues Intended for the Use of Young Persons* (1795), written in praise of Miranda, 'Nature's ingenuous child'.[8] The poem is interspersed with dialogue between Mrs Woodfield and her niece Caroline, centring on two young women of very different dispositions. Maria, represented by the showy, scentless tulip, is fashionable and vain of person whereas Miranda is as 'mild, generous and unassuming' as the lily:[9]

Miranda! mark, where, shrinking from the gale,
Its silken leaves yet moist with morning dew
That fair faint flower, the Lily of the vale,
Drops its meek head, and looks, methinks like you![10]

The retiring lily provides a stark contrast to the forward florist's tulip:

With bosom bar'd to meet the garish day,
The glaring tulip, gaudy, undismay'd
Offends the eye of taste, that turns away,
And seeks the Lily in her fragrant shade.[11]

'[W]rapp'd in its modest veil of tender green ... and bending, as reluctant to be seen', the native lily of the valley evokes the realm of the private and virtuous; in contrast, the exotic tulip symbolises the wantonness which was commonly associated with highly public women or even 'savages'.[12] We learn from Mrs Woodfield that Maria, who resembled the gaudy tulip, was so fond of painting her face that 'she was frequently insulted in the streets, being taken for one of those unhappy women who walk there for the purpose of being remarked and followed'.[13] The laws of sexual conduct are learned through dialogues on flowers, and the feminisation of botany in relation to the gendered dichotomy of the public and private spheres again reveals itself.

The poetic treatment of florist flowers has its counterpart in debates on gardening; the untainted beauty of the snowdrop or violet and the monstrous prostitution of the tulip are similar to those English perceptions of French formal gardens where the 'virgin blush of innocence' has been eclipsed by 'the harlotry of art'.[14] The sexualised imagery which surrounds cultivated varieties of flower is, of course, another strand of the symbolic association of women and gardens.[15]

Aware of current debates around botany, women educators developed comparisons between botanists' and florists' flowers and used them to teach young women about sexual conduct. Mary Wollstonecraft draws on the language of flowers in her early educational writing. *A Vindication*, as I have demonstrated, contained an attack on 'flowery diction' in books for female education. In *Original Stories From Real Life* (1788, 1791), Wollstonecraft takes the conventional comparison between woman and flower and moves it in the opposite direction, shifting away from connotations of the luxurious and the decorative towards the rational and utilitarian.[16] The flamboyant (Turkish/Dutch) tulip is unfavourably compared with the modest, sweet-smelling, English rose. The young protagonists, Caroline and Mary, are encouraged to observe the difference between the two flowers by their governess, whose aim is to banish from their minds superficial 'notions of beauty' which are not founded upon any 'principle of utility'. The girls must learn to discriminate between 'mere bodily beauty', represented by the cosmetically perfected tulip, and a virtuous soul symbolised by the English rose.[17] The flowers are assigned human counterparts as Wollstonecraft's focus slides from the flower to the female sex (a device also employed by Smith).

Betty, the housemaid, has regular features like the cultivated tulip, whereas the elegant Mrs Trueman possesses 'an excellent understanding' and a feeling heart, and is 'not like the flaunting tulip, that forces itself forward into notice, but resembles the modest rose, you see yonder, retiring under its elegant foliage.'[18] Like Smith, Wollstonecraft selects the archetypal English flower to represent virtue and characterises the foreign tulip as vulgar and tasteless, suggesting that English persons of taste and judgement would not be seduced by a beauty having neither grace nor utility. The gaudiness of the tulip is, therefore, seen to appeal to the servant classes or those whose minds are 'uninformed': 'The lower class of mankind and children are fond of finery; gaudy dazzling appearances catch their attention.'[19] Thus the vulgarity of the tulip is associated with social inferiority – of class, but also, implicitly, of nation.

Floristry was considered to be tainted by the activities of unscrupulous Dutch merchants during tulipomania in Holland and was understood by the English to have originated in Dutch artisan communities. In Wollstonecraft, Dutch tulips are depicted as the playthings of those deficient in taste or breeding, the lower orders or the foreign-born. Thus, while these shifting attitudes to florist flowers accord with late eighteenth-century discourse on the dangers of luxury, texts such as Wollstonecraft's suggest that a number of other factors were involved; among them, nationalism and class.[20]

Moralising botanists and vulgar florists

The art of elaborate plant breeding was brought to Britain by artisan refugees, especially weavers from Flanders and later from France.[21] Flemish workers fled to England during the governorship of the Duke of Alba in the sixteenth century and improved English market gardens with their methods of cultivation. Anna Pavord traces tulip breeding in England back to the activities of protestant Huguenots in the second half of the sixteenth century when tulip bulbs were brought to England from Flanders during Philip II's Catholic crusades.[22] Many immigrants were weavers who settled in Norwich, a city of some importance at this time.

It is frequently suggested that florists' societies were introduced into England by these Flemish artisans as Flemish florists' societies were active in the mid-seventeenth century long before they became popular in eighteenth-century England. In *The Dutch Gardener* (1703), Hendrik Van Oosten describes the formation of a society of florists in the Netherlands to regulate the Dutch tulip trade at the height of tulipomania in 1637.[23] However, English florists' meetings do not appear in local newspapers until the early eighteenth century. Ruth Duthie documents an advertisement for a florist's feast in the Norwich Gazette as early as 1707.[24] The Ancient Society of York Florists was founded in 1768 while another famous club, the Paisley Florist Society, the majority of whose members were skilled weavers renowned for their 'Paisley Pinks', was not formed until 1782. These florists' societies ran competitions and flower shows which became occasions for feasts. Here, English florists again imitated the Flemish, whose florists' feasts commemorated St Dorothy, the patron saint of flower-lovers.[25] By 1770, William Hanbury recorded that 'feasts are now become general, and are regularly held at towns, at proper distance, all over England'.[26] The local landowner would often be the patron and, while his gardener was allowed to compete for the prizes, the majority of the competitors at flower shows throughout the country were cottage craftsmen and tradesmen.

Floristry became the ideal occupation for cottagers with small gardens, weavers or agricultural workers.[27] Lancashire weavers, for example, were famous for their show auriculas. Gentleman, especially clergymen, and nurserymen occasionally competed for prizes alongside tradesmen but the weavers generally claimed all the prizes on such feast days. Home-based workers such as handloom weavers were always close at hand to shield their plants from adverse weather conditions. One of the humble tradesmen celebrated by George Crabbe in *The Borough* (1810) is a florist-weaver who takes delight in the perfected properties of his prize-winning carnation:[28]

> This, this is Beauty: cast, I pray, your eyes
> On this my Glory! see the Grace, the size!
> Was ever stem so tall, so stout, so strong,
> Exact in breadth, in just proportion, long;
> These brilliant Hues are all distinct and clean,
> No Kindred Tint, no blending Streaks between;
> This is no shaded, run off, pin ey'd thing'
> A King of Flowers, a Flower for England's King;
> I own my pride, and thank the favouring Star
> Which shed such beauty on my fair *Bizarre*.[29]

Though poor, the weaver experiences an overwhelming joy unknown to the wealthier inhabitants when he wins the prize at the florists' show.

There were, of course, seedsmen and nurserymen of some repute who published lavish books and catalogues such as Robert Furber's *Twelve Months of Fruits* (1732) and Philip Miller's *Gardeners Dictionary* (1731). However, I would categorise them as gardeners rather than florists. There is no evidence to suggest that they entered florists' competitions or shows. They belonged to the 'Society of Gardeners' and were more concerned with cultivating ornamental shrubs and fruit trees than exotic 'florist' flowers. Miller's *Gardeners and Florists Dictionary* first appeared in 1724; but by the time the more ambitious *Gardeners Dictionary* was published in 1731, Miller had dropped the reference to 'Florists' from its title. It seems likely that he wished to affiliate himself with the prestigious Society of Gardeners and to dissociate himself from the activities of the florist whose feasts were increasingly dominated by competitions and prizes.

By the first half of the nineteenth century new societies were formed and a horticultural press had emerged.[30] However, as botany became the fashionable pursuit of the upper middle-class (doctors, the country clergy and gentlewomen), floristry was the occupation of the humble weaver or lace-maker (especially in the industrial North and Midlands) who met in the local public house to show off their auriculas or carnations.[31]

Of the eight so-called 'florist flowers' only the pink (sometimes found in the North of England) can be considered British.[32] The tulip was a native of Turkey, cultivated by French and Flemish florists; the hyacinth, a native of Asia, cultivated by the Dutch, and so on. Anna Pavord has suggested that

> The tulip in England was generally considered a French rather than a Dutch flower. As a result it suffered in the rejection of all things French that followed the outbreak of the Seven Years War in the middle of the eighteenth century ... the tulip lost its glamorous place in the most stylish gardens of England.[33]

It is arguable that the tulip still had very strong associations with Dutch culture in eighteenth-century Britain. Holland, the setting for the *Tulpenwoede*, or Tulipomania, was the tulip's spiritual home. According to the OED, the earliest example of the word 'tulippomania' [*sic*] occurs in an eighteenth-century satire on florists in the *Tatler* in 1710.[34] There were fears that tulip mania had spread to England from Holland; Steele's Mr Spectator observed that 'a few fanciful people spend all their time in the cultivation of a single Tulip, or Carnation'.[35] The Ancient Society of York Florists kept their own records on the history of tulipomania including the following entry on Alkamaar in Holland:

> it is in the register of this town, that the History of that folly is to be found, it is there recorded that in 1637 there were publicly sold at auction at Alkamaar 120 tulips for 90,000 guilders one of which, the Admiral C[illegible] with its roots and offsets, was sold for 5,200 guilders of the money, not only the name and price of these flowers, but also their weight, is particularly set down in this register.[36]

The minute books of this Society, which date back to 1768 when the society was formed, demonstrate that eighteenth-century English florists were still captivated by the drama of tulipomania. British tulipists such as James Justice (1698–1763), the producer of the *Scots Gardiner's Directory* (1754), modelled themselves on Dutch florists. Justice bankrupted himself by purchasing expensive tulip bulbs from Holland and importing a shipload of Dutch soil to enhance their cultivation.[37]

The decline in the number of tulips in eighteenth-century British gardens, therefore, could equally be attributed to a 'rejection of all things' Dutch, rather than French, as Pavord claims. Holland, the centre of floristry, was a former enemy of Britain during the trade wars; mercantile rivalry between the Dutch and British was at least as strong as that between Britain and France and had survived from the early seventeenth century. Trade rivalry and commercial wars continued into the eighteenth century and anti-Dutch sentiment persisted in a number of eighteenth-century texts.[38]

The majority of eighteenth-century florist flowers were improved through the exertions of Dutch, French and Flemish florists. Writing on the anemone in 1792, the English florist James Maddock declared that 'The English can claim little or no share in the advancement or improvement of this flower for all varieties of double anemones we possess in England have been imported from Holland, France and Flanders'.[39] The fourth Anglo-Dutch war was fought from 1780 to 1784 when Britain declared war on Holland because the Regents had engaged in trade with American revolutionaries.[40] Britain was again waging war between 1793 and 1815 – this time against revolutionary and Napoleonic France. Not unconnectedly, the art of floristry, pioneered by the French and Dutch, aroused suspicion and was regarded with some contempt by the British during this period. Indigenous botany gained prominence over floristry amidst a tide of patriotism and British flowers were deemed to be of greater worth than alien 'exotics'.

Such British attitudes to florist flowers were also dictated by theories of taste which, again, had ideological, nationalistic components. Horace Walpole's 'The History of the Modern Taste in Gardening' (1780) claimed that the Englishman disapproved of artifice and regularity and adopted an informal style which was modelled on nature and liberty; an appreciation of 'artificial' florist flowers was contrary to this liberated English taste.[41] In contrast, according to the florist aesthetic, each flower was expected to conform to exact criteria laid down by the florist societies. The Ancient Society of York Florists adhered to specific standards set out in their minute books. The properties desired in the auricula are listed as follows:

> 1st. The stem of the flower should be lofty and strong.
> 2nd. The footstalk of the flower should be short, that the umbel may be regular and close.
> 3rd. The pipe on the neck of each flower should be short, and the flowers large, and regularly spread, being no ways inclinable to cup.
> 4th. That the colours are very bright and well mixed.
> 5th. That the eye of the flower be large, round, and of a good white, or yellow, and the tube or neck be not too wide.[42]

James Maddock's *Florist's Directory* similarly recorded the properties that were demanded of certain flowers such as the 'Fine Double Hyacinth':

> The stem should be strong, tall and erect, supporting numerous large bells, each suspended by a short and strong peduncle, or foot-stalk, in a horizontal position, so that the whole may have a compact pyramidal form, with the crown, or uppermost bell, perfectly erect.[43]

268 DESCRIPTION

PLATE III.

Fig. 1. A corolla, or bloſſom, of a fine variegated double Carnation, of the common ſize. Vide page 202 and 203.

Fig. 2. A calyx, or pod, of ditto, tied on the approach of bloom, to prevent its burſting. Page 163 and 164.

Fig. 3. An empty calyx of ditto, of the common ſize. Page 204.

Fig. 4. A corolla of a fine double laced Pink, of the middle ſize. Page 217.

Fig. 5. A ſingle petal of ditto, the broad end of which is its *lamina*, or plate, and the lower end its *unguis*, or baſe. Page 217.

Fig. 6. An empty calyx of ditto, of the middle ſize. Page 216.

16 The Variegated Double Carnation – Description. Reproduced from James Maddock, *The Florist's Directory*

Maddock spends two and a half pages describing the properties of the variegated tulip and four or five pages on the variegated double carnation (see Fig. 16). These flowers bore little resemblance to their original type: even British pinks, when cultivated by Dutch or French florists, 'so materially differ, in some of their properties, from the original species, that it is not easy to ascertain to which of them, as described by Linnaeus, they most properly belong'.[44] Maddock here asserts the incommensurability of florist and botanical thought; Linnaeans similarly upheld this division.

The increasing adoption of, and interest in, Linnaean botany contributed to the shift in attitudes concerning floristry; compared to the botanist, the florist was considered an artificer whose creations were nothing more than a corruption of nature. To their fiercest critics, florist's flowers were a violation of natural law, an immoral attempt to improve on 'the sovereign Planter's primal work'.[45] Artificial hybrid varieties were produced by florists whereas virtuous native plants, in the words of the botanist Sarah Hoare, were created by the 'Artificer divine'.[46]

Unlike florists, botanists did not make aesthetic judgements about plants or rank flowers according to their beauty. The parent of modern botany, Linnaeus, had dissociated his science from the frivolous art of floristry:

> The grand objects of [florists'] attention are the most beautiful flowers such as Tulips, Hyacinths, Anemones, Ranunculi, Carnations, Auriculas and Polyanthus. To hidden varieties of these flowers they have given such pompous names as excite wonder and astonishment ... These men cultivate a science peculiar to themselves, the mysteries of which are only known to the adepts; nor can such knowledge be worth the attention of the botanist; wherefore let no sound botanist ever enter into their societies.[47]

The reputations of English florists were sullied by the charlatan activities of their Flemish predecessors. Excessively high prices were paid for rare blooms by the rich but the florists themselves often excited contempt, especially from botanists who accused them of carrying out vulgar and unnatural practices; their unsavoury recipes for floral improvement included goose dung, bullock's blood, pigeon droppings or urine.[48]

On the other hand, Maddock, in the *Florist's Directory*, defended floristry ('a most rational and pleasing amusement') against its critics. He claimed to have written it at the request of 'many *respectable* florists' and devised rules for fellow florists that rejected the more indelicate methods of cultivation. However, while the botanist represented constancy and order, a certain aura of irrationality and madness still attached itself to the florist. Jean-Jacques Rousseau ridiculed the flower connoisseurs 'who swoon at the sight of a ranuncula, and bow down before tulips', condemning the practices of the florist as 'unsuited to the reasonable man'.[49] In the comic sketch on 'tulipophobes' in *The Tatler* referred to earlier, Bickerstaff converses with a gentleman suffering with the distemper known as 'tulippomania' who 'would talk very rationally upon any subject in the world but a tulip.'[50] The dialogue satirises the taste of florists who esteemed a flower all the more for its rarity and novelty. In contrast, the rational Bickerstaff rhapsodises over the beauty of the common daisy or violet, the daffodil and cowslip that he sees in a meadow, and reflects on 'the Bounty of Providence, which has made the most pleasing and most beautiful objects the most ordinary and most common.'[51]

The growing emphasis on the cataloguing of distinct species and compilation of both local and national floras meant that florist flowers were further denigrated. The English botanist, William Withering, excluded flowers which were 'under the influence of garden culture' from his *Arrangement of British Plants* insisting that, however different they may appear, they 'are not to be considered distinct species but only varieties':

> No variations are more common than those of colour; but desirable as these changes are to the Florist, they have little weight with the Botanist who considers them as variable accidental circumstances, and, therefore, by no means admissible in the discrimination of the species.[52]

An evaluative language can be traced in botanical texts where pure species are revered while florist flowers or 'varieties' are disparaged. Robert Thornton reported that the 'beautiful nurselings' of the florist are disregarded, or taken for 'monsters', by botanists: Withering, for example, held that 'Many flowers, under the influence of garden culture, become double; but double flowers are monsters, and, therefore, can only rank in a System of Botany, as varieties'.[53] In Priscilla Wakefield's systematic introduction to botanical science, Felicia announces her intention to disregard flowers 'of foreign extraction' which have been produced 'by the art of the florist': 'I shall pass them over as objects of admiration only, and search among the humble plants of our own growth for a few, worthy of minute description' (78). Elsewhere, she explains that the botanical scholar will learn to consider 'all double flowers, either as the sport of nature, or the effect of art, and consequently improper for [her] investigation' (19–20).

Charlotte Smith, an admirer of Withering, was eager to distance botanising women like herself from the vulgar practices of floristry:

> The extravagant fondness for the cultivation of those flowers which the art of the gardener can improve, such as Tulips, Auriculas, and Carnations, has excited laughter and contempt; and was, I think, sometimes confounded with the Science of Botany, with which it has little to do. A Florist, however, has very different pursuits and purposes from a Botanist.[54]

This is clearly a preoccupation of Smith's. Plumptre may well have had Smith in mind again when he has his female botanist, Veronica (who has already fantasised about writing a gothic romance with a botanising heroine), recite a poem she has written entitled 'The Triumph of Botany'. The poem (said to be in twenty cantos) shares the theme of Flora descending to earth in a carriage, the subject of Smith's Darwin-inspired poem, 'Flora', and it has another of Smith's concerns as its focus:

> *Veronica:* I mentioned my poem: the subject is, I think, extremely interesting, and purely classical. You know, Sir, that the botanist and florist have long been at variance; the florist only esteems a few, and those chiefly the double flowers, which the botanist considers as monsters. Now, I suppose, that after repeated hostilities, which are the subject of the former part of the poem, *Lonicera Sempervirens,* or trumpet honeysuckle, is sent, as a herald, to call a parley, and the parties meet on the plain of *Enna*, so much celebrated by the poets for its flowers and the rape of Proserpina. *Flora* enters in a wheel-barrow, the garden carriage, driving Hyacinthus, Carnatia, Auricula, Tulippa, Anemonia, Jonquilla, Ranunculas, and Polyanthus, eight in hand, and is attended by Cupids, as gardeners, bearing silver cream pots and all the prizes given as florists' feasts. *Botania* is borne in a tin box, the botanists conveyance, by eight of her favourites; and after debating the matter, as we do at Coachmakers Hall … it is agreed that they shall henceforth unite their powers, and live promiscuously in fields, or gardens: a pageant takes place, in which all their adherents appear two and two, attended by Gnomes and Sylphs: Botania and Flora change their cars, and a triumphal song is chanted to their joint honour. (II.1.29)

Whether Plumptre is satirising Smith or not here (and again it seems likely given Veronica's literary pretensions and penchant for botanical poems), he is making light of the female botanist's attempt to dissociate herself from the florist. In Plumptre the two opposing schools of thought are united to comic effect through Botania's truce with Flora in the poem. When the two types of flower, native and exotic, the attendants of the two goddesses, agree to 'live promiscuously in fields and gardens', the result is one indiscriminate union that spreads throughout the land in the manner of the Tahiti interlude in Darwin's *Loves of the Plants*. Through the introduction of this poem, Plumptre satirises the fashion for feminine Darwiniana. He is astute in identifying botany's opposition to floristry as a major preoccupation of the female botanist and 'literary lady'.

Smith continues her attack on florists in 'A Walk in the Shrubbery'.[55] She portrays the pensive botanist conducting a spontaneous outdoor exploration of shrubs in their 'natural' state, while the trifling florist idles indoors, concerned only with curios or novelties:

The Florists, who have fondly watch'd
Some curious bulb from hour to hour,
And, to ideal charms attach'd,
Derive their glory from a flower;

Or they, who lose in crouded rooms,
Spring's tepid suns and balmy air,
And value Flora's fairest blooms,
But in proportion as they're rare:

Feel not the pensive pleasures known
To him, who, thro' the morning mist,
Explores the bowery shrubs new blown,
A moralizing botanist.[56]

The self-interested florist scrutinises his prize blooms, motivated by fame and monetary gain, whereas the selfless botanist nobly contemplates the flora of the hedgerow or bower. The florist is superficially attached to the 'ideal charms' of every flower, the botanist delights in the work of the Divine Gardener Himself.

Withering's *Arrangement of British Plants* included a dictionary of botanical terms and instructed the novice in the careful dissection of flowers and the use of a botanical microscope. Aided by *Withering's Botany*, as it became known, Smith parades her botanical knowledge before the reader, using terms such as 'calyx', 'hybernacle', or 'spatha'.[57] In 'Flora', the universal names *Saxifrage, Convolvulus*, and *Scandix* appear in the main body of the text while the plants' colloquial or local names, 'Ladies Cushion', 'Morning Glory' and 'Venus's comb', are confined to footnotes. Here, Smith deviates from Wakefield and Hoare, who always placed botanical nomenclature in footnotes. However, she is inconsistent in this and does not always follow the same convention.[58] This is a poetry born out of the tension between general and particular, local and universal. Smith exhibits a Linnaean tendency of describing general characteristics of species while simultaneously writing a poetry of minute description which allows the reader to contemplate the microscopic parts of the flower, to number the streaks of the tulip.

Smith's botanical knowledge is transformed through the microscope from precise, factual data into food for the poetical imagination. Her notes to the poem, 'Flora', illustrate this process: 'The silk-like tuft within the plant called *Tradescantia* appears to the eye composed of very fine filaments; but on examining one of these fine silky threads through a microscope, it looks like a string of amethysts.'[59] Elsewhere, the gossamer thread of a spider's web is metamorphosed into something resembling the work of 'fairy fingers': 'A thousand trembling orbs of lucid dew / Spangle the texture of the fairy loom.'[60]

Judith Pascoe argues that Charlotte Smith's 'advocacy of realistic detail ... is in absolute opposition to the dominant aesthetic formulations of her day, to a Royal Academy that considered "mechanical" imitation vulgar and placed value instead on the ability to generalise and abstract from the particular'.[61] However, while she remains true to the observed characteristics of the plant, she is rarely confined to plain realistic detail and often arrives at the fanciful via the scientific. Her attack on floristry also suggests that she did not completely oppose the aesthetic theories of those such as Reynolds and Johnson who saw the florist, or flower painter, as devoting themselves to a particularity which they themselves scorned.

Flower painting was well established as a genteel accomplishment for women by the mid-century.[62] Like floristry, it also had strong associations with Dutch culture as Ann Bermingham explains:

> As a genre, feminine and otherwise, flower painting in England arose in large part due to the popularity of Dutch flower pieces and furniture styles in the late seventeenth and early eighteenth centuries. Flower painting was introduced into England in the seventeenth century, and during the reign of William and Mary it coincided with the craze for Dutch bulbs and flower gardens.[63]

By the end of the eighteenth century, flower painting was increasingly sneered at by a Royal Academy whose privileging of the universal over the particular asserted the gentlemanly authority of the English elite.[64] Smith made close studies of flowers and leaves as a child and was instructed in painting by the landscape artist, George Smith.[65] Her drawings were an artistic expression of an early interest in botany but, as her passion for plants became more theorised, she increasingly detached herself from floral accomplishments and flaunted the knowledge of universal botany she cultivated throughout her life.

What is made manifest through her interest in botany is her patriotism; we see her rejecting foreign hybrids or 'luxuriants' and embracing wild or indigenous species. 'A moralising botanist', Smith shared Rousseau's distaste for floristry and Maria Jacson's preference for 'distinct tribes'. Rousseau scorned the artistry of the florist, who cultivated luxuriants which flourished in conditions of luxury; for Rousseau, luxury sapped vigour from the army and diminished love for the fatherland.[66] Smith displays her patriotism through botany in a similar fashion, rejoicing in the simplicity of the native wild flower, rejecting

Art's unnecessary dominance over Nature and rating botanical study as infinitely to superior to fickle floristry.

Priscilla Wakefield saw botany as an antidote to the dangers of luxury. Felicia, in Wakefield's *An Introduction to Botany*, for example, examines the dust of the anthers on the Marshmallow through a botanical microscope. Discovering it is 'curiously toothed like the wheels of a watch', she concludes that 'the most minute parts of nature are finished with an elegant nicety, that surpasses the utmost efforts of art'.[67] Elsewhere, Felicia observes that cultivated Hyacinths have attractive blossoms of various colours and yet she warns her sister Constance that

> whatever pleasure they yield us ... we must reject them for the wild Harebell, in which we shall be able to trace their original features, unimproved by the polishing hand of art.[68]

Wakefield uses Linnaean botany to divert women from adornment and artifice and to shield them from the harmful effects of luxury. Again, Felicia informs Constance that:

> I intend to select our examples from plants of British growth, you must seek for them growing wild in their native fields, nor confine your walks within the limits of the garden wall.[69]

Both sisters confine their observations to the 'humble productions of the field or hedge' and delight in the 'wild Harebell', the 'humble Bindweed', and the 'little, disregarded daisy'. Charlotte Smith similarly preferred the wild 'uncultured rose', the 'freckled cowslip' or the 'odorous violet' to the showy tulip. 'Luxuriant' garden varieties hold no interest for Rowden who coveted the 'untainted' wild flower of the woods and meadow. This new taste in flowers was typically British: the simple wild flower was totally absent from Dutch flower pieces which epitomised the Dutch taste for 'exotics' or 'luxuriants' from Persia or Turkey. Norman Bryson writes that:

> Dutch flower paintings are non-pastoral or even anti-pastoral in that the flowers chosen for depiction are those which require for their existence a high level of horticultural sophistication.[70]

Such portraits of plants represent Dutch affluence at the height of the market for luxury goods in seventeenth-century Holland; in late eighteenth-century Britain, however, there were growing fears over the pernicious effects of luxury and a newer nationalistic interest in native species which caused British taste to shift away from cultivated flowers of 'foreign extraction' such as the tulip or carnation towards the humble wild flower.

Numbering the streaks of the tulip again: floristry and particularity

Maria Jacson's *Florist's Manual* was crucial in bringing these debates into the early nineteenth century. Despite the title, Jacson induces her 'sister florists' – those women with a fondness for flowers – to progress from flower gardening and floristry, from the gathering of flowers for a common nosegay to the development of a knowledge of botany. Once women have been enlisted into the science of botany they are encouraged to take up the works of Linnaeus. The 'female florist', insists Jacson, will

> increase her amusement ten-fold by making herself familiar with the ingenious system of the great parent of botany, Linnaeus, some knowledge of which seems unavoidable in those ladies who, in cultivating their favourite flowers, exercise the mental along with the corporeal faculty. (39)

Thus, it is anticipated that women's delight in flowers will pass beyond floristry to botany in order to develop the intellectual faculties as well as the physical.

Jacson's text has much in common with the educational works of Wollstonecraft and Smith. Her utilitarian discourse advocates the care and culture of a flower garden as a means of counteracting the luxuriant femininity which Wollstonecraft decried.[71] Interestingly, in this context of female cultivation, her hostility towards luxury extends to the raw material of flower gardening, to the very character of the flowers themselves. Jacson aimed to convince the 'fashionable novice' that 'humble' British flowers 'should not be neglected, even by those who have the power of cultivating exotics in their highest perfection' (9). Her mixed flower gardens were specifically designed to display common native species and to encourage a taste for borders planted with 'distinct tribes' as opposed to foreign 'varieties'.[72] Those 'Sister gardeners' who have stocked their borders with exotics selected from 'the catalogue of some celebrated name' are instructed that 'the commonest primula which presents a fresh shade of red, blue, yellow ... ought to be esteemed more valuable than the most rare American plant which does not bring a similar advantage' (7). Her advice to the novice is intended to quell 'the prevalent solicitude for rarity' and foster a taste for familiar British flowers at a time when there was a new enthusiasm in England for American plants.[73]

Jacson saw floristry as enabling the self-improvement of women, anticipating that those women who successfully mastered the art of flower gardening would come to undertake a botanic 'investigation of the habits and properties of these elegant playthings' (74). She distinguished between florist and botanist thus: the 'fashionable' florist receives gratification from the 'superficial contemplation of her cultivated borders'; she 'observes and is amused by such appearances, but exerts her intellect no further' (40), whereas the 'philosophic botanist reasons from effect to cause, until she cannot refuse her belief that the curious and beautiful economy of vegetable existence must proceed from laws not purely mechanical' (38). To become 'botanic philosophers', women must do more than 'confine their admiration to the greater or lesser number of stripes in the petals of a tulip or a carnation' (37), in contrast with the florist who concentrates on the individual and disregards the species.

Jacson's 'stripes in the petals of a tulip' recalls the passage in Johnson's *Rasselas* where the philosopher Imlac asserts that

> The business of the poet ... is to examine not the individual but the species; to remark general properties and large appearances: he does not number the streaks of the tulip, or describe the different shades in the verdure of the forest.[74]

She draws on Johnson's debate about universality and particularity in order to differentiate between floristry and botany. Sir Joshua Reynolds shares this Johnsonian preference for the general and abstract over contingent empirical particularity and draws attention to the limitations of the florist, who is likened to the lesser sort of flower painter:

> the florist or collector of shells, [will] exhibit the minute discriminations, which distinguish one object of the same species from another ... the philosopher, will consider nature in the abstract, and represent in everyone of his figures the character of its species.[75]

Thus, Jacson similarly endorses universal botany with its emphasis on species in preference to the 'minute discriminations' of the florist.

While Linnaean botany exemplified order during a period of uncertainty and instability, floristry was subject to 'continual changes and alterations'. Maddock claimed that the value attached to florist flowers was 'governed by their novelty, scarcity, or merit, and also by the introduction of new sorts, and extinction of others'.[76] Botany offered a scheme of constancy, uncovering the divine order of the natural world. The readers of Jacson's *A Florist's Manual* are similarly informed that the study of botany will lead to 'the contemplation of the creator' and 'to finding a more certain panacea to the daily chagrins of human life, than all the dissipation that the gilded hours of indiscriminate society has ever been able to afford' (41). The study of botany was deemed particularly appropriate for women and children for this very reason – as a means by which the unlearned or undisciplined were socialised into order. In Robert Thornton's *Juvenile Botany,* for example, in a pedagogical dialogue, a father informs his son that we study botany to learn that 'all is done in order'; whereas 'the Botanist beholds order and contrivance, where the uninformed spectator sees but the splendour of colour'.[77] Similarly, in Jacson's *Florist's Manual*, the 'uninformed eye' of the florist sees 'a profusion of gay and varied colours' whereas the 'philosophic botanist' perceives 'a scene of order, renovation and beauty' even when she is examining the most desolate landscape.[78] Methodical and systematic, Linnaean botany was a paradigm of order and was recommended to women for this very reason, as the discussion of Rousseau and Wakefield's letters on botany in Chapter 2 demonstrated.

Floristry, then, was subject to a politicised aesthetic in the late eighteenth and early nineteenth century. The low status of those who practised floristry, namely artisan refugees and the English artisan classes; hostility to French and Dutch culture and patriotic fervour; the tension between concepts of nature and culture, the universal and the particular; debates concerning luxury – these all contributed to the demise of the fashion for luxuriant varieties of florist flower and the consequent elevation of pure, non-hybrid, native species, accompanied by the new prominence given to botany as a discourse.

During the course of this book, I have argued that the fashion for documenting native flora was involved with both the development of national identity and the feminisation of botany; in short, it was an attempt to parade botany in 'an English dress'. William Withering anticipated that 'Botany in an English dress would become a favourite amusement with the Ladies', and set about anglicising Linnaeus's Latin classification of plants.[79] Having embarked on a project to classify all known native plants using Linnaeus's binomial system, Withering went on to produce *A Botanical Arrangement of all Vegetables Naturally Growing in Great Britain* (1776) a comprehensive flora of the British Isles.[80] Subsequent editions of this work inspired a number of imitations, all of which were specifically intended to 'facilitate and promote the study of indigenous botany'.[81]

Translations and adaptations from the works of Linnaeus established botany as a female pursuit in England. Priscilla Wakefield observed that botany was once confined to the 'circle of the learned' – those who could read the principal texts in Latin.[82] This exclusivity ended when English translations from the botanical works of Linnaeus dominated the market for natural history texts in the second half of the eighteenth century. Wakefield acknowledged that the new interest in women's botany was 'due to those of our own countrymen, who first introduced this delightful volume of nature to popular notice, by presenting it in our native language'.[83] By the 1790s, when Wakefield's *An Introduction to Botany* appeared, botanical knowledge was regarded as a 'necessary addition to an accomplished education' for women.[84] Maria Edgeworth wrote that

> The mother, who now aspires to be the esteemed and beloved instructress of her children, must have a considerable portion of knowledge ... Botany has become fashionable; in time it may become useful, if it be not so already.[85]

Thus, botany was absorbed into a maternal discourse of self-improvement. I have argued that women's texts in particular demonstrated ambivalence in the process of the feminisation of botany, but they are not simply didactic works; they offer women access to scientific botany for the first time and are open to a liberationist reading. The British 'botanical lady' herself, though stereotyped by some, offered confirmation that the age was one of ingenious and learned women, many of whom excelled in this branch of science. Botany then, was fashionable and in time it had 'become useful'.

Notes

1 From William Mason's *The English Garden* (1772–79; Dublin: S. Price, W. and H. Whitestone, W. Sleater, R. Moncrieffe, T. Walker, H. Chamberlaine, J. Beatty, L. White, R. Burton, and P. Byrne, 1782), III, lines 137–8, p. 76. William Withering uses these lines from Mason to introduce the third edition of his popular text, *An Arrangement of British Plants*, 3rd edn.

2 [Anon.], 'The Acorn and Pine. A Tale for the Ladies', attributed to 'M', *Lady's Monthly Museum*, May 1799, lines 26–7, pp. 416–17. All further references are given in parentheses after quotations in the text.

3 Maria Jacson, *A Florist's Manual* (London: Henry Colburn, 1816), p. 3. All further references are to this edition and are given in parentheses after quotations in the text. Jacson was not descended from a family of gardeners as the phrase 'hereditary liking' suggests here but she was the cousin of Sir Brooke Boothby, a member of the Botanical Society at Lichfield.

A Florist's Manual (1816) seems to have been the most successful of Jacson's works; a second edition was published in 1822. It is mentioned in the 1834 edition of J. C. Loudon's Encyclopaedia of Gardening in the section on Floriculture. For a discussion of Jacson's work, see Shteir, *Cultivating Women. A Florist's Manual* is largely overlooked by critics. Shteir, for example, has mainly been concerned with Jacson's botanical dialogues, see for example, 'Botanical Dialogues: Maria Jacson and Women's Popular Science Writing in England', *Eighteenth-Century Studies*, 23:3 (1990), 301–17. Jacson is discussed in a brief article by Fussell, 'Some Lady Botanists of the Nineteenth Century'.

4 According to Nicholas Penny, the motif of the broken lily can be found on a marble urn at Harefield in Middlesex to commemorate Diana Ball who died aged 18 in 1765. Penny states that 'there are several other late eighteenth-century monuments which use this motif. But it was popularised by Westmacott, usually in monuments to children, maidens or young wives "cut off in the flower of their youth"' (*Church Monuments in Romantic England* (New Haven, CT and London: Yale University Press, 1977), p. 33).

5 Anna Seward, note to 'Eyam' (41–8), in Lonsdale (ed.), *Eighteenth-Century Women Poets*, p. 317.

6 Cordelia Skeeles's untitled poem is printed opposite the coloured plate of the snowdrop in Thornton, *Temple of Flora*, unpag.

7 Rowden, 'Violet', in *A Poetical Introduction to the Study of Botany*, p. 114.

8 Smith, [sonnet to Miranda], *Rural Walks*, I, line 14, p. 130. For botany in the poetry of Charlotte Smith, see Pascoe, 'Female Botanists and the Poetry of Charlotte Smith'; Landry, 'Green Languages'; Ruwe, 'Charlotte Smith's Sublime'. For discussions around flowers and gardens, see Rachel Crawford, 'Troping the Subject: Behn, Smith, Hemens and the Poetics of the Bower', *Studies in Romanticism*, 38 (Summer 1999), 249–79; Deborah Kennedy, 'Thorns and Roses: the Sonnets of Charlotte Smith', *Women's' Writing*, 12:1 (1995), 43–53. For discussions around natural history and Smith's educational works, see Fletcher, *Charlotte Smith*, pp. 260–302.

9 Smith, *Rural Walks*, I, p. 129.

10 Smith, 'Sonnet', *Rural Walks*, I, lines 1–4, p. 128.

11 *Ibid.*, lines 9–12, p. 128.

12 *Ibid.*, lines 5 and 7, p. 128. Cultivated varieties of tulip were grown solely for competition or show and were often likened to immodest women who are seen to make a spectacle of themselves. For a discussion of tulip imagery in relation to femininity, see Chapter 1 above, pp. 66–8.

13 Smith, *Rural Walks*, I, p. 128.

14 Mason, *The English Garden*, I, lines 523–4, p. 31.

15 Carole Fabricant attaches political and economic significance to the sexual dimension of Augustan gardening. She states that 'throughout the period nature was variously described as a coy or seductive maiden, as a promiscuous or chaste consort, as a naked or over adorned damsel' ('Binding and Dressing Nature's Loose Tresses: The Ideology of Augustan Landscape Design', *Studies in Eighteenth-Century Cul-*

ture, 8 (1979), 109–35 (p. 110).

16 Wollstonecraft's insistence on grace and utility as prerequisites for beauty reproves aesthetic treatises such as Burke's and shows disdain for the florists' fatuous attempts to judge flowers by their conformity to ideal standards (see those of James Maddock). Besides 'colour', 'order' and 'proportion', 'grace and usefulness' are required 'to render the idea of beauty complete' (Mary Wollstonecraft, 'The Tulip and the Rose', *Original Stories From Real Life* (London: J. Johnson, 1791; facs. repr. Oxford and New York: Woodstock Books, 1990), p. 28).

17 *Ibid.*

18 *Ibid.*, p. 29.

19 *Ibid.*, p. 28. Here, Wollstonecraft's treatment of servants differs considerably from her later work. In her early work, such as *Thoughts on the Education of Daughters* (London: J. Johnson, 1787; repr. Oxford and New York: Woodstock Books, 1994), servants are usually a disastrous influence on the children of the house due to their vulgarity of taste and manners. In *Letters Written During a Short Residence in Sweden, Norway and Denmark*, ed. Carol H. Poston (1796; Lincoln, NE and London: University of Nebraska Press, 1976), however, she shows compassion for the servant women that she comes across and indicates their double disadvantage of sex and class.

20 The demand for unusual species of flower is discussed in McKendrick, Brewer and Plumb, *The Birth of a Consumer Society*, pp. 323–7.

21 For a brief account of the history of floristry, see Scott-James, *The Cottage Garden*, pp. 80–9. A comprehensive study of English floristry is Ruth Duthie's *Florists' Flowers and Societies* (Aylesbury: Shire Publications, 1988).

22 Pavord, *The Tulip*, p. 15. Pavord also associates the tulip with French Huguenots who arrived in England in the 1680s, fleeing the persecution of Louis XIV, and started a vogue for growing tulips in England between 1680 and 1710.

23 Hendrik van Oosten, *The Dutch Gardener* (London: D. Midwinter & T. Leigh, 1703), p. 188 (Part III, Chapter 21).

24 Duthie, *Florists' Flowers and Societies*, p. 14.

25 A Flemish society dedicated to St Dorothy, the patron saint of flower-lovers, is mentioned in Van Oosten, *The Dutch Gardener*, p. 188 (Part III, Chapter 21). Florists met to celebrate Mass and hold a feast in her honour on her saints day of 6 February. Ruth Duthie states that 'such St Dorothy societies continued to exist in Flanders and between 1648 and 1651 were established in Brussels, Ghent and Bruges' (*Florists' Flowers and Societies*, p. 14).

26 William Hanbury, *A Complete Body of Planting and Gardening*, 2 vols (London: Printed for the author and sold by Edward and Charles Dilly, in the Poultry, 1770), I, p. 286.

27 Town house gardens should be mentioned here too. For a recent survey see Todd Longstaffe-Gowan, *The London Town Garden, 1740–1840* (New Haven, CT: Published for the Paul Mellon Centre for British Art by Yale University Press, 2001).

28 Ruth Duthie refers to the flower in this poem as an auricula (*Florists' Flowers and Societies*, p. 36). However, in most areas carnation shows were even more numerous than those for auriculas. Robert Thornton names four types of florist's carnations: 'Flakes, Painted Ladies, Bizarres, Piquettes' (*Temple of Flora*, text accompanying plate, 'A group of Carnations', unpag.) and Crabbe's florist refers to his 'Bizarre' in the final line of the poem. The flower, therefore, is more likely to be a carnation.

29 George Crabbe, 'Trades', *The Borough* (London: J. Hatchard, 1810), lines 96–105.

30 *The Floricultural Cabinet* ran from 1833 to 1859 and *The Florist* from 1848 to 1884, while Loudon's *Gardener's Magazine* recorded florists' shows from local ones to grand events in London.

31 Florist feasts and gatherings were invariably held in public houses. After dinner the prize flowers, having been judged, were passed round the table.

32 Pinks were included towards the end of the eighteenth century for it was only then that the flower was regarded as sufficiently improved to be considered a florist's flower. See Oscar. C. Moreton, *Old Carnations and Pinks*, intr. Sacheverell Sitwell (London: G. Rainbird in association with Collins, 1955) and Duthie, 'The Pink', *Florists' Flowers*, pp. 81–7.

33 Pavord, *The Tulip*, p. 16.

34 *The Tatler*, no. 218, Thursday, 31 August 1710.

35 Richard Steele, *The Spectator*, no. 455, Tuesday, 12 August 1710.

36 York Public Library, The Ancient Society of York Florist's Record Books, *Rules, Officers, Minutes, Reports of Shows 1791–1824 With Sundry Memorandums*, unpag.

37 For James Justice, see Duthie, *Florists' Flowers*, pp. 52 and 64.

38 Notably, Defoe's *Roxana* (1724) and Swift's *Gulliver's Travels* (1726).

39 James Maddock, *The Florist's Directory* (London: B. White & Sons, 1792), p. 9. All further references are to this edition.

40 See E. N. Williams, *The Ancien Régime in Europe: Government and Society in the Major States 1648–1789* (Harmondsworth, Penguin, 1972), p. 74. Joseph Rosenblum's study of Swift and the Dutch throws light on Britain's relationship with Holland throughout the eighteenth century (Joseph Rosenblum, 'Gulliver's Dutch Uncle: Another Look at Swift and the Dutch', *British Journal for Eighteenth-Century Studies*, 24:1 (Spring 2001), 63–76).

41 Walpole's essay on garden design champions William Kent and his successor Lancelot 'Capability' Brown, satirising earlier styles especially formal, geometrical and regular gardens. The fundamental assumption that informs Walpole's essay is that the English landscape garden was the direct result of the growth of British political liberties. The essay was probably written during the 1750s and 1760s and was revised in 1770 in response to Thomas Whateley's *Observations on Modern Gardening* (London: T. Payne, 1770). This piece originally appeared in Walpole's four-volume *Anecdotes of Painting in England* in 1780, and it was included with some minor changes in punctuation in the 1782 edition of *Anecdotes*. It was first printed as a separate work in 1785 under the title *Essay on Modern Gardening* by the Strawberry Hill Press. For a reproduction of the 1780 text see Horace Walpole, *The History of the Modern Taste in Gardening*, ed. John Dixon Hunt (New York: Ursus Press, 1995). For a discussion of Walpole, see Stephen Bending, 'Horace Walpole and Eighteenth-Century Garden History', *Journal of the Warburg and Courtauld Institutes*, 57 (1994), pp. 209–26.

42 York Public Library, Ancient Society of York Florist's Record Books, *Rules, Officers, Minutes, Reports of Shows 1791–1824 With Sundry Memorandums*, unpag.

43 Maddock, *Florist's Directory*, p. 43.

44 *Ibid.*, p. 15.

45 Mason, *The English Garden*, I, line 452, p. 25.

46 Hoare, *A Poem On the Pleasures and Advantages of Botanical Pursuits*, p. 18.

47 Linnaeus, as quoted by Robert Thornton, in the text accompanying the plate 'A Group of Carnations' (Thornton, *Temple of Flora*, unpag.).

48 James Maddock recommends a 'stratum of two year old rotten cow dung' for Tulips, while urine is said to work for other 'exotics'. Novices are instructed that 'The dung of pigeons and other fowls also that of horses, sheep and deer ... is most eligible for cold wet soils and for the culture of such plants as are natives of a warm climate' (Maddock, *The Florist's Directory*, p. 236).

49 Rousseau, *Julie, or the New Héloïse*, in *The Collected Writings of Rousseau*, ed. Masters and Kelly, VI, p. 395.

50 *The Tatler*, no. 218, 31 August, 1710.

51 *Ibid.*

52 Withering, *An Arrangement of British Plants*, p. 7.

53 *Ibid.*

54 Smith's annotations to 'A Walk in the Shrubbery', *The Poems of Charlotte Smith*, ed. Curran, p. 303.

55 First published in Charlotte Smith, *Beachy Head; With Other Poems* (London: J. Johnson, 1807).

56 Smith, 'A Walk in the Shrubbery', *Poems*, p. 303.

57 'Calyx': the outer most part of the flower, its cup; 'Hybernacle': the winter covering of a bud; 'Spatha': the sheath from which many flowers such as the Narcissus spring.

58 See my discussion of 'Flora' in Chapter 4.

59 From Smith's annotations to 'Flora', *Poems*, p. 282.

60 Smith, 'The Gossamer', *Poems*, p. 55.

61 Pascoe, 'Female Botanists and the Poetry of Charlotte Smith', p. 203. More recently Jacqueline M. Labbe has argued that Smith and Seward's 'accurate rendering not only of nature but of nature mediated through pictorial and textual practice enrols them in a visual economy reliant on close, detailed, imaginative representation' ('Every Poet Her Own Drawing Master', p. 201).

62 Norman Bryson states that, 'In the second half of the eighteenth century there were between fifty and a hundred women flower painters exhibiting in London alone, but in the amateur reaches of the art world, well away from the centre stages of the Royal Academy' (*Looking At the Overlooked: Four Essays On Still Life Painting* (Cambridge, MA: Harvard University Press, 1990), p. 174).

63 Bermingham, *Learning to Draw: Studies in the Cultural History of a Polite and Useful Art*, p. 203.

64 Artists such as Mary Lawrence were rejected from the Academy's 1799 exhibition (see Bermingham, *Learning to Draw*, p. 205).

65 For Smith and the painter George Smith, see Fletcher, *Charlotte Smith*, p. 13.

66 Rousseau stated that when the arts and sciences prevailed in Rome military discipline was neglected and the Fatherland forgotten. He later expands on the theme of the relationship between luxury and patriotism: 'arts are perfected and luxury spreads, true courage is enervated, military virtues disappear and this too is the work of the sciences and all those arts which are exercised in the shade of the study' ('Discourse on the Sciences and Arts' (1750), *Collected Writings of Rousseau*, II, pp. 10 and 16.

67 Wakefield, *Introduction*, p. 122 (Letter XXI).

68 *Ibid.*, p. 80 (Letter XIV).

69 *Ibid.*, pp. 43–4 (Letter VIII).

70 Bryson, *Looking at the Overlooked*, p. 104.

71 See my discussion of luxuriant femininity in Wollstonecraft's *A Vindication of the Rights of Woman* in Chapter 1. Conventionally, flower gardens were associated with the aristocracy and suggested superfluous luxury.

72 Withering's definition of 'varieties' is helpful here; they do not figure in a system of botany because they are not distinct species:

> Both leaves and flowers are subject to variations, some of them evidently dependent upon soil and situation: but others owing to causes hitherto unascertained ... Some authors, therefore, have reckoned [such plants] as distinct species; but, let them change situations, and the appearances will be changed likewise ... it is evident therefore, that these, however different in appearance, are not to be considered distinct species, but only varieties (Withering, *An Arrangement of British Plants,* I, p. 7).

73 The new enthusiasm for American plants marked a change in gardening style. The last years of the eighteenth century and the beginning of the nineteenth saw a rage for improvement that had begun with Lancelot Brown and which continued with his successor Humphrey Repton. Miles Hadfield comments on the implications of these trends for the British Garden: 'Not only was there this vast change in garden design: David Douglas made his first introductions from Western North America of plants and trees which were to be of almost equal significance in changing not only our gardens but our woodlands' (Miles Hadfield, *Gardening in Britain* (London: Hutchinson, 1960), p. 242).

William Cobbett (1762–1835) was among those who advocated the cultivation of American plants in British gardens. He introduced the tulip tree and false acacia and later published *The American Gardener* (London: C. Clement, 1821).

74 Samuel Johnson, *The History of Rasselas, Prince of Abissinia,* ed. D. J. Enright (1754; Harmondsworth: Penguin Books, 1976), pp. 61–2. Jacson has an aesthetic approach to gardening. When instructing ladies on how to perfect a mingled flower garden, for example, she insists elsewhere that 'separate parts, in their appearance, should constitute a whole' (7).

Both writers articulate the eighteenth-century aesthetic that Geoffrey Tillotson discusses in his examination of periphrasis in poetry of the period as illustrating a scientific and humanist view of nature, where the epithets assigned to creatures place each species in genera according to their common properties (G. Tillotson, 'Eighteenth-century Poetic Diction', in James L. Clifford (ed.), *Eighteenth-Century English Literature: Modern Essays in Criticism* (Oxford: Oxford University Press, 1959), pp. 212–32).

Given the importance of the tulip to Dutch culture and as a favourite subject for Dutch painters such as Breughel, Vermeer, and Van Huysum, Johnson's quote and Jacson's reference to it may be read as an oblique comment on Dutch taste. (Anti-Dutch feeling in English patriotic discourse is seen on other occasions in this context; see my discussion of Wollstonecraft on p. 156.)

75 Sir Joshua Reynolds, *Discourses on Art*, ed. Robert R. Wark (New Haven, CT and London: Yale University Press, 1975), p. 50 (Discourse III). British writers on painting such as Shaftesbury repeatedly expressed a dislike for minuteness. However, the words 'minute' and 'minuteness' could also used to describe high finishing as well as referring to small paintings or small details within paintings. See Harry Mount, 'Morality, Microscopy and the Moderns: the Meaning of Minuteness in Shaftesbury's Theory of Painting', *British Journal for Eighteenth-Century Studies*, 21:2 (Autumn 1998), 125–41 (p. 126).

76 Maddock, *The Florist's Directory*, p. 2.

77 Robert Thornton, 'Preface', *Juvenile Botany: Being an Easy Introduction to that Delightful Science through the Medium of Familiar Conversations* (London: Printed

for Sherwood, Neely, and Jones, 1818), pp. iv, iii.

78 Jacson, *A Florist's Manual*, p. 33.

79 Withering, 'The Design', *A Botanical Arrangement of All Vegetables*, I, p. v.

80 Withering's work on indigenous botany began in 1776 with *A Botanical Arrangement of All Vegetables*. One of the most popular introductions to botany, it went through a number of editions and revisions. The most authoritative of these was the third edition referenced above, published under the title *An Arrangement of British Plants; According to the Latest Improvements of the Linnaean System. To Which is Prefixed, An Easy Introduction to the study of Botany*.

81 The subtitle to William Mavor's *The Ladies and Gentleman's Botanical Pocket* Book (London: Vernor & Hood, 1800), which was modelled on Withering's work.

82 Wakefield, 'Preface', *An Introduction to Botany*, p. ii.

83 Wakefield, 'Preface', *An Introduction to Botany*, p. iii.

84 *Ibid.*, p. iv.

85 Edgeworth, *Letters for Literary Ladies*, p. 21. (This edition reproduces the 2nd rev. edn of 1798.)

Conclusion

The sequel: the Natural System and the language of flowers

Sadly, this unique blend of science and literature, poetry and microscopy, which characterised women's botany in the Enlightenment, was missing from the Victorian flower books which superseded them. In the mid-nineteenth century, scholarly botany gradually split away from botany for ladies and – as the culmination of a movement begun earlier and affecting science in general – the scientific and literary modes separated further into two distinct discourses. The discourse surrounding plants shifted away from systematising towards mythologising in women's texts such as Maria Montolieu's *The Enchanted Plants, Fables in Verse* (1800), Mary Roberts's *Wonders of the Vegetable Kingdom Displayed* (1822) and Elizabeth Kent's *Flora Domestica* (1823). Montolieu, for example, abandoned any attempt at classification, employing flowers simply as fabula:

> the author conceiving that any illusion to the botanic distinctions of plants would be inconsistent with the simplicity intended to be preserved in the following Fables, has waved the attempt, and has hazarded in personifying them, to give to each individual the sex she thought best adapted to the moral the fable is meant to convey.[1]

Elizabeth Kent also kept botanical description to a minimum, preferring to mythologise plants and anthologise romantic verses on flowers. While Jacson combined systematic botany with hints on flower gardening in *A Florist's Manual*, Kent replaced Linnaean botany with what she called 'biographies of plants', which were purely anecdotal and drawn from plant lore.[2] Mary Roberts similarly turned her back on scientific botany using flowers merely as moral and religious emblems. We learn, for example, that the evening primrose is a 'nun-like flower' that 'opens not 'til [the sun] is gone ... like Charity, doing her good deeds in secret'.[3] Roberts epitomised the new religiosity: a convert from Quakerism she sought a new form of piety in the evangelicalism of the established church.[4] The nineteenth-century works of Montolieu, Mary Roberts and Elizabeth Kent offer a counter-narrative to the progressive Enlightenment texts of Maria Jacson, Priscilla Wakefield and Arabella Rowden.

Elsewhere, in Rebecca Hey's *The Moral of Flowers* (1833) and Louisa Anne Twamley's *Flora's Gems* (1830),[5] a sentimental and purely arbitrary language of flowers replaced the language of Linnaeus which Rousseau had insisted was as necessary to botanists as algebra was to mathematicians.[6] Nineteenth-century flower books were inspired by Charlotte de la Tour's *Le langage des fleures* (1819).[7] They were informed by notions of romantic love, read purely for pleasure, and given as love tokens.[8] The language of flowers is oriental in origin as Robert Tyas, one of the most prolific producers of nineteenth-century English flower books, explains:

> The custom of using flowers as a means of conveying thoughts and sentiments is of Eastern origin, and of very remote antiquity; we find them as images of some poetical idea, or as representing a virtuous or vicious quality, frequently introduced in Oriental writings, both sacred and profane. Some, consecrated to tender and affectionate remembrance, serve to feed the melancholy mind: while others, more numerous than the latter, awaken ideas of glory and happiness, or form a secret and mysterious language for the use of friends and lovers.[9]

Lady Wortley Montagu made this eastern custom known to Europeans when she described a Turkish love letter consisting of a purse containing a number of items such a *caramsil* or clove, and a *pul* or jonquil, all of which had specific meanings attached to them. The *ingi* or pearl meant 'fairest of the young'; the *caramsil* or clove, 'you are as slender as this rose ... I have long loved you and you have not known it'; the *pul* or jonquil, 'have pity on my passion', and the *gul* or rose meant 'may you be pleased, and your sorrows mine'.[10] 'There is no flower, no weed, no fruit, herb, pebble, or feather, that has not a verse belonging to it ... you may send letters of passion, friendship, or civility ... without ever inking your fingers', wrote Montagu.[11] The 'first principles of this mysterious language' are described in Robert Tyas's *Handbook of the Language and Sentiment of Flowers* (1840):

> By the first rule, a flower presented inclining to the right, expresses a thought; reversed it is understood to convey the contrary of that sentiment ... A rose-bud, with the thorns and leaves is understood to say 'I fear, but I hope'. The same reversed, would signify that 'You must neither fear nor hope.' You may convey your sentiments very well by a single flower. As the second rule: take the rose-bud ... and strip it of its thorns, it tells you that 'There is everything to hope' strip it of its leaves it will express that 'There is everything to fear'. The expression of nearly all flowers may be varied by changing their positions. Thus, the marigold, for example, placed upon the head, it signifies, 'distress of mind' upon the heart, 'the pains of love'; upon the breast, 'ennui' it is also necessary to know that the pronoun I is understood by inclining the flower to the right, and the pronoun thou by inclining the flower to the left.[12]

Pocketbooks featuring the language of flowers were popular with Victorian women who conversed in this secret language in Valentine cards and love letters.[13]

A bifurcation of botany had occurred whereby women's botany had become increasingly 'feminine' and ornamental and its serious scientific component had become more exclusively 'masculine' work.[14] When Elizabeth Kent's brother-in-law, Leigh Hunt, reviewed *Flora Domestica* in the *Examiner* in 1824, he described it as 'tying up its lady like bunches with posies and ends of verses'. His conception of floral femininity was clearly gendered but he somehow managed to convey the 'lady-like' limitations of nineteenth-century floriculture when he wrote 'no pretension is made to anything great; but a great deal is done, which is very pretty and small'.[15] Instruction books and manuals on the floral arts became more feminine and 'lady-like' too, as if mirroring the smallness of women's sphere and the particularity of the minute works they inspired, they shrunk in size in the nineteenth-century becoming dainty pocketbooks and miniatures designed for the delicate hand of a Victorian lady.[16]

By 1887, botany was feminised to such an extent that an article was published in the scientific journal, *Science*, which set out four 'good and cogent reasons' why botany was a suitable study for young men. Dr J. F. A. Adams wrote:

> An idea seems to exist in the minds of some young men that botany is not a manly study; that it is merely one of the ornamental branches, suitable enough for young ladies and effeminate youths, but not adapted to able-bodied and vigorous-brained young men who wish to make the best use of their powers. I wish to show that this idea is wholly unfounded, but that, on the contrary, botany ought to be ranked as one of the most useful and most manly studies, and an important, if not indispensable, part of a well-rounded education.[17]

Adams's article endeavours to defend botanical study against any accusations of effeminacy by reinventing it as a challenging scientific study for 'able-bodied and vigorous-brained young men'. Earlier in the century, attempts were made in academic science to rescue botany from its status as an 'amusement for ladies'.[18] Academicians such as John Lindley, the fellows of the Linnaean Society, and the members of the Royal Horticultural Society instigated botany's departure from feminised polite culture, reinventing it as an occupation 'for the serious thoughts of man'.[19] If there was to be a distinction between science and polite literature, the professionalisation of botany would also be an attempt at masculinisation – defining a scientific botany for gentlemen. Lindley wanted botany to develop into 'a more advanced state of science' and to move away from Linnaeus's legacy which, he claimed, encouraged identification and naming at the expense of concern with plant structure, thwarting the progress of botanical science.[20] He launched an attack on Linnaean botany in his inaugural lecture as the first professor of botany at London University, delivered in 1824:

> The simplicity of the Linnaean system was found to be only a disguise of its superficial character; it was in short, a positive and serious evil rather than an advantage; for Botanists contented themselves with just as much knowledge as was sufficient to enable them to understand the system, and looked no further.[21]

Lindley blamed the Linnaean system for emasculating botany, rendering it 'unworthy of the attention of men of enlightened minds'.[22] He sought to de-feminise botany by advocating a break with the Linnaean system and botany's links to taxonomy in favour of a 'natural' system and the study of morphology.[23]

Lindley appropriated 'ladies botany', condemning British Linnaeans who had 'continued to convert one of the most curious and interesting of all sciences into a meagre and aimless system of names'.[24] *Ladies' Botany* rendered previous texts written for the use of ladies, such as Rousseau's *Letters*, 'incomplete and obsolete'.[25] Lindley was adamant that it had now been 'admitted on all hands' that 'the principles of the artificial system of Linnaeus, which were so important and useful at the time when they were first propounded, are altogether unsuited to the present state of science'.[26] Lindley and Loudon triumphed over their Linnaean rivals and succeeded in introducing women to the Natural System of classification. By the 1840s the familiar format of epistolary or dialogic botanical works, which epitomised Linnaean botany 'for ladies' and championed the Enlightenment ideal of rational amusement, had given way to the drier schoolbook-type narratives that we find in the anti-Linnaean works of Jane Loudon. The Linnaean era, which saw published the more progressive Enlightenment texts by women, was sadly at an end.

Botanical texts which retained something of the familiar format – Harriet Beaufort's *Dialogues on Botany* (1819) and Elizabeth and Sarah Fitton's *Conversations on Botany* (1817), for example – became increasingly didactic. The young people who featured in these texts were almost interchangeable and were only allowed the most minimal responses to the all-knowing mothers' or aunts' delivery of scientific knowledge. When, prior to her *An Introduction to Botany* of 1796, Wakefield adopted the dialogue form in *Mental Improvement* (1794–97), she promoted the conversational approach made manifest in the parent–child, pupil–teacher dialogue as an innovative educational method which marked a departure from 'the austere manners of former times' when children had been secluded from the advantages of 'conversing with their parents or instructors'.[27] The new liberality enabled by the familiar style, was one of the 'ingenious methods' authors used for facilitating the acquisition of knowledge:

> The familiar intercourse, that is now maintained with young people by their parents, and those who preside over their education affords them an agreeable opportunity of enlarging their minds and attaining a fund of knowledge, by the easy medium of conversation.[28]

The Enlightenment dialogues of Wakefield and Jacson are open and exploratory: influenced by Rousseau and the Edgeworths, they promote inquiry and learning by experience, contrasting with the closed discourse of the catechism (a narrative form, comprising model sets of questions and answers which had been transposed from theology).[29] Jean-Jacques Rousseau was explicitly against catechism because his teaching methods were founded on establishing the child's autonomous judgement:

> If I had to depict sorry stupidity, I would depict a pedant teaching the catechism to children. If I wanted to make a child go mad, I would oblige him to explain what he says in saying his catechism.[30]

However, even progressive writers like Barbauld occasionally adopt the catechistic method in published texts, especially those written for younger children. *Hymns in Prose for Children* (1781) is an example of this where she teaches through a kind of relentless insistence on a particular answer to a particular question. The botanical writing in her collaborative work, *Evenings at Home* is, by way of contrast, largely free of catechism, encouraging a questioning empirical approach to plant study and discouraging rote learning. Enlightenment botany then, successfully shook off the confines of catechism, and embraced dialogue, though there is some cross-over, especially in works for young people (educational texts can sometimes use a catechism that looks like conversation, but is entirely one-sided, a monologue disguised as a dialogue; this is rare in botanical texts).[31] Botanical catechisms began to appear in the nineteenth century: William Mavor's *Catechism of Botany* was published in 1800 and a series of catechisms on scientific topics published by William Pinnock followed, including *A Catechism of Botany By A Friend To Youth* (1820). Mid-century examples are Anne Pratt's *Pictorial Catechism of Botany* (1842) and Wilson's *Catechism of Botany* (*c.* 1845). With the re-emergence of the catechism, scientific discourse in education gradually shifted away from the familial, intimate and domestic towards the impersonal textbook style which better served the Gradgrindian school of factual education or learning by rote.[32]

Scientific botany became less woman-centred in the nineteenth century too. Elizabeth and Sarah Fitton's botanical *Conversations* marked a change in emphasis from mother–daughter dialogues to those of mother and son. This text may have been designed to fill a gap in the market for botany books directed at young men.[33] The female tradition in botanical dialogues is never acknowledged; the mother figure claims that her knowledge about plants has been drawn from travel narratives such as Samuel Hearne's *Journey to the Northern Ocean* (1795).[34] The Fittons were writing at a time when Linnaeus was being challenged: there is a new emphasis on plant structure and any engagement with Linnaeus is filtered though Withering.[35] Sarah Waring's *A Sketch of the Life of Linnaeus in a Series of Letters Designed for Young Persons* (1827) retains the epistolary format of previous Linnaean texts such as Rousseau's *Letters* and Wakefield's *Introduction* but like Fittons' *Conversations on Botany* it marks a departure from exclusively female texts. Waring assumes the authoritative narrative voice of a father who endeavours to persuade his son that the feminine science of botany is not 'unsuited to the dignity of the manly character'.[36] Unlike the pioneering *Introduction* of Wakefield, which gave many women access to botanical knowledge for the first time, this work only serves to emphasise the division of knowledge; the daughter is well versed in botany but she has no vehicle for her botanical knowledge other than to teach her brother about plants whenever he is at home. He is encouraged to learn the rudiments of botany from his sister until he can undertake his medical training outside the home and become a professional in the public sphere.

I have argued during the course of this study that the most progressive texts on women's botany were produced during the Linnaean years. Linnaeus supplied 'subjects for conversation' in numerous dialogues between women, from the mother and daughter in Rousseau's *Letters* and the two sisters and their governess in Wakefield's *Introduction*, to Mrs Woodfield and her niece in Charlotte Smith's *Rural Walks*. Elsewhere, in periodicals such as *The New Lady's Magazine*, botanising women conversed in a new Linnaean language, classifying the indigenous flowers in their gardens in the manner of Maria Jacson, who had urged her 'sister florists' to make themselves familiar with 'the ingenious system of the great parent of botany, Linnaeus'.[37] Darwin found the Linnaean system a 'happy subject for the muse' and his *Loves of the Plants* gave rise to a new kind of scientific poetry by women, exemplified in Charlotte Smith's 'Flora' and Sarah Hoare's 'The Pleasures of Botanical Pursuits, A Poem'. Through their engagement with Linnaeus, enlightened women learnt to examine plants through science's 'illuminating ray'; no longer perceiving flowers merely as decorations for a nosegay or flower garden, they applied their microscopes and learnt to classify:

> But not to casual glance display'd
> Alone: by microscopic aid,
> We view a wondrous store:
> The cups nectareous now appear;
> The fringe, the down, the glandular hair;
> The germ, enclos'd with curious care,
> And petals spangled o'er.[38]

Ignored by scientists because of their dialogic, poetic or epistolary format and overlooked by literary scholars because of their scientific content, these texts by women are remarkable and unique to the eighteenth century. I have attempted to rescue them from obscurity and to assign them a proper place in the histories of science, eighteenth-century literature and women's writing.

Notes

1 From the 'Advertisement' to Maria Henrietta Montolieu, *The Enchanted Plants, Fables in Verse* (London: T. Bensley, 1800), unpag. This text consists of a number of plant fables in verse with botanical endnotes. Montolieu uses plants to explore qualities such as 'Ambition', 'Pride', 'Prejudice', 'Sensibility', and 'Vulgarity'. The overriding themes are of patriotism, humility, and the importance of knowing one's place. In 'Ambition', for example, a lowly Hemlock 'craving power' attempts to overthrow his 'sovereign flower', the Queen Lily (pp. 9–10). In 'Pride', the *Polyanthus*, a flower 'of high degree', snubs her 'country cousin', the common cowslip (pp. 41–7) and in 'Prejudice', an Orange Tree, 'a wretched exile' from its 'native shore', shows gratitude to Britain, this 'generous nation' that has raised it at vast expense. A rival, the native myrtle, learns to tolerate the exotic foreigner (p. 16).

2 In *Flora Domestica, or, The Portable Flower-Garden* (London, Taylor & Hessey, 1823), Kent informally describes approximately 200 species of plants. Species are alphabetically arranged with tips on watering and cultivation, and each entry contains additional information gleaned from mythology and folklore. Kent includes many illustrations from her favourite poets, especially Keats, Shelley and John Clare.

Despite her unscientific approach here, Kent taught Linnaean botany for several years, changing to the natural system when Linnaeus fell out of favour. For a brief description of *Flora Domestica*, see Molly Tatchell, 'Elizabeth Kent and "Flora Domestica"', *Keats–Shelley Memorial Bulletin*, 27 (1976), 15–18, and Shtier, *Cultivating Women*, pp. 135–9.

3 Mary Roberts, *Flowers of the Matin and Even Song, or Thoughts for Those Who Rise Early* (London: Grant and Griffiths, 1845), p. 99.

4 Ann Shteir comments on the religious imagery in *Wonders of the Vegetable Kingdom*, in which Roberts writes:

> Society at large may be compared to a tree. The poor may be designated by the roots; the middle classes by the stem and branches; the dignified and noble ... by the flower, leaves and fruit ... to each an allotted duty is assigned. (Mary Roberts, *Wonders of the Vegetable Kingdom Displayed in a Series of Letters* (London: Whitaker, 1822), p. 72; cited in Ann Shtier, *Cultivating Women*, p. 98.) Roberts later became known as 'Sister Mary' through her *Sister Mary's Tales in Natural History* (London: [n. pub.], 1834).

5 [Louisa Anne Twamley,] *Flora's Gems, or, the Treasures of the Parterre* (London: Charles Tilt, 1830); Rebecca Hey, *The Moral of Flowers, Illustrated By Coloured Engravings* [by William Clark] (London: Longman, 1833) For a brief discussion of these works, see Nicolette Scourse, *The Victorians and Their Flowers* (London: Croom Helm, 1983). For Rebecca Hey, see pp. 54–7, and for Louisa Anne Twamley (neé Meredith), see pp. 31–2, 56–57, and 188.

6 Ann Bermingham briefly traces the history of the language of flowers from its orientalist origins through the French texts of Charlotte de la Tour to the nineteenth-century English flower books of Robert Tyas in *Learning To Draw*, pp. 208–10. For a further discussion of nineteenth-century English flower books, see Scourse, *The Victorians and Their Flowers*, pp. 10, 37–8; floral femininity in the eighteenth and nineteenth centuries is discussed by Jennifer Bennett in *Lilies of the Hearth*, pp. 93–102. For a discussion of gender and Victorian representations of plants see Jackson-Houlston, '"Queen Lilies"?'

7 See [C. de La Tour,] *The Language of Flowers*, trans. L. Cortambert (London: Saunders & Otley, 1834). Most English texts imitated La Tour in varying degrees. One of the best known authors of English flower books was Robert Tyas whose work included the much-reprinted *Handbook of the Language and Sentiment of Flowers* (London: Robert Tyas, 1840). His flower books began appearing in the 1840s and versions of his language of flowers were still in print in 1875. Many English flower books were anonymous, from the *Language of Flowers* (London: James Williams, 1844) to *The Language and Poetry of Flowers* (London: Marcus Ward, 1882).

8 As Ann Bermingham says:

> The image of Victorian courtship that emerges is of a highly elaborate ritual in which indirection is raised to an art form. The language of flowers reinforced cultural notions of feminine modesty and delicacy in the matters of love. If one is to believe Lady Mary [Montagu], it was a veiled language from a veiled culture, one which allowed women to express emotions obliquely, and to see without being seen. (Bermingham, *Learning to Draw*, p. 209).

9 Tyas, *Handbook of the Language and Sentiment of Flowers*, pp. 10–13.

10 Montagu, *Letters of the Rt Hon Lady M...y W...y M...e; Written During Her Trav-*

els in Europe, Asia and Africa 3 vols (London: Printed for T. Becket & P. A. De Hondt, 1763), III, pp. 1–2 (Letter XL).

11 Montagu, *Letters of the Rt Hon Lady M...y W...y M...e*, III, pp. 4–5 (Letter XL).

12 Tyas, *Handbook of the Language and Sentiment of Flowers*, pp. 24–9.

13 For example, bluebell/constancy, basil/hatred; the four leaved clover meant 'be mine'; saffron, 'my best days are past' and the white rose, 'I am worthy of you' ([Anon.], *The Language and Poetry of Flowers*, pp. 148–89).

14 As botany became increasingly professionalised and masculinised in this way, there was a counter current that expressed itself in the dismissal of Sir Joseph Banks as a feminised fop; however, this does not seriously undermine the general direction of development. Banks had a reputation as an extravagant macaroni. The macaroni was an effeminate figure, associated with fashion and luxury; it was a term also linked to travel, often referring to foppish young men who embarked on the grand tour. Banks, a well-born, well-travelled, extravagant man fitted this popular stereotype; a certain femininity also attached itself to him.

Factions within the Royal Society, fearing that this botanist and dilettante figure had trivialised the important work of the society, attempted to undermine his scientific authority and status as the society's president. A power struggle ensued between the mathematicians, who thought themselves the 'real' men of science, and the leisured botanist Banks. In these debates the rigour and professionalism of mathematical science was contrasted with the feminised science of botany, represented by Banks, the virtuoso collector. Banks was unfavourably compared to Newton during this rift between mathematicians and naturalists. The mathematician James Glenie accused Banks of turning the Royal Society, once the home of philosophers, into 'a virtuoso's closet decorated with plants and shells' (See Gascoigne, *Joseph Banks and the English Enlightenment*, p. 62). Appointing a botanist as president had resulted in a traditionally 'masculine', vigorous, scholarly, scientific society being made to resemble a women's boudoir.

15 Leigh Hunt, *Examiner*, no. 881, 19 December 1824, pp. 303–4. For Kent and Leigh Hunt, see Shtier, *Cultivating Women*, pp. 142–3. For Kent and the Romantics, see Tatchell, 'Elizabeth Kent and Flora Domestica', 15–18.

16 [Anon.], *The Wax Bouquet; A Manual of Clear Instructions For Ladies Making Their Own Wax Flowers, By A Lady* [London: [n. pub.], 1855) is one such diminutive text, as is [Anonymous,] *The Wreath, or Ornamental Artist; Containing Instructions For Making Flowers of Wax Rice Paper, Lamb's Wool, and Cambric, By A Lady* (Exeter: Besley, 1835). Jennifer Bennett has observed that 'these books, true pocketbooks, are usually tiny – no more than three by five inches – painstakingly illustrated' (Bennett, p. 95). However, this trend was not exclusively confined to manuals; the 1840 edition of Robert Tyas's *Handbook* was miniature, measuring no more than one by one and a half inches.

17 Adams, 'Is Botany Suitable', 116–117 (p. 116). The four reasons are listed as: 1. The study of botany is an admirable mental discipline; 2. The study of botany promotes physical development; 3. The study of botany is of great practical utility; 4. The study of botany is a source of lifelong happiness.

18 'It has been very much the fashion of late years, in this country, to undervalue the importance of this science, and to consider it an amusement for ladies' (Lindley, *An Introductory Lecture Delivered to the University of London on April 30th, 1824*; reproduced in full in *John Lindley 1799–1865*, ed. Stearn (Suffolk: Antique Collectors, 1999), pp. 73–88 (p. 81)).

19 Lindley, 'Introductory Lecture', *John Lindley*, p. 81.
20 *Ibid.*, p. 78.
21 *Ibid.*
22 *Ibid.*
23 This term was coined by Goethe, who was a keen botanist and a great admirer of Linnaeus, but who sought to introduce the idea of process into the static concepts of botany. Ernst Cassirer discusses how Goethe's morphological conception of the 'formation and transformation of organic natures' was 'an important and crucial methodological change ... for the biology of the eighteenth century' (Cassirer, *Rousseau, Kant and Goethe*, pp. 68–72).
24 Lindley, *Ladies' Botany*, I, p. 3.
25 Lindley, 'Preface', *Ladies' Botany*, I, p. iv.
26 *Ibid.*, I, p. v.
27 Wakefield, *Mental Improvement*, II, p. 66 (Conversation 14).
28 *Ibid.*
29 I wish to make a distinction here between botanical dialogues of the Enlightenment and scientific catechisms of the nineteenth century. However, Greg Myers makes no such distinction between these genres of popular science writing. He argues that such educational texts are all examples of the didactic dialogue which differs in form from the dialectical Platonic dialogue of, say, Boyle's *The Sceptical Chymist* (1661) (See Greg Myers, 'Science For Women and Children: The Dialogue of Popular Science in the Nineteenth-Century', in John Christie and Sally Shuttleworth (eds), *Nature Transfigured: Science and Literature, 1700–1900* (Manchester and New York: Manchester University Press, 1989), pp. 171–200 (pp. 173–4.))
30 Rousseau, *Emile*, cited in Alan Richardson, 'The Politics of Childhood, Wordsworth, Blake and Catechistic Method', *ELH*, 56:4 (Winter 1989), 853–68 (p. 856).
31 For a further discussion around this travesty of dialogue, see Alan Richardson, *Literature, Education and Romanticism: Reading as Social Practice 1780–1832* (Cambridge: Cambridge University Press, 1994).
32 Thomas Gradgrind, inspecting the schoolchildren in Dickens's *Hard Times* (1854), exemplifies this kind of factual education. When girl number twenty, Sissy Jupe, is unable to define a horse it is defined for her by one of Gradgrind's more compliant pupils as follows: 'Quadruped. Graminivorous. Forty teeth, namely twenty-four grinders, four eye teeth, and twelve incisive' (Charles Dickens, *Hard Times*, ed. David Craig (1854; London: Penguin Books, 1985), p. 50).
33 The text proved popular, running to nine editions and was last reprinted in 1840. The sex of the child, Edward, allows for some interesting moralisings with regard to women. He is told not to 'expect to find in plants ... many perfections united – those that look best are seldom the most useful'; this is simultaneously applied to flowers and the whole female sex: the tulip, for example, is 'vain in gaudy colours drest, / 'Tis rather gazed at than carest' ([Fitton,] *Conversations on Botany*, p. 16).
34 Samuel Hearne, *Journey From Fort Prince Wales in Hudson's Bay in the Northern Ocean* (London: [n. pub.], 1785), cited in [Fitton,] *Conversations on Botany*, p. 121.
35 'It is not without regret, that the classification of Linnaeus has been in part relinquished, in order to conform to that of Dr. Withering' ([Fitton,] 'Preface', *Conversations on Botany*, p. iii).
36 Sarah Waring, *A Sketch of the Life of Linnaeus in a Series of Letters* (London: Harvey and Darton, 1827), p. 6.

37 Jacson, *A Florist's Manual*, p. 39.
38 Hoare, 'The Pleasures of Botanical Pursuits, A Poem', lines 64–70, appended to Wakefield, *An Introduction to Botany*, 8th edn, p. 183.

Appendix 1: Key of the Sexual System

Erasmus Darwin, from Linnaeus, *The Families of Plants, with their Natural Characters*, trans. by Erasmus Darwin (Lichfield: 1787)

KEY OF THE SEXUAL SYSTEM

MARRIAGES OF PLANTS
Florescence.

PUBLIC MARRIAGES.
Flowers visible to every one.

IN ONE BED
Husband and wife have the same bed.
All the flowers hermaphrodites: stamens and pistils in the same flower.

WITHOUT AFFINITY.
Husbands not related to each other.
Stamens not joined together in any part.

WITH EQUALITY.
All the males of equal rank.
Stamens have no determinate proportion of length.

1. ONE MALE
2. TWO MALES.
3. THREE MALES.
4. FOUR MALES.
5. FIVE MALES.
6. SIX MALES.
7. SEVEN MALES.
8. EIGHT MALES.
9. NINE MALES.
10. TEN MALES.
11. TWELVE MALES.
12. TWENTY MALES.
13. MANY MALES.

WITH SUBORDINATION.
Some males above others.
Two stamens are always lower than the others.

14. TWO POWERS.
15. FOUR POWERS.

WITH AFFINITY.
Husbands related to each other.
Stamens cohere with each other, or with the pistil.

16. ONE BROTHERHOOD.
17. TWO BROTHERHOODS.
18. MANY BROTHERHOODS.
19. CONFEDERATE MALES.
20. FEMININE MALES.

IN TWO BEDS.
Husband and wife have separate beds.
Male flowers and female flowers in the same species.

21. ONE HOUSE.
22. TWO HOUSES.
23. POLYGAMIES.

CLANDESTINE MARRIAGES.
Flowers scarce visible to the naked eye.

24. CLANDESTINE MARRIAGES.

CHARACTERS OF CLASSES

I. ONE MALE.
One husband in marriage.
One stamen in an hermaphrodite flower.

II. TWO MALES.
Two husbands in the same marriage.
Two stamens in an hermaphrodite flower.

III. THREE MALES.
Three husbands in the same marriage.
Three stamens in an hermaphrodite flower.

IV. FOUR MALES.
Four husbands in the same marriage.
Four stamens in the same flower with the fruit.
(if the two nearest stamens are shorter, it is referred to Class. 14)

V. FIVE MALES.
Five husbands in the same marriage.
Five stamens in an hermaphrodite flower.

VI. SIX MALES,
Six husbands in the same marriage.
Five stamens in an hermaphrodite flower.
(if the two opposite stamens are shorter, it belongs in Class. 15)

VII. SEVEN MALES.
Seven husbands in the same marriage.
Seven stamens in the same flower with the pistil.

VIII. EIGHT MALES.
Eight husbands in the same marriage.
Eight stamens in the same flower with the pistil.

IX. NINE MALES.
Nine husbands in the same marriage.
Nine stamens in an hermaphrodite flower.

X. TEN MALES.
Ten husbands in the same marriage.
Ten stamens in an hermaphrodite flower.

XI. TWELVE MALES.
Twelve husbands in the same marriage.
Twelve stamens to nineteen *in an hermaphrodite flower.*

XII. TWENTY MALES.
Generally twenty husbands, often more.
Stamens inserted on the calyx (not on the receptacle) *in an hermaphrodite flower.*

XIII. MANY MALES.
Twenty males or more in the same marriage.
Stamens inserted on the receptacle, *from* 20 *to* 100 *in the same flower with the pistil.*

XIV. TWO POWERS.
Four husbands, two taller than the other two.
Four stamens of which the two nearest are longer.

XV. FOUR POWERS.
Six husbands, of which four are taller.
Six stamens: of which four are longer, and the two opposite ones shorter.

XVI. ONE BROTHERHOOD.
Husbands, like brothers, arise from one base.

Stamens are united by their filaments into one body.

XVII. TWO BROTHERHOODS.
Husbands arise from two bases, as if from two mothers.
Stamens are united by their filaments into two bodies.

XVIII. MANY BROTHERHOODS.
Husbands arise from more than two mothers.
Stamens are united by their filaments into three or more bodies.

XIX. CONFEDERATE MALES.
Husbands joined together at the top.
Stamens are connected by the anthers forming a cylinder (seldom by the filaments).

XX. FEMININE MALES.
Husbands and wives growing together.
Stamens are inserted on the pistils, (not on the receptacle).

XXI. ONE HOUSE.
Husbands live with their wives in the same house, but have different beds.
Male flowers and female flowers are on the same plant.

XXII. TWO HOUSES.
Husband and wives have different houses.
Male flowers and female flowers are on different plants.

XXIII. POLYGAMIES.
Husbands live with wives and concubines.
Hermaphrodite flowers, and male ones, or female ones in the same species.

XXIV. CLANDESTINE MARRIAGES.
Nuptials are celebrated privately.
Flowers concealed within the fruit, or in some irregular manner.

ORDERS are taken from the Females or Pistils, as classes from the Males or Stamens; but in the class of Confederate Males the Orders differ from others, as in

ONE FEMALE, Two Females, Three Females, &c. according to the number of Pistils.
The number of the pistils is reckoned from the Base of the styles; but if there is no style, the calculation is made from the number of Stigmas.

EQUAL POLYGAMY, consists of many marriages with promiscuous intercourse.
That is *of many florets furnished with stamens and pistils.*
The flowers of these are vulgarly called Flosculous.

SPURIOUS POLYGAMY, where the beds of the married occupy the disk, and those of the concubines the circumference.

That is, *the hermaphrodite florets occupy the disk, and the female florets without stamens surround the border, and that in three manners:*

(a) SUPERFLUOUS POLYGAMY, when the married females are fertile, and thence the concubines superfluous.

That is, *when the hermaphrodite flowers of the disk are furnished with a stigma, and produce seeds; and the female flowers also, which constitute the circumference, produce seeds likewise.*

(b) FRUSTRANEOUS POLYGAMY, when the married females are fertile, and the concubines barren.

That is, *when the hermaphrodite flowers of the disk are furnished with a stigma, and produce seeds; but the florets which constitute the circumference, having no stigma produce no seeds.*

(c) NECESSARY POLYGAMY, when the married females are barren, and the concubines fertile.

That is, *when the hermaphrodite flowers from defect of the stigma of the pistil, produce no seed; but the female flowers in the circumference produce perfect seeds,*

(d) SEPARATE POLYGAMY, when many beds are so united that they constitute on common bed.

That is, *when many flower-bearing calyxes are contained in one common calyx; so as to constitute one flower.*

Appendix 2: Botanical poems by women

[Anna Seward (?)], from Linnaeus, *A System of Vegetables*, 1783

'The Backwardness of Spring Accounted for'[1]

[p. 1]

Last Wednesday[2] when Jupiter rose to survey
The annual return & procession of May
Concluding the Lady with Venus and Flora
Would come in full dress in the Coach of Aurora
That a string of attendants as usual would follow
And the rear of the Show be bought up by Apollo
He looked & enquired and gave orders in vain
Time seemed to stand still and to wait for the train
Aurora was sulky and loath to appear
And the Devil an Hour, Flower on Sunshine was there
May came it is true But in strange deshabille
Was wrapp'd up in flannels & looked very ill
The God shook his Curls for he little expected
To see an old favourite of his so neglected
Besides he was vexed to see things out of Season
And Mercury straight was dispatched for a reason
From his Mother a full information he got
And importantly thought he discover'd a plot
On Flora he seiz'd as the cause & contriver
And up to Jove's throne he determined to drive her
The God who rules all things but home & his wife
And was ne'er contradicted elsewhere in his life
Bounc'd about in a passion as soon as he saw her
And swore thro' the Kennel his Servants shou'd draw her

[p. 2]

"Do you think I am to wait here for you Ma'm all day
"Why are you not ready to set out with May
"You are wanted you know as a principal Guest
"But you wont go yourself & you keep back the rest
"Will Spring do you think whose chief beauty depend
"Upon you stir a Step unless you will attend

1 [Transcribed and edited by Sam George and Bill Hughes from the manuscript in the endpapers of the British Library copy of the Botanical Society at Lichfield's translation of Linnaeus's *A System of Vegetables*]

2 May Day

"I too am prepared with a genial Shower
"And to hold it much longer is not in my power
"In short Ma'am be quick & repair your transgressions
"Or I'll bind you by Styx to our next Quarter Sessions
Poor Flora wept sighed & begg'd hard to be heard
But till he was blown cou'd not get in a word
When seizing occasion to open his cause
She spoke much in praise of good order & laws
She went round the globe, called on every nation
Haranguing at large upon civilisation
Her own reputation in Sweden she hit on
And that brought her home to it's state in Great Britain
Where an ignorant treatment of her & her System
Encouraged her subjects she said to resist them
Vegetation of course was o'er run with disorder
From the wood & the wall to the bank & the border
Her wisest Oeconomy strangely distorted
And her government cou'd not be longer supported
"Here rank & high titles, says she have no merit

[p. 3]

"And my Weeds are brought up in a leveling spirit
"You vagabond Fungus what else cou'd provoke
"To tread on the toes of his highness the oak
"Or down in the Meadows, that flag a vile slave
"In the face of my nobles his banners to wave
"Observe to what irregularity passes
"From the want of distinction of Sexes & Classes
"No wonder we see such a grinning of Corols[3]
"Amidst this confusion of Manners and Morals
"Shall a Hammersmith Girl or a Gardener's boy
"My fairest arrangements at pleasure destroy
"Shall a birds nesting brat my chief quality throttle
"Or a Chambermaid stick a great Prince in a bottle
"By the legs shall a right perfect flower & his bride
"With Mules and Hermaphrodites daily be ty'd
"Can Marriage made public & Marriage clandestine
"The same common bed with strict decency rest in
"Shall a Couple as constant as Darby and Joan
"In a basket with libertine flaunters be thrown

3 Corolla the blossom grinning of Corols, some corols are said to grin as Snap Dragon, Sage &c

"Ye wives with ten husbands, say will they content ye
"Whilst a neighbour lies by you with no less than twenty
"Ye husbands in wives tho' not stinted to few
"Don't you envy the Flower that has Concubines too
"Ye ladies with Eunuchs, now is it not hard
["]That your virtue should seem to require such a guard

[p. 4]

"While your gay painted Cowslip may gad where she will
"Yet her Husband good Creature suspecteth no ill
"Patricians stand forth & say what lady's bosom
"Makes amends for your joining a plebian blossom
"And will you tho' in a laced button hole stoop
"Any longer with Soldiers & Servants to group
"No no my gay empire will sooner dissever
"And my Colonists claim independence forever
"But Sir I have lately adopted a measure
"The prospect of which gives me infinite pleasure
"Some Scholars of Litchfield that came recommended
"By the Muses who there on their *Seward* attended
"Now constitute wholly my administration
"Indeed they are men of no small reputation
"And they are compiling my Classification
"The People who hear and the People who read
"Hence forward in vain ignoramus will plead
"No tongue can excusably drop a rude word
"Before Flowers that are parted from bed & from board
"Or put to distress those unfortunate Spouses
"Who live from their husbands in separate houses
"These great legislators will shortly prescribe
"The Laws rules & habits of every tribe
"Thus their manners no longer each other will shock
"What is wrong in a rose may be right in a dock

[p. 5]

"Rejoice then my Children the hour is at hand
"When Botanical knowledge shall govern the land
"When the people of England with small pocket glasses
"Shall spend all their time in examining grasses
"When every School boy that pulls up a hex [?]
"With pliars and needles shall search for its sex
"When Gardener's Girls their boquets shall compose
"Corresponding in rank with their Customers nose
"Yes, yes, I perceive the great moment approaches
"When buds of distinction shall ride in their Coaches

"When family weight shall their blossoms promote
"And titles advance them to noses of note
"My Commoners too whom less honours attend
"From highest to lowest shall each have a friend
"This the Captain's high nostrils shall please with its prickles
"Whilst that with soft wings a fat Alderman tickles
"Those velvet ones give to a Counsellor smooth
"Or take them to Sessions their Worships to soothe
"But who is that Lady who turns up her eyes
"And the ways of the Country affects to despise
"Tis Miss Haberdasher brought up in Cheapside
"And she'll surfeit us all with her dear London Pride
"Gather Heartsease for Damon that Lover so blest
"Let sweet williams cling to fond Phillida's breast
"And the pale pining swain who despairs of succeeding
["]May indulge his soft sorrows with Love-lies-a-bleeding

[p. 6]

"With a Sprig of Parnassus[4] the Poet elate
"Will conceive his has much of the fruit in his pate
"And mad with the Charms of its honey-cups quarrel
"With all the World round till you give him his Laurel
"Old Chalkstone some twinge-wort will feelingly chuse
"May nolime tangere save him a bruise
"Ye flowers of good name & good habits I warn you
"To keep clear of the gripe of a low-lived attorney
"Let Dodder & mud-weed depicture his heart
"And rope-grass & Devil-bit mark his desert
"You thick cluster'd Stems any Tradesman may crop
"To make a huge beesom of sweets for his shop
"Those strong-scented Plants in the Corner may serve
"To cherish a Chandler's Olfactory Nerve
"Bid the Field preacher square up that rank herb of grace
"To imbitter his long hypocritical face
"Let Goose-tongue the Clerk of the Parish be sent to
"And the Watchman from Wake-robin take a Memento
"A Taylor the fumes of his Cabbage & hell
"May with rag-wort & flea-wort & louse-wort expel
"And the tinker so drunk after mending a kettle

4 Parnassus, a flower very remarkable for its parts called honey-cups.

["]May keep up the fire in his nose by a nettle
"My subjects will thus be employed with decorum
"And till this is done Sir I'll not march before them

[p. 7]

Jove was glad when she finished accepted her reason
So called for the Jordan & put back the Seasons

Elizabeth Moody, from *Poetic Trifles*, 1798

To Dr. Darwin,
ON READING HIS LOVES OF THE PLANTS

No Bard e'er gave his tuneful powers,
Thus to traduce the fame of flowers;
Till Darwin sung his gossip tales,
Of females woo'd by *twenty* males.
Of *plants* so give to amorous pleasure;
Incontinent beyond all measure.
He sings that in botanic schools,
Husbands[1] adopt licentious rules;
Plurality of Wives they wed,
And all they like—they take to bed.
That Lovers sigh with *secret* love,
And marriage rites clandestine, prove.
That, fann'd in groves their mutual fire,
They to some Gretna *Green* retire.

Linnaeus things, no doubt, reveal'd,
Which prudent *Plants* would wish conceal'd;
So free of *families* he spoke,
As must that modest race provoke.
Till he invaded Flora's bowers
None heard of marriage among flowers;
Sexual distinctions were unknown;
Discover'd by the Swede alone.
He blab'd through all the list'ning groves,
The mystick rites of *flow'ry loves.*
He pry'd in every blossom's fold,
And all he saw unseemly—told.
Blab'd tales of many a *feeble* swain;[2]
Unmeet to join in Flora's train;
Unless appointed by her care,
Like Turkish guards to watch the fair.
These *vegetable monsters* claim,
Alliance with the Eunuch's name.

[All footnotes are the original notes to the poems.]

1 See classes of Flowers, Polygamy, Clandestine Marriage, & Co.

2 See class—Vegetable Monsters and Eunuchs.

In every herb and tree that grows;
Some frail propensity he shows.

But then in prose Linneus [sic] prattles,
And soon forgot is all he tattles.
While memory better pleas'd retains,
The frolicks of poetic brains.

So when the Muse with strains like thine
Enchantment breathes through every line;
That Reason pausing makes a stand,
Control'd by Fiction's magic hand.
Enamour'd we the verse pursue,
And feel each fair delusion true.

Luxuriant thought thy mind o'ergrows;
Such painting from thy pencil flows;
Warm to my sight the visions rise,
And thy rich fancy mine supplies.
Thy themes rehearsing in my bower;
From those I picture ev'ry flower;
With thy descriptive forms impress,
I see them in thy colours drest;
Rememb'ring all thy lays unfold,
The snow-drop[3] *freezes* me with *cold.*
I hear the *love-sick* violet's sighs,
And see the hare-bell's *azure eyes.*
See *jealous cowslips* hang their heads,
And *virgin lilies*—pine in beds.
The primrose meets my tinctur'd view,
Far paler than before—she grew.
While Woodbines wanton seem to twine,
And reeling shoots the *maud'ling* [4] *vine.*

If e'er I seek the *Cypress* shade,
Whose branches contemplation aid.

3 How snow-drops cold and blue eye'd hare bells blend
Their tender tears as o'er the stream they bend;
The love-sick violet, and the primrose pale,
Bow their sweet heads and whisper to the gale,
With secret sighs the virgin lily droops,
And jealous cowslips hang their tawny cups.
DARWIN'S LOVES OF THE PLANTS.

4 "Drink deep, sweet youths", seductive Vitis cries,
The maudlin tear-drop glittering in her eyes. DARWIN.

Of learned lore my thoughts possest,
Might dwell on mummies in a chest.
Unperishable chests 'tis said,
Where the Egyptian dead were laid,
Are of the Cypress timber made.
And gates of Rome's fam'd church they say,
Defying mould'ring time's decay;
From Constantine to Pope Eugene,
Eleven hundred years were seen,
In perfect state of sound and good,
Form'd of this Adamantine wood.
Then, DARWIN! Were it not for thee,
I sure must venerate this tree.
But as his boughs hang o'er my head,
I recollect from you I read,
His wife he exiles from his bed[5]

Since thus thy fascinating art,
So takes possession of the heart,
Go bid thy Muse a wreath prepare,
"To bind some charming Chloe's hair."
But tune no more thy Lyre's sweet powers,
To libel harmless trees and flowers.

[5] Cupressus dark disdains his dusky bride,
One dome contains them—but TWO beds divide. DARWIN

Arabella Rowden, from *A Poetical Introduction to the Study of Botany,* 1801

'Cistus or Rock Rose'

Polyandra Monogynia (many stamens, one pistil)

In vain *a hum'rous race of gentle swains*
Around fair Cista thrill'd their tender strains;
In vain their ardent pray'r, there artless lay;
Of tyrant Vice she fell the hapless prey.
Borne in Destruction's car the spoiler Man
With lawless passion to the beauty ran;
But, at his touch, gay pleasure fled from thence
Ere its sweet fragrance charm'd his eager sense;
The promis'd joys he scatter'd o'er the land,
And g[r]asp'd a shadow in his murd'rous hand.
So fades the mother's hope, when flatt'ry's art
Robs the young virgin of her simple heart;
O'er the spoil'd flow'r she droops with pensive air,
The flow'r she rear'd with sweet Affection's care;
And fondly ling'ring where she saw it bloom,
The grave of innocence becomes her tomb.
Then the fell Furies, sailing through the air,
Aim their dread weapons at the tortur'd fair,
Scorn in her bleeding bosom strikes his dart,
And sad Repentance writhes around her heart.
Remorse her stinging snakes in fury throws,
And Madness heightens her exalted woes.
Poor injur'd suff'rer! bid adieu to peace;
Not in this world of sin thy pangs will cease:
Not till kind Mercy takes thee to her breast;
And bears thy spirit to the realms of rest.

Charlotte Smith, from *Beachy Head and Other Poems*, 1807

'Flora'

Remote from scenes, where the o'erwearied mind
Shrinks from the crimes and follies of mankind,
From hostile menace, and offensive boast,
Peace, and her train of home-born pleasures lost;
To Fancy's reign, who would not gladly turn,
And lose awhile the miseries they mourn
In sweet oblivion? —Come then Fancy! deign,
Queen of ideal pleasure, once again
To lend thy magic pencil, and to bring
Such lovely forms, as in life's happier Spring
On the green margin of my native Wey,
Before mine infant eyes were wont to play,
And with that pencil, teach me to describe
The enchanting Goddess of the flowery tribe,
Whose first prerogative it is to chase
The clouds that hang on languid beauty's face;[1]
And, while advancing Suns, and tepid showers,
Lead on the Laughing Spring's delicious hours,
Bid the wan maid the hues of health assume,
Charm with new grace, and blush with fresher bloom,

The vision comes!—While slowly melt away
Night's hovering shades before the eastern ray,
Ere yet declines the morning's humid star,
Fair Fancy brings her; n her leafy car
Flora descends, to dress the expecting earth,
Awake the germs, and call the buds to birth,
Bid each hybernacle its cell unfold,
And open silken leaves, and eyes of gold!

Of forest foliage of the firmest shade
Enwoven by magic hands the Car was made,
Oak and ample Plane, without entwin'd,
And Beech and Ash the verdant concave lined;
The Saxifrage,[2] that snowy flowers emboss,

1 "The spleen is seldom felt where Flora reigns, / The lowering eye, the petulance, the frowns, / And sullen sadness, that do shade, distort, / And mar the face of beauty, when no cause / For such immeasurable grief appears, / These flora banishes." Cowper.

2 Saxifrage. *Saxifraga hypnoides*, Moss Saxifrage, commonly called Ladies' cushion.

Supplied the seat; and of the mural Moss
The velvet footstool rose, where lightly rest
Her slender feet in Cypripedium drest.
The tufted Rush[3] that bears a silken crown,
The floating feathers of the Thistle's[4] down,
In tender hues of rainbow lustre dyed,
The airy texture of her robe supplied;
And wild Convolvulas,[5] yet half unblown,
Form'd with their wreathing buds her simple zone;
Some wandering tresses of her radiant hair
Luxuriant floated on the enamour'd air,
The rest were by the Scandix[6] points confin'd,
And graced, a shining knot, her hair behind—
While as a sceptre of supreme command,
She waved the Anthoxanthum[7] in her hand.

Around the Goddess, as the flies that play
In countless myriads in the western ray,
The Sylphs innumerous throng, whose magic powers
Guard the soft buds, and nurse the infant flowers,
Round the sustaining stems weak tendrils bind,
And save the Pollen from dispersing wind,
From Sun's too ardent shade their transient hues,
And catch in odorous cups translucent dews.
The ruder tasks of others are, to chase
From vegetable life the Insect race,
Breath the polluting thread the Spider weaves,
And brush the Aphis[8] from the unfolding leaves.

For conquest arm'd the pigmy warriors wield
The thorny lance, and spread the hollow shield
Of Lichen[9] tough; or bear, as silver bright,

3 Rush. *Eriophorum angustifolium.*
4 Thistle. *Carduus*
5 Convolvulas. *Convolvulas arvenis*, a remarkably pretty plant, but no favourite with the husbandman.
6 Scandix. *Scandix pectum*, Venus's comb, or Shepherd's needle.
7 Anthoxathum. *Anthoxanthum odoratum*, Vernal Meadow Grass. It is to this grass that hay owes its fine odour.
8 Aphis. *Aphis*, or *Aphides*. These are the "myriads brushed from Russian wilds;" the blights, cankers, lice, or vermin, to use common phrases, that so often disfigure and destroy the fairest vegetable productions.
9 Lichen. *Lichen*. Of these many have the forms of shields, when in fructification.

Lunaria's[10] pearly circlet, firm and light.
On the helm'd head the crimson Foxglove[11] glows,
Or Scutellaria[12] guards the marital brows,
While the Leontodon[13] its plumage rears,
And o'er the casque in waving grace appears;
With stern undaunted eye, one warlike Chief
Grasps the tall club from Arum's[14] blood-dropped leaf,
This with the Burdock's[15] hooks annoys his foes,
The purple Thorn, *that* borrows from the Rose.
In honeyed nectaries couched, some drive away
The forked insidious Earwig from his prey,
Fearless, the scaled Libellula[16] assail,
Dart their keen lances at the encroaching Snail,
Arrest the winged Ant,[17] on the pinions light,
And strike the headlong Beetle[18] in his flight.

Nor less assiduous round their lovely Queen,
The lighter forms of female Fays are seen;
Rich was the purple vest Floscella wore,
Spun of the tufts the Tradescantia[19] bore,
The Cistus[20] flowers minute her temples graced,
And threads of Yucca[21] bound her slender waist.

From the wild Bee,[22] whose wondrous labour weaves,
In artful folds the Rose's fragrant leaves,
Was borrow'd from fair Petalla's light cymarre;

10 Lunaria. *Lunaria annua*, Moon wort, usually called Honesty.
11 Foxglove. *Digitalis purpurea*, common Fox-glove.
12 Scutellaria. *Scutellaria galericulata*, small Skull-cap.
13 Leontodon. *Leontodon officinalis*, Common Dent-de-lion.
14 Arum. *Arum maculatum*, vulgarly Cuckoo pint, or Lords and Ladies.
15 Burdocks. *Archum lappa*.
16 Libellula. The Dragonfly, or as it is called in the southern countries, the Horse-stinger, though it preys only on other insects. Several sorts of these are seen about water, but its introduction here is a poetical licence, as it does not feed on or injure flowers.
17 Ant. *Formica* In one state of their existence the male Ants have wings.
18 Beetle. *Scaraberus*.
19 Tradescantia. The silk-like tuft within the plant called *Tradescantia* appears to the eye composed of very fine filaments; but on examining one of these small silky threads through a microscope, it looks like a string of amethysts.
20 Cistus. *Cistus helianthemum*, Dwarf Cistus.
21 Yucca. *Yucca*, Thready Yucca, an aloe I believe.
22 The wild bee. *Apis centuncularis*. This insect weaves or rather cements rose leaves together to form its cell.

And the Hypericum,[23] with spangling star,
O'er her fair locks its bloom minute enwreathed;
Then, while voluptuous odours round her breathed,
Came Nectarynia; as the arrowy rays
Of lambent fire round pictured Seraph's blaze,
So did the Passiflora's[24] radii shed
Cerulean glory o'er the Sylphid's head,
While round her form the pliant tendrils twined,
And clasp'd the scarf that floated in the wind.

More grave, the para-nymph Calyxa drest;
A brown transparent spatha[25] formed her vest.
The silver scales that bound her raven hair,
Xeranthemum's[26] unfading calyx bear;
And a light sash of spiral Ophrys[27] press'd
Her filmy tunic, on her tender breast.

But where shall images or words be found
O paint the fair ethereal forms, that round
He Queen of flowers attended? and the while
Basked in her eyes, and wanton'd in her smile.

Now towards the earth the gay procession bends,
Lo! From the buoyant air, the Car descends;
Anticipating then the various year,
Flowers of all hues and every month appear,
From every swelling bulb its blossoms rise;
Here blow the Hyacinths of loveliest dyes,
Breathing of heaven; and there her royal brows
Begemmed with pearl, the Crown Imperial shews;
Peeps the blue Gentian from the softning ground,
Jonquils and Violets shed their odours round;
High rears the Honeysuck his scallop'd horn;
A snow of blossoms whiten on the Thorn.
Here, like the fatal fruit to Paris given,
That spread fell feuds throughout the fabled Heaven,

23 Hypericum. An elegant shrub, of which Cowper thus speaks: "Hypericum all bloom, so thick a swarm / Of fowers like flies clothing her slender rods / That scarce a leaf appears". It seems admirably adapted to a fairy garland.

24 Passiflora. *Passiflora cerulea*, the passion flower.

25 spatha. The sheath from which many flowers spring such as the Narcissus, &c.

26 Xeranthemum. The scales of one species of the *Xeranthemum* are particularly elegant.

27 Ophrys. *Ophrys spiralis*, Spiral Ophrys, Ladies traces. The following lines describing well known flowers, notes would be superfluous.

The yellow Rose her golden globe displays;
There, lovelier still, among their spiny sprays
Her blushing Rivals glow with brighter dyes'
Than paints the Summer Sun, on western skies;
And the scarce ting'd, and paler Rose unveil
Their modest beauties to the sighing gale.

Thro' the deep woodland's wild uncultured scene,
Spreads the soft influence of the floral Queen.
A beauteous pyramid, the Chestnut[28] rears,
Its crimson tassels on the Larch[29] appears;
The Fir,[30] dark native of the sullen North,
Owns her soft sway; and slowly springing forth
On the rough Oak[31] are buds minute unfurl'd,
Whose giant produce may command the World!
Each forest thicket feels the balmy air,
And plants that love the shade are blowing there,
Rude rocks with Filices and Bryum smile,
And wastes are gay with Thyme and Chamomile.

Ah! Yet prolong the dear delicious dream,
And trace her power along the mountain stream.
See! From its rude and rocky source, o'erhung
With female Fern, and glossy Adder's-tongue,[32]
Slowly it wells, in pure and crystal drops,
And steals soft-gliding thro' the upland copse,
Then murmuring on, along the willowy sides,
The Reed-bird[33] whispers, and the Halcyon hides;[34]
While among Sallows pale, and birchen bowers,
Embarks in Fancy's eye the Queen of flowers—

O'er her light skiff, of woven bull-rush made,
The water Lily[35] lends a polish'd shade,

28 Chestnut. *Hippocastanum*, Horse chestnut.

29 Larch. *Pinus Lariæ*.

30 Fir. *Pinus sylvestris*, Scotch Fir.

31 Oak. *Quercus rober*.

32 Female fern. *Polypodium*, *Silix femina*. Adder's-tongue. *Asplenium Scolopendrium*, Hart's tongue, more usually called Adder's tongue.

33 Reed-bird. *Motacilla salicaria*, the reed Sparrow, or willow Wren. A bird that in a low and sweet note imitates several others, and sings all night.

34 Halcyon. *Alcedo ispida*, The Kingfisher or Halcyon, one of the most beautiful of English birds.

35 Water lily. *Nymphæ alba*.

While Galium[36] there of pale and silver hue,
And Epilobiums[37] on the banks that grew,
Form her soft couch; and as the Sylphs divide,
With pliant arms, the still encreasing tide,
A thousand leaves along the stream unfold;
Amid its waving swords, in flaming gold
The Iris[38] towers; and here the Arrowhead,[39]
And water Crowfoot,[40] more profusely spread,
Spangle the quiet current; higher there,
As conscious of her claims, in beauty rare,
Her rosy umbels rears the flow'ring Rush[41]
While with reflected charms the waters blush.

The Naiad now the Year's fair Goddess leads,
Thro' richer pastures, and more level meads,
Down to the Sea; where even the briny sands
Their product offer to her glowing hands;
For there, by Sea-dews nurs'd, and airs marine,
The Chelidonium[42] blows; in glaucous green,
Each refluent tide the thorn'd Eyrngium[43] laves
And its pale leaves seem tinctured by the waves;
And half way up the clift, whose rugged brow
Hangs o'er the ever toiling Surge below,
Springs the light Tamarisk[44]—The summit bare
Is tufted by the Statice;[45] and there,
Crush'd by the fisher, as he stands to mark
Some distant signal or approaching bark,
The Saltwort's[46] starry stalks are thickly sown,

36 Galium. *Galium palustre*, White Lady's bed straw.
37 Epilobiums. Various species of Willow herbs.
38 Iris. *Iris paustris*, common Flag, or yellow Iris.
39 Arrowhead. *Sagittaria sagittfolia*.
40 Crowfoot. *Ranunculus aquaticus*, while water Crowfoot.
41 Rush. *Bustomus umbellatus*, the flow'ring Rush, or water Gladiole.
42 Chelidonium. *Chelidonium galaucium*, the horned or sea Poppy.
43 Eyrngium. *Eryngium maritimum*, Sea Holly.
44 Tamarisk. *Tamarix gallica*. This elegant plant is not very uncommon on cliffs in the West of England, and was in 1800 to be found on an high rock to the Eastward of the town of Hastings, in Sussex.
45 Statice. *Statice armeria*. Sea Pink, Sea Lavender, commonly called Thrift, is frequently used for borders of flower beds. It covers some of the most sterile cliffs.
46 Saltwort. *Salsola Kali*. This plant when burnt affords a fossile alkali, and is used in the manufacture of glass. The best is brought from the Mediterranean, and forms a considerable article of commerce. It is very frequently on the cliffs on the Sussex coast.

Like humble worth, unheeded and unknown!—

From depths where Corals spring from crystal caves,
And break with scarlet branch the eddying waves,
Where Algae[47] stream, as change the flowing tides,
And were half flower, half fish, the Polyp[48] hides,
And long tenacious bands of Sea-lace twine
Round palm-shaped leaves empearl'd with Coralline,[49]
Enamour'd Fancy now the Sea-maids calls,
And from their grottos dim, and shell-paved halls,
Charm'd by her voice, the shining train emerge,
And buoyant float above the circling surge
Green Byssus,[50] waving in the sea born gales,
Form'd their thin mantles, and transparent veils
Panier'd[51] in shells, or bound with silver strings
Of silken Pinna,[52] each her trophy brings
Of plants, from rocks and caverns sub-marine,
With leathery branch, and bladder'd buds between;
There its dark folds the pucker'd Laver spread
With trees in miniature of various red;
There flag-shaped Olive leaves depending hung,
And fairy fans from glossy pebbles sprung:
Then her terrestrial train the Nereids meet,
And lay their spoils saline at Flora's feet.

O! fairest of the fabled forms that stream,
Dress'd by wild Fancy, thro' the Poet's dream,
Still may thy attributes, of leaves and flowers,
Thy gardens rich, and shrub—o'ershadowed bowers,
And yellow meads, with Spring's first honors bright,

47 Algæ. Sea weeds of many sorts. Sea Lace, line 183, is one of them. *Algæ, Fuci* and *Conferva*, include, I believe, all sea plants.

48 *Polyp*. The Polypus, or sea Anemone.

49 Coralline. Coralline is, if I do not misunderstand the only book I have to consult, a shelly substance, the work of sea insects, adhering to stones and to sea weeds.

50 Green Byssus. *Flos aquæ*, Paper Byssus; a semi-transparent substance floating on the waves.

51 Panier'd: Panier'd is not perhaps a word correctly English, but it must here be given me.

52 Pinna. The Pinna, or Sea-Wing, is contained in a two-valved shell. It consists of fine long silk-like fibres—The Pinna on the coast of Provence and Italy, is called the silk-worm of the sea. Stockings and gloves of exquisite fineness have been made of it. See note 27th to the Œconomy of vegetation [.] The subsequent lines attempt a description of sea plants, without any correct classification.

The child's gay heart, and frolic step invite;
And, while the careless wanderer explores
The umbrageous forest, or the rugged shores,
Climbs the green down, or roams the broom-clad waste,
May *Truth* and *Nature* form his future taste.
Goddess! On Youth's bless'd hours thy gifts bestow,
Bind the fair wreath on Virgin Beauty's brow,
And still may fancy's brightest flowers be wove
Round the gold chains of Hymeneal love;
But most for those, by Sorrow's hands oppress'd,
May thy beds blossom, and thy wilds be drest;
And where, by Fortune, and the World, forgot,
The Mourner droops in some sequester'd spot,
("Sad luxury to vulgar minds unknown")
O'er blighted happiness, for ever gone,
Yet the dear image seeks not to forget,
But woos his grief, and cherishes regret,
Loving, with fond and lingering pain, to mourn
O'er joys and hopes that never will return,
Thou, visionary Power, may'st bid him view
Forms not less lovely—and as transient too,
And, while they soothe the wearied Pilgrim's eyes,
Afford an antepast of Paradise.

Sarah Hoare, Appended to Priscilla Wakefield, *An Introduction to Botany in a Series of Familiar Letters*, 1818, attributed to 'S.H.' .

THE PLEASURES OF BOTANICAL PURSUITS. A POEM

SCIENCE, illuminating ray,
Pure wisdom's beam, extend thy sway,
And shine from pole to pole;
From thy accumulated store,
O'er every mind thy riches pour,
Excite from low pursuits to soar,
And dignify the soul.

Science, thy charms have ne'er deceiv'd,
Are safely trusted and believ'd,
Will strengthen and refine;
Nor ever leave on mem'ry's page,
A pang repentance would assuage,
But purest, happiest thoughts engage,
To sweeten life's decline.

O Botany!
The ardent glow
Of pure delight to thee I owe,
Since childhood's playful day;
E'en then I sought the sweet perfume,
Exhal'd along the banks of Froome,
Admir'd the rose's op'ning bloom,
And nature's rich array.

The exhilarating mountain gale,
The velvet slope, the shady vale,
Have giv'n their sweets to me:—
Eager to find the fav'rite flow'r,
I heeded not the tempest's low'r,
Nor mid-day sun's exhausting pow'r,
Impell'd by love of thee.

The search repays by health improv'd,
Richly supplies the mind with food
Of pure variety,
Awak'ning hopes of brighter joy,
Presents us sweets that never cloy,
And prompts the happiest employ
Of praise to Deity.

You, who curious search pursue,
Proclaim, does not a closer view

The patient toil repay:
'Tis worthy of the heart benign,
The chief, the intended good to find;
And, for the love of human kind,
The wond'rous work display.

For not alone to please the eye,
Nor deck our fields, this rich supply
Of ornaments profuse;
Medicinal their juices flow;
Nor void of use their colours glow,
And He who dress'd the beauteous show,
Assign'd to each its use.

They who with scientific eye,
Explore the vast variety,
To find the hidden charm;
'Tis to allay the fever's rage,
The pang arthritic to assuage,
To aid the visual nerve of age,
And fell disease disarm.

Linné, by thy experience taught,
And ample page so richly fraught
With scientific lore,
We scan thy sexual system clear,
Of plants that court the mountain air,
That bloom o'er hills, o'er meadows fair,
The forest and the moor.

But not to casual glance display'd
Alone; by microscopic aid,
We view a wondrous store:
The cups nectareous now appear;
The fringe, the down, the glandular hair;
The germ, enclos'd with curious care,
And petals spangled o'er.

Blest be the Pow'r, at whose command,
The grassy tribes o'er spread the land
With "sight-refreashing green;"
Food for the flocks, and for the swain
The exhilarating golden grain,
To cheer his heart, his hopes sustain,
And gladden every scene.

Adoxa loves the greenwood shade;
There, waving thro' the verdant glade,

Her scented seeds she strews:
Laurel that soothes the throb of pain,
Arbutus with its scarlet grain,
That richly crowns Irene's plain,
Fit subject for the muse.

Profuse of flowers *her* verdant plain,
Her glens, her hills her vales retain
Flora's perpetual smile;
The bee-flow'rs in her shades appear,
Orchis, Satyrion blossom there,
Inhaling each its native air,
They grace the emerald isle.

Mid scents as varied as the scene,
Distinct is thine, fair Meadow's Queen.
With buds of crimson dye;
Graceful thy foliage and thy hue,
In softest shades of green and blue,
Attracting still a closer view,
They fix the admiring eye.

The haughty chief, whose thirst to reign,
Spreads desolation o'er the plain,
And mingles want and woe;
Might learn of thee, and throw aside
His baneful, sanguinary pride:—
'Tis *thine* to stop the ruddy tide
'Tis *his* to bid it flow.

Oft where the stream meandering glides,
Our beauteous Monyanthes hides
Her clustering, fringed flowers;
Nor mid the garden's sheltering care,
Of fam'd exotics, rich and fair,
Purple or roseate, brown or fair,
A plant more lovely tow'rs.

Of humbler growth, tho' brighter dyes,
But not by rural swains less priz'd,
The trailing stems allure,
Of Pimpernel, whose brilliant flow'r
Closes against the approaching show'r,
Warning the swain to sheltering bow'r,
From humid air secure.

Sunk with disease and throbbing with pain,
When friendship's aid essay'd in vain.

To soothe the tort'ring hour;
Thy balm, Pistactœia, could allay;
The dire disease obey'd its sway;
I still enjoy a happier day,
And less thy healing pow'r.

Papaver! Thou pale "misery's friend,"
The soothing lymph the fibres send
Thro devious veins to weep,
With care we seek, for sorrow knows
Its pow'r to tranquillize our woes,
To give the wearied calm repose,
And sweetly lull to sleep.

The Foxglove's leaves, with caution giv'n,
Another proof of favouring Heav'n
Will happily display;
The rapid pulse it can abate;
The hectic flush can moderate;
And, blest by Him whose will is fate,
May give a lengthen'd day.

Lovely exotic, thou shalt share,
Fair Calla, all my fostering care,
To guard thy tender bloom;
Superbly raise thine ivory head,
Thine arrowy leaves umbrageous spread,
Thy fragrant odours round us shed;
We prize the rich perfume.

Averse from evning's chilly breeze,
How many close their silken leaves,
To save the embryo flowr's;
As if, ambitious of a name,
They sought to spread around their fame,
And bade the infant buds proclaim
The parent's valu'd pow'rs.

Where'er we search, the scene presents
Wonders to charm th' admiring sense,
And elevate the mind;
Nor even blooms a single spray,
That quivers in departing day,
Or turns to meet the morning ray,
But speaks a Pow'r Divine.

Great source of true felicity!
Father Omnipotent! 'tis thee

We view in grove and mead;
Thy name, thy pow'r, that we revere,
Sublime, intelligent and clear,
Inscrib'd on all around appear,
That he who runs may read.

Bibliography

Primary texts

Abbot, Charles, *Flora bedfordiensis, Comprehending Such Plants As Grow Wild in the County of Bedford, Arranged According to the System of Linnaeus, With Occasional Remarks* (Bedford: Printed and sold by W. Smith; may be had of the booksellers in Oxford & Cambridge, and of G. G. & J. Robinson, 1798)

Adams, George, *Essays on the Microscope Containing A Practical Description of the Most Improved Microscopes: A General History of Insects, Their Transformations, Peculiar Habits, and Oeconomy: An Account of the Various Species, and Singular Properties, of the Hydrae and Vorticellae: A Description of Three Hundred and Eighty Three Animalcula With A Concise Catalogue of Interesting Objects: A View of the Organisation of Timber, and the Configuration of Salts, When Under the Microscope. Illustrated With Thirty Two Folio Plates By the Late George Adams Mathematical Instrument Maker to his Majesty, & Co. ... With Considerable Additions and Improvements by Frederick Kanmacher, F. L. S.*, 2nd edn, 3 vols (1787; London: Dillon and Keating, W. and S. Jones, 1798)

Adams, H. G. (ed.), *Flowers: Their Moral Language and Poetry* (London: H. G. Clarke, 1844)

Adams, J. F. A., 'Is Botany a Suitable Study for Young Men?', *Science: An Illustrated Journal*, 9 (1887), 116–17.

Addison, Joseph and Richard Steele, *The Spectator*, ed. Gregory Smith, 4 vols, (1711–12; London: J. M. Dent, 1909)

Aikin, John, *An Essay on the Application of Natural History to Poetry* (London: J. Johnson, 1777)

Aiton, William, *Hortus Kewensis; or A Catalogue of the Plants Cultivated in the Royal Botanic Garden at Kew, etc.*, 3 vols (London: George Nicol, 1789)

Alexander, William, *The History of Women, From the Earliest Antiquity To the Present Time: Giving An Account of Almost Every Interesting Particular Concerning That Sex, Among All Nations, Ancient and Modern. With A Complete Index By William Alexander M. D.*, 2 vols (Dublin: printed by J. A Husband, for Messrs. S. Price, R. Cross, J. Potts, L. Flin [and 6 others in Dublin, 1779])

Alston, Charles, *A Dissertation on Botany by Charles Alston M. D., The King's Botanist in Scotland, Fellow at the Royal College of Physicians etc., Translated from the Latin by a Physician* (London: Benj. Dod., 1754)

——'A Dissertation on the Sexes of Plants', in *Essays and Observations Physical and Literary Read Before the Philosophical Society in Edinburgh*, 2nd edn, 5 vols (1756; Edinburgh: Printed for John Balfour, 1771), I, pp. 263–316

Ancient Society of York Florists, *Rules of the Society, 1768. List of Members, Autographs, Offices and Accounts, Rough Notes and Memorandums 1789–1803*

——*Rules, Officers, Minutes, Reports of Shows 1791–1824 With Sundry Memorandums*

Andrews, James, FRHS, *Flora's Gems: or, The treasures of the parterre: Twelve bouquets, drawn and coloured from nature by James Andrews; with poetical illustrations by Louisa Anne Twamley* (London: Charles Tilt, [1830])

[Anonymous,] *The Dutchmens Pedigree; or a Relation Shewing How They Were First Bred and Descended from a Horse-Turd by Dutchmen* (London: [n. pub.], 1653

[Anonymous,] 'Life of Boerhaave', *Gentleman's Magazine*, no. 9, March 1739

[Anonymous,] *An Epistle From Mr Banks, Voyager, Monster-Hunter, and Amoroso to Oberea, Queen of Otaheite, Transfused by A. B. C. Esq. Second Professor of Otaheite, and of every other unknown Tongue Enriched With the Finest Passages by the Queen's Letters to Mr Banks, Printed at Batavia, for Jacobus Opano* (London: sold by John Swan and Thomas Axiell, 1773)

[Anonymous,] 'Miss C to Mr H', 'Moral Reflections on Plants and Flowers', *Westminster Magazine, Or the Pantheon of Taste Containing a View of the History, Politics, Literature, Manners, Gallantry & Fashions of the Year 1777*, 5, June 1777, pp. 302–3

[Anonymous,] 'Ingeana and Flora', *New Lady's Magazine, or, Polite and Entertaining Companion for the Fair Sex*, May 1786, p. 177

[Anonymous,] *The Poetical Flower Garden, With Moral Reflections For the Amusement of Children, etc.*, (London: Darton & Harvey, 1794)

[Anonymous,] 'The Loves of the Triangles. A Mathematical and Philosophical Poem. Inscribed to Dr. Darwin', *The Anti-Jacobin; or, Weekly Examiner*, 16th April, 23rd April, 7th May 1798

[Anonymous,] 'To the Snow Drop', by E. A., *Lady's Monthly Museum, or Polite Repository*, September, 1798, p. 245

[Anonymous,] 'On the Good Effects of Bad Novels', by E. A., *Lady's Monthly Museum, or Polite Repository*, October 1798, pp. 258–63

[Anonymous,] 'Rose Bud and Tulips: A Fable For Young Ladies', by 'M', *Lady's Monthly Museum, or Polite Repository*, October 1798, pp. 330–1

[Anonymous,] [Review of] 'An Introduction to Botany, in a Series of Familiar Letters, with Illustrations and Engravings, by Priscilla Wakefield', *Lady's Monthly Museum, or Polite Repository*, November 1798, p. 404

[Anonymous,] 'The Acorn and Pine: A Tale for the Ladies', by 'M', *Lady's Monthly Museum, or Polite Repository*, May 1799, pp. 416–17

[Anonymous,] 'Mrs Charlotte Smith', by 'O', *Lady's Monthly Museum, or Polite Repository*, May 1799, pp. 337–41

[Anonymous] 'Methods of Making Artificial, or, Gum Flowers', *The Lady's Monthly Museum, or Polite Repository*, September 1799

[Anonymous] 'Various Sorts of Flowers ... Form'd From Shells', *Lady's Monthly Museum, or Polite Repository*, November 1799

[Anonymous,] [Review of] 'A Poetical Introduction to the Study of Botany, by Frances Arabella Rowden', *The Anti-Jacobin; or, Weekly Examiner*, no. 10, December 1801, pp. 356–67

[Anonymous,] [Review of] 'Erasmus Darwin, Temple of Nature', *The Critical Review*, 39, October 1803

[Anonymous,] [Review of 2nd edn, 1812] *A Poetical Introduction to the Study of Botany*, by Frances Arabella Rowden, *The Monthly Review*, no. 70, January 1813, pp. 98–9

[Anonymous,] *A Catechism of Botany By a Friend to Youth* (London: Printed by W, Clownes, For Pinnock and Maunder, Mentorian Press, and Sold by Law and Whittaker, 1817–20)

[Anonymous,] *A Catechism of Botany By A Friend to Youth* (London: Pinnock & Maunder, 1820)

[Anonymous,] *The Young Lady's Book: A Manual of Elegant Recreations, Exercises and Pursuits* (London: Vizetelly, Branston, 1829)

[Anonymous,] *Flora and Thalia: gems of flowers and poetry: being an alphabetical ar-*

rangement of flowers with appropriate poetical illustrations. By a Lady (London: [n. pub.], 1835)

[Anonymous,] *The Wreath, or ornamental artist; containing instructions for making flowers of wax rice-paper, lamb's-wool, and cambric ... By a Lady* (Exeter: Besley, 1835)

[Anonymous,] *The Young Lady's Book of Botany* (London: [n. pub.], 1838)

[Anonymous,] *The Language of Flowers: containing the name of every flower to which a sentiment has been assign(ed.) With introductory observations* (London: James Williams, 1844)

[Anonymous,] *The Wax-Bouquet ... a manual of clear instructions for ladies making their own wax flowers. By a Lady* (London: [n. pub.], [1855])

[Anonymous,] *The Language and Poetry of Flowers. With floral illustrations* (London: Marcus Ward, 1882)

Anson, Lord, *A Voyage Round the World in the Years 1740–4*, (London: J. M. Dent, 1911)

Astell, Mary, *A Serious Proposal To the Ladies for the Advancement of Their Time and Greatest Interests*, 2nd edn., corrected by the author (1694; London: R. Wilkin, 1695)

Bacon, Francis, *Essays* (London: J. M. Dent, 1950)

Baker, Henry, *The Microscope Made Easy: The Nature, Uses and Magnifying Powers of the Best Kinds of Microscopes, Described, Calculated and Explained: For the Instruction of Such Particulars as Desire to Search Into the Wonders of the Minute Creation, Tho' They Are Not Acquainted With Opticks*, 3rd edn, 2 vols (1742; London: R Dodsley, 1744)

Banks, Joseph, *The Endeavour Journals of Joseph Banks, 1768–1771* (ed.) J. C. Beaglehole, 2 vols (1768–71; Sydney: Angus & Robertson, 1963)

——*Journal of the Right Honourable Sir Joseph Banks,* BART, K. B., P. R. S., *During Captain Cook's First Voyage in H. M. S. Endeavour in 1768–71 to Terra del Fuego, Otahite, New Zealand, Australia, the Dutch East Indies, etc.*, (ed.) Sir Joseph Dalton Hooker (London: Macmillan, 1896)

Barbauld, Anna Laetitia, *Hymns in Prose for Children* (London: J. Johnson, 1781)

——*An Address to the Opposers of the Repeal of the Corporation and Test Acts, signed 'A Dissenter'* (London: J. Johnson, 1790)

——*Epistle to William Wilberforce, Esq. on the rejection of the bill for abolishing the slave trade* (London: J. Johnson, 1791)

——*The Works of Anna Laetitia Barbauld, with a Memoir by Lucy Aiken*, 2 vols (London: Longman, Hurst, Rees, Orme, Brown & Green, 1825)

——*The Poems of Anna Laetitia Barbauld*, ed. William McCarthy and Elizabeth Kraft (Athens, GA: University of Georgia Press, 1994)

[Barbauld, Anna Laetitia,] *Sins of government, sins of the nation; or , A discourse for the fast, appointed on April 19, 1793, By a Volunteer* (London: J. Johnson, 1793)

——*Civic Sermons to the People* (London: Printed for J. Johnson, 1792)

Barbauld, Anna Laetitia and John Aikin, *Evenings At Home; or, The Juvenile Budget Open(ed.) Consisting of a Variety of Miscellaneous Pieces, for the Instruction and Amusement of Young Persons*, 6 vols (London: J. Johnson, 1792–96)

Barbauld, Anna Laetitia and Dr Aikin, *Evenings at Home; or, The Juvenile Budget Opened* (1792–96; London: Ward & Lock, 1860)

Bastard, William, 'On the Cultivation of Pine-apples', *Philosophical Transactions*, 68 (1777)

Bauhins, John and Casper, *Historia plantarum universalis* (Yverdon, Switzerland: [n. pub], 1650–51)

[Beaufort, Harriet (?),] *Dialogues on Botany for the Use of Young Persons; Explaining the Structure of Plants, and the Progress of Vegetation* (London: R. Hunter, 1819)

Behn, Aphra, *A Discovery of New Worlds* (London: William Ganning, 1688)

Berkeley, George, *Theory of Vision and Other Writings* (London: J. M. Dent, 1910)

Berkenhout, John, *A Volume of Letters from Dr Berkenhout to his Son at the University* (Cambridge: For T. Cadell; London: J. Archdeacon, 1790)

Bevis, Richard (ed.), *Eighteenth-Century Drama: Afterpieces* (Oxford: Oxford University Press, 1970)

Blackwell, Elizabeth, *A Curious Herbal, Containing Five Hundred Cuts, of the Most Useful Plants, Which Are Now Used in the Practice of Physic ... To Which Is Added a Short Description of ye Plants; and Their Common Uses In Physick*, 2 vols (London: Samuel Harding, 1737)

Blake, William, *The Complete Poems*, ed. Alicia Ostriker (Harmondsworth: Penguin, 1977)

Bonnefons, Nicholas de, *Le Jardinier français qui enseigne à cultiver les arbres et herbes potagères* (Paris: P. Des-Hayes, 1651)

Boyle, Robert, *The Sceptical Chymist* (London: Printed by J. Cadwell for J. Crooke, 1661)

Breen, Jennifer (ed.), *Women Romantic Poets 1785–1832* (London: J. M. Dent, 1992)

Brown. G., *A New Treatise on Flower Painting; or, Every Lady Her Own Drawing Master Containing the Most Familiar and Easy Instructions; With Directions How to Mix the Various Tints and Obtain a Complete Knowledge of Drawing Flowers with Taste by Practice Alone* (London: Printed for the Author, 1799–1803)

Buffon, George Louis Leclerc, comte de, *Barrs Buffon: Buffon's Natural History, Containing A Theory of the Earth, A General History of Man, of the Brute, Creation, and of Vegetables, Minerals, From the French, With Notes by the Translator* [Barr] 10 vols (London: Printed for the Proprietor, and sold by H. D. Symonds, 1797)

Burke, Edmund, *A Philosophical Enquiry Into The Origins of Our Ideas of the Sublime and Beautiful*, ed. Adam Phillips (1757; Oxford: Oxford University Press, 1990)

——*Reflections on the Revolution in France and on the Proceedings in Certain Societies in London Relative to that Event*, ed. and intr. Connor Cruise O'Brien (1790; Harmondsworth: Penguin, 1969)

Candolle, Augustin Pyramus de, *Catalogus plantarum horti botanici Monspeliensis: addito observationum cica species novas aut non satis cognitas fasciculo* (Montpellier, France: J. Martel, 1813)

[Canning, George & John Hookham Frere,] 'The Loves of Triangles: A Mathematical and Philosophical Poem Inscribed to Dr Darwin', *The Anti-Jacobin; or, Weekly Examiner*, nos. 23–6, 16 April, 23 April, 7 May 1798

Centlivre, Susan, *Dramatic Works of the Celebrated Mrs Centlivre with a New Account of her Life* (London, J. Pearson, 1872)

Chapone, Mrs, *Letters on the Improvement of the Mind Addressed to a Lady and A Fathers Legacy to His Daughters By Dr Gregory* (1773; London: J. Walker, 1810)

——*Miscellanies in Prose and Verse* (London: E. & C. Dilly, 1775)

[Charlotte, Elizabeth Phelen,] Charlotte Elizabeth, *Chapters on Flowers* (London: R. B. Seeley & W. Burnside, 1836)

Chesterfield, Lord, *Letters to His Son* (1774; London: J. M. Dent, 1946)

Cleland, John, *Memoirs of a Woman of Pleasure*, 2 vols (London: G. Fenton, 1749)

Cobbett, William, *The American Gardener, or A Treatise on the Situation, Soil, Fencing and Laying Out of Gardens* (London: C. Clement, 1821)

Colman, George, *Polly Honeycombe*, in *Eighteenth-Century Afterpieces* ed. Richard Bevis (London: Oxford University Press, 1970), IV, pp. 137–61.

Condillac, Etienne Bonnot de, *An Essay On the Origin of Human Knowledge: Being A Supplement To Mr Locke's Essay On The Human Understanding*, trans. Thomas Nugent (London: 1756; facs. repr. Gainsville, FL: Scholar's Facsimiles and Reprints, 1971)

Condorcet, Jean-Antoine-Nicolas de Caritat, marquis de, 'On the Admission of Women to the Rights of Citizenship' (1790), in *Selected Writings*, ed. Keith Michael Baker (Indianapolis, IN: Bobbs-Merrill, 1976), pp. 97–104

Cook, Capt. James, *Captain Cook's Journal During His First Voyage Round the World Made in H. M. Bark Endeavour, 1768–71*, ed. Captain W. J. L. Wharton (London: E. Stock, 1893)

——*The Journals of Captain Cook on His Voyages of Discovery,* ed. J.C. Beaglehole, 4 vols (Cambridge: Cambridge University Press for The Hakluyt Society, 1955)

Cowper, William, *Complete Poetical Works*, ed. H. S. Milford (London: Henry Frowde, Oxford University Press, 1907)

Crabbe, George, *The Borough: A Poem in Twenty-Four Letters* (London: J. Hatchard, 1810)

——*Poems of George Crabbe*, ed. Adolphus William Ward, 3 vols (Cambridge: Cambridge University Press, 1906)

Craven, Elizabeth, *A Journey Through the Crimea to Constantinople* (1789; New York: Arno Press, 1970)

Curtis, William, *The Botanical Magazine; or, Flower Garden Displayed: In Which the Most Ornamental Foreign Plants, Cultivated in the Open Ground, the Green-House, and the Stove, Will Be Accurately Represented in their Natural Colours. To Which Will Be Added, Their Names, Class, Order, Generic and Specific Characters, According to the Celebrated LINNAEUS; Their Places of Growth, and Times of Flowering: Together With The Most Approved Methods of Culture, A Work Intended For the Use of Such Ladies, Gentleman, and Gardeners, As Wish to Become Scientifically Acquainted With the Plants They Cultivate*, 2 vols (London: Printed by Fry and Couchman, for W. Curtis, 1787)

D'Alembert, Jean le Rond, *Preliminary Discourse to the Encyclopedia of Diderot*, trans. Richard Schwab (1751; New York: Bobbs-Merrill, 1963)

D'Ardène, Rome J. P., *Traité des Tulipes ... Par l'auteur du Traité des Renoncules* (Avignon: [n. pub.], 1760)

Darwin, Charles, *The Origin of Species By Means of Natural Selection*, 6th edn (1859; London: J. M. Dent, 1928)

Darwin, Erasmus, 'Key of the Sexual System', in *The Families of Plants, With Their Natural Characters ... Translated from ... the Genera Plantarum, and of the Mantissae Plantarum of the Elder Linnaeus; and from the Supplementum Plantarum of the Younger Linnaeus ... By A Botanical Society at Lichfield*, 2 vols (London: printed by John Jackson; sold by J. Johnson, 1787), I, pp. lxxvii-lxxx

——*The Botanic Garden: A poem in Two Parts. Part I containing The Economy of Vegetation, Part II The Loves of the Plants, with Philosophic Notes* (London: J. Johnson, 1791; facs. repr. Menston: Scolar Press, 1973)

——*A Plan For the Conduct of Female Education in Boarding Schools* (Derby: Printed by J. Drewry for J. Johnson, 1797)

Davison, Dennis, (ed.), *The Penguin Book of Eighteenth-Century English Verse* (Harmondsworth: Penguin, 1973)
Day, Thomas, *The History of Sandford and Merton*, 3 vols (1783–89; London: John Stockdale, 1801)
Defoe, Daniel, *An Essay Upon Projects* (London: Printed by R.R. for Tho. Cockerill, at the Three Legs in the Poultrey, 1697; facs. repr. Menston: Scolar Press, 1969)
——*A Journal of the Plague Year: Being Observations or Memorials, of the Most Remarkable Occurrences, as well Publick as Private, Which Happened in London During the Last Great Visitation in 1665. Written By a Citizen Who Continued all the While in London. Never Made Public Before* (London: E. Nutt, J. Roberts, A. Dodd and J.Graves, 1722)
——*Roxana: The Fortunate Mistress*, ed. John Mullan (1724; Oxford: Oxford University Press, 1996)
Dickens, Charles, *Hard Times*, ed. David Craig (1854; London: Penguin Books, 1985)
Dryden, John, *Poems of John Dryden*, ed. James Kinsley (Oxford: Clarendon Press, 1958)
——*Poems and Fables of John Dryden*, ed. James Kinsley (Oxford: Oxford University Press, 1970)
Dumas, Alexandre, *The Black Tulip*, ed. David Coward, trans. Franz Demmler (1850; Oxford: Oxford University Press, 1993)
Edgeworth, Maria, *The Parent's Assistant*, 3rd edn, 6 vols (1796; London: J. Johnson, 1800)
——*Letters For Literary Ladies, to which is added an Essay on the Noble Science of Self-Justification*, ed. Claire Connolly (2nd edn, 1798; London: J. M. Dent, 1993)
——*Early Lessons, Frank, Rosamond, Harry and Lucy*, 6 vols (1801; London: J. Johnson, 1809)
——*Moral Tales By Miss Edgeworth*, 5th edn, 3 vols in 1 (1801; London: J. Johnson, 1809)
——*Popular Tales*, new edn (1804; London: Simpkin and Marshall, 1850)
——*Chosen Letters*, ed. F. W. Barry (London: Jonathan Cape, 1931)
Edgeworth, Maria and Richard Lovell Edgeworth, *Practical Education*, 2nd edn, 3 vols (1798; London: J. Johnson, 1801)
[Elmy, Elizabeth Wolstenholme] Ethelmer, Ellis, *Baby Buds* (Congleton: W. Elmy, 1895)
Evelyn, Charles, *The Lady's Recreation or the Art of Gardening Further Improved by C. E. To Which Are Added Observations Concerning Variegated Greens by J, Laurence*, 2nd edn (London: [n. pub.], 1718)
——*The Ladies Recreation, or, the Art of Gardening Further Improv'd ...*, rev. edn (London: E. Curll, 1719)
Fielding, Sarah, *The Governess or, Little Female Academy, Being the History of Mrs Teachum and Her Nine Girls With Their Nine Days Amusement Calculated For the Entertainment and Instruction of Young Ladies in Their Education*, ed. Jill E. Grey (London: A. Miller, 1749; facs. repr. London: Oxford University Press, 1968)
Fiennes, Celia, *The Journeys of Celia Fiennes*, ed. Christopher Morris (1685–1712; London: Cresset Press, 1947)
Firmager, Gabrielle M. (ed.), *The Female Spectator: Being Selections From Mrs Eliza Haywood's Periodical, First Published in Monthly Parts* (1744–46; London: Bristol Classical Press, 1993)
[Fitton, Elizabeth and Sarah Mary Fitton (?),] *Conversations on Botany* (London: Longman, Hurst, Rees, Orme & Brown, 1817)
——*Conversations on Botany*, 3rd edn (1817; London: Longman, Hurst, Rees and Orme,

1820)
Fontenelle, Bernard le Bovier de, *Conversations On the Plurality of Worlds*, trans. H. A. Hargreaves (1686; Berkeley and Los Angeles, CA: University of California Press, 1990)
——*A Discovery of New Worlds*, trans. Aphra Benn (London: William Ganning, 1688)
Fordyce, James, *The Character and Conduct of the Female Sex, and the Advantages to be Derived From the Society of Virtuous Women*, 2nd edn (London: T. Cadell, 1776)
——*Sermons for Young Women* (London: A. Millar, 1776; facs. repr. London: William Pickering, 1996)
Forster, Johann Reinhold, *Observations Made During a Voyage Round the World* (1778), ed. Nicholas Thomas, Harriet Guest and Michael Dettelbach (Honolulu, HI: University of Hawaii Press, 1996)
Forster, Nathaniel, *An Enquiry Into the Causes of the Present High Price of Provisions. In two parts: I. Of the general causes of this evil. II. Of the causes of it in some particular instances* (London: printed for J. Fletcher & Co; and sold by J. Fletcher in Oxford, 1767)
Gay, John, *Fables* (1727–38; Los Angeles, CA: William Andrews Clark Memorial Library, University of California, 1967)
Gerard, John, *The Herball, or Generall Histoire of Plantes* (London: J. Norton, 1597)
——*The Herball or Generall Historie of Plantes ... Very Much Enlarged and Amended by Thomas Johnson, etc.*, 2nd edn (1633; London: A. Islip, J. Norton and R. Whitakers, 1636)
Godwin, William, *Memoirs of the Author of A Vindication of the Rights of Woman* (London: J. Johnson, 1798)
Goethe, Johann Wolfgang von, 'Goethe's Botany. The Metamorphosis of Plants', (1790), trans. Agnes Arber, *Chronica Botanica*, 10:2 (1946), 63–124
——*Selected Verse*, trans. David Luke (Harmondsworth: Penguin, 1964)
Goldsmith, Oliver, *Poems and Plays* (London: J. M. Dent, 1910)
Halsted, Caroline, *The Little Botanist; or, Steps to the Attainment of Botanical Knowledge*, 2 vols (London: John Harris; Dublin: John Cummings; Edinburgh: William Wilson, 1835)
Hanbury, William, *A Complete Body of Planting and Gardening.* [etc.], 2 vols (London: Printed for the author and sold by Edward and Charles Dilly, in the Poultry, 1770)
Hawkesworth, John, *An Account of the Voyages Undertaken by the Order of His Present Majesty For Making Discoveries in the Southern Hemisphere and Successfully Performed by Commodore Byron, Captain Cartaret and Captain Wallis and Captain Cook in the Dolphin, the Swallow and the Endeavour: Drawn up From the Journals Which Were Kept By the Several Commanders, and From the Papers of Joseph Banks, Esq.*, 3 vols (London: printed for W. Strahan & T. Cadell, 1773)
——*An Account of the Voyages and Discoveries in the Southern Hemisphere*, 2nd edn, 3 vols (London: W. Strahan and T. Cadell, 1773)
Hawkins, Laetitia Matilda, *Letters on the Female Mind, its Powers and Pursuits. Addressed to Miss H. M. Williams, With Particular Reference to Her Letters From France*, 2 vols (London: Hookham & Carpenter, 1793)
Hearne, Samuel, *Journey From Fort Prince Wales in Hudson's Bay to the Northern Ocean* (London: [n. pub.], 1785)
Heath-Stubbs, John and Phillip Salman (eds), *Poems of Science* (Harmondsworth: Penguin, 1984)

Heckle, Augustin, *Bowles's Drawing Book for Ladies; or, Complete Florist: Being an Extensive and Curious Collection of the Most Beautiful Flowers All Drawn After Nature by A. Heckle With a Short Introduction to Drawing, and Directions for Mixing and Using Colours. Also Several Proper and Easy Examples. The Whole Adapted for the Improvement of* LADIES *in Needlework* (London: Carington Bowles, [*c.* 1785])

Hegel, G. W. F., *Elements of the Philosophy of Right*, ed. Allen W. Wood, trans. H. B. Nisbet (1821; Cambridge and New York: Cambridge University Press, 1991)

Helvétius, Claude-Adrien, *A Treatise On Man, His Intellectual Faculties and His Education*, trans. W. Hooper, 2 vols (1773; New York: Burt Franklin, 1969)

Hemens, Felicia, *Poetical Works of Mrs Hemens* (London: E. H. Wells, [n.d.])

Herschel, Mrs John (ed.), *Memoir and Correspondence of Caroline Herschel* (London: John Murray, 1879)

Hervey, James, 'Reflections on a Flower Garden In a Letter to a Lady,' in *Meditations and Contemplations in two volumes by James Hervey, Rector of Weston-Favell, in Northamptonshire,* 2 vols, 25th edn (1746; London: Charles Rivington, 1791)

[Hey, Rebecca,] *The Moral of Flowers. Illustrated by Coloured Engravings*, illus. by William Clark (London: Longman, 1833)

——*The Spirit of the Woods, illustrated by coloured engravings. By the author of 'The Moral of Flowers'* (London: [n. pub.], 1837)

Hoare, Sarah, 'The Pleasures of Botanical Pursuits, A Poem', appended to Priscilla Wakefield, *An Introduction to Botany*, 8th edn (London: Darton, Harvey, 1818)

——*A Poem on the Pleasures and Advantages of Botanical Pursuits, with Notes; and Other Poems By a Friend to Youth, Addressed to Her Pupils* (Bristol: Philip Rose, [1826 (?)])

——*Poems on Conchology and Botany With Plates and Notes by Sarah Hoare* (London: Simkin & Marshall; Bristol: Wright & Bagnall, 1831)

——*Memoirs of Samuel Hoare By His Daughter Sarah and His Widow Hannah* (London: Headley Brothers, 1911)

Hume, David, *A Treatise On Human Nature*, ed. L. A. Selby-Bigge (1739–40; Oxford: Clarendon Press, 1978)

——'Of National Characters', in *Essays Moral, Political, and Literary*, ed. Eugene F. Miller, rev. edn (Indianapolis, IA: Liberty Fund, 1985), pp. 197–215

Hunt, Leigh, [review of Elizabeth Kent, *Flora Domestica*], *Examiner*, no. 881, 19 December 1834, pp. 303–4

Jacson, Maria Elizabetha, *Botanical Dialogues Between Hortensia and Her Four Children, Charles, Harriet, Juliet and Henry. Designed for the Use in Schools by a Lady* (London: J. Johnson, 1797)

——*Botanical Lectures By A Lady, Altered From 'Botanical Dialogues For the Use of Schools' By the Same Author* (London: J. Johnson, 1804)

——*Sketches of the Physiology of Vegetable Life By the Authoress of Botanical Dialogues* (London: John Hatchard, 1811)

——*A Florist's Manual; or, Hints For the Construction of a Gay Flower Garden, With Observations On the Best Methods of Preventing the Depredations of Insects, By the Authoress of Botanical Dialogues and Sketches of the Physiology of vegetable Life* (London: Henry Colburn, 1816)

Jaques, E. J., *A Handbook to the Art of Wax-Flower Making* (London: [n. pub.], 1862)

Jodrell, Richard Paul, 'The Female Patriot' (1779), in *The Poetical Works of Richard Paul Jodrell* (London: [n. pub.], 1814)

Johnson, Samuel, 'The folly of annual retreats into the countryside', *The Rambler*, no. 135, 2 July 1751, in *The Yale Edition of the Works of Samuel Johnson*, ed. Herman W. Liebert, et al., 15 vols (Harvard & London: Yale University Press, 1958–1985), IV: *The Rambler (The Second of Three Volumes)*, ed. W. J. Bute & Albrecht B. Strauss (1969), pp. 349–54

——*A Dictionary of the English Language, Abstracted From the Folio Edition by the Author, etc.*, 2 vols (London: printed for J. Knapton; C. Hitch and L. Hawes; A. Millar, R. and J. Dodsley; and M. and T. Longman, 1756)

——*The History of Rasselas, Prince of Abissinia*, ed. D. J. Enright (1759; Harmondsworth: Penguin, 1976)

Joyce, Jeremiah, *Scientific Dialogues for the Instruction of Young People,* 7 vols (London: Bye & Law for J. Johnson, 1803–9)

Jussieu, Antoine Laurent de, *Genera plantarum secundum ordines naturales disposita: juxta methodum in horto regio Parisiensi exaratam* (Paris: Apud viduam Herissant, 1789)

Kant, Immanuel, *Observations On the Feeling of the Beautiful and Sublime*, trans. John T. Goldthwait (1763; Berkeley, CA and London: University of California Press, 1991)

——*Political Writings* ed. Hans Reiss, trans. H. B. Nisbet, 2nd edn (Cambridge and New York: Cambridge University Press, 1996)

Kent, Elizabeth, *Flora Domestica, or The Portable Flower Garden By Elizabeth Kent Largely Compiled From Material Supplied to the Author From Leigh Hunt*, 2nd edn (London: Taylor & Hessey, 1823)

[La Tour, Charlotte de] *The Language of Flowers,* trans. L. Cortambert (London: Saunders & Otley, 1834)

Lawson, William, *A New Orchard and Garden, ... With the Country Housewife's Garden for Hearbes of Common Use* (London: R. Aesop for R. Jackson, 1617–18)

Lee, James, *An Introduction to Botany, Containing An Explanation of the Theory of That Science, And an Interpretation of its Technical Terms, Extracted From the Works of Dr Linnaeus With an Appendix Containing Upwards of Two Thousand Names of English Plants By James Lee* (London: J. & R. Tonson, 1760)

——*An Introduction to Botany*, 5th edn (1760; London: S. Crowder, 1794)

Lemprière, J., *A Classical Dictionary Containing a Copious Account of All the Proper Names Mentioned in Antient Authors*, new edn, ed. F. D. Lemprière (1788; London: T. Cadell, 1839)

L'Enclos, Ninon de [Douxménil], *The Memoirs of Ninon de L'Enclos, with her Letters to Monsr de St Evremond and to the Marquis de Sevigné. Collected and Translated from the French by a Lady*, [trans. Elizabeth Griffith (?)], 2 vols (London: R. & J. Dodsley, 1761)

Lightfoot, John, *Flora Scotica: A Systematic Arrangement in the Linnaean Method of the Native Plants of Scotland and the Hebrides*, 2 vols (London: [n. pub.], 1777)

Lindley, John, *Collectanea botanica; or, Figures and Botanical Illustrations of Rare and Curious Plants By John Lindley* (London: printed by R. & A. Taylor, 1821)

——*An Introductory Lecture Delivered to the University of London on April 30th, 1824* (London: John Taylor, 1829)

——*An Introduction to the Natural System of Botany: or, A Systematic View of the Organisation, Natural Affinities, and Geographical Distribution of the Whole Vegetable Kingdom; together with the uses of the most important Species in Medicine, the Arts and Rural and Domestic Economy* (London: Longman, Rees, Orme, Brown and Green, 1830)

——*Ladies' Botany, or A Familiar Introduction to the Study of the Natural System of Botany*, 2 vols (London: [n. pub.], 1834–37)

——*Ladies' Botany ... New Edition for Use in Schools and for Young Persons*, 2 vols (London: Henry G. Bohn, 1841)

——*The Vegetable Kingdom; the Structure, Classification and Use of Plants* (London: Bradbury & Evans, 1846)

Linnaeus, Carl [Carl von Linné], *Systema naturae, sive regna tria naturae systematice proposita per classes, ordines, genera & species*, (Leiden, Netherlands: Apud Theodorum Haak, 1735)

——*Systema naturae* (1735; facs. repr. with intr. by M. S. J. Engel-Ledeboer and H. Engel, Nieuwkoop: Published for the Netherlands Society for the History of Medicine, Mathematics and Exact Sciences, by B. De Graaf, 1964)

——*Species Plantarum* (Uppsala: 1753; facs. repr. with intr. by W. T. Stearn, 2 vols, London: Printed For Ray Society, Sold by B. Quaritch, 1957–59)

——*Genera Plantarum*, 5th edn (Stockholm, [n. pub.], 1754; facs. repr. with intr. by W. T. Stearn, Weinheim: Engelmann, 1960)

——*A System of Vegetables, According to Their Classes, Genera, Orders, Species With Their Characters and Differences ... Translated from the Thirteenth Edition of the Systema Vegetabilium of the Late Professor Linnaeus and from the Supplementum Plantarum of the Present Professor Linnaeus*, trans. A Botanical Society at Lichfield, 2 vols (Lichfield: printed by John Jackson for Leigh and Sotheby, York Street, Covent Garden, London, 1783)

——*A Dissertation on the Sexes of Plants. Translated From the Latin of Linnaeus by James Edward Smith F.R.S.* (London: George Nicol, 1786)

——*The Families of Plants, With Their Natural Characters ... Translated from the last Edition (as Published by Dr Reichard) of the Genera Plantarum, and of the Mantissae Plantarum of the Elder Linnaeus; and from the Supplementum Plantarum of the Younger Linnaeus, With All the New Families of Plants, From Thunberg and L'Heriter ... By A Botanical Society at Lichfield*, 2 vols (London: printed by John Jackson; sold by J. Johnson, 1787)

——*A General System of Nature: Through the Three Grand kingdoms of Animals, Vegetables and Minerals By Sir Charles Linné Translated ... by William Turton* (London: Lackington, Allen, 1806)

——*Lachesis Lapponica, or, A Tour in Lapland. Now First Published from the Original Manuscript Journal of the Celebrated Linnaeus; by James Edward Smith*, 2 vols (London: printed for White & Cochrane by Richard Taylor, 1811)

——*A Selection of the Correspondence of Linnaeus, and Other Naturalists, From the Original manuscripts By Sir James Edward Smith M.D., F.R.S.C.C. & C. President of the Linnaean Society*, 2 vols (London: Longman, Hurst, Rees, Orme, & Brown, 1821)

Linnea, Elisabeth Christina [Miss E. C Linné], 'Om Indianska Krassens Blickande', *Svenska Kongliga Vetenskaps Academiens Handlingar*, 23 (1762), 284–6

Llanover, A. (ed.), *Autobiography and Correspondence of Mary Granville, Mrs Delaney*, 6 vols (London: Richard Bentley, 1861)

Locke, John, *Essay Concerning Human Understanding*, ed. and abridged by Raymond Willburn (1690; London: J. M. Dent, 1947)

——*Some Thoughts Concerning Education* [1693]: and, *Of the Conduct of the Understanding* [1706], ed. Ruth W. Grant and Nathan Tarcov (Indiana, IN: Hackett Publishing Company, 1996)

Lonsdale, Roger (ed.), *Eighteenth-Century Women Poets* (Oxford: Oxford University Press, 1989)

Loudon, Jane, *The Young Ladies Book of Botany: Being A Popular Introduction to that Delightful Science* (London: Robert Tyas, 1838)

——*Instructions on Gardening for Ladies* (London: Murray, 1840)

——*The Ladies Companion to the Flower Garden Being An Alphabetical Arrangement of all the Ornamental Plants Usually Grown in Gardens and Shrubberies With Directions for Their Culture* (London: [n. pub.], 1841)

——*The First Book of Botany: Being a Plain and Brief Introduction to that Science for Schools and Young Persons By Mrs Loudon* (London: G. Bell, 1841)

——*Botany For Ladies, or, A Popular Introduction to the Natural System of Plants According to the Classification of De Candolle By Mrs Loudon*, 2 vols (London: John Murray, 1842)

——*British Wildflowers* (London: [n. pub], 1845)

——*Ladies Country Companion; or, How to Enjoy a Country Life Rationally* (London: Longman, Brown & Green, 1845)

——*The Ladies Flower Garden*, 4 vols (London: [n. pub.], 1848)

——*Ladies Companion to the Flower Garden by Mrs Loudon*, 6th edn (London: Bradbury & Evans, 1853)

——*Mrs Loudon's First Book of Botany Being A Plain and Brief Introduction to That Science For Schools and Young Person*, new edn, rev. by David Wooster (London: Bell & Daldy, 1870)

[Jane Webb, neé Loudon,] *The Mummy: A Tale of the Twenty Second Century*, 3 vols (London: Henry Colburn, 1827)

Loudon, John Claudius, *An Encyclopedia of Gardening: Comprising the Theory and Practice of Horticulture, Floriculture, Arboriculture and Landscape Gardening, Including all the Latest Improvements* (London: Longman, Hurst, Rees, Orme & Brown, 1822)

——(ed.), *An Encyclopaedia of Plants; Comprising the Description, Specific Character, Culture, History, Application in the Arts, and Every Other Desirable Particular Respecting all the Plants Indigenous, Cultivated in, or Introduced to Britain* (London: Longman, Rees, Orme, Brown & Green, 1836)

Macaulay, Catherine, *Letters On Education* (1790; London: Dilly, 1790; facs. repr. Oxford: Woodstock Books, 1994)

Maddock, James, *The Florist's Directory, Or A Treatise on the Culture of Flowers to Which is Added a Supplementary Dissertation on Soils, Manures* (London: B. White & Sons, 1792)

[Marcet, Jane,] *Conversations on Chemistry, in which the elements of that science are familiarly explained and illustrated by experiments*, 2 vols (London: Longman, Rees, & Orme, 1806)

——*Conversations on Vegetable Physiology; comprehending the elements of botany, with their application to agriculture. By the author of Conversations on Chemistry*, 2 vols (London: Longman, Rees, Orme, Brown & Green, 1829)

Martyn, Thomas, *Plantæ Cantabrigienses; or, a Catalogue of the Plants which Grow Wild in the County of Cambridge, Disposed According to the System of Linnaeus. Herbationes Cantabrigienses, or Directions to the Places where they May be Found, Comprehended in 13 Botanical Excursions. To Which are Added, Lists of the More Rare Plants Growing in Many Parts of England and Wales* (London: [n. pub.],

1763)
——*The Language of Botany: Being a Dictionary of the Terms Made Use of in that Science, Principally by Linnaeus* (London: B. and J. White, 1793)
Mason, William, *The English Garden, A Poem in Four Books* (1772–79; Dublin: S. Price, W. and H. Whitestone, W. Sleater, R. Moncrieffe, T. Walker, H. Chamberlaine, J. Beatty, L. White, R. Burton, and P. Byrne, 1782)
Mathias, Thomas James, *The Pursuits of Literature: A Satirical Poem in Four Dialogues*, 16th edn (1798; London: Becket & Porter, 1812)
Mavor, William, *The Ladies and Gentleman's Botanical Pocket-book: Adapted to Withering's Arrangement of British Plants Intended to Facilitate and Promote the Study of Indigenous Botany* (London: Vernor & Hood, 1800)
——*A Catechism of Botany; or, An Easy Introduction to the Vegetable Kingdom. For the Use of Schools and Families*, 3rd edn (London: Lackington, Allen, 1810)
Meen, Margaret, illus., *Exotic Plants From the Royal Gardens of Kew: nos. i–ii* (London: [n. pub.], 1790
Mettrie, Offray La, *L'Homme plante* (Potsdam: [n. pub.] 1748)
——*L'Homme plante*, intr. by Francis L. Rougier (1748; New York: The Institute of French Studies, 1936)
——*Ouvrage de Pénélope ou Machiavel en Médecine* (Geneva: Heirs of Cramer & P. Philibert, 1748)
Millar, John, *The Origin of the Distinction of Ranks: or, An Inquiry Into the Circumstances Which Give Rise to Influence and Authority In the Different Members of Society*, 4th edn (1771; Edinburgh and London: William Blackwood and, Longman, Hurst, Rees and Orme, 1806)
Miller, John, *An Illustration of the Sexual System of Linnaeus by John Miller* (London: John Miller, 1777)
Miller, Philip, *The Gardener's and Florist's Dictionary; or, A Complete System of Horticulture ... to which is added , a catalogue of curious trees, plants and fruits , etc.* 2 vols (London: Printed for Charles Rivington, 1724)
——*The Gardener's and Botanist's Dictionary ... by Philip Miller; newly arranged by Thomas Martyn* (London: Printed for F.C. & J. Rivington, 1807)
[Miller, Philip,] *Catalogus Plantarum* (London: A Society of Gardeners, 1730)
Miller, Vincent, *The Man-Plant; or, Scheme for Increasing and Improving the British Breed by Vincent Miller, M.E. and Professor of Philosophy* (London: M. Cooper, 1752)
Molière, J. B., 'The Ridiculous Précieuses', in *Tartuffe and Other Plays*, trans. Donald Frame (New York: New American Library, 1981), pp. 19–47
Montagu, Lady Wortley, *Letters of Right Honourable Lady M...y W...y M...e written during her travels in Europe, Asia and Africa, to persons of distinction, men of letters, &c in different parts of Europe: which contain among other curious relations, accounts of the policy and manners of the Turks; drawn from sources that have been inaccessible to other travellers*, 3 vols (London: Printed T. Becket & P. A. De Hondt, 1763)
Montolieu, Maria Henrietta, *The Enchanted Plants, Fables in Verse. Inscribed to Miss Montolieu, and Miss Julia Montolieu* (London: Thomas Bensley, 1800)
Moody, Elizabeth, 'To Dr Darwin, on Reading his Loves of the Plants', in *Poetic Trifles* (London, printed by H. Baldwin and Son for T. Cadell, Jun. and W. Davies, 1798), pp. 8–12; facs. repr. in *Literature and Science, 1660–1834*, ed. Judith Hawley and others, 8 vols (London: Pickering and Chatto, 2003–4), IV: *Flora*, ed. Charlotte

Grant (2003), pp. 251–5
——'Sappho Burns Her books and Cultivates the Culinary Arts', in *Eighteenth-Century Women Poets*, ed. Roger Lonsdale (Oxford: Oxford University Press, 1989), p. 406

More, Hannah, *Strictures on the Modern System of Female Education, With A View of the Principles and conduct Prevalent Among Women of Rank and Fortune*, 3rd edn, 2 vols (1799; London: T. Cadell & W. Davies, 1799)

Moriarty, Henrietta Maria, *A Viridarium: Coloured Plates of Greenhouse Plants with the Linnean Names, and with Concise Rules for Their Culture* (London: [n. pub.], 1806)

——*Fifty Plates of Greenhouse Plants, Drawn and Coloured From Nature; With Concise Descriptions and Rules for Their Culture: Intended also for the Improvement of Young Ladies in the Art of Drawing*, 2nd edn (London: T. Bensley, 1807)

——*Brighton in an Uproar: Comprising Anecdotes of Sir Timothy Flight, Mr. Abrahams ... A Novel Founded on Facts* (London: Printed by the Author, 1811)

——*Crim. Con. A Novel, Founded on Facts* (London: [n. pub.], 1812)

Murray, Ann, *Mentoria, or The Young Ladies Instructor* (London: C. Dilly, 1778)

Murray, Lady Charlotte, *The British Garden. A Descriptive Catalogue of Hardy Plants Indigenous or Cultivated in the Climate of Great Britain With Their Generic and Specific Characters, Latin and English Names, Native Country, and Time of Flowering. With Introductory Remarks by Lady Charlotte Murray*, 2 vols (Bath: S. Hazard, 1799)

Oosten, Hendrik Van, *The Dutch Gardener: Or, the Compleat Florist. Containing, The most successful Method of Cultivating all sorts of Flowers; the Planting, Dressing, and Pruning of all manner of Fruit Trees. Together with a particular Account of the Nursing of Lemon and Orange Trees in Northern Climates. Written in Dutch, By Henry van Oosten, the Leyden Gardener. And made English* (London: D. Midwinter & T. Leigh, 1703)

Paine, Thomas, *The Rights of Man*, ed. Henry Collins (1791–92; Harmondsworth: Penguin, 1969)

Parkinson, John, *Paradisi in Sole Paradisi Terrestris; or a garden of all sorts of flowers which our English ayre will permit to be noursed up : with a kitchen garden of all manner of herbes, rootes and fruites, for meate or sause used with us, and an orchard of all sorte of fruit-bearing trees and shrubbes fir for our land, together with the right orderinge planting and preserving of them and their uses and virtues. Collected by John Parkinson Apothecary of London, 1629* (London: Printed by Humfrey Lownes and Robert Young, 1629)

Parley, Peter, *Tales About Plants* (London: Thomas Tegg, 1839)

Penn, William, *Some Fruits of Solitude In Reflections and Maxims Relating To Conduct* (1693; London: Edward Arnold, 1901)

[Perry, James], *Mimosa: or, The Sensitive Plant: A Poem Dedicated to Mr. Banks and Addressed to Kitt Frederick, Duchess of Queensbury, Elect* (London: Printed for W. Sandwich, 1779)

Philosophical Society of Edinburgh, *Essays and Observations: Physical and Literary. Read before the Philosophical Society in Edinburgh, and published by them*, 2nd edn, 5 vols (Edinburgh: printed for John Balfour, 1771)

Pliny, *Natural History*, trans. H. Rackham, 10 vols, Loeb Classical Library (Cambridge, MA: Harvard University Press; London: William Heinemann, 1942–52)

Plumptre, James, *The Lakers: A Comic Opera in Three Acts* (London: Printed for W. Clarke, 1798; facs. repr. Oxford and New York: Woodstock Books, 1990)

Polwhele, Richard, *Historical Views of Devonshire*, 5 vols (Exeter: Trewman & Son; London: Cadell, Dilly and Murray, 1793)

——*The Influence of Local Attachment with Respect to Home, A Poem* (London: J. Johnson, 1796)

——*The Unsex'd Females* (London: Cadell & Davies, 1798; facs. repr. New York: Garland Press, 1974)

——*The Unsex'd Females*, US edn (New York: W. Cobbett, 1800)

——*The History of Cornwall: in respect to its population; and the health ... and diseases of its inhabitants; with illustrations from Devonshire* (London: Cadell & Davies, 1806)

——*Poems: Chiefly, The Local Attachment, The Unsex'd Females, The Old English Gentleman; The Pneumatic Revellers and The Family Picture by M. Polwhele, of Polwhele*, 5 vols (Truro: J. Michell, S. Highcross, for Messrs. Rivingtons, London: 1810)

Pope, Alexander, *The Poems of Alexander Pope: A One Volume Edition of the Twickenham Pope*, ed. John Butt (London: Routledge, 1968)

——'On Topiary', *The Guardian*, no. 73, 1713

Pratt, Anne, *The Pictorial Catechism of Botany* (London: [n. pub.], 1842)

Pulteney, Richard, *A General View of the Writings of Linnaeus* (London: T. Payne & B. White, 1781)

——*Historical and Biographical Sketches of the Progress of Botany in England From its Origin to the Introduction of the Linnaean System*, 2 vols (London: T. Cadell, 1790)

Ray, John, *The Ornithology Of Francis Willughby* (London: Printed by A.C. for John Martyn, Printer to The Royal Society, 1678)

——*De variis plantarum methodis dissertatio brevis* (London: [n. pub.], 1696)

——*Methodus Plantarum* (London: [n. pub.], 1703)

——*The Wisdom of God Manifested in the Works of Creation: In Two Parts, viz. The Heavenly Bodies, Elements, Meteors, Fossils, Vegetables, Animals, (Beasts, Birds, Fishes, and Insects) more particularly in the Body of the Earth, its Figure, Motion, and Consistency, and in the admirable Structure of the Bodies of Man, and other Animals, as also in their Generation, &c. With Answers to some Objections*, 4th edn (1691; London: Printed by J. B. for Sam Smith, 1704)

Reeve, Clara, *Plans of Education; with remarks on the systems of other writers. In a series of letters between Mrs. Darnford and her friends* (London: T. Hookham and J. Carpenter, 1792)

——*The Flowers at Court by Mrs Reeve* (London: Printed and published for the author, by C. and R. Baldwin, 1809)

Repton, Humphrey, *Observations on the Theory and Practice of Landscape Gardening* (London: J. Taylor, 1830; facs. repr. Oxford: Phaidon, 1980)

Reynolds, Joshua Sir, *Discourses on Art*, ed. Robert R. Wark (New Haven, CT and London: Yale University Press, 1975)

Rice-Oxley, L. (ed.), *Poetry of the Anti-Jacobin* (Oxford: Blackwell, 1924)

Richardson, Samuel, *Clarissa Harlowe*, 4 vols (1748; New York and London: J. M. Dent, 1932)

Roberts, Mary, *Wonders of the Vegetable Kingdom Displayed in A Series of Letters* (London: Whittaker, 1822)

——*Sister Mary's Tales in Natural History* (London: [n. pub.], 1834)

——*Flowers of the Matin and Even Song; or Thoughts For Those Who Rise Early* (London: Grant and Griffiths, 1845)

Rogers, Samuel, *Recollections of the Table Talk of Samuel Rogers*, ed. Rev. Alexander Dyce (New Southgate: H. A. Rogers, 1887)

Rose, Hugh, *The Elements of Botany ... Being A Translation of the Philosophia Botanica, and Other Treatises of Linnaeus. To Which is Added, An Appendix, Wherein Are Described Some Plants Lately Found in Norfolk and Suffolk etc. By Hugh Rose* (London: T. Cadell & M. Hingeston, 1775)

Rousseau, Jean-Jacques, *Discourse on the Origin of Inequality*, ed. Patrick Coleman, trans. Franklin Philip (1755; Oxford: Oxford University Press, 1994)

——*Julie ou la Nouvelle Héloïse: Lettres de deaux amants, habitants d'une petite ville au pied des Alps*, 6 vols (Amsterdam: Marc Michel Rey, 1761)

——*Eloisa: Or, a Series of Original Letters Collected and Published by J .J. Rousseau. Translated from the French. In four volumes*, 4 vols (London: R. Griffiths, T. Becket, P. A. De Hondt, 1761)

——*Emile, Or Education*, trans. Barbara Foxley (1762; London: J. M. Dent, 1950)

——*Letters on the Elements of Botany Addressed To A Lady. By The Celebrated J. J. Rousseau, Translated into English With Notes and Twenty-Four Additional Letters, Fully Explaining the System of Linnaeus, By Thomas Martyn, B.D. F.R.S. Professor of Botany in the University of Cambridge*, 2nd edn (London: Printed for B. White & Son, 1787)

——*Letters on the Elements of Botany Addressed To A Lady*, 5th edn (London: Printed for B. & J. White, 1796)

——*Confessions*, trans. J. M. Cohen (1782; Harmondsworth: Penguin, 1953)

——*Œuvres completes*, ed. Bernard Gagnebin and Marcel Raymond, 4 vols (Paris: Gallimard, Biblioteque de la Pléiades, 1959–1969)

——*Lettres sur la botanique*, ed. Ernest J. Bonnet and Bernard Gagnebin (Paris: Saverne, 1962)

——'A Discourse on the Origin of Inequality' (1755), in *The Social Contract and Discourses*, trans. G. D. H. Cole, new edn (London: Everyman, 1973), pp. 31–126

——*On the Social Contract, with Geneva Manuscript and Political Economy*, ed. Roger D. Masters, trans. Judith R. Masters (New York: St Martin's Press, 1978)

——*Pure Curiosity: Botanical Letters and Notes Towards A Dictionary of Botanical Terms*, trans. Kate Ottevanger, illus. P. J. Redouté (New York and London: Paddington Press, 1979)

——*Reveries of the Solitary Walker*, trans. Peter France (1782; Harmondsworth: Penguin, 1979)

——*The Collected Writings of Rousseau*, ed. Roger D. Masters and Christopher Kelly, 8- vols (Hanover, NH and London: University Press of New England, 1990–)

——'Discourse on the Arts and Sciences' (1750), in *The Collected Writings of Rousseau*, II, ed. Roger D. Masters and Christopher Kelly, trans. Judith R. Bush, Roger D. Masters and Christopher Kelly (1992)

——'Luxury, Commerce and the Arts', in *The Collected Writings of Rousseau*, IV, ed. Roger D. Masters and Christopher Kelly, trans. Judith R. Bush and others (1994), pp. 44–51

——*The Social Contract*, trans. Christopher Betts (1762; Oxford and New York: Oxford University Press, 1994)

——*The Confessions and Correspondence Including the Letters to Malsherbes*, in *The Collected Writings of Rousseau*, V, ed. Christopher Kelly, Roger D. Masters and Peter G. Stillman, trans. Christopher Kelly (1995)

——*Julie, or the New Héloïse: Letters of Two Lovers Who Live in a Small Town at the*

Foot of the Alps (1761), in *The Collected Writings of Rousseau*, VI, trans. and annotated by Philip Stewart and Jean Vaché (1997)
——*The Collected Writings of Rousseau*, VIII: *The Reveries of the Solitary Walker, Botanical Writings, and Letter to Franquières*, ed. Christopher Kelly, trans. Charles E. Butterworth, Alexandra Cook, and Terence E. Marshall (2000)
Rowden, Frances Arabella, *A Poetical Introduction to the Study of Botany* (London: T. Bensley, 1801)
——*The Pleasures of Friendship. A Poem in Two Parts* (London: [n. pub.], 1810)
——*A Poetical Introduction to the Study of Botany*, 2nd edn (London: Printed by A. J. Valpy; sold by Longman, Hurst, Rees, Orme, and Browne; J. White and Cochrane; J. Murray and J. Harris, 1812)
——*A Poetical Introduction to the Study of Botany*, 3rd edn (London: Printed for G. & W. B. Whittaker by Weed and Rider, 1818)
——*A Christian Wreath for the Pagan Deities, or An Introduction to Greek and Roman Mythology* (London: A. J. Valpy, 1820)
——*A Biographical Sketch of the Most Distinguished Writers of Ancient and Modern Times* (London: Longman, Hatchard & Son, Seely, Laker, Uxbridge, [n.d.])
Sancho, Ignatius, *Letters of the Late Ignatius Sancho, An African*, ed. Vincent Carretta (1782; Harmondsworth: Penguin, 1988)
Scott, Sarah, *Millenium Hall*, ed. Gary Kelly (1762; Ontario, Canada: Broadview Press, 1999)
Serle, John, *A Plan of Mr Pope's Garden* (London, R. Dodsley,1745; facs. repr. New York: Garland Press, 1982)
Seward, Anna, *Elegy on Captain Cook. To Which is Added Ode to the Sun By Miss Anna Seward*, 2nd edn (London: J. Dodsley, 1780)
——*Llangollen Vale With Other Poems* (London: G. Sael. 1796)
——*Memoirs of the Life of Dr Darwin: Chiefly During His Residence at Lichfield, With Anecdotes of His Friends and Criticisms on His Writings by Anna Seward* (London: J. Johnson, 1804)
——*Letters of Anna Seward: written between the years 1784 and 1807* (Edinburgh: A. Constable and Company, 1811)
——*Bluestocking Feminism: Writings of the Bluestocking Circle, 1738–1790*, ed. Gary Kelly and others, 6 vols (London: Chatto & Pickering, 1999), IV: *Anna Seward*, ed. Jennifer Kelly
[Anna Seward (?),] 'The Backwardness of Spring Accounted For', in Linnaeus, *A System of Vegetables ... Translated from the Thirteenth Edition of the Systema Vegetabilium of the Late Professor Linnaeus and from the Supplementum Plantarum of the Present Professor Linnaeus ... By A Botanical Society at Lichfield*, 2 vols (Lichfield: printed by John Jackson for Leigh and Sotherby ... London, 1783), II, manuscript in endpapers (British Library, 447.c.18)
Shenstone, William, *Unconnected Thoughts on Gardening, A Description of the Leasowes* (1764; facs. repr. New York: Garland Press, 1982)
Sheridan, Richard, *The School For Scandal and Other Plays*, ed. Michael Cordner (Oxford: Oxford University Press, 1988)
Smart, Christopher, *Selected Poems*, ed. Karina Williamson and Marcus Walsh (Harmondsworth: Penguin, 1990)
Smellie, William, *The Philosophy of Natural History* (Edinburgh: Printed for the Heirs of Charles Elliot and T. Kay; London: T. Cadell and G. G. & J. Robinson, 1790)
Smellie, William (ed.), *Encyclopaedia Britannica, or A Dictionary of Arts and Sciences*

(Edinburgh: Printed for A. Bell and C. Macfarquhar; sold by Colin Macfar, 1771)

Smith, Charlotte, *Desmond, A Novel By Charlotte Smith*, 3 vols (London: Printed for G. G. & J. Robinson, 1792)

——*Rural Walks in Dialogues: Intended For the Use of Young Persons by Charlotte Smith*, 2nd edn, 2 vols (London: T. Cadell and W. Davies, 1795)

——*Rambles Farther: A Continuation of Rural Walks: In Dialogues: Intended for the Use of Young Persons* (Dublin: P. Wogan, P. Byrne, J. Moore. B. Dugdale, H. Fitzpatrick, 1796)

——*The Young Philosopher: A Novel; in Four Volumes, By Charlotte Smith*, 4 vols (London: T. Cadell & W. Davies, 1798)

——*The Letters of a Solitary Wanderer: Containing Narratives of Various Description*, 3 vols (London: printed by and for Sampson Low, 1800–1)

——*Conversations Introducing Poetry Chiefly on the Subject of Natural History for the Use of Children and Young Persons by Charlotte Smith*, 2 vols (London: J. Johnson, 1804)

——*Beachy Head; With Other Poems* (London: J. Johnson, 1807)

——*The Poems of Charlotte Smith*, ed. S. Curran (Oxford: Oxford University Press, 1993)

——*The Young Philosopher*, ed. Elizabeth Kraft, Eighteenth-Century Novels by Women (1798; Lexington, KY: University Press of Kentucky, 1999)

Smith, David Nichol (ed.), *The Oxford Book of Eighteenth Century Verse* (Oxford: Clarendon Press, 1926)

Smith, Edward James, *Memoir and Correspondence of the Late Sir James Edward Smith*, ed. Lady Pleasance Smith, 2 vols (London, Longman, Rees, Orme, Brown, Green, 1832)

Sprat, Thomas, *History of the Royal Society*, ed. Jackson I. Cope and Harold Whitmore Jones (1667; St Louis, WA: Washington University Press, 1966)

Steele, Richard, *Plays*, ed. G. A. Aiken (London and New York: T. Fisher Unwin, 1903)

——*The Tatler*, ed. G. A. Aiken, 4 vols (1709–11; London, 1898–99)

Stoever, D. H., *Life of Sir Charles Linnaeus, Knight of the Swedish Order of the Polar Star & C, To Which is Added a Copious List of his Works and a biographical Sketch of the Life of His Son, Translated From the Original German by Joseph Trapp, A. H. ...* (London: B and J. White, 1794)

[Stretser, Thomas (?),] *The Natural History of the Arbor Vitae, or Tree of Life* (London: Printed for the Company of Gardeners, J. Grage, 1732)

Stubbs, John Heath and Phillips Salman (eds), *Poems of Science* (Harmondsworth: Penguin, 1984)

Swift, Jonathan, *The Conduct of the Allies* (1712; Oxford: Clarendon Press, 1951)

——*Gulliver's Travels*, ed. Paul Turner (1726; Oxford: Oxford University Press, 1986)

——*A Complete Collection of Genteel and Ingenious Conversation*, intr. by Michael Foot (1755; facs. repr. Bristol: Thoemmes Press, 1995)

——*Prose Works*, ed. H. Davies (Oxford: Oxford University Press, 1951)

——*Complete Poems*, ed. Pat Rogers (Harmondsworth: Penguin, 1983)

Switzer, Stephen, *Iconographia rustica; or, the nobleman, gentleman, and gardener's recreation*, 3 vols (London: [n. pub.], 1718; facs. repr. New York: Garland Press, 1982)

Temple, William, *Observations Upon the United Provinces of the Netherlands* (London: Printed by A. Maxwell for Sa. Gellibrand, 1673)

Thomson, James, *Spring, A Poem* (London: A. Millar & G. Straham, 1728)

——*The Poems of James Thomson*, ed. J. Logie Robertson (Oxford: Oxford University Press, 1963)

Thornton, Robert John, *The Politician's Creed: Being the Great Outline of Political Science From the Writings of Montesquieu, Hume, Gibbon, Paley, Townsend etc., by an Independent* (London: T. Cox, 1795)

——*Botanical Extracts, or, Philosophy of Botany*, 3 vols (1799; London: White, Johnson, 1810)

——*An Account of Dr Thornton's Exhibition of Botanical Paintings: Now Open at No. 49 New Bond Street; With the Poetic Compositions Made on the Different Subjects, And Explanatory Notes*, 4th edn (London: C. Whittingham, 1804)

——*New Illustration of the Sexual System of Carolus von Linnaeus: Comprehending an Elucidation of the Several Parts of Fructification; A Prize Dissertation on the Sexes of Plants; A Full Explanation of the Classes, and Orders, of the Sexual System; And The Temple of Flora, or Garden of Nature, Being Picturesque, Botanical Coloured Plates, of select Plants, Illustrative of the same, With Descriptions* (London: T. Bensley, 1807)

——*An Easy Introduction to the Science of Botany Through the Medium of Familiar Conversations Between a Father and His Son by Robert John Thornton, M.D.* (London: Sherwood, Jones, 1813)

——*Juvenile Botany: Being an Easy Introduction to that Delightful Science Through the Medium of Familiar Conversations* (London: Printed for Sherwood, Neely and Jones, 1818)

——*The Temple of Flora By Robert Thornton*, Abridged and intr. by Ronald King (London: Weidenfeld and Nicholson, 1981)

——*Temple of Flora, or, Garden of the botanist, poet, painter, and philosopher* (London: Robert Thornton, 1812) http://digital.library.wisc.edu/1711.dl/DLDecArts.ThornTempFlo (accessed 17 September 2003)

Tournefort, Joseph Pitton de, *Elémens de botanique, ou methode pour connoître les plantes*, 3 vols (Paris: [n. pub.], 1694)

——*Institutiones Rei Herbariae*, 3 vols (Paris, [n. pub.], 1700)

Trimmer, Sarah, *An Easy Introduction to the Knowledge of Nature, and Reading the Holy Scriptures Adapted to the Capacities of Children* (London: J. Dodsley, 1780)

——*Fabulous Histories: Designed For the Instruction of Children, Respecting Their Treatment of Animals* (London: T. Longman, and G. G. J. & J. Robinson 1786; facs. repr. New York and London: Garland Publishing, 1977)

Trussler, Simon (ed.), *Eighteenth-Century Comedy* (Oxford: Oxford University Press, 1969)

Twamley, Louisa Anne, *Flora's Gems, or, the Treasures of the Parterre: Twelve Bouquets, Drawn and Coloured From Nature By James Andrews; With Poetical Illustrations By Louisa Anne Twamley* (London: Charles Tilt, 1830)

——*The Romance of Nature; or, the flower-seasons illustrated* (London: Charles Tilt, 1836)

——*An Autumn Ramble by the Wye* (London: Charles Tilt, 1839)

Tyas, Robert, *The Language of Flowers; or, Floral Emblem of Thoughts, feelings, and Sentiments ... With twelve coloured groups of flowers* (London, [n. pub.], 1875)

[Tyas, Robert,] *The Sentiment of Flowers ... Twelve coloured plates* (London, [n. pub.], 1836)

——*Handbook of the Language and Sentiment of Flowers: containing the name of every flower to which a sentiment has been assigned* (London: Robert Tyas, 1840)

van Kampen, Nicholas, *The Dutch Florist*, 2nd edn (1763; London: R. Baldwin, 1764)
Wakefield, Priscilla, *Mental Improvement; or the Beauties and Wonders of Nature and Art Conveyed in A Series of Instructive Conversations*, 2 vols (London: Darton and Harvey, 1794)
——*Mental Improvement*, intr. Ann Shteir (1794; East Lansing, Michigan: Colleagues Press, 1995)
——*Leisure Hours: or Entertaining Dialogues, etc.* (London: [n. pub.], 1794–96)
——*Juvenile Anecdotes, Founded on Facts*, 2nd edn (1795; London: Allen & West; Darton & Harvey, 1796)
——*An Introduction to Botany In A Series of Familiar Letters, With Engravings By Priscilla Wakefield* (Dublin: Printed by Thomas Burnside. For Messrs P. Wogan, P. Byrne, J. Milliken, J. Rice, B. Dugdale, J. Gough, P. Moore and George Johnston, 1796)
——*Reflections on the Present Condition of the Female Sex; with Suggestions for its Improvement* (London: J. Johnson, 1798)
——*Reflections on the Present Condition of the Female Sex; with Suggestions for its Improvement* (London: J. Johnson, Darton & Harvey, 1798; facs. repr. New York and London: Garland Publishing, 1974)
——*The Juvenile Travellers; containing the remarks of a family during a tour through the principle states and kingdoms of Europe, etc.* (London: Darton & Harvey, 1801)
——*A Family Tour Through the British Empire; containing some account of its manufactures, natural and artificial curiosities, history and antiquities; interspersed with biographical anecdotes. Particularly adapted to the amusement and instruction of youth* (London: Darton & Harvey, 1804)
——*Domestic Recreations: Or, Dialogues Illustrative of Natural and Scientific Subjects* (London: Printed for Darton & Harvey, 1805)
——*Excursions in North America, described in letters from a gentleman and his young companion, to their friends in England* (London: Darton & Harvey, 1806)
——*An Introduction to the Natural History and Classification of Insects, in a Series of Familiar Letters* (London: [n. pub.], 1816)
——*An Introduction to Botany*, 8th edn (London: Darton Harvey & Co., 1818)
Walpole, Horace, *The History of the Modern Taste in Gardening* (1780; New York: Ursus Press, 1995)
——*The Yale Edition of Horace Walpole's Correspondence*, ed. W. S. Lewis and A. Dayle Wallace, 31 vols (London: Oxford University Press; New Haven: Yale University Press, 1937–61
Waring, Sarah, *A Sketch of the Life of Linnaeus in a Series of Letters Designed for Young Persons* (London: Harvey & Darton, 1827)
——*The Wild Garland; or, Prose and Poetry Connected with English Wild Flowers Intended as an Embellishment to the Study of Botany* (London: Printed for Harvey & Darton, 1827)
——*The Meadow Queen; or, the Young Botanists with the Wild Flower Alphabet. By the author of the Wild Garland*, (London: [n. pub.], 1836)
Whately, Sir Thomas, *Observations on Modern Gardening* (London: T. Payne, 1770; facs. repr. New York: Garland Press, 1982)
White, Gilbert, *The Natural History of Selborne*, ed. Richard Mabey (1789; Harmondsworth: Penguin, 1977)
Wilkes, John, M. P. *An Essay on Woman and Other Pieces, Printed at the Private press in Great George Street, Westminster in 1763 and Now Reproduced in Fac-simile*

From A Copy Believed to Be Unique To Which Are Added Epigrams and Miscellaneous Poems Now First Collected Preceded By An Introductory Narrative of the Circumstances Connected With the Prosecution of the Author in the House of Lords (London: [n. pub], 1871)

Williams, Annie M., *Wax Flower Modelling made easy ... With coloured frontispiece and illustrations* (London: [n. pub.], 1871)

Wilson, Lucy Sarah, *Botanical Rambles Designed as an Early and Familiar Introduction to the Study of Botany By the Author of the India Cabinet* (London: [n. pub.], 1822)

Wilson, T., *A Catechism of Botany: The Tribes of Plants* (London: Darton, 1845)

Withering, William, *A Botanical Arrangement of All The Vegetables Naturally Growing in Great Britain. With Descriptions of the Genera and Species, According to the System of the celebrated Linnæus. Being an Attempt to render them familiar to those who are unacquainted with the Learned Languages*, 2 vols (Birmingham: Printed by M. Swinney, for T. Cadell and P. Elmsley in the Strand, and G. Robinson in Pater-noster-row, London, 1776)

——*An Arrangement of British Plants, According to the Latest Improvements of the Linnaean System To Which Is Prefixed An Easy Introduction to the Study of Botany. Illustrated By Copper Plates By William Withering*, 3rd edn, 4 vols (Birmingham: Printed by M. Swinney for G. G. & J. Robinson, and B. & J. White, London, 1796)

——*An Arrangement of British Plants according to the latest improvements of the Linnean system; with an easy introduction to the study of botany*, 6th edn, 4 vols (London: Cadell and Davies, Cuthell [etc.], 1818)

Withering, Jnr, William, 'Memoir of his Life, Character and Writings', in *Miscellaneous Tracts of the Late William Withering, M.D., F.R.S.* (London: Longman, Hurst, Rees, Orme & Browne, 1822)

Wollstonecraft, Mary, *Thoughts on the Education of Daughters* (London: J. Johnson, 1787; facs. repr. Oxford and New York: Woodstock Books, 1994)

——*Original Stories From Real Life* (London: J. Johnson, 1791; facs. repr. Oxford and New York: Woodstock Books, 1990)

——*A Vindication Of the Rights of Woman*, ed. Carol H. Poston, 2nd edn (1792; New York and London: W. W. Norton, 1988)

——*Letters Written During a Short Residence in Sweden, Norway and Denmark,* 1796, ed. Carol H. Poston, (Lincoln, NE and London: University of Nebraska Press, 1976)

——*Works*, ed. Janet Todd and Marilyn Butler, 7 vols (London: William Pickering, 1989)

Wu, Duncan (ed.), *Romantic Women Poets* (Oxford: Blackwell, 1997)

Young, Arthur, *Observations on the Present State of the Waste Lands of Great Britain. Published on occasion of the establishment of a new colony on the Ohio. By the author of the Tours through England* (London: printed for W. Nicholl, 1773)

——*Travels in France and Italy During the Years 1787, 1788 and 1789* (London: J. M. Dent, 1915)

Secondary texts

Abir-Am, Pnina and Dorinda Outram (eds), *Uneasy Careers and Intimate Lives: Women and Science, 1789–1979* (New Brunswick and London: Rutgers University Press, 1987)

Adhemar, Jean, *Graphic Art in the Eighteenth-Century* (London: Thames and Hudson, 1964)

Aldis, Janet, *Madame Geoffrin: Her Salon and Her Times 1750–1777* (London: Methuen, 1905)

Allen, David Elliston, *The Victorian Fern Craze: A History of Pteridomania* (London: Hutchinson, 1969)

——*The Naturalist in Britain: A Social History* (London: Allen Lane, 1976)

——*The Botanists: A History of the Botanical Society of the British Isles* (Winchester: St. Paul's Bibliographies, 1986)

——*Naturalists and Society: the Culture of Natural History in Britain 1700–1900* (Aldershot: Ashgate, 2001)

Anscomb, Lisa, 'As far as a woman's reasoning can go': Scientific Dialogue and Sexploitation', *History of European Ideas*, 31:2 (2005) 193–208

Arber, Agnes, *Herbals, Their Origin and Evolution: A Chapter in the History of Botany, 1470–1670* (Cambridge: Cambridge University Press, 1986)

Armstrong, Isobel, *Women's Poetry in the Enlightenment: the Making of a Canon, 1730–1820* (Basingstoke: Macmillan, 1999)

Armstrong, Isobel (ed.), *New Feminist Discourses* (London and New York: Routledge, 1992)

Armstrong, Nancy, *Desire and Domestic Fiction: A Political History of the Novel* (Oxford and New York: Oxford University Press, 1987)

Armstrong, Patrick, *The English Parson-Naturalist: A Companion Between Science and Religion* (Leominster: Gracewing, 2000)

Ashmun, Margaret, *The Singing Swan: an account of Anna Seward and her acquaintance with Dr Johnson, Boswell and others of their time* (New Haven, CT: Yale University Press, 1931)

Ashton, T. S., *An Economic History of England: The Eighteenth Century* (London: Methuen, 1955)

——*The Industrial Revolution 1760–1830* (Oxford: Oxford University Press, 1968)

Barker-Benfield, G. J., *The Culture of Sensibility: Sex and Society in Eighteenth- Century Britain* (Chicago: Chicago University Press, 1992)

Barnard, Teresa, 'Anna Seward and the Battle for Authorship', *Corvey CW3 Journal*, no. 1: Papers from the inaugural Chawton House Conference, Women's Writing in Britain 1660–1830, July 2003 (Summer 2004), www2.shu.ac.uk/corvey/cw3journal/Issue%20one/barnard.html (accessed 24 August 2006)

Barnes, Barry, *T. S. Kuhn and Social Science* (London: Macmillan Press, 1982)

Barnes, Barry and Steven Shapin (eds), *Natural Order: Historical Studies of Scientific Culture* (Beverley Hills, CA and London: Sage Publications, 1979)

Barrell, John, *The Political Theory of Painting From Reynolds to Hazlitt: The Body of the Public* (New Haven, CT and London: Yale University Press, 1986)

——*Poetry, Politics and Language* (Manchester: Manchester University Press, 1988)

——'"The Dangerous Goddess": Masculinity, Prestige and the Aesthetic in Early Eighteenth-Century Britain', *Cultural Critique*, 12, *Discursive Strategies and the Economy of Prestige* (Spring 1989), 101–31

Barrell, John (ed.), *Painting and the Politics of Culture: New Essays on British Art 1700–1850* (Oxford and New York: Oxford University Press, 1992)

Barrell, John and Stephen Heath (eds), *The Birth of Pandora and the Division of Knowledge* (Basingstoke: Macmillan, 1992)

Batey, Mavis, *Regency Gardens* (London: Shire, 1995)

Beer, Sir Gavin de, 'Jean-Jacques Rousseau: Botanist', *Annals of Science: A Quarterly Review of the History of Science Since the Renaissance*, 10:3 (1954), 189–223

Bender, John, 'A New History of the Enlightenment', *Eighteenth-Century Life: Studies in the Eighteenth Century*, 16:1 (February 1992), 1–20

Bending, Stephen, 'William Mason's "An Essay on the Arrangement of Flowers in Pleasure Grounds"', *Journal of Garden History*, 19:4 (1989), 217–20

——'Horace Walpole and Eighteenth-Century Garden History, *Journal of the Warburg and Courtauld Institutes*, 57 (1994), 209–26

——'The Improvement of Arthur Young: Agricultural Technology and the Production of Landscape in Eighteenth-Century England', in David E. Nye (ed.), *Technologies of Landscape: Reaping to Recycling* (Amherst, MA: University of Massachusetts Press, 2000), pp. 241–53

Bendyshe, Thomas, 'On the Anthropology of Linnaeus', in *Memoirs Read Before the Anthropological Society of London: 1863–4*, 3 vols (London: Trübner, 1865), I, pp. 421–58

Benedict, Barbara, *Curiosity: A Cultural History of Early Modern Inquiry* (Chicago and London: University of Chicago Press, 2003)

Benhabib, Seyla and Drucilla Cornell (eds), *Feminism As Critique* (Minneapolis, MN: University of Minnesota Press, 1988)

Benjamin, Marina (ed.), *Science and Sensibility: Gender and Scientific Enquiry 1780–1945* (Oxford: Blackwell, 1991)

Bennett, Jennifer, *Lilies of the Hearth: the Historical Relationship Between Women and Plants* (Willowdale, Ontario: Camden House, 1991)

Bennett, Sue, *Women and Gardens* (London: National Portrait Gallery, 2000)

Bergström, Ingvar, *Dutch Still Life Painting in the Seventeenth Century*, trans. Christine Hedström and Gerald Taylor (London: Faber and Faber, 1956)

Bermingham, Ann, *Learning to Draw: Studies in the Cultural History of a Polite and Useful Art* (New Haven, CT and London: Yale University Press, 2000)

Bevis, Richard, *English Drama: Restoration and the Eighteenth Century, 1660–1789*, Longman Literature in English Series (New York: Longman, 1988)

Bewell, Alan, 'Jacobin plants: botany as social theory in the 1790s', *Wordsworth Circle,* 20 (1989), 132–9

——'"On the Banks of the South Sea"': Botany and Sexual Controversy in the Late Eighteenth-Century', in David Philip Miller and Peter Manns Reill (eds), *Visions of Empire: Voyages, Botany and Representations of Nature* (Cambridge: Cambridge University Press, 1996), pp. 173–91

Bleir, Ruth, *Science and Gender: A Critique of Biology and its Theories on Women* (New York and London: Pergamon, 1984)

Bloch, R. H., 'Ideals in Transition: The Rise of the Moral Mother 1785–1815', *Feminist Studies* (1978), 101–27

Bloch, Maurice, and Jean H. Bloch, 'Women and the Dialectics of Nature in Eighteenth-Century French Thought', in Carol MacCormack and Marilyn Strathern (eds), *Nature, Culture, Gender* (Cambridge: Cambridge University Press, 1980), pp. 25–92

Blunt, Wilfrid, *Tulipomania* (Harmondsworth: Penguin, 1950)

——*The Compleat Naturalist: A Life of Linnaeus* (London: Collins, 1971)

——*Tulips and Tulipomania* (London: Basilisk Press, 1977)

Blunt, Wilfrid and William T. Stearn, *The Art of Botanical Illustration* (first pub. London: Collins, 1950; rev. edn Woodbridge, Suffolk: Antique Collector's Club, 1994)

Bolla, Peter de, *The Discourse of the Sublime: Readings in History, Aesthetics and the Subject* (Oxford: Basil Blackwell, 1989)

Bowler, Peter J., *The Fontana History of the Environmental Sciences*, The Fontana History of Science (London: Fontana, 1992)

Bowles, Paul, 'John Millar, The Four Stages Theory and Women's Position In Society', *The History of Political Economy*, 16:4 (1984), 619–38

Bradshaw, Penny, 'Gendering the Enlightenment: Conflicting Images of Progress in the Poetry of Anna Laetitia Barbauld', *Women's Writing*, 5:3 (1998), 353–71

Brewer, John, *The Pleasures of the Imagination: English Culture in the Eighteenth Century* (London: Harper Collins, 1997)

Britten, James, 'Mrs Moriarty's *Viridarium*', *Journal of Botany*, 55 (1917), 52–4

Britten, James and G. S. Boulger, *A Biographical Index of British and Irish Botanists* (London: West, Newman, 1893)

Broadie, Alexander (ed.), *The Scottish Enlightenment: An Anthology* (Edinburgh: Canongate Books, 1997)

Brockway, Lucille H., *Science and Colonial Expansion: The Role of the British Botanic Gardens* (London: Academic Press, 1975)

Brown, Jane, *The Pursuit of Paradise: A Social History of Gardens and Gardening* (London: Harper Collins, 1999)

Brown, Laura, 'Reading Race and Gender: Jonathan Swift', *Eighteenth-Century Studies*, 23 (1990), 425–43

——*Ends of Empire: Women and Ideology in Early Eighteenth-Century Literature* (Ithaca, NY and London: Cornell University Press, 1993)

Browne, Alice, *The Eighteenth-Century Feminist Mind* (Brighton: Harvester Press, 1987)

Browne, Janet, 'Botany for Gentleman: Erasmus Darwin and the Loves of the Plants', *ISIS: Journal of the History of Science Society*, 80:304 (December 1989), 593–621

——'Botany in the Boudoir and Garden: The Banksian Context', in David Philip Miller and Peter Hanns Reill (eds), *Visions of Empire, Visions of Empire: Voyages, Botany and Representations of Nature* (Cambridge: Cambridge University Press, 1996), pp. 153–72

Brownell, Morris R., *Alexander Pope and the Arts of Georgian England* (Oxford: Clarendon, 1978)

Bryson, Norman. *Looking at the Overlooked: Four Essays On Still Life Painting* (Cambridge, MA: Harvard University Press, 1990)

Buchan, Ursula and Nigel Colborn, *The Classic Horticulturalist* (London: Cassell, 1987)

Burbidge, Robert Brinsley, *A Dictionary of British Flower, Fruit, and Still Life Painters*, 2 vols (Leigh-on-Sea: F. Lewis, 1974), I: *1515–1849*

Bush, Clive, 'Erasmus Darwin, Robert John Thornton, and Linnaeus' Sexual System', *Eighteenth-Century Studies*, 7:3 (Spring, 1974), 295–320

Bushnell, Rebecca, *Green Desire: Imagining Early Modern English Gardens* (Ithaca, NY: Cornell University Press, 2002)

Butler, Marilyn, *Romantics, Rebels and Reactionaries: English Literature and its Background 1760–1830* (Oxford: Oxford University Press, 1981)

Butler, Melissa A., 'Wollstonecraft Versus Rousseau: Natural Religion and the Sex of Virtue and Reason', in Donald C. Mell, Jr, Theodore E. D. Braun and Lucia M. Palmer (eds), *Man, God, and Nature in the Enlightenment* (East Lansing, MI: Colleagues Press, 1998), pp. 65–73

Calè, Luisa, '"A Female Band Despising Nature's Law": Botany, Gender and Revolution in the 1790s', *Romanticism on the Net*, 17 (February, 2000) www.erudit.org/revue/ron/2000/v/n17/005889ar.html (accessed 4 July 2003)

Calhoun, Craig (ed.), *Habermas and the Public Sphere* (Cambridge, MA: MIT Press, 1992)

Cantor, Paul, 'The Metaphysics of Botany: Rousseau and the New Criticism of Plants',

South West Review, 70:3 (Summer 1985), 362–80

Carey, John, 'Erasmus Darwin: The Big Bang and Vegetable Love', in John Carey (ed.), *The Faber Book of Science* (London: Faber, 1995), pp. 47–50.

Carr, D. J. (ed.), *Sidney Parkinson: Artist of Cook's 'Endeavour Voyage'* (Canberra: Australia University Press, 1983)

Carter, Harold B., *Sir Joseph Banks, 1743–1820* (London: British Museum, 1988)

Cassirer, Ernst, *The Philosophy of Enlightenment*, trans. Fritz C. A. Koellin and James P. Pettegrove (Boston, MA: Beacon Press, 1955)

——*Rousseau, Kant and Goethe*, trans. James Gutmann, Paul Oskar Kristeller and John Herman Randall Jr (New York: Harper and Row, 1963)

Castiglione, Dario and Lesley Sharpe (eds), *Shifting the Boundaries: The Transformation of the Languages of Public and Private in the Eighteenth-Century* (Exeter: University of Exeter Press, 1995)

Chambers, Douglas, *Planters of the English Landscape Garden: Botany, Trees and the Georgics* (Yale: Yale University Press, 1993)

——*The Reinvention of the World: English Writing 1650–1750* (London: Arnold, 1996)

——'Stories of Plants: The assembling of Mary Capel Somerset's botanical collection at Badminton', *Journal of the History of Collections*, 9:1 (1997), 49–60

Chapple, J. A. V., *Science and Literature in the Nineteenth Century* (London: Macmillan, 1986)

Chard, Chloe, *Pleasure and Guilt on the Grand Tour: Travel Writing and Imaginative Geography 1600–1830* (Manchester, Manchester University Press, 1999)

Christie, John and Sally Shuttleworth (eds), *Nature Transfigured: Science and Literature 1700–1900* (Manchester: Manchester University Press, 1989)

Clark, A. J., 'Swift and the Dutch', *Huntington Library Quarterly*, no. 17 (1954), 345–56

Clark, William, Jan Golinski and Simon Schaffer, *The Sciences in Enlightened Europe* (Chicago and London: University of Chicago Press, 1999)

Clarke, H. F., 'Eighteenth-Century Elysiums: The Role of "Association" in the Landscape Movement', *Journal of the Warburg Institute*, no. 6 (1943), 165–89

——*The English Landscape Garden* (Gloucester: Alan Sutton, 1980)

Clifford, James L. (ed.), *Eighteenth-Century English Literature: Modern Essays in Criticism* (New York and Oxford: Oxford University Press, 1959)

Clinton, Katherine B., 'Femme et Philosophe: Enlightenment Origins of Feminism', *Eighteenth-Century Studies*, 8:3 (1975), 283–99

Cobban, Alfred, *A History of Modern France*, 3 vols (Harmondsworth: Penguin, 1957), I: *Old Régime and Revolution 1715–1799*

Coffey, Donna, 'Protecting the Botanic Garden: Seward, Darwin, and Coalbrookdale', *Women's Studies*, 31 (2002), 141–64

Colley, Linda, *Britons: Forging the Nation 1707–1837* (London: Vintage, 1996)

Collingwood, R. G., *The Idea of Nature* (Oxford: Clarendon Press, 1945)

Colton, Judith, 'Merlin's Cave and Queen Caroline: Garden Art as Political Propaganda', *Eighteenth-Century Studies*, 10:1 (Autumn 1976), 1–20

Conway, Alison, 'Nationalism, Revolution and the Female Body: Charlotte Smith's *Desmond*', *Women's Studies*, 24:5 (1995), 395–409

Cook, Alexandra, 'Jean-Jacques Rousseau and Exotic Botany', *Eighteenth-Century Life*, 26:3 (Autumn, 2002), 181–201

Cook, G. C., *Erasmus Darwin and the Foxglove Conspiracy* (London: Royal Society of Medicine, 1993)

Coombe, D. E., 'The Wordsworths and Botany', *Notes and Queries*, 197 (1952), 298–9

Cope, Kevin (ed.), *Compendious Conversations: The Method of Dialogue in the English Enlightenment* (Frankfurt: Peter Lang, 1992)

Copleston, S. J., Frederick, *A History of Philosophy*, 6 vols (New York: Image Books, 1964), VI, Part II: *Modern Philosophy: Kant*

Copley, Stephen and John Whale (eds), *Beyond Romanticism: New Approaches to Texts and Contexts 1780–1832* (London and New York: Routledge, 1992)

Cosslett, Tess, '"Animals Under Man"? Margaret Gatty's *Parables from Nature*', *Women's Writing*, 10:1, (2003), 137–53

Cox, Virginia, *The Renaissance Dialogue in its Social and Literary Contexts: Castiglione to Galileo*, Cambridge Studies in Renaissance Literature and Culture, 2 (Cambridge: Cambridge University Press, 1992)

Crabbe, George [Jnr], *The Life of George Crabbe by his Son*, intr. Edmund Blunden (London: Cresset Press, 1947)

Craske, Matthew, *Art in Europe 1700–1830* (Oxford: Oxford University Press, 1977)

Crawford, Rachel, 'Troping the Subject: Behn, Smith, Hemans and the Poetics of the Bower', *Studies in Romanticism*, 38 (1999), 249–79

Curran, Stuart (ed.), *The Cambridge Companion to British Romanticism* (Cambridge, Cambridge University Press, 1993)

Dantec, Denise le, *Reading the French Garden: Story and History*, trans. Jessica Levine (Cambridge, MA: MIT Press, 1990)

Dart, Gregory, *Rousseau, Robespierre and English Romanticism* (Cambridge: Cambridge University Press, 1998)

Day, Aidan, *Romanticism* (London: Routledge, 1996)

Dean, John, 'Controversy Over Classification: A Case Study From the History of Botany', in Barry Barnes and Steven Shapin (eds), *Natural Order: Historical Studies of Scientific Culture* (Beverley Hills, CA and London: Sage Publications, 1979), pp. 211–31

Delaporte, François, *Nature's Second Kingdom: Explorations of Vegetality in the Eighteenth Century*, trans. Arthur Goldhammer (Cambridge, MA: MIT Press, 1982)

Desmond, Ray, *Dictionary of British and Irish Botanists and Horticulturists* (London: Taylor and Francis, 1977)

Donald, Diana, *The Age of Caricature: Satirical Prints in the Reign of George III* (New Haven, CT and London: Yale University Press, 1996)

Douglas, Aileen, 'Popular Science and the Representation of Women: Fontenelle and After', *Eighteenth-Century Life*, 18:2 (May 1994), 1–15

Dunn, John, *Locke* (Oxford and New York: Oxford University Press, 1984)

Duthie, Ruth, *Florists' Flowers and Societies* (Aylesbury: Shire Publications, 1988)

Eagleton, Terry, *The Rape of Clarissa* (Oxford: Blackwell, 1982)

——*The Function of Criticism: From the Spectator to Poststructuralism* (London: Verso, 1984)

——*The Ideology of the Aesthetic* (Oxford: Blackwell, 1990)

——*The Idea of Culture* (Oxford: Blackwell, 2000)

Edmunds, Dave and John Eidinow, *Rousseau's Dog: Two Great Thinkers at War in the Age of Enlightenment* (London: Faber and Faber, 2006)

Eliot, Simon and Beverley Stern (eds), *The Age of Enlightenment: An Anthology of Eighteenth Century Texts*, 2 vols (Sussex: Ward Lock, 1990), II

Fabricant, Carole, 'Binding and Pressing Nature's Loose Tresses: The Ideology of Augustan Landscape Design', *Studies in Eighteenth-Century Culture*, 8 (1979), 109–35

——*Swift's Language* (Baltimore, MD and London: Johns Hopkins University Press,

1982)

——'Review of Peter Martin, *Pursuing Innocent Pleasures: The Gardening World of Alexander Pope*, and Robert P. Maccubbin; Peter Martin, *British and American Gardens in the Eighteenth Century: Eighteen Illustrated Essays on Garden History*', *Eighteenth-Century Studies*, 20: 4 (Summer 1987), 500–9

Fara, Patricia, *Sex, Botany and Empire* (Cambridge: Icon Books, 2003)

Fletcher, Loraine, 'Four Jacobin Women Novelists', in John Lucas (ed.), *Writing and Radicalism* (Edinburgh: Longman, 1996), pp. 103–27

——*Charlotte Smith: A Critical Biography* (London: Macmillan, 1998)

Folger Collective on Early Women Critics (eds), *Women Critics 1660–1820: An Anthology* (Bloomington and Indianapolis, IN: Indiana University Press, 1995)

Foxon, David, *Libertine Literature in England, 1660–1745: With an Appendix on the Publication of John Cleland's Memoirs of a Woman of Pleasure Commonly Known as Fanny Hill* (London: Book Collector, 1955)

Frängsmyr, Tore (ed.), *Linnaeus: The Man and the Work* (Berkeley, CA and London: University of California Press, 1983)

Fryer, Peter, *Mrs Grundy: Studies in English Prudery* (London: Dennis Dobson, 1963)

Fulford, Tim, 'Coleridge, Darwin, Linnaeus: The Sexual Politics of Botany', *Wordsworth Circle*, 28:3 (1997), 124–30

Fussell, G. E., 'The Rt. Hon. Lady Charlotte Murray', *Gardener's Chronicle*, 127 (1950), 238–9

——'Some Lady Botanists of the Nineteenth Century', *Gardener's Chronicle*, 130 (1951), 63–4

Gage, Andrew Thomas, *A History of the Linnaean Society of London* (London: Taylor & Francis for The Linnaean Society, 1938)

Gallagher, Catherine and Thomas Laqueur (eds), *The Making of the Modern Body: Sexuality and Society in the Nineteenth Century* (Berkeley, CA and London: University of California Press, 1987)

Garfinkle, Norton, 'Science and Religion in England, 1790–1800: The Critical Response to the Work of Erasmus Darwin', *Journal of the History of Ideas*, 16:3 (June 1955), 376–88

Gascoigne, John, *Joseph Banks and the English Enlightenment: Useful Knowledge and Polite Culture* (Cambridge: Cambridge University Press, 1994)

Gates, Barbara, T., *Kindred Nature: Victorian and Edwardian Women Embrace the Living World* (Chicago and London: University of Chicago Press, 1998)

Gates, Barbara, T. (ed.), *In Nature's Name: An Anthology of Women's Writing and Illustration 1780–1930* (Chicago and London: University of Chicago Press, 2002)

Gates, Barbara T. and Ann Shtier (eds), *Natural Eloquence: Women Reinscribe Science* (Madison, WI: University of Wisconsin Press, 1997)

Gay, Peter, *The Enlightenment: An Interpretation*, 2 vols (New York: Norton, 1969), II: *The Science of Freedom*

Geertz, Clifford, *Local Knowledge: Further Essays In Interpretative Anthropology* (New York: Basic Books, 1983)

George, Sam, 'The Cultivation of the Female Mind: Enlightened Growth, Luxuriant Decay and Botanical Analogy in Eighteenth-century Texts', *History of European Ideas*, 31 (2005), 209–23

——'Linnaeus in Letters and the Cultivation of the Female Mind: "Botany in an English Dress"', *British Journal for Eighteenth-Century Studies*, 28:1 (Spring 2005), 1–18

——'"Not Strictly Proper for A Female Pen": Eighteenth-Century Poetry and the Sexuality of Botany', *Comparative Critical Studies*, 2:2 (2005), 191–210

——'Cultivating the Botanical Woman: Rousseau, Wakefield and the Instruction of Ladies in Botany', *Zeitschrift für pädagogische Historiographie*, 12:1 (2006), 3–11

Gibs, Denis, 'Erasmus Darwin's Interest in Female Education', *Journal of Medical Biography*, 7:4 (November 1999), 243–4

Gleadle, Kathryn, *The Early Feminists: Radical Unitarians and the Emergence of the Women's Rights Movement 1831–51* (New York: St Martins Press; London: Macmillan, 1995)

——*British Women in the Nineteenth Century* (Hampshire: Palgrave, 2001)

Goodman, Dena, *The Republic of Letters: A Cultural History of the French Enlightenment* (Ithaca and London: Cornell University Press, 1984)

Gould, Stephen Jay, *Dinosaur In A Haystack: Reflections In Natural History* (Harmondsworth: Penguin, 1996)

Grafton, Anthony, *The Footnote: A Curious History* (London: Faber and Faber, 1997)

Granziera, Patrizia, *Ideology of the English Landscape Garden* (Coventry: University of Warwick, 1996)

Green, Reynolds J., *A History of Botany in the United Kingdom From the Earliest Times to the End of the Nineteenth Century* (London: J. M. Dent, 1914)

Grigson, Geoffrey (ed.), *Before The Romantics: An Anthology of the Enlightenment* (London: George Routledge, 1946)

Guest, Harriet, 'A Double Lustre: Femininity and Sociable Commerce, 1730–1760', *Eighteenth-Century Studies*, 23:4, *The Politics of Difference* (Summer 1990), 479–501

——'The Great Distinction: Figures of the Exotic in the Work of William Hodges', in Isobel Armstrong (ed.), *New Feminist Discourses: Critical Essays on Theories and Texts* (London and New York: Routledge, 1992), pp. 296–342

——'Curiously Marked: Tattooing, Masculinity, and Nationality in Eighteenth-Century British Perceptions of the South Pacific', in John Barrell (ed.), *Painting and the Politics of Culture: New Essays on British Art 1700–1850* (Oxford and New York: Oxford University Press, 1992), pp. 101–34

——*Small Change: Women, Learning, Patriotism, 1750–1810* (Chicago and London: Chicago University Press, 2000)

——'Eighteenth-Century Femininity: 'A Supposed Sexual Character'', in Vivien Jones (ed.), *Women and Literature in Britain 1700–1800* (Cambridge: Cambridge University Press, 2000), pp. 46–68

Gutting, Gary (ed.), *Paradigms and Revolutions: Appraisals and Applications of Thomas Kuhn's Philosophy of Science* (Notre Dame, IN and London: University of Notre Dame Press, 1980)

Habermas, Jürgen, 'Modernity: An Incomplete Project', trans. Seyla Ben-Habib, in Hal Foster (ed.), *The Anti-Aesthetic: Essays on Postmodern Culture* (Washington: Bay Press, 1983), pp. 3–15

——*The Structural Transformation of the Public Sphere An Enquiry Into the Category of Bourgeois Society*, trans. Thomas Berger (Cambridge: Polity Press, 1989)

——*The Philosophical Discourse of Modernity: Twelve Lectures*, trans. Frederick Lawrence (Oxford: Blackwell, 1987)

Hadfield, Miles, *Gardening in Britain* (London: Hutchinson, 1960)

——*The English Landscape Garden* (London: Shire Publications, 1977)

Hagberg, Knut, *Carl Linnaeus*, trans. Alan Blair (London: Jonathon Cape, 1952)

Halkett, Samuel and John Laing, *Dictionary of Anonymous and Pseudonymous English Literature*, ed. Dennis E. Rhodes and Anna E. C. Simoni, continuing the work of

James Kennedy, W. A. Smith, and A. F. Johnson, 9 vols (Edinburgh: Oliver and Boyd, 1926–62)

Hamilton, Paul, *Historicism* (London: Routledge, 1996)

Hankins, Thomas, *Science and the Enlightenment* (Cambridge: Cambridge University Press, 1985)

Harding, Sarah, 'Feminism, Science and the Anti-Enlightenment', in Linda J. Nicholson (ed.), *Feminism/Postmodernism* (New York: Routledge, 1993), pp. 83–106

Hartcup, Adeline, *Angelica: The Portrait of an Eighteenth-Century Artist* (London: Heinemann, 1954)

Harth, Erica, *Cartesian Women: Versions and Subversions of Rational Discourse in the Old Regime* (Ithaca, NY and London: Cornell University Press, 1992)

Hartley, Lodwick, 'Johnson, Reynolds, and the Notorious Streaks of the Tulip Again', *Eighteenth Century Studies*, 8:3 (1975), 329–37

Harvey, F. J. Darton, *Children's Books in England* (Cambridge: Cambridge University Press, 1960)

Hayden, Ruth, *Mrs Delany and Her Flower Collages* (London: British Museum Press, 1980)

Hazlitt, W. Carew, *Gleanings in Old Garden Literature* (London: Elliot Stock, 1892)

Hedley, Owen, *Queen Charlotte* (London: J. Murray, 1975)

Heller, John L., 'Classical Mythology in the *Systema Naturae* of Linnaeus', *Transactions and Proceedings of the American Philological Association*, 76 (1945), 333–57

Henrey, Blanche, *British Botanical and Horticultural Literature Before 1800*, 3 vols (Oxford: Oxford University Press, 1975)

Hepper, Nigel F., *Kew: Gardens for Science and Pleasure* (London: HMSO, 1982)

Hilbish, Florence Mary Anna, *Charlotte Smith, Poet and Novelist 1749–1806* (Philadelphia, PA: University of Pennsylvania, 1941)

Hill, Bridget, *Republican Virago: the Life and Times of Catherine Macaulay* (Oxford: Clarendon Press, 1992)

——*Women, Work and Sexual Politics in Eighteenth-Century England* (Montreal, Canada: McGill-Queen's University Press, 1994)

——'Priscilla Wakefield as a Writer of Children's Educational Books', *Women's Writing*, 4:1 (1997), 3–13

Hobsbawm, Eric, *Nations and Nationalism Since 1780* (Cambridge: Cambridge University Press, 1990)

Hoffmeister, Gerhart (ed.), *Goethe in Italy, 1786–1986* (Amsterdam: Rodopi B.V., 1988)

Hort, Sir Arthur, 'Linnaeus and the Naming of Plants', *Blackwood's Magazine*, 230:1393 (1931), 682–700

Hoskin, Michael and Brian Warner, *Caroline Herschel's Comet Sweepers* (Bath: The William Herschel Society, 1996)

Hoskins, W. G., *The Making of the English Landscape* (London: Hodder and Stoughton, 1955)

Howe, Bea, *Lady With Green Fingers: The Life of Jane Loudon* (London: Country Life, 1961)

Howells, Robin, 'Reading Rousseau's Sexuality' in Sarah Knott and Barbara Taylor (eds), *Women, Gender and Enlightenment* (Basingstoke: Palgrave Macmillan, 2005) pp. 174–88

Huet, Marie-Hélène, 'The Revolutionary Sublime', *Eighteenth-Century Studies*, 28:1 (Autumn 1994), 51–64

Hunt, John Dixon and Peter Willis (eds), *The Genius of Place: The English Landscape*

Garden 1620–1820 (Cambridge, MA and London: MIT Press, 1988)
Hunt, Peter, *Children's Literature: An Illustrated History* (Oxford: Oxford University Press, 1995)
Hunter, Michael, *Science and Society in Restoration England* (Cambridge and New York: Cambridge University Press, 1981)
——*Establishing the New Science: The Experience of the Early Royal Society* (Woodbridge: Boydell, 1989)
Hussey, Christopher, *English Gardens and Landscapes 1700–1750* (London: Country Life, 1967)
Hutchinson, John, *Common Wild Flowers* (Harmondsworth: Penguin, 1945)
——*More Common Wild Flowers* (Harmondsworth: Penguin, 1948)
——*Uncommon Wild Flowers* (Harmondsworth: Penguin, 1950)
Jackson, Benjamin Daydon, *Guide to the Literature of Botany; Being A Classified Selection of Botanical Works* (London: Longmans, Green & Company, 1881)
Jackson-Houlston, Caroline, '"Queen Lilies"? The Interpretation of Scientific, Religious and Gender Discourses in Victorian Representations of Plants', *Journal of Victorian Culture*, 12:1 (2006), 84–110
Jacob, Margaret, *The Newtonians and the English Revolution 1689–1720* (Sussex: Harvester, 1976)
Jacobus, Mary, '"The Science of Herself": Scenes of Female Enlightenment', in Tilottama Rajan and Julia M. Wright (eds), *Romanticism, History, and the Possibilities of Genre: Re-forming literature 1789–1837* (Cambridge: Cambridge University Press, 1998), pp. 240–69
Janson, Albert, *Jean-Jacques Rousseau als Botaniker* (Berlin: Reimer, 1885)
Janson, Frederic H., *Pomona*'s *Harvest: An Illustrated Chronicle of Antiquarian Fruit Literature* (Portland, OR: Timber Press, 1996)
Johnson, Claudia (ed.), *The Cambridge Companion to Mary Wollstonecraft*, (Cambridge, Cambridge University Press, 2002)
Johnson, Pauline, 'Feminism and the Enlightenment', *Radical Philosophy*, 63 (1993), 3–12
Jones, Peter (ed.), *Philosophy and Science in the Scottish Enlightenment* (Edinburgh: J. Donald, 1989)
Jones, Vivien (ed.), *Women in the Eighteenth Century: Constructions of Femininity* (London and New York: Routledge, 1994)
——*Women and Literature in Britain 1700–1800* (Cambridge, Cambridge University Press, 2000)
——'Advice and Enlightenment: Mary Wollstonecraft and Sex Education', in Sarah Knott and Barbara Taylor (eds), *Women, Gender and Enlightenment* (Basingstoke: Palgrave Macmillan, 2005), pp. 140–55
Joppien, Rüdiger and Bernard Smith, *The Art of Captain Cook's Voyages*, 3 vols (New Haven, CT and London: Published for the Paul Mellon Centre for Studies in British Art by Yale University Press, 1985–88)
Jordonova, Ludmilla, 'Natural Facts: A Historical Perspective on Science and Sexuality', in Carol MacCormack and Marilyn Strathern (eds), *Nature, Culture, Gender* (Cambridge: Cambridge University Press, 1980), pp. 42–70
——*Sexual Visions: Images of Gender in Science and Medicine Between the Eighteenth and Twentieth Centuries* (Madison, WI: University of Wisconsin Press, 1989)
Jordonova, Ludmilla (ed.), *Languages of Nature: Critical Essays on Science and Literature* (London: Free Association Press, 1986)

Jump, Harriet (ed.), *Women's Writing of the Romantic Period 1789–1836: An Anthology* (Edinburgh: Edinburgh University Press, 1997)

Kamuf, Peggy, *Fictions of Feminine Desire: Disclosures of Heloise* (Lincoln, NE: University of Nebraska Press, 1982)

Kastner, Joseph, *A World of Naturalists* (London: John Murray, 1997)

Kauffman, Linda, *Discourses of Desire: Gender, Genre and Epistolary Fiction* (Ithaca, NY: Cornell University Press, 1986)

Kauffman, Linda (ed.), *Gender and Theory: Dialogues of Feminist Criticism* (Oxford: Blackwell, 1989)

Keane, Angela, *Women Writers and the English Nation in the 1790s: Romantic Belongings* (Cambridge: Cambridge University Press, 2000)

Keeney, Elizabeth B., *The Botanizers: Amateur Scientists in Nineteenth-Century America* (Chapel Hill, NC and London: University of North Carolina Press, 1992)

Kellaway, Deborah (ed.), *The Virago Book of Women Gardeners* (London: Virago Press, 1996)

Keller, Evelyn Fox, *Reflections on Science and Gender* (New Haven, CT: Yale University Press, 1985)

Kelly, Jennifer (ed.), *Bluestocking Feminism: Writings of the Bluestocking Circle, 1738–1790*, ed. Gary Kelly and others, 6 vols (London: Chatto & Pickering, 1999), IV: *Anna Seward*

Kennedy, Deborah, 'Thorns and Roses: the Sonnets of Charlotte Smith', *Women's Writing*, 12:1 (1995), 43–53

King, Amy M., 'Linnæus's Blooms: Botany and the Novel of Courtship', *The Eighteenth-Century Novel*, 1 (2001), 127–60

King-Hele, Desmond, *Erasmus Darwin* (New York: Charles Scribner's Sons, 1963)

King-Hele, Desmond (ed.), *The Essential Writings of Erasmus Darwin* (London: MacGibbon & Key, 1968)

Klonk, Charlotte, *Science and Perceptions of Nature: British Landscape Art in the Eighteenth and Early Nineteenth Century* (New Haven, CT and London: Yale University Press for The Paul Mellon Centre for Studies in British Art, 1996)

Knight, David, *Natural Science Books in English 1600–1800* (London: Batsford, 1972)

——*Ordering the World: A History of Classifying Man* (London: Burnett Books, 1981)

Knott, Sarah and Barbara Taylor (eds), *Women, Gender and Enlightenment* (London: Palgrave, 2005)

Koerner, Lisbet, 'Goethe's Botany: Lessons of a Feminine Science', *ISIS*, 84:3 (1993), 470–95

——*Linnaeus: Nature and Nation* (Cambridge, MA and London: Harvard University Press, 1999)

Korner, S., *Kant* (Harmondsworth: Penguin, 1955)

Kramer, Jack, *Women of Flowers: A Tribute to Victorian Women Illustrators*, photographed by Eric Strachan, designed by Mary Tiegreen, ed. Linda Sunshine (New York: Stewart, Tabori & Chang, 1996)

Kramnick, Isaac (ed.), *The Portable Enlightenment Reader* (Harmondsworth: Penguin, 1995)

Kusch, Manfred, 'The River and the Garden: Basic Spatial Models in *Candide* and *La Nouvelle Héloïse*', *Eighteenth-Century-Studies,* 24:1 (1978), 1–15

Kuhn, Thomas S., *The Structure of Scientific Revolutions* (Chicago: University of Chicago Press, 1970)

Labbe, Jacqueline, M., 'Cultivating One's Understanding: the female romantic garden',

Women's Writing, 4:1 (1997), 39–56

——'Every Poet Her Own Drawing Master: Charlotte Smith, Anna Seward and *ut pictura poesis*', in Thomas Woodman (ed.), *Early Romantic Perspectives in British Poetry From Pope to Wordsworth* (London: Macmillan, 1998), pp. 200–14

——'"Transplanted into More Congenial Soil": Footnoting the Self in the Poetry of Charlotte Smith', in Joe Bray, Miriam Handley and Anne C. Henry (eds), *Ma(r)king the Text: The Presentation of Meaning on the Literary Page* (Aldershot: Ashgate, 2000), pp. 71–86

——*Charlotte Smith: Romanticism, Poetry and the Culture of Gender* (Manchester: Manchester University Press, 2003)

Laird, Mark, *The Flowering of the Landscape Garden: English Pleasure Grounds, 1720–1800* (Philadelphia, PA: University of Pennsylvania Press, 1999)

Lakatos, Imre and Alan Musgrove (eds), *Criticism and the Growth of Knowledge* (London: Cambridge University Press, 1970)

Lamb, Jonathan, 'Minute Particulars and the Representation of the Pacific', *Eighteenth-Century Studies*, 28:3 (1995), 281–94

——*Preserving the Self in the South Seas, 1680–1840* (Chicago and London: University of Chicago Press, 2001)

Lamb, Jonathan, Vanessa Smith and Nicholas Thomas (eds), *Exploration and Exchange: a South Seas Anthology, 1680–1900* (Chicago and London: Chicago University Press, 2000)

Landes, Joan B., *Women and the Public Sphere in the Age of the French Revolution* (Ithaca, NY: Cornell University Press, 1988)

Landry, Donna, *The Muses of Resistance: Labouring Class Women's Poetry in Britain, 1739–1796* (Cambridge: Cambridge University Press, 1990)

——'Green Languages? Women Poets As Naturalists in 1653 and 1807', *Huntington Library Quarterly*, 63:4 (2000), 467–89

Larson, James L., 'Goethe and Linnaeus', *Journal of the History of Ideas*, 28:4 (Oct.–Dec. 1967), 590–6

——*Reason and Experience: the Representation of Natural Order in the Works of Carl Von Linné* (Berkeley and Los Angeles, CA: University of California Press, 1971)

Leach, Camilla and Joyce Goodman, 'Educating the Women of the Nation: Priscilla Wakefield and the Construction of National Identity', *Quaker Studies*, 5:2 (2001), 165–82

Leask, Nigel, *Curiosity and the Aesthetics of Travel Writing, 1770–1840: 'From An Antique Land'* (New York: Oxford University Press, 2002)

Leatherbarrow, D., *Ideas of Character and Situation in the Theory of the Eighteenth-Century Landscape Garden* (Colchester: University of Essex, 1983)

Leatherdale, W. H., *The Role of Analogy, Model and Metaphor in Science* (Amsterdam: North Holland Publishing Company, 1974)

Leslie, Michael and Timothy Raylor (eds), *Culture and Cultivation in Early Modern England: Writing and the Land* (Leicester: Leicester University Press, 1992)

Levey, Michael, *Rococo To Revolution: Major Trends In Eighteenth-Century Painting* (London: Thames and Hudson, 1977)

Linney, Verna, 'A Passion for Art, A Passion for Botany: Mary Delany and Her Floral Mosaiks', *Eighteenth-Century Women: Studies in Their Lives, Work and Culture*, 1 (2001), 203–35.

Lipson, E., *The Growth of English Society: A Short Economic History* (London: A. & C. Black, 1949)

Lloyd, Genevieve, *The Man of Reason: 'Male' and 'Female' in Western Philosophy* (London: Routledge, 1994)

Longstaffe-Gowan, Todd, *The London Town Garden, 1740–1840* (New Haven, CT: Published for the Paul Mellon Centre for British Art by Yale University Press, 2001)

Lougee, Carolyn, *Le Paradis des Femmes: Women, Salons and Social Stratification in Seventeenth-century France* (Princeton, NJ: Princeton University Press, 1976)

Lovejoy, Arthur O., *The Great Chain of Being*, 2nd edn (Cambridge, MA: Harvard University Press, 1970)

Lovell, Terry, *Consuming Fiction* (London: Verso, 1997)

Lovibond, Sabina, 'Feminism and Postmodernism', *New Left Review*, 178 (Nov.–Dec. 1989), 5–28

Lucas, E. V., *A Swan and her Friends* (London: Methuen, 1907)

MacCormack, Carol and Marilyn Strathern (eds), *Nature, Culture, Gender* (Cambridge: Cambridge University Press, 1980)

MacCubbin, Robert P. (ed.), *'Tis Nature's Fault: Unauthorised Sexuality During the Enlightenment* (New York: Press Syndicate of the University of Cambridge, 1987)

MacCubbin, Robert P., and Peter Martin (eds), *British and American Gardens in the Eighteenth Century: Eighteen Illustrated Essays on Garden History* (Williamsberg, VA: Colonial Williamsburg Foundation, 1984)

Mack, Phyllis, 'Women and the Enlightenment', *Women and History*, 9 (1984), 1–11

Maniquis, Robert M., 'The Puzzling *Mimosa*: Sensitivity and Plant Symbols in Romanticism', *Studies in Romanticism*, 8:3 (Spring 1969), 129–55

Martin, Peter, *Alexander Pope and the Arts of Georgian England* (Oxford: Clarendon Press, 1978)

——*Pursuing Innocent Pleasures: The Gardening World of Alexander Pope* (Hamden: Archon Books, 1984)

Mavor, Elizabeth, *The Ladies of Llangollen: A Study in Romantic Friendship* (London: Michael Joseph, 1971)

McKendrick, Neil, John Brewer and J. H. Plumb, *The Birth of a Consumer Society: The Commercialisation of Eighteenth-Century England* (London: Hutchinson, 1983)

McKeon, Michael, '"Natural History" as a Narrative Model', in *The Origin of the English Novel 1600–1740* (Baltimore, MD: Johns Hopkins University Press, 1991), pp. 69–73

McNeil, Maureen, *Under The Banner of Science: Erasmus Darwin and His Age* (Manchester: Manchester University Press, 1987)

Mears, James A. (ed.), *Plant Taxonomic Literature: Bibliographic Guide* (Cambridge: Chadwyck-Healey, 1989)

Mee, Jon, *Romanticism, Enthusiasm, and Regulation: Poetics and the policing of culture in the Romantic period* (Cambridge: Cambridge University Press, 2003)

Merquior, J. G., *Foucault* (London: Fontana Press, 1991)

Meyer, Gerald Dennis, *The Scientific Lady in England 1650–1760: An Account of Her Rise With Emphasis on the Major Roles of the Telescope and Microscope* (Berkeley and Los Angeles, CA: University of California Press, 1955)

Miller, Casey and Kate Swift, *Words and Women: Language and the Sexes* (Harmondsworth: Penguin, 1979)

Miller, David Philip and Peter Hanns Reill (eds), *Visions of Empire: Voyages, Botany and Representations of Nature* (Cambridge: Cambridge University Press, 1996)

Mitchell, M. E., 'The Authorship of Dialogues in Botany', *Irish Naturalist's Journal*, 19:11 (1979), 407

Monk, Samuel Holt, *The Sublime: A Study of Critical Theories in Eighteenth-Century England* (Ann Arbor, MI: University of Michigan Press, 1960)

Moore, Patrick, *Caroline Herschel: Reflected Glory* (Bath: Ralph Allen Press, 1988)

——*William Herschel: Astronomer and Musician of 19 New King Street, Bath* (Bath: The William Herschel Society, 1991)

Moreton, Oscar C., *Old Carnations and Pinks*, intr. Sacheverell Sitwell (London: G. Rainbird in association with Collins, 1955)

Morton, A. G., *History of Botanical Science: An Account of the Development of Botany From Ancient Times to the Present Day* (London: Academic Press, 1981)

Mount, Harry, 'Morality, Microscopy and the Moderns: the Meaning of Minuteness in Shaftesbury's Theory of Painting', *British Journal for Eighteenth-Century Studies*, 21:2 (Autumn 1998), 125–41

Myers, Greg, 'Science For Women and Children: the Dialogue of Popular Science in the Nineteenth Century', in John Christie and Sally Shuttleworth (eds), *Nature Transfigured: Science and Literature 1700–1900* (Manchester and New York: Manchester University Press, 1989), pp. 171–200

Myers, Mitzi, 'Impeccable Governesses, Rational Dames and Moral Mothers: Mary Wollstonecraft and the Female Tradition in Georgian Children's Books', *Children's Literature,* 14 (1986), 31–59

Newman, Gerald, *The Rise of English Nationalism: A Cultural History 1740–1830* (London: Weidenfeld and Nicholson, 1987)

Nicolson, Marjorie Hope, *Science and Imagination* (Ithaca, NY: Great Seal Books, 1956)

——*Newton Demands the Muse: Newton's Opticks and the Eighteenth-Century Poets* (Princeton, NJ: Princeton University Press, 1966)

Nussbaum, Felicity, A., *The Brink of All We Hate: English Satires On Women 1660–1750* (Lexington, KY: Kentucky University Press, 1984)

——*Torrid Zones: Maternity, Sexuality and Empire in Eighteenth-Century English Narratives* (Baltimore, MD and London: John Hopkins University Press, 1995)

Nussbaum, Felicity, A. (ed.), *Eighteenth-Century Studies*, 23:4, Special Issue: *The Politics of Difference* (1990)

Nussbaum, Felicity and Laura Brown (eds), *The New Eighteenth Century: Theory, Politics, English Literature* (New York and London: Routledge, 1987)

Olby, R. C., *Late Eighteenth-Century European Scientists* (Oxford and London: Pergamon Press, 1966)

Oliver, F. W. (ed.), *Makers of British Botany: A Collection of Biographies* (Cambridge, Cambridge University Press, 1913)

Oliver, Marc, 'Lessons for the Four-Year Old Botanist: Rousseau's "Forgotten Science" of Childhood', in Norman Buford (ed.), *The Child in French Francophone Literature*, (New York: Rodopi Editions, 2004), pp. 161–9

Outram, Dorinda, *The Enlightenment* (Cambridge: Cambridge University Press, 1995)

Pascoe, Judith, 'Female Botanists and the Poetry of Charlotte Smith', in Carol Shiner Wilson and Joel Haefner (eds), *Re-Visioning Romanticism: British Women Writers, 1776–1837* (Philadelphia, PA: University of Pennsylvania Press, 1994), pp. 193–209

Pateman, Carole, *The Sexual Contract* (Cambridge: Polity, 1988)

Patterson, Sylvia, *Rousseau's Emile and Early Children's Literature* (Metuchen, NJ: Scarecrow Press, 1971)

Pavord, Anna, *The Tulip* (London: Bloomsbury, 1999)

Pearson, Hesketh (ed.), *The Swan of Lichfield. Being a selection from the correspon-*

dence of Anna Seward, with a short biography and preface (London: Hamish Hamilton, 1936)
Pearson, Jacqueline, '"Books, My Greatest Joy": Constructing the Female Reader in *The Lady's Magazine*', *Women's Writing*, 3:1 (1996), 3–15
Peck, T. W. and K. D. Wilkinson, *William Withering of Birmingham, M.D., F.R.S., F.L.S.* (Bristol: John Wright & Sons, 1950)
Penny, Nicholas, *Church Monuments in Romantic England* (New Haven, CT and London: Yale University Press, 1977)
Percy, Carol, 'In the Margins: Hawkesworth's Editorial Emendations to the Language of Captain Cook's *Voyages*', *English Studies*, 77:6 (November 1996), 549–78
Percy, Joan, 'Maria Elizabetha Jacson and her Florist's Manual', *Garden History*, 20:1 (1992), 45–56
Pettit, Alexander and Patrick Spedding (eds), *Eighteenth-Century British Erotica*, 5 vols (London: Pickering and Chatto, 2001)
Phillips, M. and W. S. Tomkinson, *English Women in Life and Letters* (Oxford: Oxford University Press, 1927)
Phillips, Patricia, *The Scientific Lady: A Social History of Women's Scientific Interests 1520–1918* (London: Weidenfeld and Nicholson, 1990)
Picciotto, Joanna, 'Optical Instruments and the Eighteenth-Century Observer', *Studies in Eighteenth-Century Culture*, 29 (2000), 123–53
Plumb. J. H., *England In the Eighteenth Century 1714–1815* (Harmondsworth: Penguin, 1950)
Pollard, Sidney, *The Idea of Progress* (London: C. A. Watts, 1968)
Poovey, Mary, *The Proper Lady and the Woman Writer: Ideology as Style in the Works of Mary Wollstonecraft, Mary Shelley and Jane Austen* (Chicago, IL: University of Chicago Press, 1984)
Porter, Dennis, 'Jean-Jacques Rousseau: Policing the Aesthetic From the Left', in Richard Burt (ed.), *The Administration of Aesthetics; Censorship, Political Criticism and the Public Sphere*, Cultural Politics, 7 (Minneapolis, MN and London: University of Minnesota Press, 1994), pp. 106–22
Porter, Roy, 'Erasmus Darwin: Doctor of Revolution', in James R. Moore (ed.), *History, Humanity and Evolution: Essays for John Greene* (Cambridge: Cambridge University Press, 1989), pp. 39–70
——*English Society in the Eighteenth Century* (Harmondsworth: Penguin, 1990)
——*Enlightenment: Britain and the Creation of the Modern World* (London: Penguin, 2000)
Praeger, Lloyd, R., *Some Irish Naturalists: A Biographical Notebook* (Dundalk: Dundalgan Press, 1949)
Pratt, Mary Louise, *Imperial Eyes: Travel Writing and Transculturation* (London: Routledge, 1992)
Prochaska, Frank, *Women and Philanthropy in Nineteenth-century England* (Oxford: Oxford University Press, 1980)
Punter, David, '1789: The Sex of Revolution', *Criticism: A Quarterly For Literature and the Arts*, 24:3 (1982), 201–17
Ranson, Florence, *British Herbs* (Harmondsworth: Penguin, 1954)
Rauch, Alan, *Useful Knowledge: The Victorians, Morality and the March of Intellect* (Durham, NC: Duke University Press, 2001)
Raven, Charles, E., *English Naturalists From Neckam to Ray: A Study of the Making of the Modern World* (Cambridge: Cambridge University Press, 1947)

——*John Ray: Naturalist* (1942; Cambridge: Cambridge University Press, 1986)
Real, Hermann J. and Heinz J. Vienken, 'Swift's "Trampling on the Crucifix" Once More', *Notes and Queries*, 228 (1983), 513–14
Reeds, Karen, 'When the Botanist Can't Draw: The Case of Linnaeus', *Interdisciplinary Science Reviews*, 29:3 (2004), 248–58
Rees, Christine, *Utopian Imagination and Eighteenth-Century Fiction* (London: Longman, 1996)
Rendall, Jane, *The Origins of the Scottish Enlightenment 1707–1776* (London: Macmillan, 1978)
——*The Origins of Modern Feminism: Women in Britain, France and the United States, 1780–1860* (London: Macmillan, 1985)
——'"The Grand Causes Which Combine to Carry Mankind Forward": Wollstonecraft, History and Revolution', *Women's Writing*, 4:2 (1997), 155–72
Reynolds, Myra, *The Learned Lady in England 1650–1760* (Gloucester, MA: Peter Smith, 1964)
Richardson, Alan, 'The Politics of Childhood, Wordsworth, Blake and Catechistic Method', *ELH,* 56:4 (Winter 1989), 853–68
——*Literature, Education and Romanticism: Reading As Social Practice 1780–1832* (Cambridge: Cambridge University Press, 1994)
Ridge, Antonia, *The Man Who Painted Roses: The Story of Pierre Redouté* (London: Faber and Faber, 1974)
Ritterbush, Philip, *Overtures to Biology: The Speculations of Eighteenth-Century Naturalists* (New Haven, CT: Yale University Press, 1964)
Rix, Martyn, *The Art of the Botanist* (Guildford: Lutterworth, 1981)
Robertson-Stewart, Charles, 'The Pneumatics and Georgics of the Scottish Mind', *Eighteenth-Century Studies*, 20:3 (1987), 296–312
Robinson, Eric, 'John Clare (1793–1864) and James Plumptre (1771–1832): A Methodistical Parson', *Transactions of the Cambridge Bibliography Society*, 11:1 (1996), 59–88
Rohde, Eleanour Sinclair, *The Old English Herbals* (New York: Dover Publications, 1971)
Rosenblaum, Joseph, 'Gulliver's Dutch Uncle: Another Look at Swift and the Dutch', *British Journal for Eighteenth-Century Studies*, 24:1 (Spring 2001), 63–76
Ross, Stephanie, '*Ut Hortus Poesis*: Gardening and her Sister Arts in Eighteenth-Century England', *British Journal of Aesthetics*, 25:1 (Winter 1985), 17–32
——*What Gardens Mean* (Chicago, IL and London: Chicago University Press, 1988)
Rose, R. B., 'The Priestley Riots of 1791', *Past and Present*, 18 (1960), 68–88
Rousseau, G. S., 'Science Books and Their Readers in the Eighteenth Century', in Isabel Rivers (ed.), *Books and Their Readers in Eighteenth-Century England* (New York: St Martin's Press, 1982), pp. 197–255
——*Perilous Enlightenment: Pre- and Post-modern Discourses: Sexual, Historical* (Manchester and New York: Manchester University Press, 1991)
Rousseau, G. S. and Roy Porter (eds), *The Ferment of Knowledge: Studies in the Historiography of Eighteenth-Century Science* (Cambridge: Cambridge University Press, 1980)
Russell, Colin A., *Science and Social Change 1700–1900* (London: Macmillan, 1983)
Russell, Gillian and Clara Tuite (eds), *Romantic Sociability: Social Networks and Literary Culture in Britain, 1770–1840* (Cambridge: Cambridge University Press, 2002)
Ruwe, Donelle, R., 'Charlotte Smith's Sublime: Feminine Poetics, Botany and *Beachy*

Head, Prism(s): Essays in Romanticism, 7 (1999), 117–32

Sambrook, James, *The Eighteenth Century: The Intellectual and Cultural Context of English Literature, 1700–1789* (London: Longman, 1994)

Saunders, Gill, *Picturing Plants: An Analytical History of Botanical Illustration* (Berkeley, CA: University of California Press, 1995)

Scarse, David, *Flower Drawings* (Cambridge: Cambridge University Press, 1997)

Schiebinger, Londa, *The Mind Has No Sex? Women In the Origins of Modern Science* (Cambridge, MA and London: Harvard University Press, 1989)

——'The Anatomy of Difference: Race and Sex in Eighteenth-Century Science', *Eighteenth-Century Studies*, 23:4, Special Issue: *The Politics of Difference* (Summer 1990), 479–501

——'The Private Life of Plants: Sexual Politics in Carl Linnaeus and Erasmus Darwin', in Marina Benjamin (ed.), *Science and Sensibility: Gender and Scientific Enquiry 1780–1945* (Oxford: Blackwell, 1991), pp. 121–43

——*Nature's Body: Sexual Politics and the Making of Modern Science* (London: Pandora, 1993)

Schnorrenberg, Barbara Brandon, 'A Paradise Like Eve's: Three Eighteenth-century English Female Utopias', *Women's Studies*, 9:3 (1982), 263–73

Schofield, Robert, *The Lunar Society of Birmingham: A Social History of Provincial Science and Industry in Eighteenth-Century England* (Oxford: Clarendon Press, 1962)

Schor, Naomi, *Reading in Detail: Aesthetics and the Feminine* (London: Methuen, 1987)

Scott, David, 'Rousseau and Flowers: The Poetry of Botany', *Studies on Voltaire and the Eighteenth Century*, 182 (1979), 73–86

Scott-James, Anne, *The Cottage Garden* (London: Allen Lane, 1981)

Scourse, Nicolette, *The Victorians and Their Flowers* (London: Croom Helm, 1983)

Scrase, David, *Flower Drawings* (Cambridge: Cambridge University Press, 1997)

Scully, Vincent, *French Royal Gardens: Designs of André Le Nôtre*, with photographs by Jeannie Baubiom Mackler (New York: Rizzoli, 1992)

Secord, Anne, 'Botany on a Plate: Pleasure and the Power of Pictures in Promoting Early Nineteenth-Century Scientific Knowledge', *ISIS*, 93 (2002), 28–57

Sekora, John, *Luxury: The Concept in Western Thought* (Baltimore, MD: Johns Hopkins University Press, 1977)

Shattock, Joan, *The Oxford Guide to British Women Writers* (Oxford: Oxford University Press, 1994)

Sheffield, Suzanne Le-May, *Revealing New Worlds: Three Victorian Women Naturalists* (Routledge: London and New York, 2001)

Shteir, Ann B., 'Linnaeus's Daughters: Women and British Botany', in Barbara J. Harris and Joanne K. McNamara (eds), *Women and the Structure of Society: Selected Research from the Fifth Berkshire Conference on the History of Women* (Durham, NC: Duke University Press, 1984), pp. 67–74

——'Priscilla Wakefield's Natural History Books', in Alwynne Wheeler and James H. Price (eds), *From Linnaeus to Darwin: Commentaries on the History of Biology and Geology: Natural History in the Early Nineteenth Century*, Papers from the fifth Easter Meeting of the Society for the History of Natural History (March 1983) (London: Society for the History of Natural History, 1985), 29–35

——'Botany in the Breakfast Room: Women in Early Nineteenth-Century Plant Study', in Pnina G. Abir-Am and Dorinda Outram (eds), *Uneasy Careers and Intimate Lives: Women in Science, 1789–1979* (New Brunswick, NJ: Rutgers University Press,

1987), 31–43

——'Botanical Dialogues: Maria Jacson and Women's Popular Science Writing in England', *Eighteenth-Century Studies*, 23:3 (1990), 301–17

——'*Flora Feministica*: Reflections on the Culture of Botany', *Lumen*, 12 (1993), 167–76

——*Cultivating Women, Cultivating Science: Flora's Daughters and Botany in England 1760–1860* (Baltimore, MD and London: Johns Hopkins University Press, 1996)

Shuttleworth, Sally (ed.), *Science Serialized: Representations of the Sciences in Nineteenth-Century Periodicals* (Cambridge, MA: MIT Press, 2004)

Simpson, David, *Romanticism, Nationalism, and the Revolt Against Theory* (Chicago, IL and London: University of Chicago Press, 1993)

——'Being There?: Literary Criticism, Localism and Local Knowledge', *Critical Quarterly,* 35:3 (Autumn, 1993), 3–17

Sitter, John (ed.), *The Cambridge Companion to Eighteenth-Century Poetry* (Cambridge: Cambridge University Press, 2001)

Sitwell, Sacheverell, *Old-fashioned Flowers*, illus. John Farleigh (London: Country Life, 1939)

Slaughter, M. M., *Universal Languages and Scientific Taxonomy in the Seventeenth Century* (Cambridge: Cambridge University Press, 1982)

Smith, Bernard, *European Vision and the South Pacific* (New Haven, CT and London: Yale University Press, 1988)

——*Imagining the Pacific: In the Wake of Cook's Voyages* (New Haven, CT and London: Yale University Press, 1992)

Smith, Edward, *The Life of Sir Joseph Banks* (London and New York: John Lane, 1911)

Smith, Jack, 'A Gilded Dinosaur: Reflections on the Portico Buffon', *Portico Monograph*, 7 (1996)

Smith, Joseph, *A Descriptive Catalogue of Friends' Books*, 2 vols (London: J. Smith, 1867)

Southall, Raymond, 'Botany Into Poetry: Erasmus Darwin, Coleridge & Wordsworth', *English Language Notes*, 33:1 (September 1995), 20–2

Spadafora, David, *The Idea of Progress in Eighteenth-Century Britain* (New Haven, CT and London: Yale University Press, 1990)

Spencer, Samia I. (ed.), *French Women and the Age of Enlightenment* (Bloomington, IN: Indiana University Press: 1984)

Spender, Dale, *Living By the Pen: Early British Women Writers* (New York and London: Teachers College Press, 1992)

Stafford, Barbara, *Voyage Into Substance: Art, Science, Nature and the Illustrated Travel Account, 1760–1840* (Cambridge, MA: MIT Press, 1984)

——'Voyeur or Observer? Enlightenment Thoughts on the Dilemmas of Display', *Configurations: A Journal for Literature, Science and Technology*, 1 (Autumn 1993), 95–128

——*Artful Science: Enlightenment Entertainment and the Eclipse of Visual Education* (Cambridge, MA: MIT Press, 1994)

——'Images of Ambiguity: Eighteenth-Century Microscopy and the Neither/Nor', in David Philip Miller and Peter Hanns Reill (eds), *Visions of Empire* (Cambridge: Cambridge University Press), pp. 250–7

——*Visual Analogy: Consciousness as the Art of Connecting* (Cambridge, MA and London: MIT Press, 1999)

Stafleau, Frans, *Linnaeus and the Linnaeans: The Spreading of their Ideas in Systematic*

Botany 1735–1789 (Utrecht: Oosthoek's Uitgeversmaatschappis N.V. for the International Society of Plant Taxonomy, 1971)

Stafleau, Frans A. and Richard S. Cowan (eds), *Taxonomic Literature: a Selective Guide to Botanical Publications and Collections with Dates, Commentaries and Types*, 2nd edn, 7 vols (Utrecht: Bohn, Scheltema & Holkema, 1976–78)

Stanton, Domna, 'The Fiction of *Préciosité* and the Fear of Women', *Yale French Studies*, 62, Feminist Readings: French Texts/American Contexts (1981), 107–34

Staves, Susan, *Married Women's Separate Property in England, 1660–1833* (Cambridge, MA: Harvard University Press, 1990)

Stearn, William T., 'Linnaeus's "Species Plantarum" and the Language of Botany', *Proceedings of the Linnaean Society of London*, 165, part 2 (1955), 158–64

——'Carl Linnaeus: Classifier and Namer of Living Things', *New Scientist*, 4 (1958), 401–3

——'The Origin of the Male and Female Symbols of Biology', *Taxon*, 11:4 (1962), 109–13

——'Carl Linnaeus and the Theory and Practice of Horticulture', *Taxon*, 25:1 (1976), 21–31

Stearn, William T. (ed.), *John Lindley, 1799–1865, Gardener, Botanist, and Pioneer Orchidologist* (Suffolk: Antique Collectors Club, 1999)

Steinbrügge, Lieselotte, *The Moral Sex: Women's Nature in the French Enlightenment*, trans. Pamela E. Selwyn (New York and Oxford: Oxford University Press, 1995)

Steiner, George, *Antigones: The Antigone Myth in Western Literature, Art and Thought* (Oxford: Oxford University Press, 1984)

Summerfield, Geoffrey, *Fantasy and Reason: Children's Literature in the Eighteenth Century* (London: Methuen, 1984)

Sutton, Geoffrey, *Science for a Polite Society: Gender, Culture and the Demonstration of Enlightenment* (Oxford: Westview Press, 1995)

Taboroff, June, '"Wife Unto Thy Garden": The First Gardening Books for Women', *Garden History*, 11:7 (Spring 1983), 1–5.

Tadmor, Naomi, '"In the Even My Wife Read To Me"': Women, Reading and Household Life in the Eighteenth-Century', in *The Practice and Representation of Reading in England*, ed. James Raven, Helen Small and Naomi Tadmor (Cambridge: Cambridge University Press, 1996), pp. 162–74

Tatchell, Molly, 'Elizabeth Kent and "Flora Domestica"', *Keats–Shelley Memorial Bulletin*, 27 (1976), 15–18

Taylor Barbara, *Eve and the New Jerusalem* (London: Virago, 1983)

Taylor, Geoffrey, *Some Nineteenth-Century Gardeners* (Essex: The Anchor Press, 1951)

Teute, Fredrika J., 'The Loves of the Plants; or, the Cross Fertilization of Science and Desire at the End of the Eighteenth Century', *Huntington Library Quarterly*, 63:3 (2000), 319–45

Thomas, Keith, *Man and the Natural World: Changing Attitudes in England 1500–1800* (Harmondsworth: Penguin, 1983)

Thompson, E. P., *The Making of the English Working Class*, rev. edn (Harmondsworth: Penguin, 1980)

Thompson, Roger, *Unfit for Modest Ears: A Study of Pornographic, Obscene and Bawdy Works Written or Published in England in the Second Half of the Seventeenth Century* (London: Macmillan, 1979)

Tobin, Beth Fowkes, 'Imperial Designs, Botanical Illustration and the British Empire', *Studies in Eighteenth Century Culture*, 25 (1996), 265–92

——*Picturing Imperial Power: Colonial Subjects in Eighteenth-Century British Painting* (Durham and London: Duke University Press, 1999)

Todd, Janet, *Sensibility: An Introduction* (London: Methuen, 1986)

——*Feminist Literary History* (Oxford: Blackwell, 1988)

——*The Sign of Angelica: Women, Writing and Fiction, 1660–1800* (London: Virago, 1989)

Tomaselli, Sylvana, 'The Enlightenment Debate on Women', *History Workshop Journal*, 20 (1985), 101–24

Turner, Cheryl, *Living By the Pen: Women Writers in the Eighteenth Century* (London: Routledge, 1992)

Tuer, Andrew, *Forgotten Children's Books* (London: Bracken Books, 1986)

Turrill, W. B., *The Royal Botanic Gardens at Kew* (London: Herbert Jenkins, 1959)

Uglow, Jenny, *The Lunar Men: the Friends Who Made the Future* (London: Faber and Faber, 2002)

Vickery, Amanda, *The Gentleman's Daughter: Women's Lives in Georgian England* (New Haven and London: Yale University Press, 1998)

Vickery, Roy (ed.), *A Dictionary of Plant Lore* (Oxford: Oxford University Press, 1995)

Wagner, Peter, *Eros Revived: Erotica of the Enlightenment in England and America* (London: Paladin, 1990)

Wallace, Anne D., 'Picturesque Fossils, Sublime Geology? The Crisis of Authority in Charlotte Smith's *Beachy Head*', *European Romantic Review*, 13 (2002), 77–93

Walling, Jane, 'The Imagination of Plants: Botany in Rousseau and Goethe', *Comparative Critical Studies*, 2:2 (2005), 211–25.

Ward, Bobby, Y., *A Contemplation Upon Flowers: Garden Plants in Myth and Literature* (Portland, OR: Timber Press, 1999)

Waters, Mary, *British Women Writers and the Profession of Literary Criticism 1789–1832* (Basingstoke: Macmillan, 2003)

——'Elizabeth Moody', *The Literary Encyclopedia*, www.literarydictionary.com/php/speople.php?rec=true&UID=3170 (accessed 24 August 2006)

Wexler, Victor G., '"Made for Man's Delight": Rousseau as Antifeminist', *American Historical Review*, 81:2 (April 1976), 266–91

Whigham, Maurice, J. (ed.), *Quakers in Natural History and Medicine in Ireland and Britain* (Dublin: National Botanic Gardens, 1996)

White, Daniel E., 'The "Joineriana": Anna Laetitia Barbauld, The Aikin Family Circle and the Dissenting Public Sphere', *Eighteenth-Century Studies*, 32:4, (Summer 1999), 511–33.

Willey, Basil, *The Eighteenth-Century Background: Studies On the Idea of Nature in the Thought of the Period* (London: Chatto and Windus, 1957)

Williams, Raymond, *The Long Revolution* (Harmondsworth: Penguin, 1965)

——*The Country and the City* (New York: Oxford University Press, 1973)

——*Problems in Materialism and Culture* (London: Verso, 1980)

——*Keywords: A Vocabulary of Culture and Society*, first pub. 1976, rev. edn (London: Fontana, 1983)

Williams, E. N., *The Ancien Regime in Europe: Government and Society in the Major States 1648–1789* (Harmondsworth: Penguin, 1972)

Wilson, Carol Shiner and Joel Haefner (eds), *Re-Visioning Romanticism: British Women Writers, 1776–1837* (Philadelphia, PA: University of Pennsylvania Press, 1994)

Wilson, Charles, *England's Apprenticeship 1603–1763* (London: Longman, 1971)

Wokler, Robert, *Rousseau* (Oxford and New York: Oxford University Press, 1995)

Wystrach, V. P., 'Anna Blackburne (1792–93): A Neglected Patroness of Natural History', *Journal of the Society for the Bibliography of Natural History*, 8 (1976–78), 148–68

Yolton, John W., Roy Porter, Pat Rogers and Barbara Maria Stafford (eds), *The Blackwell Companion to the Enlightenment* (Oxford: Blackwell, 1991)

Index

Note: 'n.' after a page reference indicates the number of a note on that page. Literary works can be found under authors' names. Page numbers in *italics* refer to illustrations.